Personal Injury Awards in EU and EFTA Countries

Personal Injury Awards in EU and EFTA Countries

Edited by
David McIntosh
and
Marjorie Holmes

KLUWER LAW INTERNATIONAL
THE HAGUE / LONDON / NEW YORK

Published by:
Kluwer Law International
P.O. Box 85889, 2508 CN The Hague, The Netherlands
sales@kluwerlaw.com
http://www.kluwerlaw.com

Sold and Distributed in North, Central and South America by:
Aspen Publishers, Inc.
7201 McKinney Circle
Frederick, MD 21704
USA

Sold and Distributed in all other countries by:
Turpin Distribution Services Limited
Blackhorse Road
Letchworth
Herts SG6 1HN
United Kingdom

A CIP Catalogue record for this book is available from the Library of Congress

Printed on acid-free paper.

Typeset by *Steve Lambley Information Design*, The Hague.

ISBN 90-411-2009-2

Kluwer Law International incorporates the imprint of Martinus Nijhoff Publishers

CONTENTS

PREFACE

When in 1989 we began planning the first edition of this comparative report we quickly appreciated we were attempting to fill a vacuum. We were unable to lean on other publications and we approached the launch of the first edition with trepidation in the belief that there would be national practitioners capable of correcting any misunderstandings on our part and on the part of our individual country by country collaborators. This concern proved justified but to a lesser extent than we had anticipated. We are grateful to our reviewers and others who volunteered constructive criticism. This has proved of immense help as we have tried to improve as well as expand our efforts towards our second edition (1994) and this our third edition.

Our first edition was the first comparative study of personal injury compensation awards covering all EU countries. It generated calls for a wider European survey and thus our decision to extend the second survey to embrace the formerly seven European Free Trading Area (EFTA) countries as well as the European Union jurisdictions previously included. In 1995, Austria, Finland and Sweden became members of the European Union, leaving only four members in the EFTA: Iceland, Liechtenstein, Norway and Switzerland.

As at the date of going to print there are 13 countries which have applied to join the EU, including countries as diverse as Poland and Turkey and enlargement is possibly the greatest challenge faced by the EU. This is bound to show up further anomalies in the levels of personal injury compensation and will add to the burden of preparing a Fourth Edition in due course!

A significant development since our second edition is monetary union and the introduction of a common currency, the EURO, in all but 3 of the Member States surveyed (Denmark, England and Wales and Sweden). The Euro has made it easier for us to compare awards and monetary union and may, by making the disparities easier to identify aid our plea for greater uniformity in levels of awards across Europe.

Our first edition generated interest throughout Europe and also in North America, Australia and Japan. This has no doubt encouraged our contributing lawyers whom we identify, country by country, enthusiastically to contribute their knowledge and experience. The value of this publication is enhanced by the quality of our co-authors' experience. Please see below section "contributors" for more details.

Please note that this book, as the previous two editions in 1991 and 1994 deals with civil compensation awards only. It should be noted that criminal compensation awards are generally much lower than the level of civil awards throughout Europe. It is, however, worth noting that there have been a few exceptionally high criminal awards in England and Wales. Recently, a teenager won compensation of GBP 4.75 million[1], from the Criminal Injuries Compensation Board: one of the biggest payouts to a British crime victim. This sum contrasts with the much smaller amounts usually awarded by the Board which are in the range of GBP 30,000 to 70,000.

We are pleased that our earlier editions have received judicial notice and have been referred to by parliamentary committees, including the UK Law Commission, when some of the countries we have surveyed have considered levels of damages in personal injury claims. This pleasure is, however, negated by the EU despite our lobbying for more than ten years, refusing to apply the non-discriminatory principal of Article 12 of the Treaty of Rome to the need for fairness throughout the European community in personal injury compensation. At the date of going to print we understand that the Commission is funding a research project which will compare EU legal systems and personal injury awards. We have already established that wide discrepancies exist.

We are not calling for a general increase in awards. Access to the justice of uniformly fair compensation for personal injuries is something which any one of us could need if unfortunate enough to become involved in an accident. This is not somebody else's problem: it is potentially a problem for all of us. And it is a problem which can only be solved by a European wide approach. It is a need which should be addressed by the European Institutions supported by the individual Members of the European Parliament.

Without wishing to add fuel to an increasing compensation culture, given the ingenuity of claimant lawyers and the liberal approach of many courts we pose, but do not seek to answer, the question as to whether continued reluctance to grasp the nettle of unfairness amounts to an actionable breach of Article 12.

In striving for improvement we have added:

1. Exchange rate analysis and inflation comparisons across Europe.

[1] Lloyd's List, Lloyd's Information Casualty Report 07/12/2001

2. Further categories of common injuries, namely, deafness and the concept of repetitive strain for several EU and EFTA countries and a schedule for stress (for England and Wales only)
3. Bloc graphs to cover more injuries rather than the limited selection produced in the first edition.
4. An analysis on the changes which have taken place since the surveys for our first (1991) and second (1994) editions (1994) were completed.

It was impossible to complete the survey of all 20 countries on one day. However, all reports of the EU Member States and EFTA countries for the third edition were completed between the end of the year 1999 and beginning of the year 2001.

We thank Tokio Marine and Fire Insurance Company for their continued interest and support. We also thank Isabel Sylvestre who has assisted in co-ordinating with the European lawyers' editing, and publication of this third edition throughout. We finally thank our colleagues at Davies Arnold Cooper, Fiona Gill and Andrew Higgs, Gail Sanderson, Caroline Donovan, Cheryl Salters, John Franssen and Jacqueline Cook from the Information Centre, also Sharon Kyberd, Joanne Sandiford and Leo Holmes.

We are sad to report the death of Alan K Brown, one of our Scottish correspondent co-authors for this third edition, who died tragically in December 2000.

July 2002

DAVID MCINTOSH

MARJORIE HOLMES

FOREWORD

Judge Nicholas Forwood, Court of First Instance of the EC

In its 1999 conclusions following the Tampere Summit, the European Council resolved to work towards the creation of a common judicial area across the whole of the European Union, within which European citizens should be able to achieve effective protection of their rights, irrespective of where their cause of action arises and of where it has to be enforced.

Title IV of the EC Treaty, as amended by the Treaties of Amsterdam and Nice, provides for a variety of measures improving judicial co-operation in civil cases with cross-border implications. These include measures for the mutual recognition and enforcement of judgements (already implemented in the so-called "Brussels I" and "Brussels II" regulations) and other measures promoting the compatibility of rules of civil procedure and of national rules concerning conflict of laws.

The very real problems that arise for individuals as a result of differences between the substantive laws in different Member States of the EU are, by contrast, a matter that has yet to be seriously addressed at the Community level. In the field of tort law, in particular, variations in the overall levels of awards of damages for personal injuries, depending on the states in which proceedings are brought, must inevitably give rise to both real and perceived inequalities and differences of treatment that will undermine the objectives of the common judicial area, and create a very real feeling of injustice. In the last resort, such differences may even attack the common assumptions that underlie the principles of mutual recognition and enforcement.

This book, now in its third edition, is for this reason particularly valuable in drawing attention to the enormous disparities that exist in the levels of such awards. By combining the expertise of personal injury lawyers in all the EU Member States and other western European jurisdictions, the authors have produced a unique and invaluable work for any personal injury practitioner faced with an international personal injuries claim. Moreover, by relating the awards to differences in general levels of earnings in different countries, the authors have tried to ensure that their comparisons are realistic.

For the same reasons, it will also provide an authoritative source of information valuable for judges and legislators, at national and Community level.

Luxembourg, December 2002

TABLE OF CASES

A v The National Blood Authority QBD 26 March 2001 [2001] 3 ALL E.R. 289

AB v South West Water Services [1992] 4 ALL ER 574

Allan v Scott 1972 SLT 46

Austrian Supreme Court, decision 60b 2394/96v

Conaty v Barclays Bank Plc (unreported, May 25, 2000)

Cush v Southern Health and Social Services Board 23 June 1992

Doleman and Another v Deakin The Times, 30 January 1990

Frost v Chief Constable of Yorkshire [1999] 1 All E.R. 1

Hadden v Smith, London High Court, 22/01/2002, by Mr Justice Wright

H. v Ministry of Defence [1991] 2 QB 103; [1991] 2 WLR 1192; [19911 2 All ER 834, CA

Jarvis v Swan Tours Limited 1973 IQB 233

Keely v Davies The Times 27 September 1990

Landgericht München I, decision Az 1908647/00

Luthar v Fox QBD, Birmingham District Registry, 22 March 2000

McPherson v Camden LBC (unreported 1999)

Paula Kealy v the Ministry for Health

Rames v Kapitaen Manfred Draxl Schiffahrts GmbH (unreported)

Reddy v Bates 1984 ILRM 197

Rookes v Barnard [1964] AC 1120

Rorrison v West Lothian College, 1999 2000 S.C.L.R. 245; 1999 Rep. L.R. 102

Sinnott v Quinnsworth and another Irish Supreme Court, 1984

Smith v Baker and McKenzie (MCLC) Mayor's and City of London Court 11 April 1994; [1994] C.L.Y. 1662

Sutherland v Hatton (2002) LTL 05/02/02; [2002] 2 All ER 1

Vanbraeckel v Alliance Nationale des Mutualites Chretiennes ECJ C 368/98

Wells v Wells [1999] IAC 345

COUNTRIES COVERED

EU

Austria

Belgium

Denmark

England and Wales

Finland

France

Germany

Greece

Ireland

Italy

Luxembourg

The Netherlands

Portugal

Scotland

Spain

Sweden

EFTA

Iceland

Liechtenstein

Norway

Switzerland

The Countries of Europe, 1998

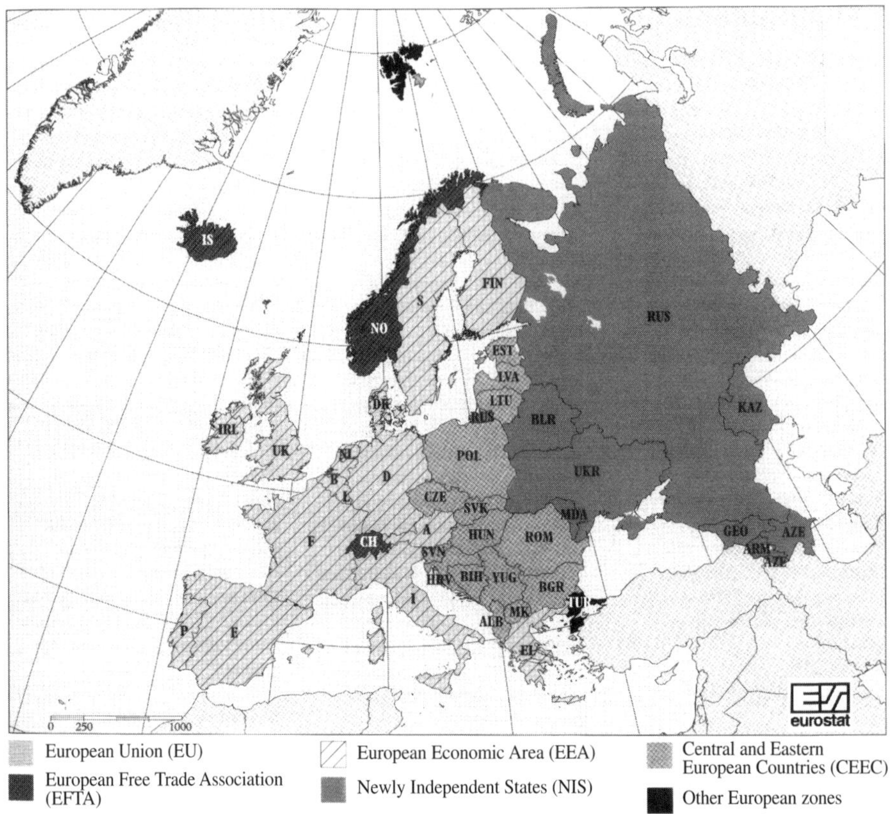

CONTRIBUTORS – EU

Austria

Dr Ivo Greiter was born in Innsbruck on November 7, 1940. After completion of his law studies at the University of Innsbruck, he received his training in a law firm in Vienna and with Booz, Allen & Hamilton Management Consultants, London, New York, Dusseldorf as well as in law firms in Innsbruck and Brussels. Dr Greiter is a Partner in the law firm of Pegger, Kofler & Partners in Innsbruck. He is a speaker at seminars on domestic and foreign law. Since 1976 he has been the Austrian Chairman of the international legal organisation, World Jurist Association, Washington DC. Since 1980 he has served on the committee of the Tyrolean Bar Association. He is a member of the Austrian National Committee of the International Chamber of Commerce, Paris, and a member of several international legal organisations.

He is a member of the editorial board of the Washington based publication *Law and Technology,* an Austrian correspondent for *European Competition Law Review,* London, and the *International Company and Commercial Law Review,* London. In addition to his legal practice, he is active as an arbitrator in international business disputes in and outside Austria.

Contact details:
Greiter Pegger Kofler & Partners
Maria- Theresien- Strasse 24
A - 6020 Innsbruck
Tel: 0043512571811
Fax: 0043512584925
Email:info@greiter.lawfirm.at

Belgium

Roger O. Dalcq – Doctor in law (1951) – graduate in Economic Sciences (1951) and in insurance law (1952). Admitted to the Brussels Bar on 19 October 1951. Member of the Bar Counsel (1967-1970). Professor at the University of Louvain in liability law (1965-1994). Partner of the cabinet Janson Baugniet (1957-1998).

Chief editor at the "Journal des Tribunaux". Director of the *Revue Générale des Assurances et des Responsabiliés.*

Contact details:
Janson Baugniet
187, Chaussée de la Hulpe
B- 1170 Bruxelles
Tel: 3226753030
Fax: 3226753031
Email:email@janson-baugniet.be

Daniel de Callatay has practised as a lawyer at the Brussels Bar since 1983. Former assistant at the University of Louvain in Insurance and liability law, he teaches the award of corporal damage. Author (in 1990 and in 1998) of Chronicle of case law relating to road accidents.

Denmark

Jørgen Rasch graduated in law from the University of Copenhagen in 1975 and subsequently qualified as a lawyer with the law firm Poul Hjermind, specialising in litigation, corporate law, financing and international tax law. Since 1981 he has been counsel of Assuranceforeningen SKULD and the Danish Shipowners' Defence Association, dealing mainly with international maritime law and marine cargo claims. He is a member of the Danish CMI and admitted to the Bar of the Supreme Court of Denmark. He has published articles in international magazines, given papers and participated at international conferences on ro-ro safety and on international maritime arbitration.

Contact details:
Frederiksborggade 15
DK-1360
København
Tel: 004533116861
Fax: 004533113341
Email:syn2.cph@skuld.com

England and Wales

Marjorie Holmes, BSc (London School of Economics) and LLB (Cambridge University) qualified as a barrister in 1980, transferred to become a solicitor in 1988 and was made a partner in the law firm of Davies Arnold Cooper in 1990. Shortly afterwards she spent three months on secondment to Tokio Marine and Fire Insurance at their head office in Tokyo, lecturing on marine and European issues. She is an associate of the Institute of Arbitrators a member of the International Bar Association and has had various articles published on a wide range of European related topics, including *Civil Procedures in EC Countries* published by Lloyd's of London Press. She is currently head of the International Transport European & Competition Department (ITEC) of Davies Arnold Cooper, London.

David McIntosh has been senior partner of Davies Arnold Cooper since 1978 and is currently the President of the Law Society of England and Wales. He is a non-executive director of Markel Underwriting Agency and has considerable experience in commercial litigation including fraud investigation with international dimensions. He has a background in product liability and media orchestrated group actions. David regularly advises multinationals and UK corporations, insurers and reinsurers on liability, risk exposure and control. He has experience in professional negligence and directors and officers' litigation in the financial services sector.

He was Chairman of the International Bar Association's Consumer Affairs, Advertising; Unfair Competition and product Liability Committee 1995-1999; Member Executive Committee of the International Association of Defence Counsel 1995-1998; Member Court of Appeal Users Committee; Former member Arson Bureau Committees

He has written numerous papers on compensation, insurance and product liability, as well co-authoring *Civil Procedures in EC Countries* with Majorie Holmes.

Malcolm Henké started his career in personal injury litigation in 1976 handling both Employers liability and motor claims. He worked initially as an assistant to several high profile litigation lawyers and benefited from an early grounding in high value complex injury litigation. As he gained experience he formed a team of specialist motor litigators dealing with both high volume low value litigation and complex catastrophic claims concerning spinal cord/brain injury.

He now concentrates exclusively on high value litigation and has dealt with many high profile cases within the UK and across Europe and the USA. He had written extensively on his subject and has lectured on catastrophic claims and associated matters to lawyers, insurers and re-insurers. He sits on both the clinical negligence working party (periodical payments) and the structured settlement working party and takes a particular interest in innovative claims handling linked with rehabilitation.

Contact details:
Greenwoods Solicitors
18 Bedford Square
London WC1 3JA
Tel:0044 207 3234632
email: mch@greenwoods-law.co.uk
and
Davies Arnold Cooper
6-8 Bouverie Street
London EC4Y 8DD
Tel: 0044 207 936 2222
Fax: 0044 207 936 2020

Fiona Gill, LLB (Trinity College Dublin) joined Davies Arnold Cooper as a trainee solicitor in 1990, qualifying in 1992. She was made a partner in the Product Liability Group in 2001 and specialises in litigation with an emphasis on occupational health and industrial disease claims. She is currently involved in the defence of a group action brought by 7500 South African residents against a UK based multinational company. She regularly speaks and writes on these topics.

Isabel Sylvestre qualified as a lawyer in Germany in 1999 after studying at Mannheim/Heidelberg University and joined DAC in London shortly after. Since Isabel joined Davies Arnold Cooper she has been involved in regulatory European and domestic work, mainly in the field of maritime and free movement of goods/services law.

Finland

Henrik Langenskiold, LLM (University of Helsinki). Partner in law firm Serlachius & Ryti since 1963. Admitted to the Bar in 1965. Practised in London with Thos. R. Miller & Son in 1966 and in New York with Haight, Gardner, Poor & Havens in 1970, specialising in maritime and insurance law.

Contact details:
Serlachius & Ryti

Mannerheimintic 16 A
SF 00100
Helsinki
Tel: 0035896844710
Fax: 0035896849445

France

Gérard Honig graduated in law from the University of Paris (MA in Law and D.E.S. Private Law) and took a postgraduate qualification at the Institute of Comparative Law in New York. He qualified as a lawyer (avocat) in 1970 and founded with two partners the law firm Honig Buffat Mettetal in 1979. In 2001, Honig Buffat Mettetal merged with Durpey Preel Coulon and became known under the name H.P.M.B.C. The firm specialises in insurance, reinsurance and corporate risks in France and Europe and represents the main French and foreign insurance companies.

Contact details:
Honig Preel Mettetal Buffat Coulon
12 Rue Magellan
75378
Paris
Tel: 0033144438888
Fax: 0033144438877
Email:scp@hpmbc.com

Margareth Rebner graduated in law from the University of Paris-Sorbonne (DEA Private International Law) and took a postgraduate qualification at the University of San Diego, USA of International Business Transactions. Mrs Rebner joined H.P.M.B.C in January 1999 having worked for 6 years as a lawyer in the insurance and industrial risks areas.

Germany

Johannes Wuppermann studied law in Freiburg im Breisgau, and trained in Hamburg. Since 1981 he has been working as an independent solicitor in Hamburg in partnership with Richard Fischer. In 1986 Johannes Wuppermann was admitted to the Hanseatic Supreme Court of Hamburg, and since 1990 he has been entitled to style himself "Fachanwalt für Arbeitsrecht" [specialist in employment law]. As well as employment law, his specialist field is compensation law, including personal injury compensation.

Contact details:
Rae Fischer-Molina-Schmidt-Wuppermann
Bornstrasse 14
20146 Hamburg
Tel: 0049404500316
Fax: 0049404103200
Email: raebornstrasse@t-online.de

Greece

Evangelos Tsouroulis, BA, LLB (Cape) and Law Degree (Athens), is a partner of the law firm Deucalion Rediadis and Sons, Piraeus, Greece. He specialises in all aspects of maritime, company, civil and commercial law. He is a member of the Hellenic Maritime Law Association, the Hellenic Labour Law Association and of the Committee of EEC Affairs of the Piraeus Bar Association. He has had articles published on product liability, insurance and civil procedure.

Contact details:
Deucalion Rediadis & Sons
41 Akti Miaouli
Gr- 185 35
Piraeus
Tel: 003014294900
Fax: 003014294941
Email:main@redias.ath.forthnet.gr

Deucalion G. Rediadis qualified as a member of the Bar of Piraeus in 1992 after studying law in the Universities of Athens (Degree in Law), Southampton (LLM) and Bordeaux (under an ERASMUS postgraduate scholarship). He specialises in shipping law and private international law and has written and lectured on both the above subjects as well as on product liability. He is a member of the Hellenic Maritime Association and a founding editor of the *Athens Law Review.*

Ireland

Katherine Delahunt graduated from University College Cork in 1976 and was admitted to the roll of Solicitors in 1979. In 2000 she was a Partner with the firm of Vincent & Beatty and specialising in insurance, maritime law and defence and personal injury and product liability claims. In 2002, she was appointed as a Judge in Ireland.

Contact details:
Vincent & Beatty
67-68 Fitzwilliam Square
Dublin 2
Tel: 0035316763721
Fax: 0035316785317
Email:postmaster@vblaw.ie

Italy

Allesandro P. Giorgetti graduated in private international law from Milan State University in 1983 and was admitted to the Milan Bar in the same year. He later joined Studio Legale Giorgetti, where he specialised in insurance and reinsurance law, including insurance broking and agency. He is an active member of the International Bar Association insurance committee as well as of the International Association of Defense Counsel; he has lectured on insurance and liability topics in Italy and abroad.

Contact details:
Studio Legale Georgetti
Via Fontana 28
20121 Milan
Italy
Tel: 0039025457734
Fax: 00390255180282
Email:slg@onw.net

Luxembourg

René Diederich graduated from the University of Grenoble Law School (Master of Laws) in 1978 and from the Institut d'Etudes Politiques de Grenoble in 1979. He was admitted to the Luxembourg Bar in 1980. He is now a partner of Loesch & Wolter and head of the litigation department specialising in all aspects of general, civil and commercial law, international contracts, product liability, labour law and construction law.

Contact details:
De Bandt, Van Hecke, Lagae & Loesch
4 Rue Carlo Hemmer
B.P. 1107
1011 Luxemburg
Tel: 003522608-1
Fax: 0035226088888
Email:rdiedrich@debandt.com

The Netherlands

Marinus M MacLean is a partner at Kennedy van der Laan, in the liability and insurance and commercial litigation department. He graduated from the Vrije Universiteit of Amsterdam in 1983. He is the author of several articles both on the settlement agreement and the right of recourse and a former lecturer at the Vrije Universiteit on product liability and insurance law. He is counsel to various insurance companies and other commercial clients as well as private clients in the field of personal injury.

Contact details:
Kennedy Van der Laan
Keizersgracht 555
Postbus 15744
1001 NE
Amsterdam
Tel: 0031205506666
Fax: 0031205506777
Email:d.wachter@kvdl.nl

Portugal

Henrique Dos Santos Pereira graduated in law from the Catholic University of Lisbon, was admitted to the Portuguese Bar Association in 1985. He joined M. P. Barrocas & Associados and practises in general legal matters (mainly litigation and corporate law).

Contact details:
Barrocas & Sarmento
Amoreiras
Torre 2-16
1070 - 274 Lisbon
Tel : 00351213820360
Fax: 0035113870304
Email:barrocas@mail telepac.pt

Scotland

Alastair Lockhart is the Senior Reparation Partner in the Reparation Unit of the Litigation Division of Morison Bishop based in the firm's Glasgow Office. He has an LLB from Glasgow University (1967) and after completing his apprenticeship joined the Glasgow firm of Robertson Chalmers & Auld where he became a partner in 1970. He has been dealing with personal injury litigation, principally on the instructions of insurers, since 1970. He also has a special interest in Adoption Law. During his professional career he has been convenor of the Court House Committee of the Royal Faculty of Procurators in Glasgow; a member of the Standing Advisory Committee to Glasgow Sheriff Court and a part time tutor of Advocacy and Pleading in the Diploma of Legal Practice Course at Glasgow University.

Contact details:
Morison Bishop
2 Blythswood Square
Glasgow
G2 4AD
Tel: 01412484672
Fax: 01412219270
Email:mail@morisonbishop.co.uk

Alan K Brown graduated in Law from the University of Glasgow in 1988. He subsequently qualified as a Solicitor with the firm of Bishop and Robertson Chalmers and became a Partner in 1997. He worked in the Litigation Division undertaking a variety of work but with emphasis on personal injury cases and construction law matters. Alan sadly died in December 2000.

Spain

Mercedes Pallares, born in Madrid in 1959, has a degree in law from the Complutense University of Madrid and in 2002 became a partner of Davies Arnold Cooper working in the Spanish Office, in Madrid. Her specialisation is civil and labour law. During the last five years she has focused her professional career upon civil liability, both contentious and non-contentious. She has published a number of articles on insurance related matters in Spanish and in English.

Contact details:
Davis Arnold Cooper
Madrid Office
Pº de la Castellana No. 41.1
28046 Madrid
Tel: 0034913913200
Fax: 0034913197532
Email: mpallares@dacspain.com

Sweden

Gøran Dahlstrøm, economist specialised in personal injury awards at the Skandia Insurance Company. Member of the Traffic Injury Commission in Sweden since 1997.

Contact details:
Skkandia
Privat-Personkador
405 07
Gotenbòrg
Fax: 004631816886
Email:goran.dahlstrom@if.se

CONTRIBUTORS - EFTA

Iceland

Ingolfur Hjartarson, Supreme Court Attorney, graduated from the University of Reykjavik in 1969 with a law degree; completed postgraduate studies at the University of Oslo and Leeds University. Since 1976 he has been running a law office in Reykjavik covering a very broad practice dealing with business law, insurance and personal injury matters.

Contact details:
Lögfraedithjonustan ehf
House of Commerce
Kringlan 7
103 Reykjavik

Norway

Pål Mitsem, Supreme Court Attorney, graduated in law from the University of Oslo in 1967. He carried out postgraduate studies at the London School of Economics, Southern Methodist University, Dallas, and L'Institut Francais du Pétrole in Paris. He is the author of several books and articles, including articles on the principles of calculation of personal injury damages in Norwegian law. Admitted to practise before all courts in Norway, including the Norwegian Supreme Court. His firm has offices in Stavanger, Oslo and Bergen.

Contact details:
Advokatfirma Mitsem
Kingsgårdbakken 3
PO Box 30
N-4001 Stavanger
Tel: 004751530000
Fax: 004751535800
Email: mitsem@mitsem.no

Switzerland and Liechtenstein

Andreas Girsberger, LLD (Zurich University) and LLM (Harvard University); practising attorney in Zurich specialising in international arbitration, insurance law; teaching fellow at Zurich University on questions of personal and professional liability; currently president of the Swiss Law Association, former president of Swiss Insurance Law Association.

Contact details:
Kirchgasse 40
CH 8024
Zürich
Tel: 004112517365
Fax: 004112518128

EXPLANATORY NOTE

The purpose of this book is to compare awards across Europe at a particular point in time. It is not intended as (and could never be) a summary of the most up to date awards in each country, because of the speed and unevenness of changes across the jurisdiction. The awards were all made around the beginning of 2000.

Every case turns on its particular facts and there is no "correct" figure for compensation in a personal injury claim. It is unlikely that two lawyers in the same jurisdiction would come up with exactly the same suggested level of award even given the same facts. This is inevitable since judges have a discretion, sometimes a very wide discretion, and it is generally impossible to predict exactly what figure that the judge will award.

In addition, the same physical injury may cause different consequences to different sufferers. For example, a person blinded by an accident may be very independent and not require much nursing care after being discharged from hospital, whilst another person of less confidence but suffering the same total blindness may be much less independent and require a considerable amount of assistance. The individual may be able to continue with his or her employment, as for example with a telephonist, whereas a manual worker may be unable to resume his job. Further, the amount of medical care required can vary depending on whether there is a spouse or parent, son/daughter, sibling or friend prepared to assist in looking after the injured person.

For each of the countries included in this survey we have asked experienced lawyers to make assessments relevant to their jurisdiction. Our tables and bloc graphs identify surprising components or variations of assessments of damages across and between jurisdictions. They highlight the domestic and international difficulties which confront those who rightly expect a degree of uniformity in personal injury awards across national boundaries.

The two hypothetical injured persons we have chosen for our survey are:

a) A male doctor, aged 40, with a wife and two children aged 7 and 5 years.

b) A single female legal secretary, aged 20 years, with no dependants.

The lawyers we consulted in each EU or EFTA country were asked to assess the average income of a doctor and a legal secretary in their country. If regional differences were significant within their own country, they were asked to make an assessment of income on the basis that the injured person worked in the capital city or alternatively to explain why a different figure was taken (see Italian section).

Since the first edition of this book which was published in 1991, with regard to the English schedule, we have made assumptions, such as when the two hypothetical persons would be able to return to work. The other jurisdictions' lawyers were asked to follow the same assumptions. Early on in the original survey, we were informed by Messrs Studio Mordiglia (Genoa), that they would be unable to make an assessment of likely levels of compensation without being given a percentage of disability for the different types of injury. In Italy this percentage is normally assessed by a doctor. As we were dealing with hypothetical persons – trying to compare like with like, working on our experiences as to what percentage the Department of Social Security (DSS) in England would use for the assessment of an industrial disability pension – we asked all the lawyers to assume the following percentages of disability, unless their jurisdiction dictated another percentage:

1. Instant death – inapplicable
2. Burn types A, B and C (burns to the face with and without permanent scarring and burns to other parts of the body) – 1%-20%
3. Quadriplegia – 100%
4. Paraplegia – 70%
5. Brain damage – 80%
6. Brain damage with motor deficiency – 90%
7. Amputation of leg above knee – 35%
8. Amputation of leg below knee – 30%
9. Amputation of arm above elbow – 30%
10. Amputation of arm below elbow – 30%
11. Loss of eyesight – one eye without cosmetic disability – 30%
12. Loss of eyesight – one eye with cosmetic disability – 30%
13. Total blindness – 100%
14. Deafness – 50%
15. Repetitive strain injury – 15%-20%

In every case we have asked the lawyers to choose the most generous justifiable award.

With regard to the schedule for England and Wales, we spot-checked the assessments by asking other practising lawyers (in England) how they would assess the same injuries. In each case we found the amount assessed varied but their figures for the serious injuries were within 30% of our original figures. We have been able to cross-check in other ways. For example, the participating Luxembourg lawyer, Rene Diederich, advised us that he would anticipate Luxembourg awards to be similar to French and Belgian awards but with higher amounts awarded in respect of moral damages. The assessments made by French and Belgian lawyers independently confirm that this is indeed the case.

In the case of EFTA countries, Liechtenstein awards are somewhere between Austrian and Swiss figures. Again, assessments made by the Austrian and Swiss lawyers confirm this to be so.

We have drawn up three tables for each hypothetical case comparing all the countries showing (1) the overall award; (2) the pain and suffering elements of the award; and (3) bereavement awards.

The Dutch and the German sections do not include an assessment for medical expenses. We were advised that the variance in medical expenses in those countries is large and they have little or no experience of assessing medical expenses because most people have private permanent medical insurance in their jurisdictions. It means that in most Dutch and German cases private medical insurers claim their outlays directly against the tortfeasor's insurers.

In order to enable comparisons we have included in the overall tables a notional figure for medical expenses for Germany and the Netherlands, based on English estimates which we view as conservative (see the German and Dutch section).

Although, for our purposes, full liability was assumed, by no stretch of the imagination do the jurisdictions covered present a level playing field so far as access to the courts or establishing liability in like cases is concerned.

In every country where personal injury claims go to a full civil trial the assessment is made by a judge except in Scotland where a small number of cases are still dealt with by a jury. In Ireland assessments were made by juries until July 1988 when juries were abolished in personal injury cases. In the second edition of the book, we stated that: "Perhaps surprisingly this has not had the expected effect of a levelling off in the rate of increase in awards."[1] Our Irish correspondent

1 *Ireland—A case study,* by Brian Gregan (see source material No. 10) (Confederation of Irish industry), March 1992.

confirmed that the abolition of juries had not had the expected effect of slowing down the rate of increase in levels of awards. Our figures confirmed that awards particularly for pain and suffering in Ireland remain high. However, it is also interesting to note that some jurisdictions such as Italy are catching Ireland up.

Although for our purposes no limits of liability have been assumed it is appropriate to note that for injuries at sea and in the air (with the Athens Convention 1974, the Limitation Convention 1976 and the Warsaw Convention), limits usually apply, and in most countries (but not England and Wales, Scotland or Ireland) limits apply for road traffic accidents. In some countries, including Spain and Germany, awards for injury caused by pharmaceutical products (drugs) are also limited.

This book involves assessments of personal injury awards covering 20 jurisdictions and involving 25 contributing lawyers. As a result it does take some time to draw the work together and summarise it. The assessments here were prepared pre-the introduction of the Euro into 12 Member States within Europe. Each section is therefore in the pre-Euro national currencies. However we have prepared the country sections referring to Euros. We have also prepared comparison tables in Pound Sterling, Euros and US Dollars.

The introduction of the Euro will have very significant affect on the different level of awards across Europe. See Comments and Recommendations for further discussion.

Currencies and Inflation

On 2 May 1998 the European Council, meeting at the level of Heads of State or Government decided that eleven of Europe's Member States would join the third phase of Economic and Monetary Union (EMU): Austria, Belgium, Finland, France, Germany, Ireland, Italy, Luxembourg, the Netherlands, Portugal and Spain.

On 1 January 1999, conversion rates were fixed among currencies of participating countries and against the euro. This marked the beginning of monetary union.

The UK reserved the right to enter the third stage of EMU and to enter the final stage at a later stage after approval by its Parliament. Denmark negotiated a derogation not to participate in the third stage, unless this was approved by a new national referendum. Sweden had decided not to participate. Greece joined the EMU on 1 January 2001.

Because the Euro was introduced as the only currency in 12 (and national notes were withdrawn) of the 15 Member States from 1 January 2002 we have for this third edition of the book, prepared a summary table in Euros (€) as well as Pound Sterling (£) and US Dollars ($).

With regard to inflation, consumer price inflation in Europe declined during most of the 1990s and so did interest rates[2]. After relatively high short-term interest rates in most countries at the beginning of the 1990s, rates fell significantly EU-wide from 1992[3].

The following table outlines the average inflation rate in the 15 European Member States and Iceland and Norway for the time between the second edition of the book in 1994 and the year 2000[4]. Unfortunately, we have no figures available for the remaining two EFTA countries Switzerland and Liechtenstein.

Table 1

Belgium	1994–2000	1,7% average
Denmark	1994–2000	2,0%
Germany	1994–2000	1,4%
Greece[5]	1994–2000	6,1%
Spain	1994–2000	3,2%
France	1994–2000	1,4%
Ireland	1994–2000	2,6%
Italy	1994–2000	3,1%
Luxembourg	1994–2000	1,8%
The Netherlands	1994–2000	1,9%
Austria	1994–2000	1,5%
Portugal	1994–2000	3,0%
Finland	1994–2000	1,4%
Sweden	1994–2000	1,7%
UK	1994–2000	1,8%
Iceland	1996–2000	2,4%
Norway	1996–2000	2,1%

2 Source: eurostat datashop (Statistical Office of the European Communities in Luxembourg) "Europe in Figures", Fifth edition 2000

3 Source: eurostat "Europe in Figures", Fifth edition 2000

4 These figures have been prepared on the basis of the data given in "Europe in Figures", Fifth edition by Eurostat datashop

5 In Greece, there used to be an inflation rate of 10,9% in 1994 and 9,3% in 1995, which went down to 2.1% in 1999

Table 2

	1st edn	*2nd edn*	*Dec97*	*3rd edn*	*% change between 2nd and 3rd edns*
EU					
Austria	*	Sch. 17.55	Sch. 12.66	Sch 22.85	+ 30.2 %
Belgium	Bf. 59.60	Bf. 50.00	Bf. 61.36	Bf. 66.99	+ 33.98 %
Denmark	DKK.11.02	DKK. 9.55	DKK. 11.33	DKK 12.37	+ 30.21%
England/Wales	–	–	–	–	–
Finland	*	FMK. 8.62	FMK. 9.01	FMK 9.87	+ 14.5 %
France	Ffr. 9.73	Ffr. 8.40	Ffr. 9.96	Ffr. 10.89	+ 29.64 %
Germany	DM. 2.90	DM. 2.49	DM. 2.97	DM. 3.25	+ 30.5 %
Greece	Dr. 285	Dr. 315	Dr. 469.21	Dr. 565.86	+ 79.64 %
Ireland	I£. 1.08	I£. 1	I£. 1.16	I£ 1.31	+ 31 %
Italy	Lire. 2,124	Lire. 2,212	Lire. 2922.5	Lire. 3215.24	+ 45.35 %
Luxembourg	Lux.f. 59.55	Lux.f. 51.6	Lux.f. 60.24	Lux.f. 67.05	+ 29.94 %
Netherlands	H.fl. 3.26	H.fl. 2.79	H.fl. 3.35	H.fl. 3.66	+ 31.18 %
Portugal	Esc. 254	Esc. 216	Esc. 303.02	Esc. 332.91	+ 54.13 %
Scotland	–	–	–	–	–
Spain	Pta. 178.45	Pta. 170	Pta. 252.04	Pta. 276.29	+ 62.52 %
Sweden	*	SEK.11.225	SEK. 13.07	SEK. 15.3	+ 36.3 %

Table 3

	1st edn	*2nd edn*	*Dec97*	*3rd edn*	*% change between 2nd and 3rd edns*
EFTA					
Iceland	*	IKK. 98.42	IKK. 119.25	IKK. 145.08	+ 47.4 %
Liechtenstein	*	Sw.fr. 2.185	Sw.fr. 2.41	Sw.fr. 2.53	+ 15.79 %
Norway	*	NOK. 10.35	NOK. 12.19	NOK. 13.19	+ 27.44 %
Switzerland	*	Sw.fr. 2.185	Sw.fr. 2.41	Sw.fr. 2.53	+ 15.79 %

Percentage change in awards since 2nd edn (interest not included)

Table 4

Doctor, male, aged 40, married with 2 dependent children.

Instant death, total compensation.

	Percentage change in awards since 2nd edition in £'s Sterling[6]	*Percentage change in awards since 2nd edition in national currencies*
Austria	– 23.20%	0%
Belgium	– 12.92%	+17.00%
Denmark	– 6.84%	+20.56%
England and Wales	+38.56%	+38.56%
Finland	– 19.56%	– 7.89%
France	+11.40%	+42.59%
Germany	+0.15%	+30.79%
Greece	– 8.76%	+66.39%
Iceland	+32.44%	+94.75%
Ireland	– 1.31%%	+29.2%
Italy	+25.75%	+82.81%
Lichentenstein	– 13.65%	0%
Luxembourg	– 24.09%	– 1.36%
The Netherlands	– 16.98%	+8.84%
Norway	+30.79%	+13.29%
Portugal	– 27.87%	+11.17%
Scotland	+37.39%	+37.39%
Spain	– 42.49%	– 7.57%
Sweden	+7.89%	+46.63%
Switzerland	– 13.63%	0%

6 These figures are calculated on the basis of the sums of money shown in the tables from the second edition.

Table 5

Doctor, male, aged 40, married with 2 dependent children.

Quadriplegia, total compensation

	Percentage change in awards since 2nd edition in £'s Sterling[7]	*Percentage change in awards since 2nd edition in national currencies*
Austria	– 23.2%	0%
Belgium	– 10.89%	+17.97%
Denmark	– 6.84%	+20.56%
England and Wales	+100.22%	+102.22%
Finland	+7.4%	+22.91%
France	15.41%	+9.93%
Germany	+49.72%	+95.41%
Greece	– 7.02%	+55.08%
Iceland	+32.44%	+94.75%
Ireland	– 1.31%	+29.2%
Italy	– 8.85%	+32.55%
Lichentenstein	– 13.65%	0%
Luxembourg	– 23.07%	0%
The Netherlands	– 16.98%	+8.84%
Norway	+30.79%	+13.29%
Portugal	– 27.87%	+11.17%
Scotland	+66.60%	+66.60%
Spain	– 21.15%	+20.86%
Sweden	+7.89%	+46.63%
Switzerland	– 13.63%	0%

7 These figures are calculated on the basis of the sums of money shown in the tables from the second edition.

Table 6

Doctor, male, aged 40, married with 2 dependent children.

Quadriplegia, pain and suffering awards

	Percentage change in awards since 2nd edition in £'s Sterling[8]	*Percentage change in awards since 2nd edition in national currencies*
Austria	– 23.20%	0%
Belgium	+35.29%	+81.33%
Denmark	– 22.80%	0%
England and Wales	+40.43%	+40.43%
Finland	+40.65%	+61.04%
France	– 22.87%	0%
Germany	+78.77%	+133.33%
Greece	+122.66%	+300.00%
Iceland	+144.22%	+2600.00%
Ireland	– 15.19%	+11.11%
Italy	+103.07%	+195.18%
Lichentenstein	– 13.65%	0%
Luxembourg	– 23.04%	0%
The Netherlands	+1.64%	+33.33%
Norway	– 7.63%	+17.74%
Portugal	+399.14%	+669.23%
Scotland	+30.00%	+30.00%
Spain	–	–
Sweden	– 12.29%	+19.23%
Switzerland	– 13.63%	0%

8 These figures are calculated on the basis of the sums of money shown in the tables from the second edition.

Table 7

Doctor, male, aged 40, married with 2 dependent children.

Amputation of arm above elbow, pain and suffering awards.

	Percentage change in awards since 2nd edition in £'s Sterling[9]	*Percentage change in awards since 2nd edition in national currencies*
Austria	– 23.20%	0%
Belgium	+52.51%	+104.16%
Denmark	– 49.60%	– 34.73%
England and Wales	+25.00%	+25.00%
Finland	+0.65%	+21.95%
France	– 16.35%	8.57%
Germany	– 13.39%	0%
Greece	+85.54%	+233.33%
Iceland	+71.85%	+153.33%
Ireland	+43.13%	+87.5%
Italy	+78.25%	+159.11
Lichentenstein	– 13.65%	0%
Luxembourg	– 23.04%	0%
The Netherlands	– 23.77%	0%
Norway	– 32.72%	– 14.29%
Portugal	+199.47%	+361.54%
Scotland	+11.11%	+11.11%
Spain	–	–
Sweden	+19.27%	+62.13%
Switzerland	– 13.63%	0%

9 These figures are calculated on the basis of the sums of money shown in the tables from the second edition.

Table 8

Legal Secretary, woman, aged 20, single.

Instant death, total compensation.

	Percentage change in awards since 2nd edition in £'s Sterling [10]	*Percentage change in awards since 2nd edition in national currencies*
Austria	– 23.23%	0%
Belgium	+49.28%	+100.00%
Denmark	– 4.45%	+23.81%
England and Wales	0%	0%
Finland	–	–
France	+4.47%	+35.43%
Germany	– 4.27%	+25.00%
Greece	– 27.80%	+29.69%
Iceland	+1.77%	+50.00%
Ireland	+96.30%	+157.14%
Italy	– 21.19%	+13.41%
Lichentenstein	– 13.65%	0%
Luxembourg	– 23.04%	0%
The Netherlands	+117.69%	+185.71%
Norway	+31.14%	+67.12%
Portugal	+580.24%	+948.80%
Scotland	+64.71%	+64.71%
Spain	– 41.03%	– 4.17%
Sweden	– 26.43%	0%
Switzerland	– 13.63%	0%

10 These figures are calculated on the basis of the sums of money shown in the tables from the second edition.

Table 9

Legal Secretary, woman, aged 20, single.

Quadriplegia, total compensation.

	Percentage change in awards since 2nd edition in £'s Sterling[11]	*Percentage change in awards since 2nd edition in national currencies*
Austria	– 23.2%	0%
Belgium	– 14.60%	+14.43%
Denmark	– 34.96%	– 15.74%
England and Wales	+133.1%	+133.1%
Finland	– 15.55%	– 3.31%
France	– 17.82%	+6.54%
Germany	+68.25%	+119.61%
Greece	– 15.29%	+51.96%
Iceland	+128.02%	+236.09%
Ireland	– 18.52%	+55.26%
Italy	– 13.37%	+24.16%
Lichentenstein	– 13.65%	0%
Luxembourg	– 22.95%	+0.13%
The Netherlands	+110.42%	+176.04%
Norway	– 1.38%	+25.68%
Portugal	– 49.23%	– 20.22%
Scotland	+97.60%	+97.60%
Spain	– 10.15%	+45.88%
Sweden	+22.96%	+67.14
Switzerland	– 13.63%	0%

11 These figures are calculated on the basis of the sums of money shown in the tables from the second edition.

Table 10

Legal Secretary, woman, aged 20, single.

Quadriplegia, pain and suffering awards

	Percentage change in awards since 2nd edition in £'s Sterling[12]	*Percentage change in awards since 2nd edition in national currencies*
Austria	– 23.20%	0%
Belgium	+16.51%	+56.10%
Denmark	– 22.68%	+0.16%
England and Wales	+30.43%	+30.43%
Finland	+41.28%	+61.76%
France	– 22.87%	0%
Germany	– 14.87%	+11.11%
Greece	+33.59%	+140.00%
Iceland	+144.22%	+260.00%
Ireland	– 23.67%	0%
Italy	+128.29%	+231.50%
Lichentenstein	– 13.65%	0%
Luxembourg	– 22.08%	+1.26%
The Netherlands	+1.64%	+33.3%
Norway	– 7.10%	+16.36%
Portugal	+399.32%	+515.38%
Scotland	+13.04%	+13.04%
Spain	–	–
Sweden	– 2.00%	+38.48%
Switzerland	– 13.63%	0%

12 These figures are calculated on the basis of the sums of money shown in the tables from the second edition.

Table 11

Legal Secretary, woman, aged 20, single.

Amputation of arm above elbow, pain and suffering awards

	Percentage change in awards since 2nd edition in £'s Sterling[13]	*Percentage change in awards since 2nd edition in national currencies*
Austria	– 23.20%	0%
Belgium	+43.29%	+91.98%
Denmark	– 22.80%	0%
England and Wales	+37.5%	+37.5%
Finland	+5.09%	+20.33%
France	– 16.26%	8.57%
Germany	– 23.39%	0%
Greece	+85.54%	+233.33%
Iceland	+71.85%	+153.33%
Ireland	+66.99%	+118.75%
Italy	+0.21%	+45.59
Lichentenstein	– 13.65%	0%
Luxembourg	– 23.61%	– 0.51%
The Netherlands	– 23.77%	0%
Norway	– 31.05%	– 12.12%
Portugal	+199.47%	+361.54%
Scotland	+20.00%	+20.00%
Spain	–	–
Sweden	+7.71%	+46.43%
Switzerland	– 13.63%	0%

13 These figures are calculated on the basis of the sums of money shown in the tables from the second edition.

EMU Convergence Criteria

	Inflation: Harmonised indices of consumer prices: 09/97–09/98 (1)	*Interest Rates: Long-terms interest rates: 09/97–09/98 (2)*	*General government budgetary position: Deficit/GDP ratio 1997 (3) (4)*	*General government budgetary position: Debt/GDP ratio 1997 (3)*
B	1.0	5.1	2.0	121.9
DK	1.4	5.3	–0.5	64.1
D	1.0	4.9	2.7	61.2
EL	4.7	9.1	4.0	109.5
E	1.9	5.2	2.6	68.9
F	0.9	5.0	3.0	58.1
IRL	1.8	5.2	–0.9	63.4
I	2.0	5.3	2.7	121.6
L	1.2	5.1	–3.0	6.7
NL	2.0	5.0	0.9	71.4
A	0.9	5.0	1.9	64.3
P	2.0	5.3	2.5	61.5
FIN	1.5	5.1	1.1	55.1
S	1.7	5.4	0.8	76.6
UK	1.7	6.0	2.1	53.5
EU-15	1.5	5.3	2.3	71.9
EUR-11	1.3	5.1	2.5	74.5

(1) Inflation: arithmetic average of twelve monthly Harmonised Indices of Consumer Prices (HICP) relative to the arithmetic average of the twelve monthly HICP of the previous period.

(2) Yield on government bonds of around 10 years to maturity: average of the last 12 monthly averages.

(3) as notified by Member States in September 1998.

(4) a negative sign indicates a surplus.

This table was reproduced with kind permission from Europe in Figures, *Eurostat, Office for Official Publications of the European Communities, 2000, Fifth edition*

Exchange Rates against the ecu/euro

(Year averages, national currency per ecu/euro)

	1980	*1985*	*1990*	*1991*	*1992*
Belgium/Luxembourg (Franc)	40.6	44.91	42.43	42.22	41.59
Denmark (Krone)	7.83	8.02	7.86	7.91	7.81
Germany (Deutsche Mark)	2.52	2.23	2.05	2.05	2.02
Greece (Drachma)	59.42	105.74	201.41	225.22	247.03
Spain (Peseta)	99.70	129.14	129.41	128.47	132.53
France (Franc)	5.87	6.8	6.91	6.97	6.85
Ireland (Punt)	0.68	0.72	0.77	0.77	0.76
Italy (Lira)	1189.21	1447.99	1521.98	1533.24	1595.52
Netherlands (Guilder)	2.76	2.51	2.31	2.31	2.27
Austria (Schilling)	17.97	15.64	14.44	14.43	14.22
Portugal (Escudo)	69.55	130.25	181.11	178.61	174.71
Finland (Markka)	5.17	4.69	4.85	5.0	5.81
Sweden (Krona)	5.88	6.52	7.52		7.53
UK (Pound)	0.6	0.59	0.71	0.70	0.74
Japan (Yen)	315.04	180.56	183.66	166.49	164.22
USA (Dollar)	1.39	0.76	1.27	1.24	1.3

1993	*1994*	*1995*	*1996*	*1997*	*1998*	
40.47	39.66	38.55	39.3	40.53	40.62	Belgium/ Luxembourg
7.59	7.54	7.33	7.36	7.48	7.45	Denmark
1.94	1.92	1.88	1.91	1.96	1.97	Germany
268.57	288.03	302.99	305.55	309.36	330.74	Greece
149.12	158.92	163.0	160.75	165.89	167.18	Spain
6.63	6.58	6.53	6.49	6.61	6.6	France
0.8	0.79	0.82	0.79	0.75	0.79	Ireland
1841.23	1915.06	2130.14	1958.96	1929.30	1943.65	Italy
2.18	2.16	2.1	2.14	2.21	2.22	Netherlands
13.62	13.54	13.18	13.44	13.82	13.85	Austria
188.37	196.9	196.11	195.76	198.59	201.7	Portugal
6.7	6.19	5.71	5.83	5.88	5.98	Finland
9.12	9.16	9.33	8.51	8.65	8.92	Sweden
0.78	0.78	0.83	0.81	0.69	0.68	UK
130.15	121.32	123.01	138.08	137.08	146.42	Japan
1.17	1.19	1.31	1.27	1.13	1.12	USA

This table was reproduced with kind permission from Europe in Figures*; Eurostat, Office for Official publications of the European Communities, 2000, fifth edition*

EU COUNTRIES

Austria

Pain and suffering awards in Austria are low by comparison to many other European jurisdictions. The highest award for pain and suffering to date is the amount of EUR 127,148 (equivalent to GBP 76,586 and USD 107,726), which was awarded by the Oberster Gerichtshof (Austrian Supreme Court) in 1997[1] to a minor who suffered brain injury after lacking oxygen during birth. Nevertheless, the levels of pain and suffering awards in Austria are in the midfield along with countries such as France. Injuries giving rise to pain and suffering awards are put unofficially into four categories and damages are awarded for each day that each type of pain is suffered: light pain, moderate pain, strong pain and very strong pain. For other heads of damage such as instant death, burns or paraplegia, Austria is still at the bottom of the scale, only leaving Finland and Denmark behind.

Annuities as well as lump sum payments are common in Austria and the tortfeasor is liable to the injured person for any future deterioration after the injury for a period of up to 30 years.

Belgium

Belgian awards are generally similar to those in Germany, the Netherlands, Luxembourg and France. It is interesting to note that the income of a doctor in Belgium is close to that in England. Unlike England and Ireland there is no provision for statutory bereavement but there is a similar award described as 'indemnity for moral damages'. Any near relative of the injured person – mother, father, grandmother, grandfather, husband, wife, cohabitant companion, son, daughter, brother or sister – will be entitled to claim compensation for 'moral damage' caused by

1 Judgment of 13 February 1997 (6 Ob 2394/96v)

loss of a near relative. This is regardless of whether the deceased is a minor and/or married. In Belgium, non-dependent parents of a single person over 18 receive 'moral damages' for loss of a loved one and the amount is higher if the person killed was still living with his/her parents.

In this third edition, the 'moral damage' award has risen in the last few years from between EUR 3,717-7,434 (GBP 2,239-4,478[2] and USD 3,149-6,299) for a loss of a child or a wife or husband to EUR 7,434-12,058 (GBP 4,478-7,463 and USD 6,299-10,497). It has also increased for loss of brother and sister from EUR 1,239 (GBP 746 and USD 1,049) to EUR 2,479 (GBP 1,493 and USD 2,100) and for grandparents from EUR 744 (GBP 448 and USD 630) to EUR 2,479 (GBP 1,493 and USD 2,100). The amount awarded will also depend on whether the "relatives" are living together.

The mental stress inflicted on the wife and for the children of the injured person is furthermore taken in account in case of quadriplegia, paraplegia, and brain damage.

The term "sexual injury" has now taken the place of the previous claim known as *premium voluptatis* which was compensation for loss of chance to marry. It can only be put forward as above in claims involving injuries such as paraplegia, quadriplegia and brain damage.

In Belgium, like England and indeed most countries (not Denmark and Portugal), the paying party i.e. compensator, must reimburse the welfare service for welfare payments.

Denmark

The levels of awards in Denmark are surprisingly low given its comparatively high standard of living. One of the reasons for Denmark's lowly position in our league table is that medical expenses, which account for the major part of the awards in most countries, are not included in Denmark where there is little private health care available. State medical care is of an extremely high standard. Our Danish correspondent, Jorgen Rasch has explained that the social security system covers all contingencies such as accidents, sickness, old age and unemployment and is mainly financed out of general taxation revenue. The State pays for all medical

2 The figures in brackets in this section refer to conversion rates based on the exchange rate on 4 July 2001 unless otherwise stated (GBP 1 = USD 1. 4066 = EUR 1.6602)

expenses and does not make any claim from the parties for recoupment where compensation is awarded.

Danish pain and suffering awards are low and bereavement damages do not exist. As with the Piper Alpha and Lockerbie tragedies in Scotland (referred to below), the settlements in the *Scandinavian Star Ferry* case do not reflect normal Danish awards, being at least 50% above the legal compensation levels required by Norwegian or Danish law.

Compensation may be awarded to homosexual partners provided they are married or have lived together for more than two years. Homosexual marriage carries the same status as heterosexual marriages except that the couple are not allowed to adopt children (in the UK homosexual partners can adopt).

Jorgen Rasch has advised us of new legislation which provides for compensation in the event of an injury following a vaccination. The level of compensation follows the 1989 Liability Compensation Act.

Further, there is a new trend in claims for Post Incident Traumatic Disease. The most recent award stated the disability at 50% or equivalent to the loss of all fingers on the left hand.

England and Wales

England and Wales is a separate jurisdiction for personal injury purposes from the two other distinct jurisdictions within the United Kingdom — Scotland and Northern Ireland. Although a Scottish case, *Allan* v. *Scott,* 1972 SLT 46, declared that the Scottish and English awards should be the same, Scottish awards are in practice often noticeably lower than English awards. The two disasters in Scotland, Piper Alpha and Lockerbie, and subsequent or likely settlements of them, do not reflect normal Scottish levels of awards, as they include a "mid-Atlantic" element which takes into account the threat of litigation in the United States.

In our second edition, we reported that the Judicial Studies Board has published *Guidelines for the Assessment of General Damages in Personal Injury Cases*, which are now in their fourth edition (2000) and have become the definitive reference for practitioners [*Heal v. Rankin*]. [Damages awarded for pain, suffering and loss of amenity are expected to increase substantially following the recommendations of the Law Commission in report No 257. In that documentation document, the Law Commission debated the current level of awards provided in personal injury actions and decided that such damages should be increases by between 50% and 100%, during the course of the next three years.]

It should be noted that bereavement damages are not, under English law as it stands, paid to the parents of a single person over 18 (see *Doleman and Another* v. *Deakin,* The Times, 30 January 1990). In Scotland, the Damages (Scotland) Act 1976 allows for the recovery of damages (known as loss of society) by a wider category of relations, the amount to be awarded is within the discretion of the Court and will depend on the closeness of the relationship. There is no amount for a loss of society award fixed by statute.

The highest published English personal injury award, on completion of our first edition, was GBP 1,571,282 (see *Lambert* v. *Devon County,* The Financial Times, 28 July 1990). The highest reported personal injury lump sum award has since risen to GBP 1.7 million (USD 3,278,450 according to rates at the time of the first publication), which funded a structured settlement which with the agreement of the parties was approved by the English courts: *Kelly* v. *Dawes.*[3]

Since the second edition, the levels of awards have again risen significantly. In *Biesheuvel v Birrell*, a Dutch citizen, who was rendered tetraplegic in a road accident, was awarded a record compensation award of more than GBP 9.2 million at the English High Court in 1998[4] (USD 15,131,608 according to rates at the time of the award). Assessing the damages, the Court referred to the House of Lords' *Wells v Wells* decision and accepted that there "might be special circumstances which justify increasing multipliers where conventional discount rates were inadequate", whereas the high taxes in the Netherlands were taken into account. In *Luhar v Fox* (2001),[5] a 10-year-old boy received GBP 5.1 million (USD 7,173,660 and EUR 8,467,020) for severe high cervical spinal cord injuries sustained in a road traffic accident in 1993. The claimant was rendered tetraplegic from the neck down, and required a ventilator in order to breathe.

In another case, a 7-year-old boy who suffered brain damage after contracting the E. coli bacteria on a school visit to a farm has been awarded GBP 2.6 million (USD 3,657,160 and EUR 4,316,520) damages in a settlement at the High Court in January 2001.[6]

By means of the *Damages (Personal Injury) Order 2001*, pursuant to section 1 of the Damages Act 1996, the Lord Chancellor on 25 June 2001 set a discount rate

---

3 *The Times*, 27 September 1990

4 *Biesheuvel v Birrell (No. 2)* (QBD) 21 December 1998

5 QBD, Birmingham District Registry (HH Judge David Matthews) 22 March 2000

6 Reported in *The Independent*, dated 23 January 2001

of 2.5 percent for damages in personal injury claims, in accordance with the principle set by the House of Lords in *Wells v Wells* (1999). He decided to set a single and fixed rate to cover all cases, in order to provide certainty. The courts retain a discretion under section 1(2) of the Damages Act 1996 to adopt a different rate in any particular case in exceptional circumstances.

In a recent out of court settlement, a claimant was awarded GBP 3.3 million (USD 4,641,780 and EUR 5,478,660) in damages after suffering from cerebral palsy after being starved of oxygen during birth in an out of court settlement made by the Health Authority. It is thought that the award could have been increased by as much as GBP 100,000 (USD 140,660 and EUR 166,020) due to the discount rate being reduced from 3 % to 2.5 %. In a recent case *Hadden v Smith*[7] before the High Court, a cyclist who was involved in a road accident, was awarded damages of GBP 4.15 million (USD 5,837,390 and EUR 6,889,830) for suffering brain injuries and being dependent on expensive care for the rest of his life.

Finland

The constituents of awards in Norway, Denmark and Finland are similar in that they are made up of (1) pain and suffering, (2) permanent defect and handicap and (3) loss of income payments. For the first two occupation and income are irrelevant. Injuries giving rise to pain and suffering are put into three categories:

a) Minor

b) Moderate

c) Severe

Only moderate and severe (category (b) and (c) cases) qualify for compensation. With regard to pain and suffering awards, Finland gives low awards, but not as low as Greece, Sweden, Denmark and Portugal, whereas with regard to all remaining heads of damage, Finland is at the bottom of the scale.

The awards for permanent defect and handicap injuries are classified into 20 different groups with the minimum payment for an adult over 18 being EUR 2,354 (GBP 1,418 and USD 1,995) in Category 1 (the least serious injuries), and EUR

---

7 *Hadden v Smith* at the London High Court, 22/01/2002 by Mr Justice Wright

70,646 (GBP 42,553 and USD 59,855) for Category 20 (the most serious injuries). Children receive half that figure until Category 15 but even less than half that figure from Category 16 to 20.

Medical expenses are also paid for very serious injuries. Again, the amount awarded depends on which of the four different categories the injury falls into.

The loss of income element in the Finnish schedule is notional. It is calculated by Davies Arnold Cooper on the basis of the Finnish narrative, but applying the relevant English multiplier simply for comparison purposes.

France

The levels of awards made in France are not initially different from those in England, although structured settlements are commonplace in France. However, the methods of calculation as shown in the French section are completely different. It can be seen that general damages include future medical expenses. Another feature of the French awards is the interest payable to Sécurité Sociale (the French equivalent of DSS) on pre-trial pecuniary loss. Unlike England, bereavement damages are recoverable by the siblings as well as the parents of the 20-year-old legal secretary without dependants.

Margareth Rebner from H.P.M.B.C in Paris has advised us that there have been a number of significant awards in France in HIV and/or Hepatitis C cases in the past few years. For HIV cases, the average awards are around EUR 198,188 (GBP 119,376 and USD 167,914) and the highest can go up to over EUR 457,355 (GBP 275,482 and USD 387,493). For Hepatitis C cases, the average awards are around EUR 22,868 (GBP 13,774 and USD 19,375) and the highest reach EUR 304,904 (GBP 183,655 and USD 258,329.)

It should also be noted that pain and suffering awards are not the only non-economic awards made in France. Loss of leisure and ability to enjoy sex are additional heads of damage in respect of which compensation can be awarded.

Germany

The original survey was completed at the end of 1989, before the unification of Germany. The 1993 awards in the old East Germany are considered by our German contributor to be between 25-35% less than in the old West Germany. In accordance with our stated methodology (see pages 1-2) the highest West German awards have been adopted for our purposes.

In October 1989 the highest published judgment figure stood at DEM 500,000 (1989 worth GBP 172,414 and USD 263,630; spring 1993 worth GBP 206,612 and USD 303,340; third edition equivalent to GBP 153,846,[8] USD 216,400 and EUR 255,415). The case concerned a four-year-old girl whose injuries resulted in paraplegia which will confine her to a wheelchair for the rest of her life. By completion of this edition the highest award was given to a 33-year-old man by the Dusseldorf Court of Appeal. He was rendered paraplegic in a traffic accident. He received the equivalent of DEM 1,050,000 (GBP 323,077 and USD 454,440) comprising DEM 450,000 (GBP 138,462 and USD 194,761) lump sum payment and a monthly annuity of DEM 750 (GBP 231 and USD 325) worth DEM 600,000 (GBP 184,615 and USD 259,679.)

Since the second edition, we found that compensation amounts continue to increase slowly in Germany but our German correspondent lawyer, Johannes Wuppermann in Hamburg advised us that there have now been several cases in which compensation of EUR 255,415, or DEM 500,000, (GBP 153,846 and USD 216,400) or more was awarded. In 1998, a 54-year-old woman was awarded the equivalent of EUR 306,498, or DEM 600,000, (GBP 184,615 and USD 259,679) compensation for medical malpractice after an operation on her spine resulted in paraplegia. Further, the claimant retained the right to return to court for additional compensation if a further belated claim should arise after the judicial hearing.

We have found that only recently, in a judgment of March 2001, a victim of a road traffic accident was awarded EUR 510,830 (GBP 307,692 and USD 432,800) for pain and suffering by a Court in Munich,[9] the first time that the limit of EUR 510,830 (DEM 1 million) was reached.

German lawyers were not able to advise the highest settlement inclusive of medical expenses. The reason is that over 95% of German people have social sickness insurance and the tortfeasor's insurance companies often settle medical expense claims direct with the claimant's insurers.

Medical expenses in Germany are higher than in England with all-round medical care at home costing up to around EUR 10,217 per month (GBP 6,154 and USD 8,656); hospital beds EUR 153-357 (GBP 92-215 and USD 129-302) per day in a standard hospital in a mid-sized town; EUR 817 (GBP 492 and USD 692) per

---

8 This figure is based on the exchange rate on 4 July (GBP 1 equivalent to DEM 3.25)

9 Landgericht München I, Az 19 08647 or Deutsches Autorecht 2001/368

day for AIDS sufferers and, the cost in intensive care is EUR 767-1,532 per day (GBP 462-923 and USD 650-1,298). However, as explained above for comparison purposes only the English section medical expenses have been adopted, although conservative, they gave some basis for comparison.

As in the Netherlands (see below), for the serious injuries in the overall comparison schedules, we have included medical expenses at the English rate, to allow a comparison across the jurisdictions as far as is possible.

Greece

Greece has a written constitution and, like all EU countries save the UK and Ireland, it follows a civil code system.

Our first edition showed that the Greek awards were at the bottom of the European range of damages and this was still the case in the second edition. In the new edition, however, the Greek awards seem to be in the mid-field leaving Finland, Portugal, Sweden, Austria and even Spain behind. The Greek method of calculation is surprisingly similar to the English but there are some important differences. For example, in Greece, as in Germany and Norway but not England, in assessing the levels of pain and suffering awards the degree of fault as well as the financial and social status of both parties is taken into consideration. However, under specific provisions of the Greek Civil Code, damages payable to the relatives of the deceased for loss of support, as well as damages payable to the injured party, are paid in monthly instalments and not in a lump sum, save in exceptional circumstances.

Paradoxically, parents of the single woman over 20 receive on her instant death considerably more than in many other jurisdictions. At the other extreme England, Germany, Denmark and the Netherlands award only funeral expenses.

Our Greek correspondent co-author, Mr E. Tsouroulis of Deucalion Rediadis and Sons in Piraeus has advised us that since the 1994 edition of the book, the level of damages for pain and suffering awarded by the courts has increased considerably. Comparisons with other countries however, show they are still at the bottom end of the table.

The Greek Civil Code provides for damages payable to the relatives of a deceased for loss of support and damages payable to an injured party to be paid in monthly instalments and not in a lump sum save in exceptional cases.

The legal interest rate is quite high in Greece, currently 18% p.a., payable either from the date of the event that gave rise to the claim or from the date of service of the writ.

Ireland

In the Republic of Ireland, overall awards and the pain and suffering element are high by comparison with other countries. In the second edition in 1994, the Irish figures were at the top of the comparison tables and in this third edition they are still leading the tables. However, the England & Wales figures have become very close to the Irish figures.

In Ireland, assessments were made by juries until July 1988 when juries were abolished in personal injury cases. In the second edition of the book (1994) we stated that: "Perhaps surprisingly this has not had the expected effect of a levelling off in the rate of increase in awards.[10] Our Irish correspondent lawyer, Katherine Delahunt, confirmed that the abolition of juries had not had the expected effect of slowing down the rate of increase in levels of awards. Our figures, both in relation to overall awards and in relation to pain and suffering awards confirm that. However, it is also interesting to compare the increase in awards across Europe since the second edition. These do appear to show the Irish overall awards are not increasing in percentage as quickly as some other countries eg. English and Welsh, Scottish, German or Greek awards.

The Irish legal system follows the English system, which is not surprising since Ireland did not become an independent state until the 1920s. Ireland is still a common law jurisdiction with a split legal profession involving solicitors and barristers but only barristers enjoy rights of audience in the higher courts. Methods of calculating personal injury awards have, however, evolved differently since Irish independence.

The major differences between compensation awards in England and in the Republic of Ireland are that:

a) The Irish award for future loss of earnings incorporates an allowance for inflation and an allowance for the risk that the injured party might not be employed for all of what would otherwise have been expected to be his full working life. (Unemployment in Ireland is around 3.8%.[11] The earnings assessment set out in the Irish schedule was prepared with the assistance of an actuary.

10 *Ireland – A case study*, by Brian Gregan (Confederation of Irish Industry), March 1992

11 Source: Eurostat, the European Commission Representation in Ireland, 2 October 2001

b) Although judges have discretion to award interest on pre-trial losses, it is very rare for such interest to be awarded.

c) Statutory bereavement damages in Ireland are governed by the Civil Liability Act (as amended) 1961. The present figure is EUR 9,505 (GBP 5,725 and USD 8,053).

Katherine Delahunt from Vincent & Beatty Solicitors in Dublin has pointed out that today, in Ireland, extensive use is made of pre-trial settlement meetings, which in many cases lead to an early settlement thereby reducing legal fees and other professional fees.

Because of differing levels of damages awarded in recent Army deafness cases, the Irish Government brought in the Civil Liability (assessment of Hearing) Injuries Act 1998.

Katherine Delahunt further has explained that there is no specific limitation on the amount of general damages that can be awarded. The Supreme Court has however laid down guidelines for the High Court to follow. Recently, the Supreme Court in the case of *Ramos v. Kapitaen Manfred Draxl Schiffahrts GmbH* (unreported) reduced an award of general damages from EUR 316,833 (GBP 190,840 and USD 268,436) to EUR 190,100 (GBP 114,504 and USD 161,061) and the Chief Justice advised he was being generous even in this. While the plaintiff's injuries were life threatening, he had recovered well and therefore the Supreme Court held that the High Court was wrong in assessing the injuries in the same way as one would a catastrophic case.

We were advised that actions arising with regard to contaminated blood plasma are now being dealt with by a Tribunal, which has the power to award damages, future loss and a punitive sum against the State. It is expected that the Army deafness cases will also be heard by a Tribunal, which has proved in other claims to be both expeditious and cost effective.

Italy

Italy is the country that differs most from the English system. Calculations for fatal accidents and personal injuries were placed under three classes as follows:

a) Biological damages

b) Property damages.

c) Moral damages or personal damage.

Biological damages are defined as an award for violation of the mental, psychological and physical integrity of the injured party regardless of loss of income; property damages are defined as loss of income, and moral damages as compensation for pain and suffering where the harmful act is likened to a crime against the person.

Initially, we assumed that biological damages were part of pain and suffering awards. However, "moral damages" also appear to be compensation for pain and suffering. We understand from the participating Italian lawyer that biological damages are a new concept introduced into the Italian legal system in 1979.

With regard to biological damages, in this third edition, only figures from the Milan lawyers have been included, but biological damages are included in the schedule. Readers should be aware that some areas of Italy will include them whilst others will not (see Italian section for further explanation).

If biological damages were an Italian equivalent of pain and suffering awards as we had initially assumed, it would make sense that biological damages should not be awarded in an instant death case. However the concept of biological damages is not that simple. Since our first edition at least one Italian court has held that biological damages would not be awarded in an instant death case. The injured party must have suffered before dying before such damages can be passed on to his heirs. But other Italian courts appear to correlate biological damage with bereavement rather than pain and suffering and award biological damages in death cases on the basis of loss of companionship.

Our correspondent Allessandro Georgetti from Studio Legale Georgetti in Milan has advised us that there is still no established procedure agreed upon by the Italian courts to determine the amount to be awarded for biological damages. He explained that actuarial tables have been adopted by several Italian courts, which helped to harmonise the award-making process in Italy and the tables are now the basis for a government project of reform to address the problem of how biological damage should be liquidated all over the country. We were surprised by the definition of moral damages as "an award for pain and suffering as a result of criminal wrongdoing". On further investigation, however, it appears that "criminal wrongdoing" for the purpose of Italian civil proceedings includes personal injury caused by negligence.

Our correspondent explained that despite the new Civil Procedure Code, it is still normal that court proceedings and the final judgment take place long after the accident has occurred. It may take three or four years from the date of the commencement of proceedings before a final decision is obtained. However, contrary to what we reported in the first and second editions, courts, from 2000 onwards, have not made an award that included a devaluation factor unless the party had rigidly proven that in consequence of the damage there was a financial loss. The event of the Euro does of course mean that devaluation is no longer a consideration.

Our Italian lawyer advised us that very recently, Italian law was changed to include damages for the "trauma of facing death". Before, this could not be indemnified in relation to the victims' relatives when the victim had actually died. Examples of claims under this head include the Mont Blanc disaster victims' relatives.

Luxembourg

We reported in the first and second editions of this book that Luxembourg follows a similar system to France and Belgium. This is still the case and has been confirmed by Luxembourg lawyer Rene Diederich who said in his report that on the main principles according to which damages are recoverable for personal injuries, the Luxembourg courts tend to follow French and, to a certain extent, Belgian case law. With regard to levels of amounts, Luxembourg courts would refer to French or Belgian jurisprudence, with the exception that certain amounts that would be awarded in order to compensate the moral damages suffered by the direct and indirect injured victims might even be higher in the Grand Duchy of Luxembourg than in neighbouring France and Belgium. The results of this third survey however would appear to show that awards in both Belgium and France, (but particularly in Belgium) have increased more than the awards in Luxembourg in recent years.

Whilst structured settlements are the norm in France for serious personal injury cases, they are not common in Luxembourg. In this respect, Luxembourg is similar to Belgium.

The Netherlands

Since the first edition of this book was published, a new Civil Code is in place replacing section 1406 of the 1838 Civil Code and funeral expenses are now included in personal injury awards. However, surviving relatives as dependants are since NOT entitled to bereavement damages. The category of damages has been considered by the Supreme Court but has been neglected.

Our first edition showed that the pain and suffering awards in the Netherlands were not generous and were generally lower than in Belgium, France, Luxembourg, England, Germany and Ireland. The highest pain and suffering award in The Netherlands (up to completion of the first edition report) was NGL 300,000 (GBP 92,310 and USD 178,020 according to rates from around the time of the first publication) awarded to a patient infected with HIV through the negligence of a hospital. This represented a quantum leap for the Netherlands' courts but since then, NGL 300,000 (GBP 81,967, USD 115,295 and EUR 136,082) has been awarded for exceptional serious injuries on a number of occasions. Our correspondent, Marinus M. Mac Lean has advised us that the largest amount in damages ever awarded in the Netherlands is still the above-mentioned case with NLG 300,000 (GBP 81,967, USD 115,295 and EUR 136,082). He expects that awards for very serious injuries (such as paraplegia) will gradually become higher, but at present damages awarded in the Netherlands are still relatively modest in relation to awards in other EU countries.

With regard to awards for loss of earning capacity, Marinus M. MacLean has advised us that claims for loss of income against a paying party have become higher as social security benefits have decreased in the past few years.

Portugal

In the first and second editions, our Portuguese source, Mr Pereira of M. P. Barrocas & Associados, found it very difficult to draw up a schedule with figures. Our correspondent explained whilst preparing the figures for this third edition that there is still a lack of conformity within the country. The Portuguese awards were the lowest in Europe in the previous editions in 1991 and 1994 and this remains the case. Portuguese judges are not bound by any particular case law and as first instance decisions are not made public, awards can vary hugely. The figures provided for specific items, such as funeral expenses, are much less than in other countries.

The Portuguese have two systems, one is fault based and the other is non-fault. We have incorporated a notional schedule based on the information received from Portugal, in relation to the fault system. This has enabled us to include Portugal in the overall comparison schedule.

Portugal, unlike England, awards "moral damages" in a fatal case even where there are no dependants. Whilst civil code system lawyers refer to "moral damages" as "pain and suffering", clearly the use of the words "moral damages" can have a wider meaning. [In Portugal] "Moral damages" on instant death refers to bereavement rather than pain and suffering.

In the second edition in 1994, we reported that the usual maximum moral damages element in a fatal case award was PTE 1,300,000 (GBP 3,905[12] and USD 5,493), and the highest award in the second edition was PTE 2,000,000 (GBP 6,008 and USD 8,451). For this third edition, our Portuguese correspondent lawyer, H. de los Santos Pereira explained that, according to most recent case law, the maximum moral damage in a fatal claim payable to the widow or widower is EUR 14,960 (GBP 9,011 and USD 12,675) and the maximum moral damages attributable to the deceased's sons (descendants) is EUR 19,947 (GBP 12,015 and USD 16,900.)

Scotland

On the unification of England and Wales with Scotland in 1707, one of the agreed conditions was that the legal systems should remain separate. This is still the case today and accounts for the divergence in the way in which personal injury awards are assessed in these jurisdictions.

There is no statutory provision for bereavement damages in Scotland. Loss of society is different in that it is discretionary and dependent not just on financial dependency but social closeness of parent and child. For example, a parent living some distance away and unlikely to visit a daughter regularly is unlikely to receive and award for loss of society on her death. In the Scottish schedule B (the legal secretary) GBP 1,500 (USD 2,110 and EUR 2,490) for each parent is included on the assumption that the parents live close by in Scotland and see their daughter regularly.

In the early nineties, the use of actuarial tables was met with some resistance in Scotland, however, the House of Lords' *Wells v Wells* ruling in 1998, where it was held that actuarial tables should provide the starting point when selecting a multiplier, has been followed in Scotland and until the Secretary of State prescribes otherwise, the assumed rate of return is 3%.

Scotland is the only jurisdiction covered in this book that provides for jury trial, and there is an increasing propensity for claimants to opt for their right to jury trial.

Spain

Our Spanish correspondent lawyer for previous editions, Ruiz-Gallardon Y Muniz described the levels of personal injury awards in Spain as a "lottery". He reported that judges were not bound by case law or legislation. They did not usually break down their awards to identify what percentage of the award was made for pain and suffering or medical expenses. For this reason the Spanish figures varied hugely making it difficult to provide reliable guidelines. As a result no pain and suffering award assessments were made for Spain in previous editions.

Our correspondent for this third edition of the book, Mercedes Pallares from Davies Arnold Cooper, Madrid, advised us that the Spanish legal system is very similar to that operated by other European countries bound by a Civil Code countries in Europe. A rating system, introduced by The Treasury and Economic ministry (order dated 5 March 1991) is now applied by the courts which has resulted in greater certainty in relation to calculating awards. Further legislation on the regulations and supervision of private insurance enacted in 1995 is also of assistance in calculating awards.

In the third edition, no calculations have been made for medical, pharmaceutical and hospital costs and expenses, as the valuation arising from this concept strongly depends on individual circumstances. Those costs, however, are recoverable as personal injury awards.

Sweden

In Sweden there is strict liability by legislation in many areas including rail, motor, sea, pollution and nuclear fuel. Against the expectations of many practitioners and commentators Sweden has adopted strict product liability legislation to implement with the EU Product Liability Directive with a *development risk defence.* A form of strict liability has also been introduced through case law — for example in relation to injuries caused by blasting works.

There are also several no-fault schemes – including the Patient Insurance Scheme which covers injury caused by medical treatment and the Pharmaceutical Insurance Scheme for injuries caused by drugs. In order to succeed in a claim to these schemes, causation, but not fault, must be established. However, the assessments in this report assume that both negligence and causation have been proved. For motor claims, there is a limit of SEK 300,000,000 (GBP 19,607,843, USD 27,580,391 and EUR 32,552,940) per case.

Compensation for future loss of income or loss of maintenance is paid in the form of an annuity or a lump sum, and the annuity is the most common form of compensation. Awards under tort law in Sweden are low by comparison to most EU and EFTA countries. The Swedish figures now rank at the very low mid-field of the overall awards and are ranked even lower for awards in respect of pain and suffering. Three reasons for these low awards are: (1) the Swedish Social Security system pays 90% of an injured workers' income in the first year; (2) the scale of non-economic loss awards is low; (3) private insurance is the exception rather than the rule.

EFTA COUNTRIES

Iceland

Iceland's compensation system is similar to systems in the other Nordic countries. In 1993, Iceland passed legislation in relation to damages, using legislation in the Nordic countries as models. Under the Icelandic legislation, the tortfeasor compensates for loss of earnings, suffering, medical expenses and other financial loss. If the harmful event has permanent consequences, compensation is also paid for non-financial loss and disability. Compensation according to Icelandic legislation is partially standardised but efforts are made to take the victims' age and occupation into consideration.

Awards for pain and suffering are standardised in Iceland, the award is ISK 1,500 (GBP 10.34, USD 14.54 and EUR 17.17) for each day the victim needs to remain in bed, and ISK 850 (GBP 5.86, USD 8.24 and EUR 9.73) for each day he remains ambulant without recovery.

In Iceland, as in many countries actuaries are involved in calculating loss of income awards.

Medical expenses for medical services and nursing are usually small as they are mostly paid by public funds.

Bereavement damages are linked to dependency payments and in our model example, no bereavement damages were awarded to relatives of the secretary.

Liechtenstein

Liechtenstein generally follows Austrian practice and jurisprudence with regard to personal injury awards (see Liechtenstein Supreme Court decision, 6 May 1991).

As in Austria, no bereavement damages are awarded but there are exceptions for example, motor insurers will pay bereavement damages.

The Liechtenstein currency (the Swiss Franc) is stronger than the Austrian Schilling and the cost of living in Liechtenstein is comparatively higher than in Austria.

It will be interesting to see what effect if any the replacement of the Austrian Schilling with the Euro will have. Whilst the categories of award are the same in the two countries, the Liechtenstein awards are higher. The Liechtenstein section therefore is based on the Austrian figures with the called-for adjustments as advised by our correspondent Swiss lawyers.

Our Swiss correspondent, Dr Girsberger, reports that in Liechtenstein, both Austrian and Swiss law are applied. Liechtenstein tends to follow the example of the leading Swiss liability insurers, which is mostly written by Swiss companies who tend to apply their own standards of indemnification.

Norway

In Norway, as in most EFTA countries, there is no claim for bereavement damages. There are two types of non-economic damages as follows:

1. Common law non-economic damages.
2. Medical disability compensation

Common law non-economic damages are awarded in cases involving gross negligence. The amount of compensation where gross negligence has been established will depend on the degree of wrongdoing and also the ability of the wrongdoer to pay. Common law non-economic damages have traditionally been very conservative. A typical compensation award would be NOK 50,000 (GBP 3,791, USD 5,332 and EUR 6,294) as a lump sum payment. Medical disability compensation is considerably higher than common law non-economic damage. This system is similar to the Danish system and in the first edition we included both these elements as the equivalent of pain and suffering. The Norwegian explanation of the system does appear to confirm that was the correct approach.

Again as in Denmark and Iceland medical expenses are not included as they are paid for on a non-recoverable basis by the State.

Under Norwegian law all employers are obliged to have occupational injuries insurance. Where the employer fails to arrange an insurance policy, the employee is awarded compensation from a pooling arrangement between insurance companies.

Switzerland

In Switzerland, personal injury claims that include an element of future loss of income are compensated by a capital award instead of an annuity. The award is arrived at by use of actuarial tables of Stauffer/Schaetzle.

Of the EFTA countries, Switzerland is responsible for the highest award, with payments in excess of one million British Pounds for such serious injuries as quadriplegia, paraplegia, brain injury and total blindness.

Bereavement damages are recoverable in Switzerland, unlike most of the EFTA countries. Since 1984, National Accident Insurance is compulsory for employees. The insurer has a right of recourse against a third party liability insurer.

However, pain and suffering awards in Switzerland are low. For the legal secretary, in particular they are very low with for example pain and suffering for RSI being less than for the doctor.

PARAMETERS

Victims' personal data

Married man, aged 40, 2 dependants, doctor

Single woman, aged 20, no dependants, legal secretary

Types of Injury

1. Instant death
2. Burns (A,B,C)
   a) Burns to face with scarring
   b) Burns to face (no scars)
   c) Burns to other parts of the body (15-20%)
3. Quadriplegia
4. Paraplegia
5. Brain damage – moderate
6. Brain damage with motor deficiency
7. Amputation of leg above knee
8. Amputation of leg below knee
9. Amputation of arm above elbow
10. Amputation of arm below elbow
11. Loss of eyesight – one eye without cosmetic disability
12. Loss of eyesight – one eye with cosmetic disability
13. Loss of eyesight- total blindness
14. Total deafness
15. Repetitive strain injury

Schedule of Incomes

Table 1. Schedule A – Doctor, net income

EU

	£	$	€
Austria	30,635	43,091	50,860
Belgium	26,870	37,795	44,610
Denmark	21,423	30,134	35,566
England / Wales	36,000	50,638	59,767
Finland	30,395	42,754	50,462
France	32,140	45,208	53,359
Germany	30,769	43,280	51,083
Greece	12,724	17,898	21,124
Ireland	38,168	53,687	63,367
Italy	31,102	43,748	51,636
Luxembourg	31,320	44,055	51,997
The Netherlands	27,322	38,431	45,360
Portugal	6,008	8,451	9,974
Scotland	36,000	50,638	59,767
Spain	17,373	24,437	28,843
Sweden	32,680	45,968	54,255

EFTA

	£	$	€
Iceland	25,503	35,873	42,340
Liechtenstein	39,526	55,597	65,621
Norway	37,908	53,321	62,935
Switzerland	39,526	55,597	65,621

Table 2. Schedule B – Legal scretary, net income

	Age 20			Age 30			Age 40		
EU	£	$	€	£	$	€	£	$	€
Austria	6,565	9,234	10,899	*	*	*	*	*	*
Belgium	7,464	10,499	12,392	11,196	15,748	18,588	13,062	18,373	21,686
Denmark	11,641	16,374	19,326	11,641	16,374	19,326	11,641	16,374	19,326
England/Wales	14,372	20,216	23,860	14,717	20,701	24,433	15,804	22,230	26,238
Finland	10,132	14,252	16,821	*	*	*	*	*	*
France	9,183	12,917	15,246	14,325	20,150	23,782	14,325	20,150	23,782
Germany	7,692	10,820	12,770	10,769	15,148	17,879	12,308	17,312	20,434
Greece	4,418	6,214	7,335	*	*	*	*	*	*
Ireland	6,489	9,127	10,773	11,450	16,106	19,009	11,450	16,106	19,009
Italy	8,709	12,250	14,459	*	*	*	*	*	*
Luxembourg	10,440	14,685	17,332	14,914	20,978	24,760	18,643	26,223	30,951
The Netherlands	6,421	9,032	10,660	9,153	12,875	15,196	9,153	12,875	15,196

Portugal	4,205	5,915	6,981	5,257	7,394	8,728	6,909	9,718	11,470
Scotland	10,000	14,066	16,602	*	*	*	*	*	*
Spain	6,949	9,774	11,537	*	*	*	*	*	*
Sweden	11,765	16,549	19,232	*	*	*	*	*	*

	Age 20			Age 30			Age 40		
EFTA	£	$	€	£	$	€	£	$	€
Iceland	8,961	12,605	14,877	*	*	*	*	*	*
Liechtenstein	11,858	16,679	19,687	15,810	22,238	26,248	19,763	27,799	32,811
Norway	14,989	21,084	24,882	*	*	*	*	*	*
Switzerland	14,229	20,015	23,623	18,182	25,575	30,186	18,972	26,686	31,497

* No figures are available for a secretary's net income at the age of 30 and 40

NB. This is a rough guide of incomes suggested by our correspondents and may not reflect the level of incomes exactly

TOTAL COMPENSATION: EU COUNTRIES

Table 1. Schedule A. GBP (£)

Doctor, man, 40, married, 2 dependent children; currency at 4 July 2001

Injury	*Austria GBP 1= 22.85 ATS*	*Belgium GBP 1= 66.99 BEF*	*Denmark GBP 1= 12.37 DKK*	*England /Wales*
1. Instant death	70,818	356,462	110,752	518,750
2. Burns A. Face B. Face (no scars) C. Body	23,632 to 43,589	97,085 97,085 97,085	52,466 52,466 52,466	117,000 107,000 97,000
3. Quadriplegia	254,267	1,174,032	317,259	2,372,250
4. Paraplegia	224,858	754,531	148,424	1,223,125
5a. Brain damage (moderate)	184,683	600,230		1,112,250
5b. Brain damage with motor deficiency	198,031	1,283,207	317,259	1,904,450
6a. Amputation of leg above the knee	79,650	393,748	184,608	281,125
6b. Amputation of leg below the knee	68,709	335,278		221,133
7a. Amputation of arm above the elbow	97,155	396,020	196,605	718,125
7b. Amputation of arm below elbow	90,591	389,723		679,125
8a. Loss of eyesight – one eye without cosmetic disability	36,018	167,917	63,945	52,500
8b. Loss of eyesight – one eye with cosmetic disability	56,236	176,127		57,500
8c. Loss of eyesight total blindness	167,834	653,790	264,390	1,018,500
9. Deafness	104,070	290,982	184,608	265,000
10. RSI	—	332,114	—	169,500

<table>
<tr><th>Injury</th><th>Finland
GBP 1=
9.87 FIM</th><th>France
GBP 1=
10.89 FRF</th><th>Germany
GBP 1=
3.25 DEM</th><th>Greece
GBP 1=
565.86 GRD</th></tr>
<tr><td>1. Instant death</td><td>21,277+ Fe</td><td>306,636</td><td>401,231</td><td>210.034</td></tr>
<tr><td>2. Burns
A. Face
B. Face (no scars)
C. Body</td><td>61,649
61,649
58,010</td><td>98,749
to
114,127</td><td>123,077
to
138,462</td><td>73,496
to
90,552</td></tr>
<tr><td>3. Quadriplegia</td><td>581,896</td><td>1,009,458</td><td>1,911,923*
to
2,004,231*</td><td>685,152</td></tr>
<tr><td>4. Paraplegia</td><td>508,948</td><td>623,655</td><td rowspan="3">806,346*
to
1,706,154*</td><td>307,107</td></tr>
<tr><td>5a. Brain damage (moderate)</td><td rowspan="2">581,896</td><td rowspan="2">884,444
to
908,790</td><td rowspan="2">350,740</td></tr>
<tr><td>5b. Brain damage with motor deficiency</td></tr>
<tr><td>6a. Amputation of leg above the knee</td><td>71,233</td><td>192,593</td><td rowspan="2">148,846*
to
178,462*</td><td>134,962</td></tr>
<tr><td>6b. Amputation of leg below the knee</td><td>69,021</td><td>159,504</td><td>118,244</td></tr>
<tr><td>7a. Amputation of arm above the elbow</td><td>81,066</td><td>197,368</td><td rowspan="2">343,461*
to
379,615*</td><td>134,962</td></tr>
<tr><td>7b. Amputation of arm below elbow</td><td>79,959</td><td>169,316</td><td>118,244</td></tr>
<tr><td>8a. Loss of eyesight – one eye without cosmetic disability</td><td>63,862</td><td>56,474</td><td rowspan="2">46,154
to
55,385</td><td rowspan="2">109,638</td></tr>
<tr><td>8b. Loss of eyesight – one eye with cosmetic disability</td><td>68,927</td><td>94,169</td></tr>
<tr><td>8c. Loss of eyesight total blindness</td><td>581,896</td><td>309,120</td><td>672,308*</td><td>372,177</td></tr>
<tr><td>9. Deafness</td><td>51,777</td><td>129,624
to
130,083</td><td>256,923</td><td>175,662</td></tr>
<tr><td>10. RSI</td><td>—</td><td>—</td><td>—</td><td>69,769</td></tr>
</table>

** In these cases the cost of medical care has been added on using the medical costs suggested under the English example of the same injuries.*

Injury	*Ireland GBP 1= 1.31 IEP*	*Italy GBP 1= 3215.24 ITL*	*Luxembourg GBP 1= 67.05 LUF*	*The Netherlands GBP 1= 3.66 NLG*
1. Instant death	611,450	671,722	354,057	276,639
2. Burns A. Face B. Face (no scars) C. Body	148,855 129,771 129,771	45,856 to 126,503	86,501 86,501 86,501	59,836 59,836 59,836
3. Quadriplegia	1,340,076 to 1,378,244	931,093	1,023,043	698,839* to 1,830,628*
4. Paraplegia	994,275 to 1,032,443	634,319	473,553	
5a. Brain damage (moderate)	838,550 to 914,886	760,298	563,521	
5b. Brain damage with motor deficiency	1,336,260 to 1,374,427	847,322	974,183	
6a. Amputation of leg above the knee	232,443	237,919	92,198	156,038* to 192,869*
6b. Amputation of leg below the knee	205,954	195,919	85,226	
7a. Amputation of arm above the elbow	509,542	237,919	262,375	335,000* to 377,295*
7b. Amputation of arm below elbow	505,267	195,919	256,736	
8a. Loss of eyesight – one eye without cosmetic disability	116,412	234,187	57,085	27,322 to 35,519
8b. Loss of eyesight – one eye with cosmetic disability	137,405 to 148,855	236,053	66,034	
8c. Loss of eyesight total blindness	807,634 to 826,718	810,000	572,309	550,820* to 575,410*
9. Deafness	442,748 to 461,832	457,747	319,510	467,213 to 515,027
10. RSI	—	122,255	—	—

Injury	*Portugal GBP 1= 332.91 PTE*	*Scotland*	*Spain GBP 1= 276.29 ESP*	*Sweden GBP 1= 15.3 SEK*
1. Instant death	195,849	513,425	101,378	71,895
2. Burns A. Face B. Face (no scars) C. Body	 19,825 19,825 19,825	 87,250 74,300 87,300	 43,203 28,744 32,877	 9,477 9,477 9,477
3. Quadriplegia	253,822	1,822,787	546,832	385,131
4. Paraplegia	167,312	974,823	525,242	377,614
5a. Brain damage (moderate)	253,822	903,410	174,235	353,105
5b. Brain damage with motor deficiency		1,642,605	247,180	365,719
6a. Amputation of leg above the knee	131,267	125,725	96,424	28,889
6b. Amputation of leg below the knee		120,475	71,690	22,026
7a. Amputation of arm above the elbow	156,799	578,385	94,061	346,536
7b. Amputation of arm below elbow		568,385	75,771	342,418
8a. Loss of eyesight – one eye without cosmetic disability	20,426	45,800	32,817	13,922
8b. Loss of eyesight – one eye with cosmetic disability		50,800	43,235	—
8c. Loss of eyesight total blindness	147,788	797,579	263,829	367,288
9. Deafness	129,164	488,920	99,338	342,614
10. RSI	8,260	132,120	—	143,791

** In these cases the cost of medical care has been added on using the medical costs suggested under the English example of the same injuries.*

Table 2. Schedule B. GBP (£)

Legal scretary, woman, 20, single; currency at 4 July 2001

<table>
<tr><th>Injury</th><th>Austria
GBP 1=
22.85 ATS</th><th>Belgium
GBP 1=
66.99 BEF</th><th>Denmark
GBP 1=
12.37 DKK</th><th>England
/Wales</th></tr>
<tr><td>1. Instant death</td><td>2,188</td><td>11,196</td><td>2,102</td><td>1,250</td></tr>
<tr><td>2. Burns
A. Face
B. Face (no scars)
C. Body</td><td>12,473
to
20,832</td><td>59,766
59,766
59,766</td><td>31,609
31,609
31,609</td><td>66,500
56,500
46,500</td></tr>
<tr><td>3. Quadriplegia</td><td>186,433</td><td>1,078,128</td><td>203,371</td><td>2,267,500</td></tr>
<tr><td>4. Paraplegia</td><td>164,902</td><td>673,660</td><td rowspan="2">97,041</td><td>1,533,500</td></tr>
<tr><td>5a. Brain damage (moderate)</td><td>115,974</td><td>414,139</td><td>765,500</td></tr>
<tr><td>5b. Brain damage with motor deficiency</td><td>128,884</td><td>1,241,303</td><td>97,041
to
203,371</td><td>1,998,000</td></tr>
<tr><td>6a. Amputation of leg above the knee</td><td>67,221</td><td>204,140</td><td rowspan="2">117,672</td><td>264,000</td></tr>
<tr><td>6b. Amputation of leg below the knee</td><td>56,280</td><td>168,812</td><td>167,000</td></tr>
<tr><td>7a. Amputation of arm above the elbow</td><td>58,468</td><td>258,315</td><td rowspan="2">125,465</td><td>356,750</td></tr>
<tr><td>7b. Amputation of arm below elbow</td><td>51,904</td><td>249,926</td><td>259,500</td></tr>
<tr><td>8a. Loss of eyesight – one eye without cosmetic disability</td><td>27,046</td><td>79,064</td><td rowspan="2">41,132</td><td>31,500</td></tr>
<tr><td>8b. Loss of eyesight – one eye with cosmetic disability</td><td>35,230</td><td>90,259</td><td>36,500</td></tr>
<tr><td>8c. Loss of eyesight total blindness</td><td>100,000</td><td>461,711</td><td>170,776</td><td>590,500</td></tr>
<tr><td>9. Deafness</td><td>44,551</td><td>309,182</td><td>117,672</td><td>138,000</td></tr>
<tr><td>10. RSI</td><td>–</td><td>194,410</td><td>–</td><td>100,750</td></tr>
</table>

<table>
<tr><th>Injury</th><th>Finland
GBP 1=
9.87 FIM</th><th>France
GBP 1=
10.89 FRF</th><th>Germany
GBP 1=
3.25 DEM</th><th>Greece
GBP 1=
565.86 GRD</th></tr>
<tr><td>1. Instant death</td><td>Fe</td><td>29,844</td><td>2,307</td><td>14,668</td></tr>
<tr><td>2. Burns
A. Face
B. Face (no scars)
C. Body</td><td>18,355
18,355
14,432</td><td>56,633
to
74,777</td><td>61,538
to
76,923</td><td>14,765
to
16,223</td></tr>
<tr><td>3. Quadriplegia</td><td>262,573</td><td>975,487</td><td>2,003,280*
to
2,064,819*</td><td>572,580</td></tr>
<tr><td>4. Paraplegia</td><td>262,573</td><td>579,362</td><td rowspan="3">594,506*
to
1,824,314*</td><td>232,169</td></tr>
<tr><td>5a. Brain damage (moderate)</td><td rowspan="2">262,573</td><td rowspan="2">843,825
to
872,178</td><td rowspan="2">285,053</td></tr>
<tr><td>5b. Brain damage with motor deficiency</td></tr>
<tr><td>6a. Amputation of leg above the knee</td><td>26,825</td><td>170,294</td><td rowspan="2">195,772*
to
249,176*</td><td>86,085</td></tr>
<tr><td>6b. Amputation of leg below the knee</td><td>24,049</td><td>133,099</td><td>74,709</td></tr>
<tr><td>7a. Amputation of arm above the elbow</td><td>155,645</td><td>158,589</td><td rowspan="2">92,308
to
101,503</td><td>86,085</td></tr>
<tr><td>7b. Amputation of arm below elbow</td><td>148,656</td><td>127,521</td><td>74,709</td></tr>
<tr><td>8a. Loss of eyesight – one eye without cosmetic disability</td><td>21,135</td><td>51,798</td><td rowspan="2">519,565*</td><td rowspan="2">69,806</td></tr>
<tr><td>8b. Loss of eyesight – one eye with cosmetic disability</td><td>26,201</td><td>72,505</td></tr>
<tr><td>8c. Loss of eyesight total blindness</td><td>140,995</td><td>270,332</td><td>519,565*</td><td>247,057</td></tr>
<tr><td>9. Deafness</td><td>34,918</td><td>147,658
to
148,118</td><td>88,388</td><td>113,323</td></tr>
<tr><td>10. RSI</td><td>–</td><td>–</td><td>–</td><td>42,590</td></tr>
</table>

** In these cases the cost of medical care has been added on using the medical costs suggested under the English example of the same injuries.*

Injury	*Ireland GBP 1= 1.31 IEP*	*Italy GBP 1= 3215.24 ITL*	*Luxembourg GBP 1= 67.05 LUF*	*The Netherlands GBP 1= 3.66 NLG*
1. Instant death	17,176	176,368	6,115	5,464
2. Burns A. Face B. Face (no scars) C. Body	102,824 89,847 82,214	50,006 to 79,322	45,562 45,562 45,562	12,330 12,330 12,330
3. Quadriplegia	1,098,282	715,086	976,570	536,981* to 1,883,770*
4. Paraplegia	604,008 to 642,176	477,839	347,331	
5a. Brain damage (moderate)	365,840 to 404,008	582,277	427,797	
5b. Brain damage with motor deficiency	1,206,298 to 1,244,466	647,791	860,189	
6a. Amputation of leg above the knee	185,305	152,964	64,109	148,607* to 207,937*
6b. Amputation of leg below the knee	117,672 to 136,756	122,138	57,803	
7a. Amputation of arm above the elbow	299,408 to 318,511	152,964	60,846	228,120* to 289,031*
7b. Amputation of arm below elbow	274,542 to 285,992	122,138	55,715	
8a. Loss of eyesight – one eye without cosmetic disability	81,679	149,232	42,551	13,661 to 21,858
8b. Loss of eyesight – one eye with cosmetic disability	100,763 to 112,214		48,293	
8c. Loss of eyesight total blindness	350,573	610,469	396,490	309,462* to 323,123*
9. Deafness	217,748 to 233,015	327,627	280,510	133,350 to 140,181
10. RSI	–	56,509	–	143,443

Injury	*Portugal GBP 1= 332.91 PTE*	*Scotland*	*Spain GBP 1= 276.29 ESP*	*Sweden GBP 1= 15.3 SEK*
1. Instant death	45,658	1,500	45,045	3,268
2. Burns A. Face B. Face (no scars) C. Body	8,891 8,891 8,891	39,800 24,800 39,800	58,736 27,231 28,608	5,033 to 12,222
3. Quadriplegia	237,301	1,620,994	538,236	275,948
4. Paraplegia	150,792	421,550	517,924	267,353
5a. Brain damage (moderate)	249,317	477,975	169,652	244,771
5b. Brain damage with motor deficiency		1,416,440	241,690	252,941
6a. Amputation of leg above the knee	86,330	79,800	91,166	30,523
6b. Amputation of leg below the knee		74,550	72,444	24,771
7a. Amputation of arm above the elbow	93,028	230,710	119,588	149,412
7b. Amputation of arm below elbow		219,710	102,506	143,791
8a. Loss of eyesight – one eye without cosmetic disability	17,963	23,800	25,696	11,960
8b. Loss of eyesight – one eye with cosmetic disability		33,800	36,731	11,960
8c. Loss of eyesight total blindness	180,229	373,600	261,370	264,183
9. Deafness	87,111	128,680	96,942	232,405
10. RSI	5,677	113,680	–	94,118

** In these cases the cost of medical care has been added on using the medical costs suggested under the English example of the same injuries.*

Table 3. Schedule A. EUR (€) (£ = €1.6602)

Doctor, man, 40, married, 2 dependent children; currency at 4 July 2001

Injury	*Austria*	*Belgium*	*Denmark*	*England/Wales*
1. Instant death	117,572	591,798	183,870	861,129
2. Burns A. Face B. Face (no scars) C. Body	39,234 to 72,366	161,181 161,181 161,181	87,104 87,104 87,104	194,243 177,641 161,039
3. Quadriplegia	422,134	1,949,128	526,713	3,938,409
4. Paraplegia	373,309	1,252,672	246,414	2,030,632
5a. Brain damage (moderate)	306,611	996,502		1,846,557
5b. Brain damage with motor deficiency	328,771	2,130,380	526,713	3,161,768
6a. Amputation of leg above the knee	132,235	653,700	306,486	466,724
6b. Amputation of leg below the knee	114,071	556,629		367,125
7a. Amputation of arm above the elbow	161,297	657,472	326,404	1,192,231
7b. Amputation of arm below elbow	150,399	647,018		1,127,483
8a. Loss of eyesight – one eye without cosmetic disability	59,797	278,776	106,161	87,161
8b. Loss of eyesight – one eye with cosmetic disability	93,363	292,406		95,462
8c. Loss of eyesight total blindness	278,638	1,085,422	439,940	1,690,914
9. Deafness	172,777	483,088	306,486	439,953
10. RSI	—	551,376	—	281,404

Injury	*Finland*	*France*	*Germany*	*Greece*
1. Instant death	35,241+Fe	509,077	666,124	348,698
2. Burns A. Face B. Face (no scars) C. Body	102,350 102,350 96,308	163,943 to 189,474	204,332 to 229,875	122,018 to 150,334
3. Quadriplegia	966,064	1,675,902	3,174,175* to 3,327,424*	1,137,489
4. Paraplegia	844,955	1,035,392	1,338,696* to 2,832,557*	509,859
5a. Brain damage (moderate)	966,064	1,468,354 to 1,508,773		582,299
5b. Brain damage with motor deficiency				
6a. Amputation of leg above the knee	118,261	319,743	247,114* to 296,283*	224,064
6b. Amputation of leg below the knee	114,589	264,809		196,309
7a. Amputation of arm above the elbow	134,586	327,670	570,214* to 630,237*	224,064
7b. Amputation of arm below elbow	132,748	281,098		196,309
8a. Loss of eyesight – one eye without cosmetic disability	106,024	93,758	76,625 to 91,950	182,021
8b. Loss of eyesight – one eye with cosmetic disability	114,433	156,339		
8c. Loss of eyesight total blindness	966,064	513,201	1,116,166*	617,888
9. Deafness	85,960	215,202 to 215,964	426,544	291,634
10. RSI	—	—	—	115,830

* *In these cases the cost of medical care has been added on using the medical costs suggested under the English example of the same injuries.*

Injury	*Ireland*	*Italy*	*Luxembourg*	*The Netherlands*
1. Instant death	1,015,129	1,115,193	587,805	459,276
2. Burns A. Face B. Face (no scars) C. Body	 247,129 215,446 215,446	 76,130 to 210,020	 143,609 143,609 143,609	 99,340 99,340 99,340
3. Quadriplegia	2,224,794 to 2,288,161	1,545,801	1,698,456	1,160,213* to 3,039,209*
4. Paraplegia	1,650,695 to 1,714,062	1,053,096	786,193	
5a. Brain damage (moderate)	1,392,161 to 1,518,894	1,262,247	935,558	
5b. Brain damage with motor deficiency	2,218,459 to 2,281,824	1,406,724	1,617,339	
6a. Amputation of leg above the knee	385,902	394,993	153,067	259,054* to 320,201*
6b. Amputation of leg below the knee	341,925	325,265	141,492	
7a. Amputation of arm above the elbow	845,942	394,993	435,595	556,167* to 626,385*
7b. Amputation of arm below elbow	838,844	325,265	426,233	
8a. Loss of eyesight – one eye without cosmetic disability	193,267	388,797	94,773	45,360 to 58,969
8b. Loss of eyesight – one eye with cosmetic disability	228,120 to 247,129	391,895	109,630	
8c. Loss of eyesight total blindness	1,340,834 to 1,372,517	1,344,762	950,147	914,471* to 955,296*
9. Deafness	735,050 to 766,733	759,952	530,451	775,667 to 855,048
10. RSI	—	202,968	—	—

Injury	*Portugal*	*Scotland*	*Spain*	*Sweden*
1. Instant death	325,149	852,388	168,308	119,360
2. Burns A. Face B. Face (no scars) C. Body	32,913 32,913 32,913	144,852 123.353 144,935	71,726 47,721 54,582	15,734 15,734 15,734
3. Quadriplegia	421,395	3,026,191	907,850	639,394
4. Paraplegia	277,771	1,618,401	872,007	626,915
5a. Brain damage (moderate)	421,395	1,499,841	289,265	586,225
5b. Brain damage with motor deficiency		2,727,053	410,368	607,167
6a. Amputation of leg above the knee	217,929	208,729	160,083	47,962
6b. Amputation of leg below the knee		200,013	119,020	36,568
7a. Amputation of arm above the elbow	260,318	960,235	156,160	575,319
7b. Amputation of arm below elbow		943,633	125,795	568,482
8a. Loss of eyesight – one eye without cosmetic disability	33,911	76,037	54,483	23,113
8b. Loss of eyesight – one eye with cosmetic disability		84,338	71,779	
8c. Loss of eyesight total blindness	245,358	1,324,141	438,009	609,772
9. Deafness	214,438	811,705	164,921	568,808
10. RSI	13,713	219,346	—	238,722

* *In these cases the cost of medical care has been added on using the medical costs suggested under the English example of the same injuries.*

Table 4. Schedule B. EUR (€) (£ = €1.6602)

Legal scretary, woman, 20, single; currency at 4 July 2001

<table>
<tr><th>Injury</th><th>Austria</th><th>Belgium</th><th>Denmark</th><th>England/Wales</th></tr>
<tr><td>1. Instant death</td><td>3,633</td><td>18,588</td><td>3,490</td><td>2,075</td></tr>
<tr><td>2. Burns
A. Face
B. Face (no scars)
C. Body</td><td>20,708
to
34,585</td><td>99,224
99,224
99,224</td><td>52,477
52,477
52,477</td><td>110,403
93,801
77,199</td></tr>
<tr><td>3. Quadriplegia</td><td>309,516</td><td>1,789,908</td><td>337,637</td><td>3,764,504</td></tr>
<tr><td>4. Paraplegia</td><td>273,770</td><td>1,118,410</td><td rowspan="2">161,107</td><td>2,545,917</td></tr>
<tr><td>5a. Brain damage (moderate)</td><td>192,540</td><td>687,554</td><td>1,270,883</td></tr>
<tr><td>5b. Brain damage with motor deficiency</td><td>213,973</td><td>2,060,811</td><td>161,107
to
337,637</td><td>3,317,080</td></tr>
<tr><td>6a. Amputation of leg above the knee</td><td>111,600</td><td>338,913</td><td rowspan="2">195,359</td><td>438,293</td></tr>
<tr><td>6b. Amputation of leg below the knee</td><td>93,436</td><td>280,262</td><td>277,253</td></tr>
<tr><td>7a. Amputation of arm above the elbow</td><td>97,069</td><td>428,855</td><td rowspan="2">208,297</td><td>592,276</td></tr>
<tr><td>7b. Amputation of arm below elbow</td><td>86,171</td><td>414,927</td><td>430,822</td></tr>
<tr><td>8a. Loss of eyesight – one eye without cosmetic disability</td><td>44,902</td><td>131,262</td><td rowspan="2">68,287</td><td>52,296</td></tr>
<tr><td>8b. Loss of eyesight – one eye with cosmetic disability</td><td>93,363</td><td>292,406</td><td>95,462</td></tr>
<tr><td>8c. Loss of eyesight total blindness</td><td>278,638</td><td>1,085,422</td><td>439,940</td><td>1,690,914</td></tr>
<tr><td>9. Deafness</td><td>172,777</td><td>483,088</td><td>306,486</td><td>439,953</td></tr>
<tr><td>10. RSI</td><td>—</td><td>551,376</td><td>—</td><td>281,404</td></tr>
</table>

<table>
<tr><th>Injury</th><th>Finland</th><th>France</th><th>Germany</th><th>Greece</th></tr>
<tr><td>1. Instant death</td><td>Fe</td><td>49,547</td><td>3,830</td><td>24,352</td></tr>
<tr><td>2. Burns
A. Face
B. Face (no scars)
C. Body</td><td>30,473
30,473
23,960</td><td>94,022
to
124,145</td><td>102,165
to
127,708</td><td>24,513
to
26,933</td></tr>
<tr><td>3. Quadriplegia</td><td>435,924</td><td>1,619,504</td><td>3,325,845*
to
3,428,013*</td><td>950,597</td></tr>
<tr><td>4. Paraplegia</td><td rowspan="3">435,924</td><td>961,857</td><td rowspan="3">986,999*
to
3,028,726*</td><td>385,447</td></tr>
<tr><td>5a. Brain damage (moderate)</td><td rowspan="2">1,400,918
to
1,447,990</td><td rowspan="2">473,245</td></tr>
<tr><td>5b. Brain damage with motor deficiency</td></tr>
<tr><td>6a. Amputation of leg above the knee</td><td>44,535</td><td>282,722</td><td rowspan="2">248,391*
to
343,213*</td><td>142,918</td></tr>
<tr><td>6b. Amputation of leg below the knee</td><td>39,926</td><td>220,971</td><td>124,032</td></tr>
<tr><td>7a. Amputation of arm above the elbow</td><td>258,402</td><td>263,289</td><td rowspan="2">325,021*
to
413,682*</td><td>142,918</td></tr>
<tr><td>7b. Amputation of arm below elbow</td><td>246,799</td><td>211,710</td><td>124,032</td></tr>
<tr><td>8a. Loss of eyesight – one eye without cosmetic disability</td><td>35,088</td><td>85,995</td><td rowspan="2">153,250
to
168,515</td><td rowspan="2">115,892</td></tr>
<tr><td>8b. Loss of eyesight – one eye with cosmetic disability</td><td>114,433</td><td>156,339</td></tr>
<tr><td>8c. Loss of eyesight total blindness</td><td>966,064</td><td>513,201</td><td>1,116,166*</td><td>617,888</td></tr>
<tr><td>9. Deafness</td><td>85,960</td><td>215,202
to
215,964</td><td>426,544</td><td>291,634</td></tr>
<tr><td>10. RSI</td><td>—</td><td>—</td><td>—</td><td>115,830</td></tr>
</table>

** In these cases the cost of medical care has been added on using the medical costs suggested under the English example of the same injuries.*

<table>
<tr><th>Injury</th><th>Ireland</th><th>Italy</th><th>Luxembourg</th><th>The Netherlands</th></tr>
<tr><td>1. Instant death</td><td>28,516</td><td>292,806</td><td>10,152</td><td>9,071</td></tr>
<tr><td>2. Burns
A. Face
B. Face (no scars)
C. Body</td><td>170,708
149,164
136,492</td><td>83,020
to
131,690</td><td>75,642
75,642
75,642</td><td>20,470
20,470
20,470</td></tr>
<tr><td>3. Quadriplegia</td><td>1,823,368</td><td>1,187,186</td><td>1,621,302</td><td rowspan="4">891,496*
to
3,127,435*</td></tr>
<tr><td>4. Paraplegia</td><td>1,002,774
to
1,066,141</td><td>793,308</td><td>576,639</td></tr>
<tr><td>5a. Brain damage (moderate)</td><td>607,368
to
670,734</td><td>966,696</td><td>710,229</td></tr>
<tr><td>5b. Brain damage with motor deficiency</td><td>2,002,696
to
2,066,062</td><td>1,075,463</td><td>1,428,086</td></tr>
<tr><td>6a. Amputation of leg above the knee</td><td>307,643</td><td>253,951</td><td>106,434</td><td rowspan="2">246,717*
to
345,217*</td></tr>
<tr><td>6b. Amputation of leg below the knee</td><td>195,359
to
227,042</td><td>202,774</td><td>95,965</td></tr>
<tr><td>7a. Amputation of arm above the elbow</td><td>497,077
to
528,792</td><td>253,951</td><td>101,017</td><td rowspan="2">378,725*
to
479,849*</td></tr>
<tr><td>7b. Amputation of arm below elbow</td><td>455,795
to
474,804</td><td>202,774</td><td>92,498</td></tr>
<tr><td>8a. Loss of eyesight – one eye without cosmetic disability</td><td>135,603</td><td rowspan="2">247,755</td><td>70,643</td><td rowspan="2">22,680
to
36,289</td></tr>
<tr><td>8b. Loss of eyesight – one eye with cosmetic disability</td><td>228,120
to
247,129</td><td>109,630</td></tr>
<tr><td>8c. Loss of eyesight total blindness</td><td>1,340,834
to
1,372,517</td><td>1,344,762</td><td>950,147</td><td>914,471*
to
955,296*</td></tr>
<tr><td>9. Deafness</td><td>735,050
to
766,733</td><td>759,952</td><td>530,451</td><td>775,667
to
855,048</td></tr>
<tr><td>10. RSI</td><td>—</td><td>202,968</td><td>—</td><td>—</td></tr>
</table>

Injury	*Portugal*	*Scotland*	*Spain*	*Sweden*
1. Instant death	75,801	2,490	74,784	5,426
2. Burns				
A. Face	14,761	66,076	97,514	8,356 to 20,291
B. Face (no scars)	14,761	41,173	45,209	
C. Body	14,761	66,076	47,495	
3. Quadriplegia	393,967	2,691,174	893,579	458,129
4. Paraplegia	250,345	699,857	859,857	443,859
5a. Brain damage (moderate)	413,916	793,534	281,656	406,369
5b. Brain damage with motor deficiency		2,351,574	401,254	419,933
6a. Amputation of leg above the knee	143,325	132,484	151,354	50,674
6b. Amputation of leg below the knee		123,768	120,272	41,125
7a. Amputation of arm above the elbow	154,445	383,025	198,540	248,054
7b. Amputation of arm below elbow		364,763	170,180	238,722
8a. Loss of eyesight – one eye without cosmetic disability	29,822	39,513	42,660	19,856
8b. Loss of eyesight – one eye with cosmetic disability		84,338	71,779	
8c. Loss of eyesight total blindness	245,358	1,324,141	438,009	609,772
9. Deafness	214,438	811,705	164,921	568,808
10. RSI	13,713	219,346	—	238,722

** In these cases the cost of medical care has been added on using the medical costs suggested under the English example of the same injuries.*

Table 5. Schedule A. USD ($) (£ = $1.4066)

Doctor, man, 40, married, 2 dependent children; currency at 4 July 2001

<table>
<tr><th>Injury</th><th>Austria</th><th>Belgium</th><th>Denmark</th><th>England/Wales</th></tr>
<tr><td>1. Instant death</td><td>99,613</td><td>501,399</td><td>155,784</td><td>729,674</td></tr>
<tr><td>2. Burns
A. Face
B. Face (no scars)
C. Body</td><td>33,241
to
61,312</td><td>136,560
136,560
136,560</td><td>73,799
73,799
73,799</td><td>164,572
150,506
136,440</td></tr>
<tr><td>3. Quadriplegia</td><td>357,652</td><td>1,651,393</td><td>446,257</td><td>3,336,807</td></tr>
<tr><td>4. Paraplegia</td><td>316,285</td><td>1,061,323</td><td rowspan="2">208,773</td><td>1,720,448</td></tr>
<tr><td>5a. Brain damage (moderate)</td><td>259,775</td><td>844,284</td><td>1,564,491</td></tr>
<tr><td>5b. Brain damage with motor deficiency</td><td>278,550</td><td>1,804,959</td><td>446,257</td><td>2,678,799</td></tr>
<tr><td>6a. Amputation of leg above the knee</td><td>112,036</td><td>553,846</td><td rowspan="2">259,670</td><td>395,430</td></tr>
<tr><td>6b. Amputation of leg below the knee</td><td>96,646</td><td>471,602</td><td>311,046</td></tr>
<tr><td>7a. Amputation of arm above the elbow</td><td>136,658</td><td>557,042</td><td rowspan="2">276,545</td><td>1,010,115</td></tr>
<tr><td>7b. Amputation of arm below elbow</td><td>127,425</td><td>548,184</td><td>955,257</td></tr>
<tr><td>8a. Loss of eyesight – one eye without cosmetic disability</td><td>50,663</td><td>236,192</td><td rowspan="2">89,945</td><td>73,847</td></tr>
<tr><td>8b. Loss of eyesight – one eye with cosmetic disability</td><td>79,102</td><td>247,740</td><td>80,880</td></tr>
<tr><td>8c. Loss of eyesight total blindness</td><td>236,075</td><td>919,621</td><td>371,891</td><td>1,432,622</td></tr>
<tr><td>9. Deafness</td><td>146,385</td><td>409,295</td><td>259,670</td><td>372,749</td></tr>
<tr><td>10. RSI</td><td>—</td><td>467,152</td><td>—</td><td>238,419</td></tr>
</table>

<table>
<tr><th>Injury</th><th>Finland</th><th>France</th><th>Germany</th><th>Greece</th></tr>
<tr><td>1. Instant death</td><td>29,928+fe</td><td>431,314</td><td>564,372</td><td>295,434</td></tr>
<tr><td>2. Burns
A. Face
B. Face (no scars)
C. Body</td><td>86,715
86,715
81,597</td><td>138,900
to
160,531</td><td>173,120*
to
194,761*</td><td>103,379
to
127,370</td></tr>
<tr><td>3. Quadriplegia</td><td>818,495</td><td>1,419,904</td><td>2,689,311*
to
2,819,151*</td><td>963,735</td></tr>
<tr><td>4. Paraplegia</td><td>715,886</td><td>877,233</td><td rowspan="3">1,134,206*
to
2,399,876*</td><td>431,977</td></tr>
<tr><td>5a. Brain damage (moderate)</td><td rowspan="2">818,495</td><td rowspan="2">1,244,059
to
1,278,304</td><td rowspan="2">493,351</td></tr>
<tr><td>5b. Brain damage with motor deficiency</td></tr>
<tr><td>6a. Amputation of leg above the knee</td><td>100,196</td><td>270,901</td><td rowspan="2">209,367*
to
251,025*</td><td>189,838</td></tr>
<tr><td>6b. Amputation of leg below the knee</td><td>97,085</td><td>224,358</td><td>166,322</td></tr>
<tr><td>7a. Amputation of arm above the elbow</td><td>114,027</td><td>277,618</td><td rowspan="2">483,112*
to
533,966*</td><td>189,838</td></tr>
<tr><td>7b. Amputation of arm below elbow</td><td>112,470</td><td>238,160</td><td>166,322</td></tr>
<tr><td>8a. Loss of eyesight – one eye without cosmetic disability</td><td>89,828</td><td>79,436</td><td rowspan="2">64,920
to
77,905</td><td rowspan="2">154,217</td></tr>
<tr><td>8b. Loss of eyesight – one eye with cosmetic disability</td><td>96,953</td><td>132,458</td></tr>
<tr><td>8c. Loss of eyesight total blindness</td><td>818,495</td><td>434,808</td><td>945,668*</td><td>523,504</td></tr>
<tr><td>9. Deafness</td><td>72,830</td><td>182,329
to
182,975</td><td>361,388</td><td>247,086</td></tr>
<tr><td>10. RSI</td><td>—</td><td>—</td><td>—</td><td>98,137</td></tr>
</table>

** In these cases the cost of medical care has been added on using the medical costs suggested under the English example of the same injuries.*

Injury	*Ireland*	*Italy*	*Luxembourg*	*The Netherlands*
1. Instant death	860,066	944,844	498,017	389,120
2. Burns A. Face B. Face (no scars) C. Body	209,379 182,536 182,536	64,501 to 177,939	121,672 121,672 121,672	84,165 84,165 84,165
3. Quadriplegia	1,884,951 to 1,938,638	1,309,675	1,439,012	982,987* to 2,574,961*
4. Paraplegia	1,398,547 to 1,452,234	892,233	666,100	
5a. Brain damage (moderate)	1,179,504 to 1,286,879	1,069,435	792,649	
5b. Brain damage with motor deficiency	1,879,583 to 1,933,296	1,191,843	1,370,286	
6a. Amputation of leg above the knee	326,954	334,657	129,686	219,483* to 271,290*
6b. Amputation of leg below the knee	289,695	275,580	119,879	
7a. Amputation of arm above the elbow	716,722	334,657	369,057	471,211* to 530,703*
7b. Amputation of arm below elbow	710,709	275,580	361,125	
8a. Loss of eyesight – one eye without cosmetic disability	163,745	329,407	80,296	38,431 to 49,961
8b. Loss of eyesight – one eye with cosmetic disability	193,274 to 209,379	332,032	92,883	
8c. Loss of eyesight total blindness	1,136,018 to 1,162,862	1,139,346	805,010	774,783 to 809,372
9. Deafness	622,769 to 649,613	643,867	449,423	657,182 to 724,437
10. RSI	—	171,964	—	—

<table>
<tr><th>Injury</th><th>Portugal</th><th>Scotland</th><th>Spain</th><th>Sweden</th></tr>
<tr><td>1. Instant death</td><td>275,481</td><td>722,184</td><td>142,598</td><td>101,128</td></tr>
<tr><td>2. Burns</td><td></td><td></td><td></td><td></td></tr>
<tr><td>A. Face</td><td>27,886</td><td>122,726</td><td>60,769</td><td>13,330</td></tr>
<tr><td>B. Face (no scars)</td><td>27,886</td><td>104,510</td><td>40,431</td><td>13,330</td></tr>
<tr><td>C. Body</td><td>27,886</td><td>122,796</td><td>46,245</td><td>13,330</td></tr>
<tr><td>3. Quadriplegia</td><td>357,026</td><td>2,563,932</td><td>769,174</td><td>541,725</td></tr>
<tr><td>4. Paraplegia</td><td>235,341</td><td>1,371,186</td><td>738,805</td><td>531,152</td></tr>
<tr><td>5a. Brain damage (moderate)</td><td rowspan="2">357,026</td><td>1,270,737</td><td>245,079</td><td>496,677</td></tr>
<tr><td>5b. Brain damage with motor deficiency</td><td>2,310,488</td><td>347,683</td><td>514,420</td></tr>
<tr><td>6a. Amputation of leg above the knee</td><td rowspan="2">184,640</td><td>176,845</td><td>135,630</td><td>40,635</td></tr>
<tr><td>6b. Amputation of leg below the knee</td><td>169,460</td><td>100,839</td><td>30,982</td></tr>
<tr><td>7a. Amputation of arm above the elbow</td><td rowspan="2">220,553</td><td>813,556</td><td>132,306</td><td>487,438</td></tr>
<tr><td>7b. Amputation of arm below elbow</td><td>799,490</td><td>106,579</td><td>481,645</td></tr>
<tr><td>8a. Loss of eyesight – one eye without cosmetic disability</td><td rowspan="2">28,731</td><td>64,422</td><td>46,160</td><td rowspan="2">19,583</td></tr>
<tr><td>8b. Loss of eyesight – one eye with cosmetic disability</td><td>71,455</td><td>60,814</td></tr>
<tr><td>8c. Loss of eyesight total blindness</td><td>207,879</td><td>1,121,875</td><td>371,102</td><td>516,627</td></tr>
<tr><td>9. Deafness</td><td>181,682</td><td>687,715</td><td>139,729</td><td>481,921</td></tr>
<tr><td>10. RSI</td><td>11,619</td><td>185,840</td><td>—</td><td>202,256</td></tr>
</table>

** In these cases the cost of medical care has been added on using the medical costs suggested under the English example of the same injuries.*

Table 6. Schedule B. USD ($) (£ = $1.4066)

Legal scretary, woman, 20, single; currency at 4 July 2001

<table>
<tr><th>Injury</th><th>Austria</th><th>Belgium</th><th>Denmark</th><th>England/Wales</th></tr>
<tr><td>1. Instant death</td><td>3,078</td><td>15,748</td><td>2,957</td><td>1,758</td></tr>
<tr><td>2. Burns
A. Face
B. Face (no scars)
C. Body</td><td>17,545
to
29,302</td><td>84,067
84,067
84,067</td><td>44,461
44,461
44,461</td><td>93,539
79,473
65,407</td></tr>
<tr><td>3. Quadriplegia</td><td>262,237</td><td>1,516,495</td><td>286,062</td><td>3,189,466</td></tr>
<tr><td>4. Paraplegia</td><td>231,951</td><td>947,570</td><td rowspan="2">136,498</td><td>2,157,021</td></tr>
<tr><td>5a. Brain damage (moderate)</td><td>163,129</td><td>582,528</td><td>1,076,752</td></tr>
<tr><td>5b. Brain damage with motor deficiency</td><td>181,288</td><td>1,746,017</td><td>136,498
to
286,062</td><td>2,810,387</td></tr>
<tr><td>6a. Amputation of leg above the knee</td><td>94,553</td><td>287,143</td><td rowspan="2">165,517</td><td>371,342</td></tr>
<tr><td>6b. Amputation of leg below the knee</td><td>79,163</td><td>237,451</td><td>234,902</td></tr>
<tr><td>7a. Amputation of arm above the elbow</td><td>82,241</td><td>363,346</td><td rowspan="2">176,479</td><td>501,805</td></tr>
<tr><td>7b. Amputation of arm below elbow</td><td>73,008</td><td>351,546</td><td>365,013</td></tr>
<tr><td>8a. Loss of eyesight – one eye without cosmetic disability</td><td>38,043</td><td>111,211</td><td rowspan="2">57,856</td><td>44,308</td></tr>
<tr><td>8b. Loss of eyesight – one eye with cosmetic disability</td><td>49,555</td><td>126,958</td><td>51,341</td></tr>
<tr><td>8c. Loss of eyesight total blindness</td><td>140,660</td><td>649,443</td><td>240,214</td><td>830,597</td></tr>
<tr><td>9. Deafness</td><td>62,665</td><td>434,895</td><td>165,517</td><td>194,111</td></tr>
<tr><td>10. RSI</td><td>—</td><td>273,457</td><td>—</td><td>141,715</td></tr>
</table>

<table>
<tr><th>Injury</th><th>Finland</th><th>France</th><th>Germany</th><th>Greece</th></tr>
<tr><td>1. Instant death</td><td>Fe</td><td>41,979</td><td>3,245</td><td>20,632</td></tr>
<tr><td>2. Burns
A. Face
B. Face (no scars)
C. Body</td><td>25,818
25,818
20,300</td><td>79,660
to
105,181</td><td>86,559
to
108,200</td><td>20,768
to
22,819</td></tr>
<tr><td>3. Quadriplegia</td><td rowspan="4">369,335</td><td>1,372,120</td><td>2,817,814*
to
2,904,374*</td><td>805,391</td></tr>
<tr><td>4. Paraplegia</td><td>814,931</td><td rowspan="3">836,232*
to
2,566,080*</td><td>326,569</td></tr>
<tr><td>5a. Brain damage (moderate)</td><td rowspan="2">1,186,924
to
1,226,805</td><td rowspan="2">400,956</td></tr>
<tr><td>5b. Brain damage with motor deficiency</td></tr>
<tr><td>6a. Amputation of leg above the knee</td><td>37,732</td><td>239,536</td><td rowspan="2">210,448*
to
290,786*</td><td>121,087</td></tr>
<tr><td>6b. Amputation of leg below the knee</td><td>33,827</td><td>187,217</td><td>105,086</td></tr>
<tr><td>7a. Amputation of arm above the elbow</td><td>218,930</td><td>223,071</td><td rowspan="2">275,373*
to
350,491*</td><td>121,087</td></tr>
<tr><td>7b. Amputation of arm below elbow</td><td>209,100</td><td>179,371</td><td>105,086</td></tr>
<tr><td>8a. Loss of eyesight – one eye without cosmetic disability</td><td>29,728</td><td>72,859</td><td rowspan="2">129,840
to
142,774</td><td rowspan="2">98,189</td></tr>
<tr><td>8b. Loss of eyesight – one eye with cosmetic disability</td><td>36,854</td><td>101,986</td></tr>
<tr><td>8c. Loss of eyesight total blindness</td><td>198,324</td><td>380,249</td><td>730,820*</td><td>347,510</td></tr>
<tr><td>9. Deafness</td><td>49,116</td><td>208,343</td><td>124,327</td><td>159,400</td></tr>
<tr><td>10. RSI</td><td>—</td><td>—</td><td>—</td><td>59,907</td></tr>
</table>

** In these cases the cost of medical care has been added on using the medical costs suggested under the English example of the same injuries.*

<table>
<tr><th>Injury</th><th>Ireland</th><th>Italy</th><th>Luxembourg</th><th>The Netherlands</th></tr>
<tr><td>1. Instant death</td><td>24,160</td><td>248,079</td><td>8,601</td><td>7,686</td></tr>
<tr><td>2. Burns
A. Face
B. Face (no scars)
C. Body</td><td>144,632
126,379
115,642</td><td>70,338
to
111,574</td><td>64,088
64,088
64,088</td><td>17,343
17,343
17,343</td></tr>
<tr><td>3. Quadriplegia</td><td>1,544,843</td><td>1,005,840</td><td>1,373,643</td><td rowspan="4">755,317*
to
2,649,711*</td></tr>
<tr><td>4. Paraplegia</td><td>849,598
to
903,285</td><td>672,128</td><td>488,556</td></tr>
<tr><td>5a. Brain damage (moderate)</td><td>514,591
to
568,278</td><td>819,031</td><td>601,739</td></tr>
<tr><td>5b. Brain damage with motor deficiency</td><td>1,696,779
to
1,750,466</td><td>911,183</td><td>1,209,942</td></tr>
<tr><td>6a. Amputation of leg above the knee</td><td>260,650</td><td>215,159</td><td>90,176</td><td rowspan="2">209,031*
to
292,484*</td></tr>
<tr><td>6b. Amputation of leg below the knee</td><td>165,517
to
192,361</td><td>171,799</td><td>81,306</td></tr>
<tr><td>7a. Amputation of arm above the elbow</td><td>421,147
to
448,018</td><td>215,159</td><td>85,586</td><td rowspan="2">320,874*
to
406,551*</td></tr>
<tr><td>7b. Amputation of arm below elbow</td><td>386,171
to
402,276</td><td>171,799</td><td>78,369</td></tr>
<tr><td>8a. Loss of eyesight – one eye without cosmetic disability</td><td>114,890</td><td rowspan="2">209,910</td><td>59,852</td><td rowspan="2">19,216
to
30,745</td></tr>
<tr><td>8b. Loss of eyesight – one eye with cosmetic disability</td><td>141,733
to
157,840</td><td>67,929</td></tr>
<tr><td>8c. Loss of eyesight total blindness</td><td>493,116</td><td>858,686</td><td>557,703</td><td>435,289*
to
454,505*</td></tr>
<tr><td>9. Deafness</td><td>306,284
to
327,759</td><td>460,840</td><td>394,565</td><td>187,570
to
197,179</td></tr>
<tr><td>10. RSI</td><td>—</td><td>79,486</td><td>—</td><td>201,767</td></tr>
</table>

Injury	*Portugal*	*Scotland*	*Spain*	*Sweden*
1. Instant death	64,223	2,110	63,360	4,597
2. Burns A. Face B. Face (no scars) C. Body	12,506 12,506 12,506	55,983 34,884 55,983	82,618 38,303 40,240	7,079 to 17,191
3. Quadriplegia	333,788	2,280,090	757,083	388,148
4. Paraplegia	212,104	592,952	728,512	376,059
5a. Brain damage (moderate)	350,689	672,320	238,633	344,295
5b. Brain damage with motor deficiency		1,992,365	339,961	355,787
6a. Amputation of leg above the knee	121,432	112,247	128,234	42,934
6b. Amputation of leg below the knee		104,862	101,900	34,843
7a. Amputation of arm above the elbow	130,853	324,517	168,212	210,163
7b. Amputation of arm below elbow		309,044	144,185	202,256
8a. Loss of eyesight – one eye without cosmetic disability	25,267	33,477	36,144	16,823
8b. Loss of eyesight – one eye with cosmetic disability		47,543	51,666	
8c. Loss of eyesight total blindness	253,510	525,506	367,643	371,600
9. Deafness	122,530	181,001	136,359	326,901
10. RSI	7,985	159,902	—	132,386

** In these cases the cost of medical care has been added on using the medical costs suggested under the English example of the same injuries.*

Bloc Graphs, Total Compensation: EU Countries

Table 1. Schedule A

Doctor, man, 40, married, 2 dependent children – instant death; GBP

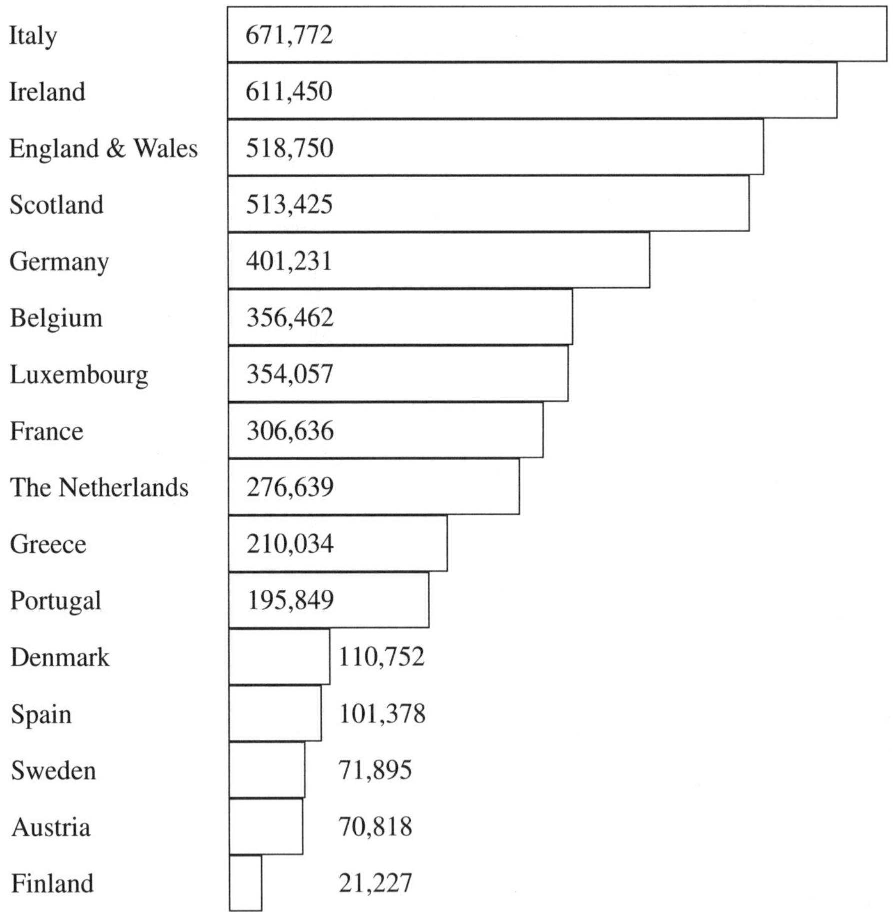

Table 2. Schedule A

Doctor, man, 40, married, 2 dependent children – burns; GBP

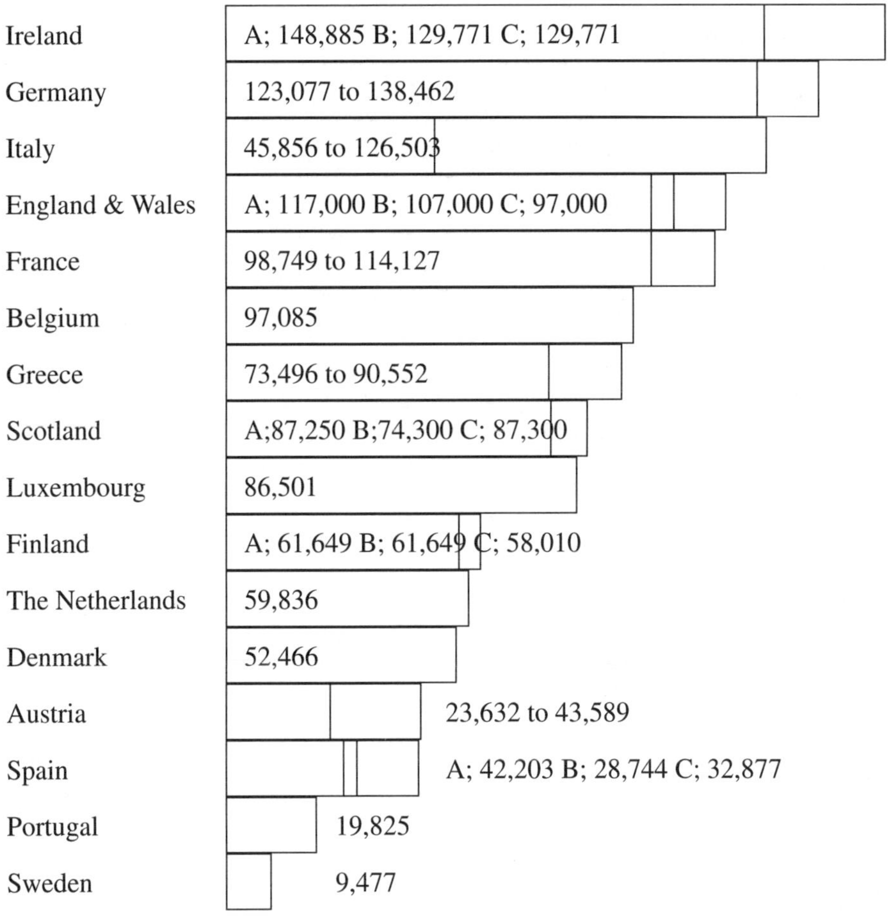

Table 3. Schedule A

Doctor, man, 40, married, 2 dependent children – quadriplegia; GBP

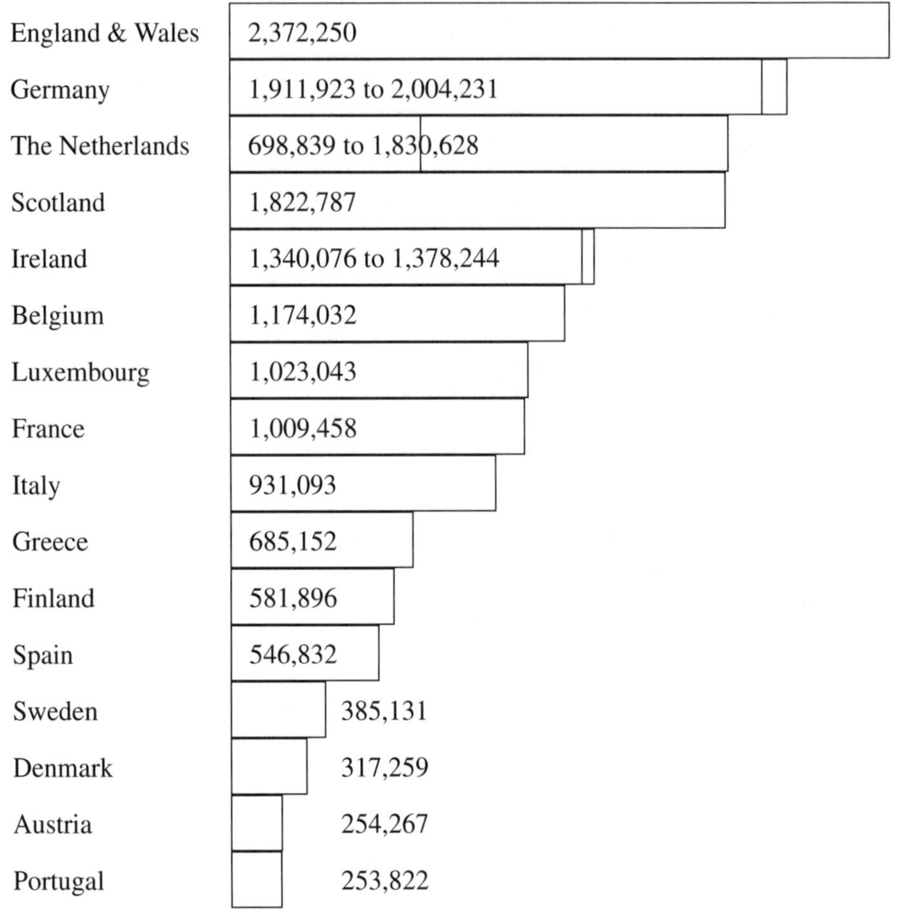

Table 4. Schedule A

Doctor, man, 40, married, 2 dependent children – paraplegia; GBP

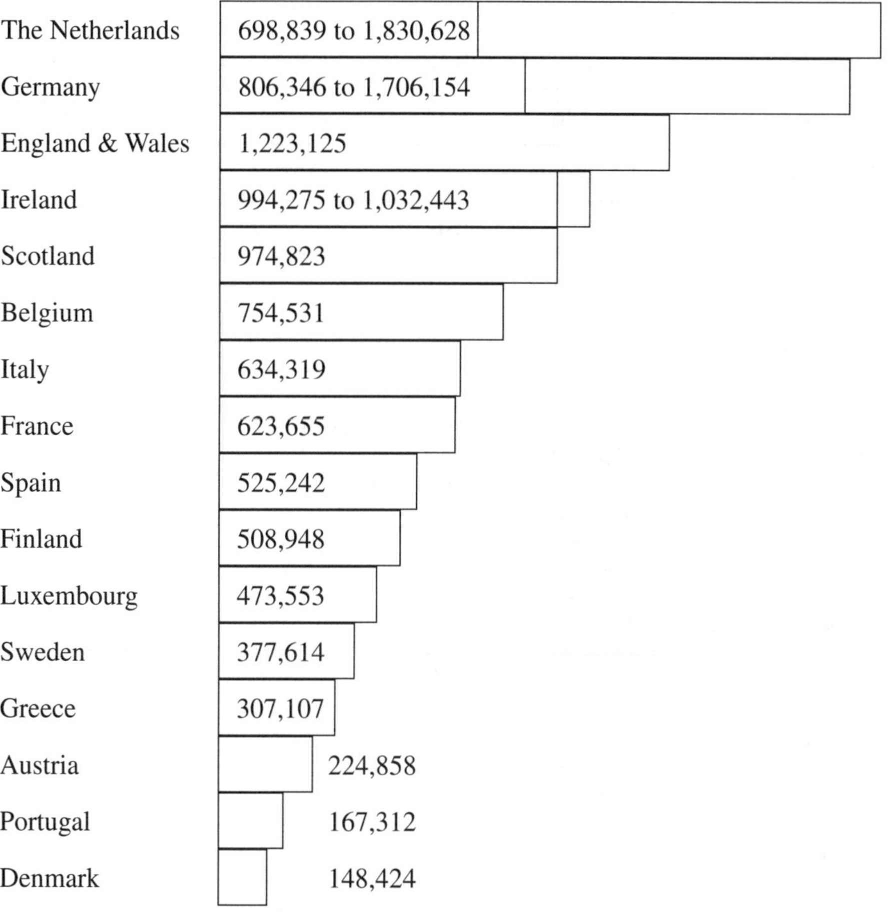

Table 5. Schedule A

Doctor, man, 40, married, 2 dependent children – brain damage (moderate); GBP

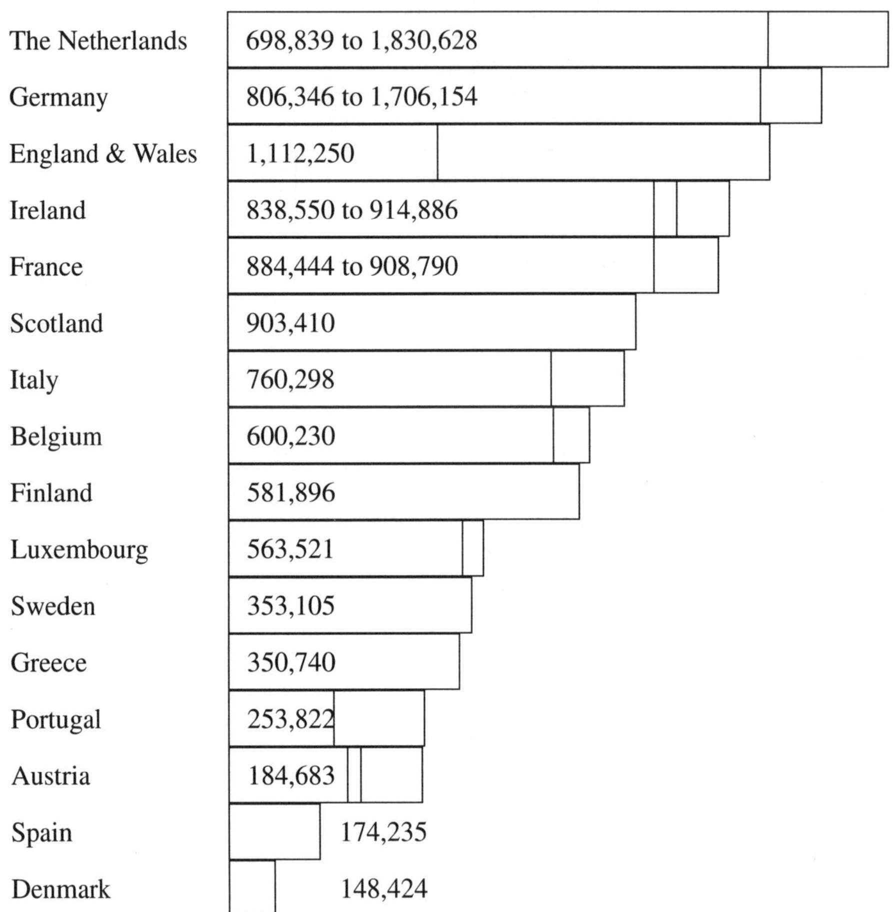

Table 6. Schedule A

Doctor, man, 40, married, 2 dependent children – brain damage (motor deficiency); GBP

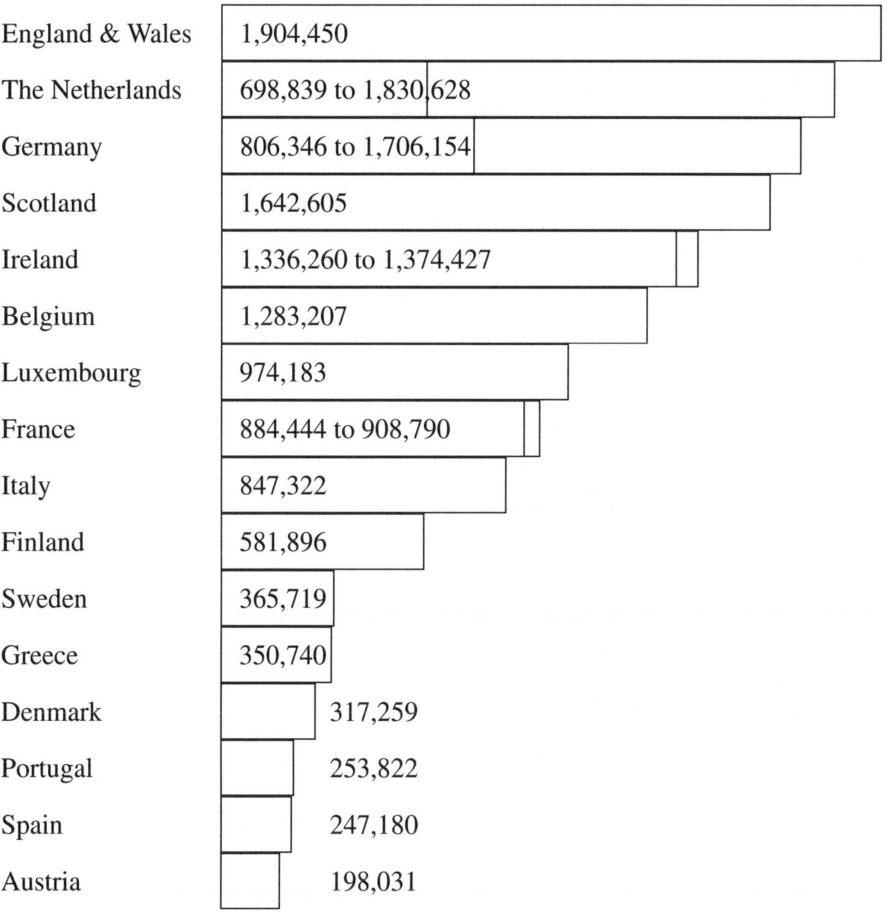

Table 7. Schedule A

Doctor, man, 40, married, 2 dependent children – amputation of leg above the knee; GBP

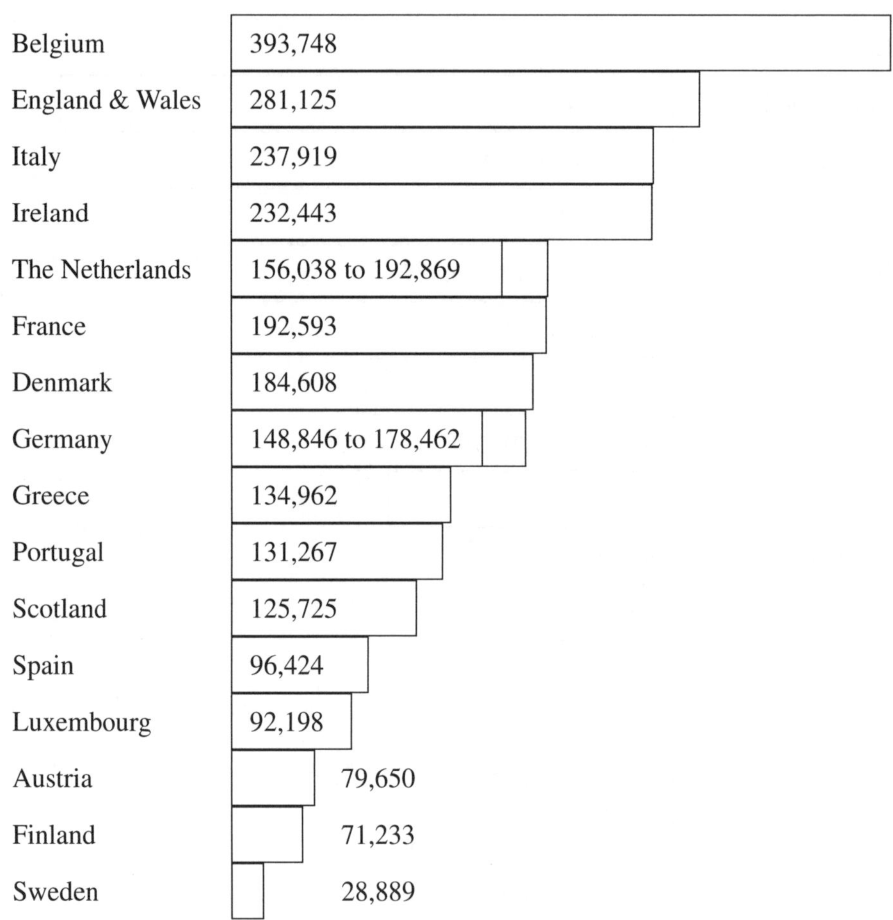

Table 8. Schedule A

Doctor, man, 40, married, 2 dependent children – amputation of leg below the knee; GBP

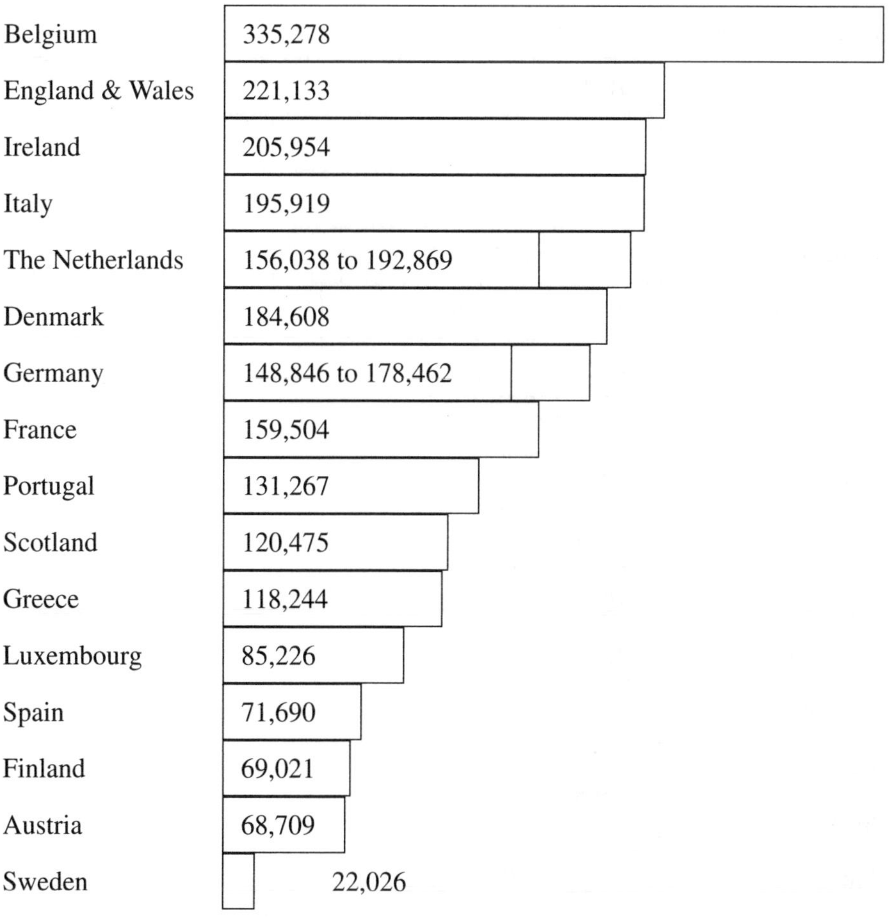

Table 9. Schedule A

Doctor, man, 40, married, 2 dependent children – amputation of arm above the elbow; GBP

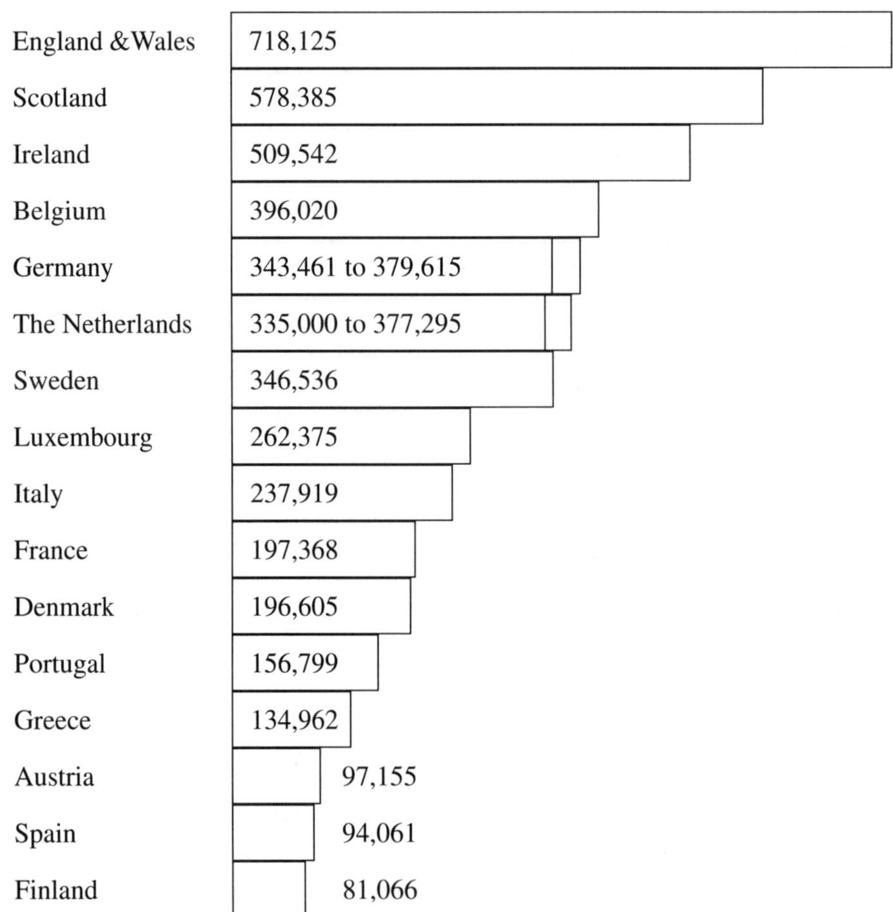

Table 10. Schedule A

Doctor, man, 40, married, 2 dependent children – amputation of arm below the elbow; GBP

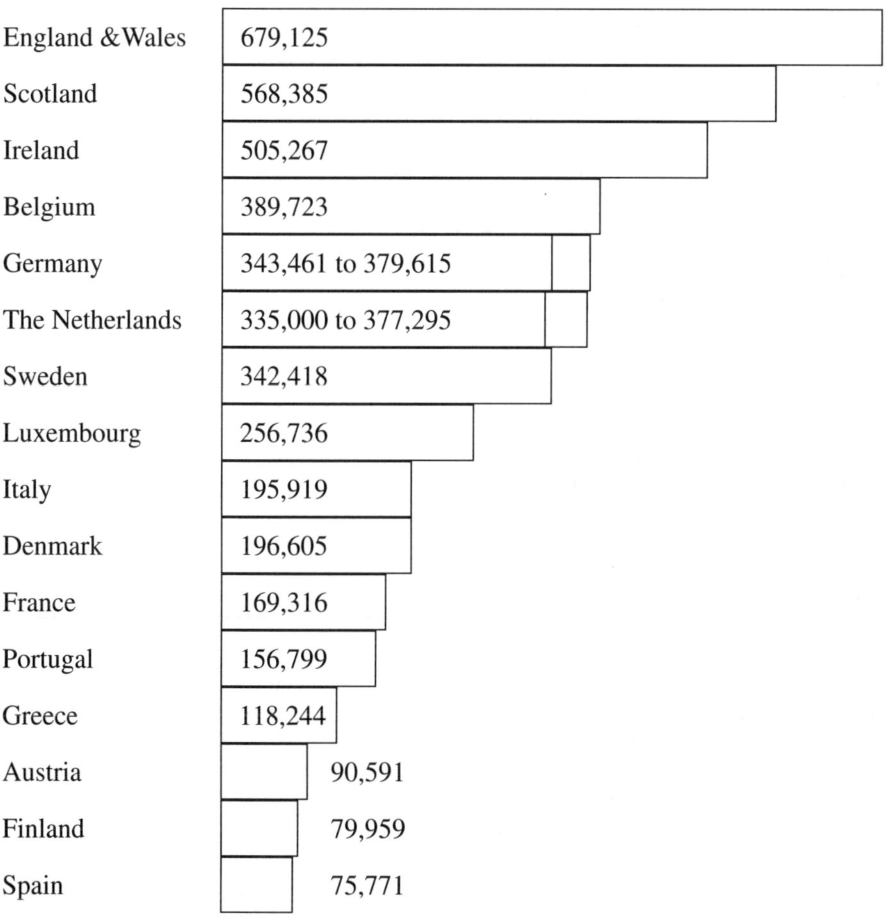

Table 11. Schedule A

Doctor, man, 40, married, 2 dependent children – loss of one eye without cosmetic injury; GBP

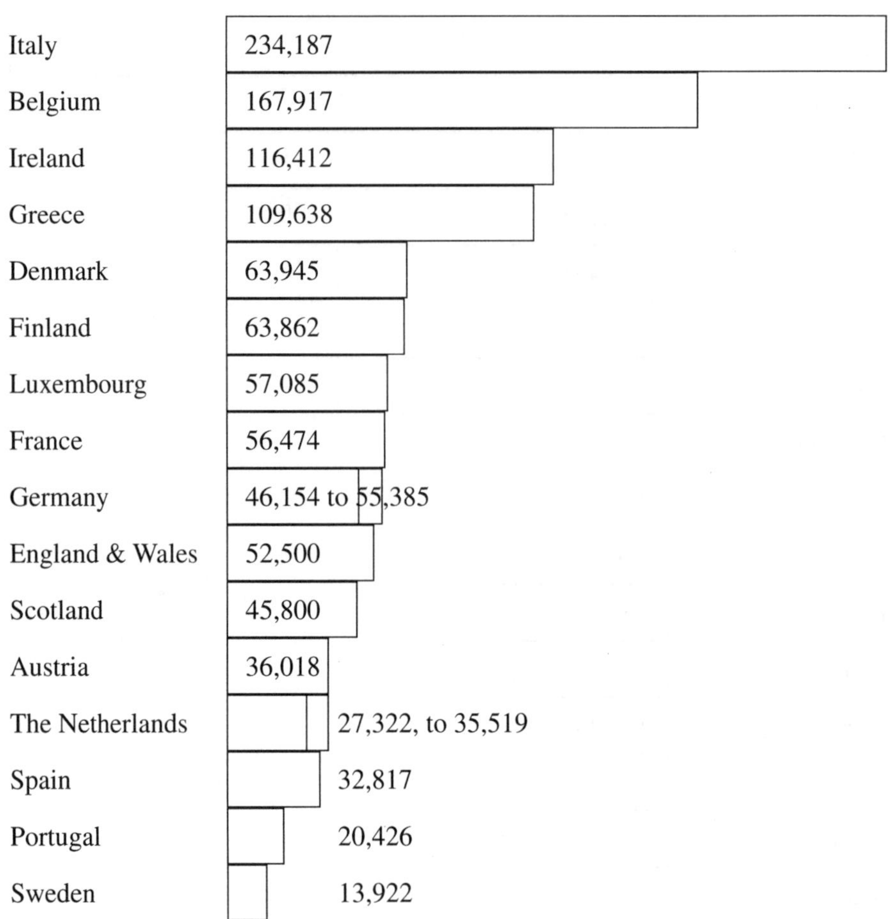

Table 12. Schedule A

Doctor, man, 40, married, 2 dependent children – loss of one eye with cosmetic injury; GBP

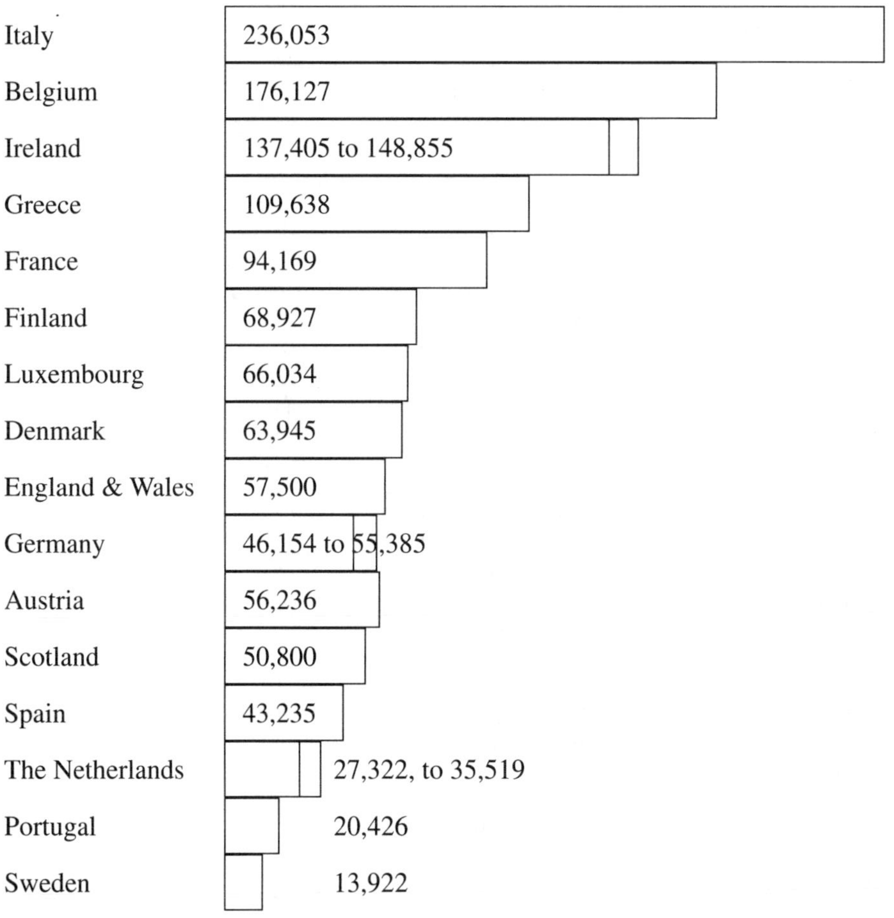

Table 13. Schedule A

Doctor, man, 40, married, 2 dependent children – loss of eyesight, total blindness; GBP

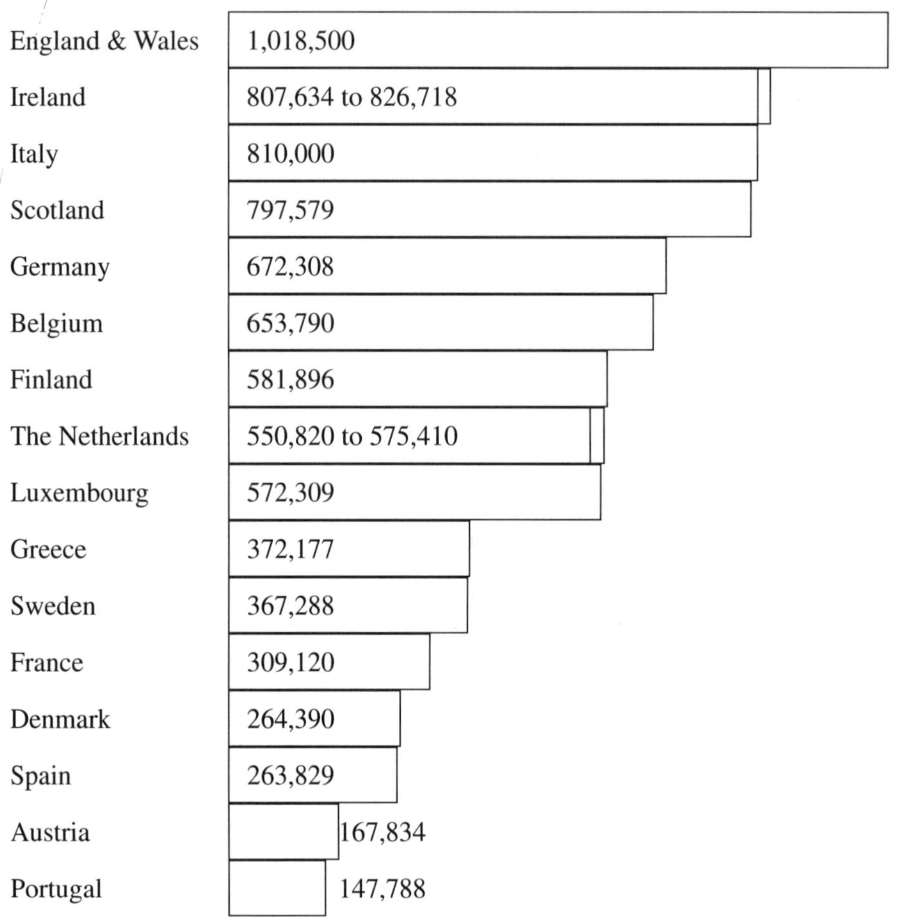

Table 14. Schedule A

Doctor, man, 40, married, 2 dependent children – deafness; GBP

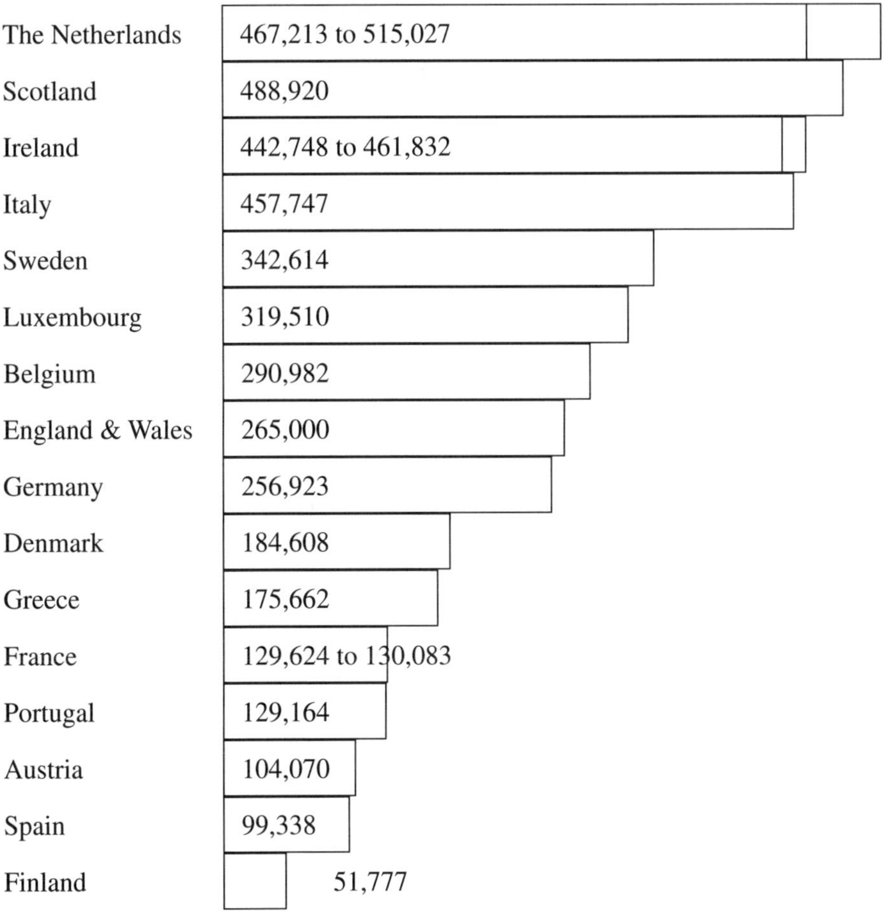

Table 15. Schedule A

Doctor, man, 40, married, 2 dependent children – RSI; GBP

Country	GBP
Belgium	332,114
England & Wales	169,500
Sweden	143,791
Scotland	132,120
Italy	122,255
Greece	69,769
Portugal	8,260

Table 16. Schedule B

Legal secretary, woman, 20, single – instant death; GBP

Country	GBP
Italy	176,368
Portugal	45,658
Spain	45,045
France	29,844
Ireland	17,176
Greece	14,668
Belgium	11,196
Luxembourg	6,115
The Netherlands	5,464
Sweden	3,268
Germany	2,307
Austria	2,188
Denmark	2,102
Scotland	1,500
England &Wales	1,250
Finland	Funeral expenses

Table 17. Schedule B

Legal secretary, woman, 20, single – burns; GBP

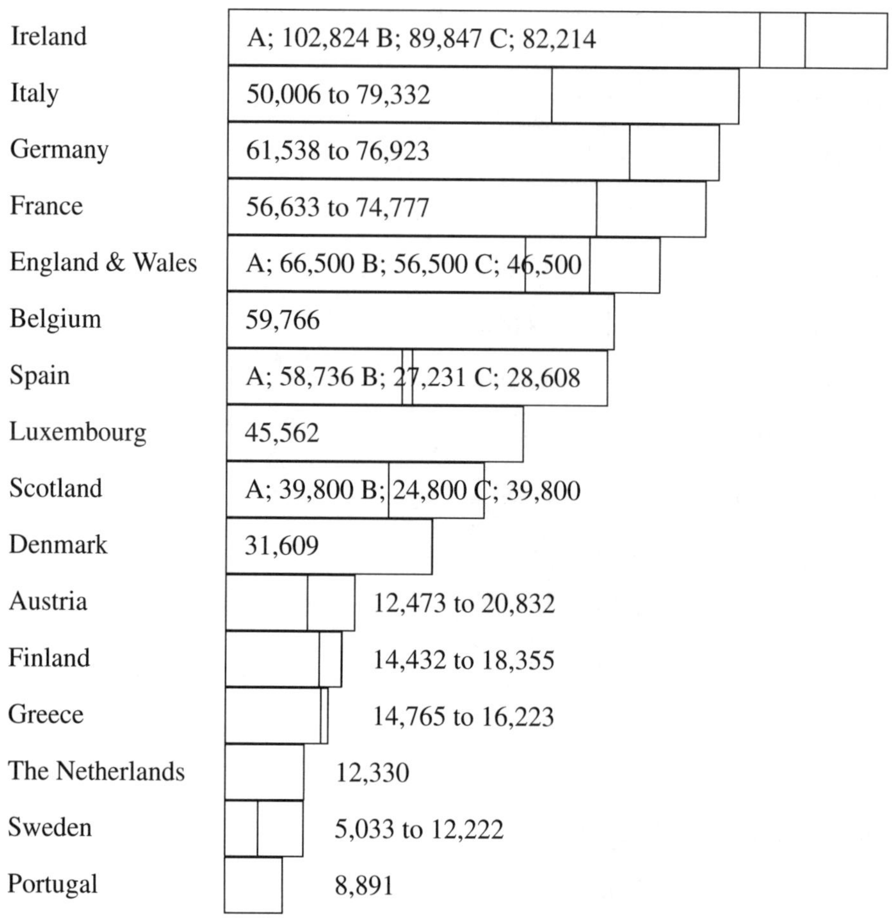

Table 18. Schedule B

Legal secretary, woman, 20, single – quadriplegia; GBP

Country	Total compensation (GBP)
England & Wales	2,267,500
Germany	2,003,280 to 2,064,819
The Netherlands	536,981 to 1,883,770
Scotland	1,620,994
Ireland	1,098,282
Belgium	1,078,128
Luxembourg	976,570
France	975,487
Italy	715,086
Greece	572,580
Spain	538,236
Sweden	275,948
Finland	262,573
Portugal	237,301
Denmark	203,371
Austria	186,433

Table 19. Schedule B

Legal secretary, woman, 20, single – paraplegia; GBP

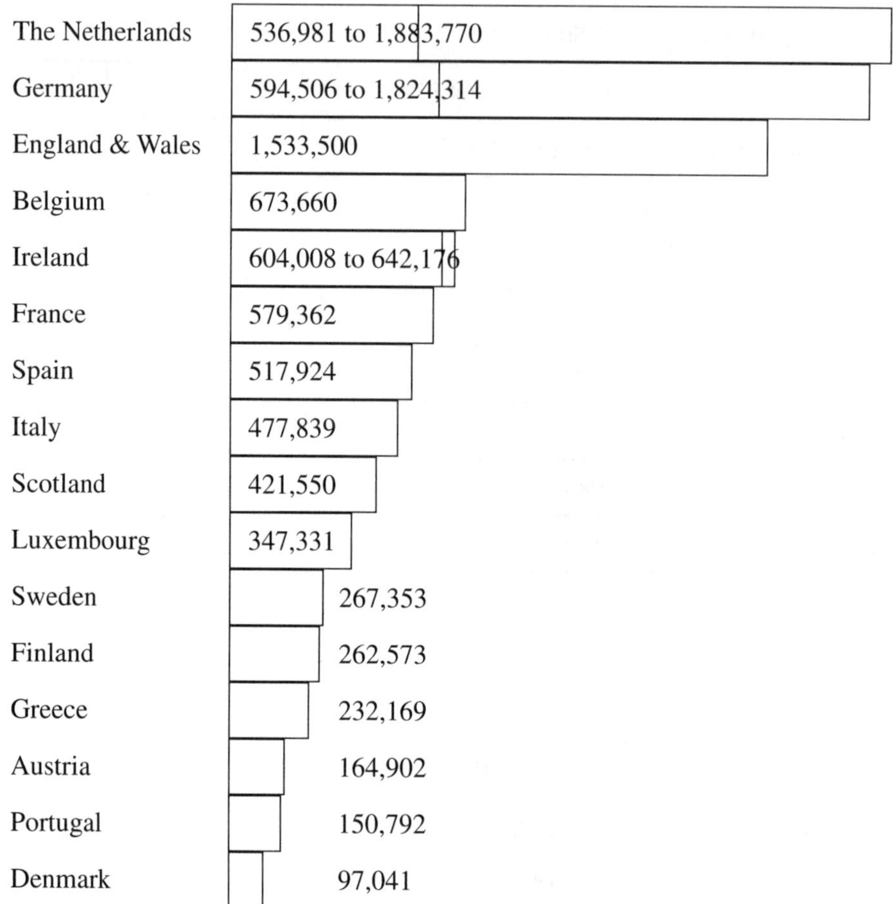

Table 20. Schedule B

Legal secretary, woman, 20, single – brain damage (moderate); GBP

The Netherlands	536,981 to 1,883,770
Germany	594,506 to 1,824,314
France	843,825 to 872,178
England & Wales	765,500
Italy	582,277
Scotland	477,975
Luxembourg	427,797
Belgium	414,139
Ireland	365,840 to 404,008
Greece	285,053
Finland	262,573
Portugal	249,317
Sweden	244,771
Spain	169,652
Austria	115,974
Denmark	97,041

Table 21. Schedule B

Legal secretary, woman, 20, single – brain damage (motor deficiency); GBP

England & Wales	1,998,000
The Netherlands	536,981 to 1,883,770
Germany	594,506 to 1,824,314
Scotland	1,416,440
Belgium	1,241,303
Ireland	1,206,298 to 1,244,466
France	843,825 to 872,178
Luxembourg	860,189
Italy	647,791
Greece	285,053
Finland	262,573
Sweden	252,941
Portugal	249,317
Spain	241,690
Denmark	97,041 to 203,371
Austria	128,884

Table 22. Schedule B

Legal secretary, woman, 20, single – amputation of leg above the knee; GBP

Country	GBP
England & Wales	264,000
The Netherlands	148,607 to 207,937
Germany	149,615 to 206,730
Belgium	204,140
Ireland	185,305
France	170,294
Italy	152,964
Denmark	117,672
Spain	91,166
Portugal	86,330
Greece	86,085
Scotland	79,800
Austria	67,221
Luxembourg	64,109
Sweden	30,523
Finland	26,825

Table 23. Schedule B

Legal secretary, woman, 20, single – amputation of leg below the knee; GBP

Country	GBP
The Netherlands	148,607 to 207,937
Germany	149,615 to 206,730
Belgium	168,812
England & Wales	167,000
Ireland	117,672 to 136,756
France	133,099
Italy	122,138
Denmark	117,672
Portugal	86,330
Greece	74,709
Scotland	74,550
Spain	72,444
Luxembourg	57,803
Austria	56,280
Sweden	24,711
Finland	24,049

Table 24. Schedule B

Legal secretary, woman, 20, single – amputation of arm above the elbow; GBP

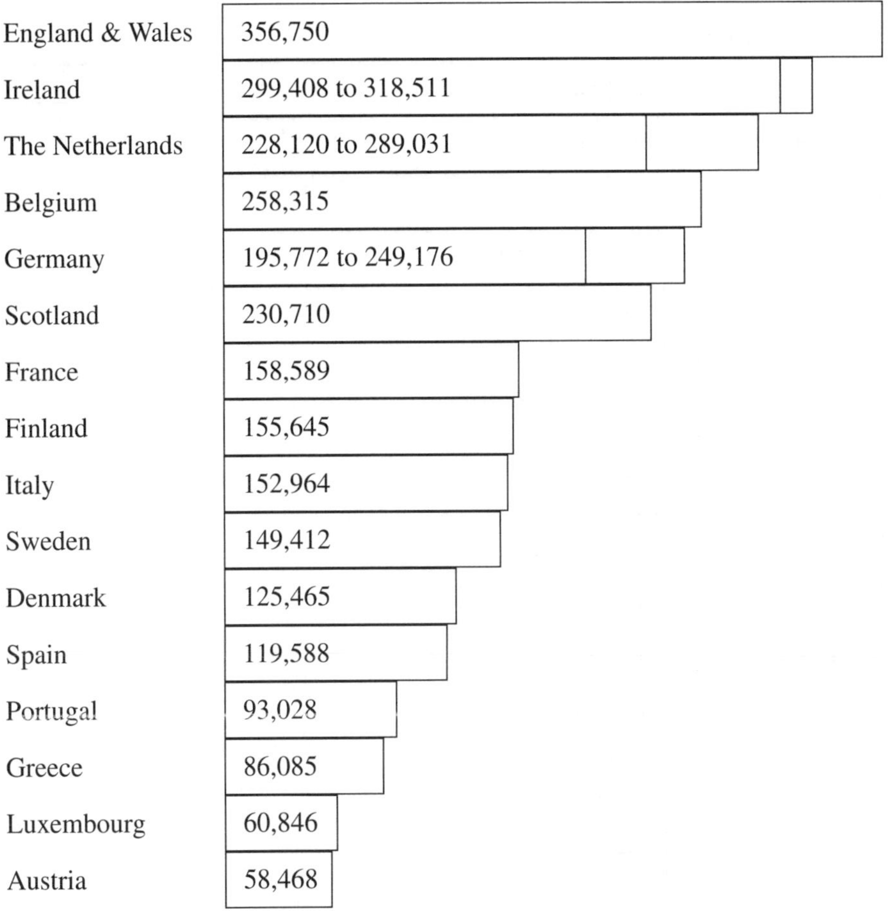

Table 25. Schedule B

Legal secretary, woman, 20, single – amputation of arm below the elbow; GBP

Country	GBP
The Netherlands	228,120 to 289,031
Ireland	274,542 to 285,992
England & Wales	259,500
Belgium	249,926
Germany	195,772 to 249,176
Scotland	219,710
Finland	148,656
Sweden	143,791
France	127,521
Denmark	125,465
Italy	122,138
Spain	102,506
Portugal	93,028
Greece	74,709
Luxembourg	55,715
Austria	51,904

Table 26. Schedule B

Legal secretary, woman, 20, single – loss of one eye without cosmetic injury; GBP

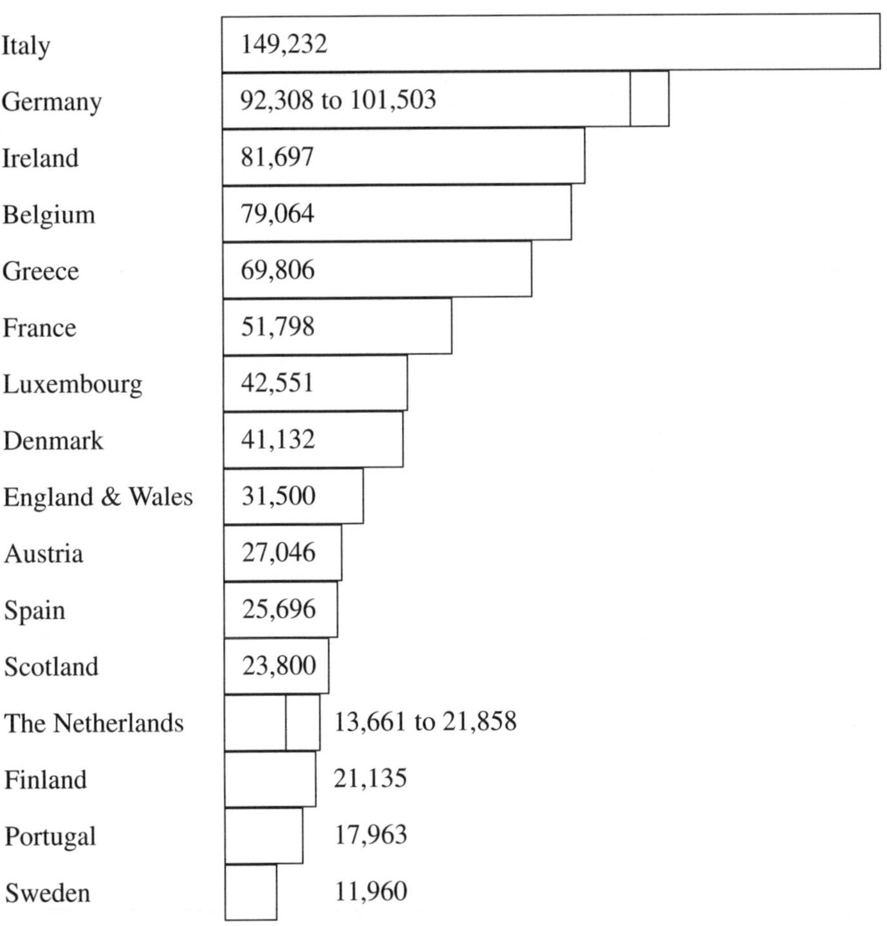

Table 27. Schedule B

Legal secretary, woman, 20, single – loss of one eye with cosmetic injury; GBP

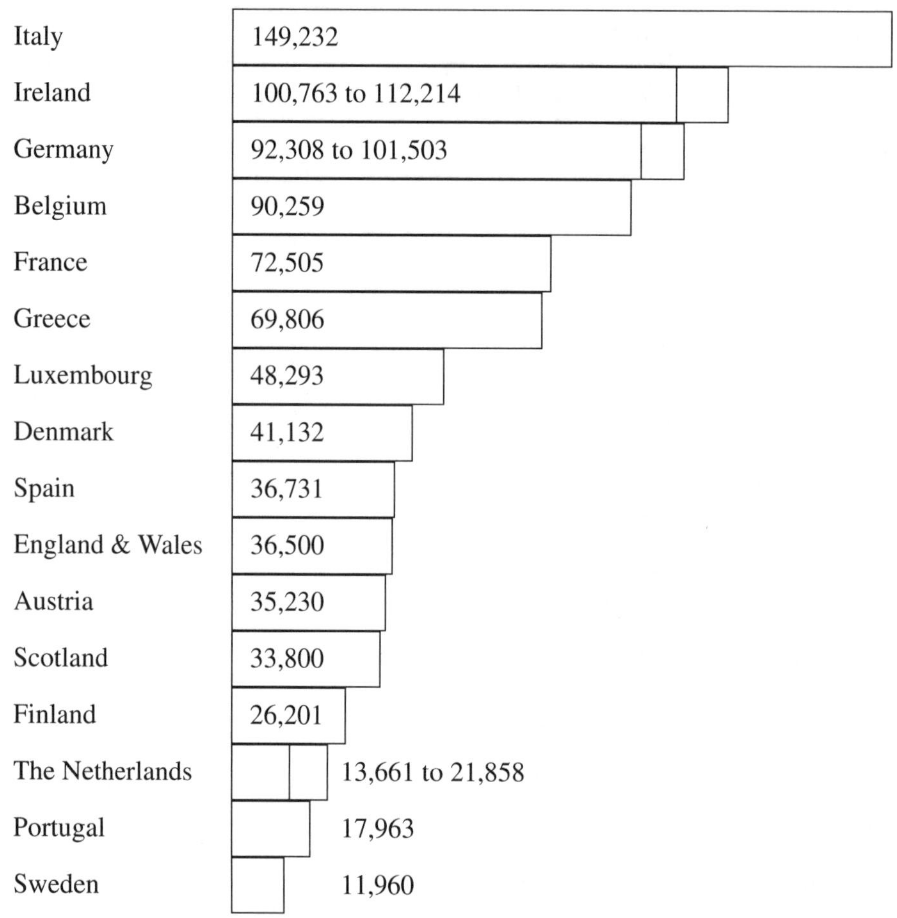

Table 28. Schedule B

Legal secretary, woman, 20, single – loss of eyesight, total blindness; GBP

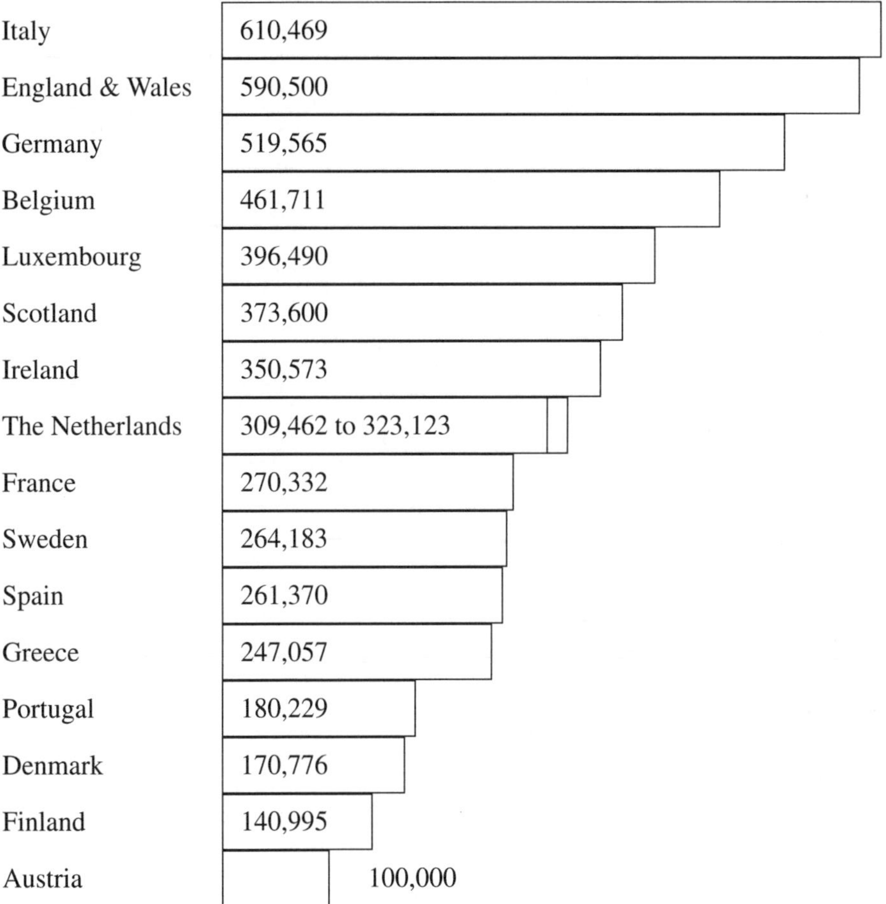

Table 29. Schedule B

Legal secretary, woman, 20, single – deafness; GBP

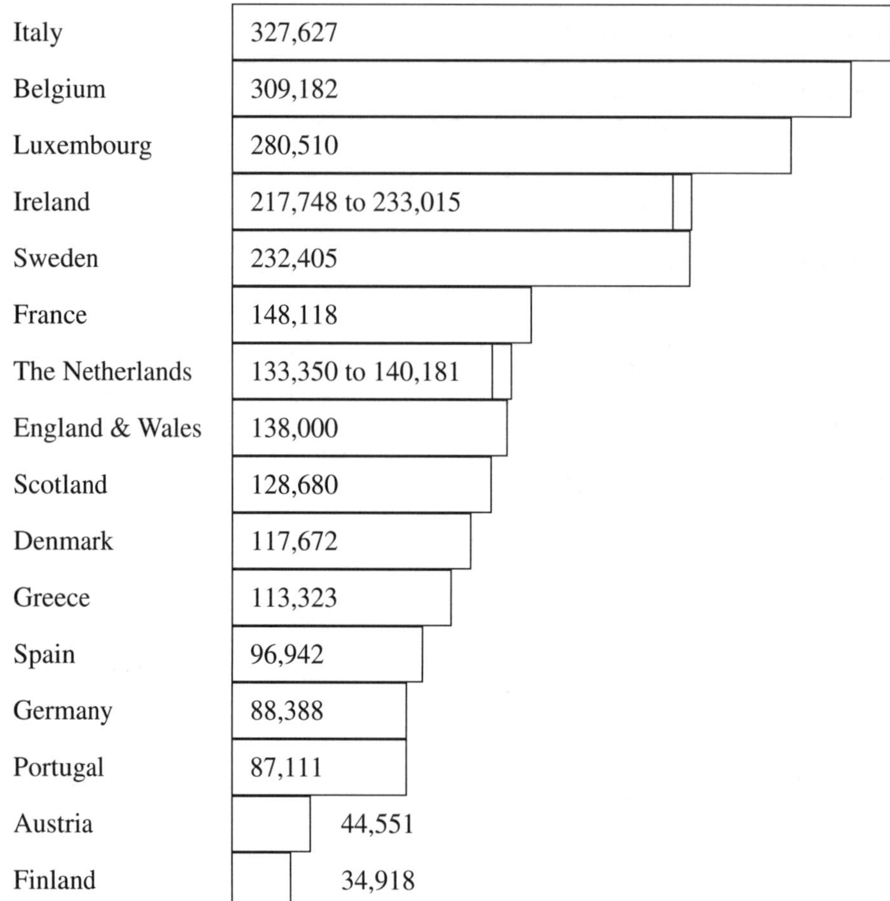

Table 30. Schedule B

Legal secretary, woman, 20, single – RSI; GBP

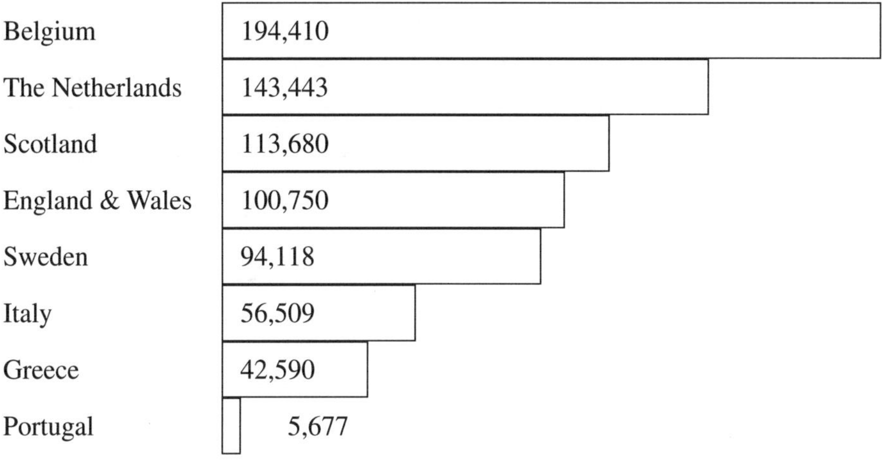

PAIN AND SUFFERING COMPENSATION: EU COUNTRIES

Table 1. Schedule A

Doctor, man, 40, married, 2 dependent children; currency at 4 July 2001

Injury	*Austria GBP 1= 22.85 ATS*	*Belgium GBP 1= 66.99 BEF*	*Denmark GBP 1= 12.37 DKK*	*England /Wales*
1. Instant death	–	–	–	–
2. Burns A. Face B. Face (no scars) C. Body	4,814 to 8,753	28,418 28,418 28,418	5,497 5,497 5,497	55,000 45,000 35,000
3. Quadriplegia	63,457	120,839	12,773 to 24,091	150,000
4. Paraplegia	45,952	97,078		110,000
5a. Brain damage (moderate)	42,451	97,078		100,000
5b. Brain damage with motor deficiency	51,641	119,469		125,000
6a. Amputation of leg above the knee	28,446	68,165	15,198	55,000
6b. Amputation of leg below the knee	21,882	49,855		45,000
7a. Amputation of arm above the elbow	21,882	65,398	15,198	55,000
7b. Amputation of arm below elbow	17,505	59,248		45,000
8a. Loss of eyesight – one eye without cosmetic disability	16,630	22,944	6,710	25,000
8b. Loss of eyesight – one eye with cosmetic disability	18,818	31,154	6,710	30,000
8c. Loss of eyesight total blindness	28,884	88,364	25,586	105,000
9. Deafness	18,818	69,931	15,198	47,500
10. RSI	–	20,899	–	11,750

<table>
<tr><th>Injury</th><th>Finland
GBP 1=
9.87 FIM</th><th>France
GBP 1=
10.89 FRF</th><th>Germany
GBP 1=
3.25 DEM</th><th>Greece
GBP 1=
565.86 GRD</th></tr>
<tr><td>1. Instant death</td><td>–</td><td>–</td><td>–</td><td>–</td></tr>
<tr><td>2. Burns
A. Face
B. Face (no scars)
C. Body</td><td>7,372
7,372
3,733</td><td>5,051
5,510
5,051</td><td>15,385
to
30,769</td><td>3,534
to
5,302</td></tr>
<tr><td>3. Quadriplegia</td><td rowspan="4">41,297</td><td>59,688</td><td>123,077
to
215,385</td><td>10,603</td></tr>
<tr><td>4. Paraplegia</td><td>45,914</td><td>61,538
to
92,308</td><td>8,836</td></tr>
<tr><td>5a. Brain damage (moderate)</td><td>27,548</td><td rowspan="2">40,000
to
92,308</td><td rowspan="2">11,487</td></tr>
<tr><td>5b. Brain damage with motor deficiency</td><td>27,548</td></tr>
<tr><td>6a. Amputation of leg above the knee</td><td>16,956</td><td>41,322</td><td rowspan="2">23,077
to
27,692</td><td>7,069</td></tr>
<tr><td>6b. Amputation of leg below the knee</td><td>14,744</td><td>39,486</td><td>5,302</td></tr>
<tr><td>7a. Amputation of arm above the elbow</td><td>20,276</td><td>34,894</td><td rowspan="2">18,462
to
24,615</td><td>7,069</td></tr>
<tr><td>7b. Amputation of arm below elbow</td><td>19,169</td><td>25,253</td><td>5,302</td></tr>
<tr><td>8a. Loss of eyesight – one eye without cosmetic disability</td><td>9,585</td><td>11,938</td><td rowspan="2">15,385
to
24,615</td><td rowspan="2">3,534</td></tr>
<tr><td>8b. Loss of eyesight – one eye with cosmetic disability</td><td>14,650</td><td>16,988</td></tr>
<tr><td>8c. Loss of eyesight total blindness</td><td>41,297</td><td>20,661</td><td>40,000
to
49,231</td><td>15,021</td></tr>
<tr><td>9. Deafness</td><td>21,382</td><td>18,825</td><td>21,538
to
23,077</td><td>5,302</td></tr>
<tr><td>10. RSI</td><td>–</td><td>–</td><td>–</td><td>884</td></tr>
</table>

<table>
<tr><th>Injury</th><th>Ireland
GBP 1=
1.31 IEP</th><th>Italy
GBP 1=
3215.24 ITL</th><th>Luxembourg
GBP 1=
67.05 LUF</th><th>The Netherlands
GBP 1=
3.66 NLG</th></tr>
<tr><td>1. Instant death</td><td>–</td><td>–</td><td>–</td><td>–</td></tr>
<tr><td>2. Burns
A. Face
B. Face (no scars)
C. Body</td><td>45,802
to
64,885</td><td>10,886
to
10,954</td><td>22,370*
22,370*
22,370*</td><td>9,563
9,563
9,563</td></tr>
<tr><td>3. Quadriplegia</td><td>152,672
to
190,840</td><td>137,704</td><td>73,264*</td><td rowspan="4">54,645
to
109,290</td></tr>
<tr><td>4. Parapeligia</td><td>114,504
to
152,672</td><td>90,784</td><td>55,070*</td></tr>
<tr><td>5a. Brain damage (moderate)</td><td rowspan="2">114,504
to
190,840</td><td>107,839</td><td>55,217*</td></tr>
<tr><td>5b. Brain damage with motor deficiency</td><td>123,314</td><td>63,420*</td></tr>
<tr><td>6a. Amputation of leg above the knee</td><td rowspan="4">114,504</td><td>28,206</td><td>43,726*</td><td rowspan="2">27,322
to
34,153</td></tr>
<tr><td>6b. Amputation of leg below the knee</td><td>21,594</td><td>36,757*</td></tr>
<tr><td>7a. Amputation of arm above the elbow</td><td>28,206</td><td>35,099*</td><td rowspan="2">20,492
to
32,787</td></tr>
<tr><td>7b. Amputation of arm below elbow</td><td>21,594</td><td>29,162*</td></tr>
<tr><td>8a. Loss of eyesight – one eye without cosmetic disability</td><td>76,336</td><td>21,594</td><td>24,273*</td><td rowspan="2">10,929
to
19,126</td></tr>
<tr><td>8b. Loss of eyesight – one eye with cosmetic disability</td><td>95,420
to
106,870</td><td>28,206</td><td>33,297*</td></tr>
<tr><td>8c. Loss of eyesight total blindness</td><td>152,672
to
171,756</td><td>123,314</td><td>83,275*</td><td>40,984
to
54,645</td></tr>
<tr><td>9. Deafness</td><td>57,252
to
76,336</td><td>72,329</td><td>86,197*</td><td>20,492
to
27,322</td></tr>
<tr><td>10. RSI</td><td>—</td><td>12,441</td><td>–</td><td>–</td></tr>
</table>

** Doesn't include interest.*

Injury	*Portugal GBP 1= 332.91 PTE*	*Scotland*	*Spain GBP 1= 276.29 ESP*	*Sweden GBP 1= 15.3 SEK*
1. Instant death	–	–	See notes on pain and suffering awards for Spain	–
2. Burns A. Face B. Face (no scars) C. Body	3,004 3,004 3,004	25,000 12,000 25,000		980 to 4,575
3. Quadriplegia	30,038	130,000		40,523
4. Parapeligia		115,000		33,007
5a. Brain damage (moderate)		90,000		19,281
5b. Brain damage with motor deficiency		115,000		26,667
6a. Amputation of leg above the knee	18,022	55,000		13,203
6b. Amputation of leg below the knee		50,000		8,497
7a. Amputation of arm above the elbow		55,000		17,908
7b. Amputation of arm below elbow		45,000		15,948
8a. Loss of eyesight – one eye without cosmetic disability	12,015	20,000		4,706
8b. Loss of eyesight – one eye with cosmetic disability		25,000		
8c. Loss of eyesight total blindness	27,034	90,000		35,425
9. Deafness	21,027	18,000		18,301
10. RSI	3,004	7,200		2,092 to 8,954

Table 2. Schedule B

Legal scretary, woman, 20, single; currency at 4 July 2001

Injury	*Austria GBP 1= 22.85 ATS*	*Belgium GBP 1= 66.99 BEF*	*Denmark GBP 1= 12.37 DKK*	*England /Wales*
1. Instant death	–	–	–	–
2. Burns A. Face B. Face (no scars) C. Body	5,689 to 10,066	29,910 29,910 29,910	5,093 5,093 5,093	55,000 45,000 35,000
3. Quadriplegia	67,834	132,027	12,773 to 25,586	150,000
4. Paraplegia	50,328	108,274		110,000
5a. Brain damage (moderate)	45,952	108,274		100,000
5b. Brain damage with motor deficiency	54,705	119,469		135,000
6a. Amputation of leg above the knee	30,635	68,165	15,198	55,000
6b. Amputation of leg below the knee	24,070	52,841		45,000
7a. Amputation of arm above the elbow	24,070	71,369	15,602	55,000
7b. Amputation of arm below elbow	19,694	62,980		45,000
8a. Loss of eyesight – one eye without cosmetic disability	19,694	23,690	6,710	25,000
8b. Loss of eyesight – one eye with cosmetic disability	21,882	34,886	6,710	30,000
8c. Loss of eyesight total blindness	33,260	88,364	25,586	105,000
9. Deafness	21,882	69,931	15,198	47,500
10. RSI	–	20,899	–	11,750

<table>
<tr><th>Injury</th><th>Finland
GBP 1=
9.87 FIM</th><th>France
GBP 1=
10.89 FRF</th><th>Germany
GBP 1=
3.25 DEM</th><th>Greece
GBP 1=
565.86 GRD</th></tr>
<tr><td>1. Instant death</td><td>–</td><td>–</td><td>–</td><td>–</td></tr>
<tr><td>2. Burns
A. Face
B. Face (no scars)
C. Body</td><td>8,223
8,223
4,300</td><td>6,887
8,264
6,887</td><td>15,385
to
30,769</td><td>1,767
to
2,121</td></tr>
<tr><td>3. Quadriplegia</td><td rowspan="4">49,807</td><td>59,688</td><td>92,308
to
153,846</td><td>10,603</td></tr>
<tr><td>4. Paraplegia</td><td>45,914</td><td>61,538
to
92,308</td><td>7,069</td></tr>
<tr><td>5a. Brain damage (moderate)</td><td>27,548</td><td rowspan="2">40,000
to
92,308</td><td rowspan="2">10,603</td></tr>
<tr><td>5b. Brain damage with motor deficiency</td><td>27,548</td></tr>
<tr><td>6a. Amputation of leg above the knee</td><td>19,226</td><td>41,322</td><td rowspan="2">23,077
to
27,692</td><td>8,836</td></tr>
<tr><td>6b. Amputation of leg below the knee</td><td>16,450</td><td>39,486</td><td>7,069</td></tr>
<tr><td>7a. Amputation of arm above the elbow</td><td>23,396</td><td>34,894</td><td rowspan="2">18,462
to
24,615</td><td>8,836</td></tr>
<tr><td>7b. Amputation of arm below elbow</td><td>22,006</td><td>25,253</td><td>7,069</td></tr>
<tr><td>8a. Loss of eyesight – one eye without cosmetic disability</td><td>11,003</td><td>11,938</td><td rowspan="2">15,385
to
24,615</td><td rowspan="2">5,302</td></tr>
<tr><td>8b. Loss of eyesight – one eye with cosmetic disability</td><td>16,069</td><td>16,988</td></tr>
<tr><td>8c. Loss of eyesight total blindness</td><td>49,807</td><td>20,661</td><td>40,000
to
49,231</td><td>14,138</td></tr>
<tr><td>9. Deafness</td><td>24,786</td><td>20,661</td><td>21,538
to
23,077</td><td>8,836</td></tr>
<tr><td>10. RSI</td><td>–</td><td>–</td><td>–</td><td>884</td></tr>
</table>

Injury	*Ireland GBP 1= 1.31 IEP*	*Italy GBP 1= 3215.24 ITL*	*Luxembourg GBP 1= 67.05 LUF*	*The Netherlands GBP 1= 3.66 NLG*
1. Instant death	–	–	–	–
2. Burns A. Face B. Face (no scars) C. Body	61,069 to 83,969	12,314 12,314 12,314	23,190* 23,190* 23,190*	9,563 9,563 9,563
3. Quadriplegia	190,840	154,810	93,119*	54,645 to 109,290
4. Paraplegia	133,588 to 171,756	102,062	67,349*	54,645 to 109,290
5a. Brain damage (moderate)	114,504 to 190,840	121,236	68,990*	54,645 to 109,290
5b. Brain damage with motor deficiency	114,504 to 190,840	138,632	78,833*	54,645 to 109,290
6a. Amputation of leg above the knee	95,420 to 152,672	31,710	46,597*	27,322 to 34,153
6b. Amputation of leg below the knee	95,420 to 152,672	24,277	40,652*	27,322 to 34,153
7a. Amputation of arm above the elbow	95,420 to 133,588	31,710	40,652*	20,492 to 34,153
7b. Amputation of arm below elbow	95,420 to 133,588	24,277	35,730*	20,492 to 34,153
8a. Loss of eyesight – one eye without cosmetic disability	76,336	31,710	30,620*	10,298 to 19,126
8b. Loss of eyesight – one eye with cosmetic disability	95,420 to 106,870	31,710	36,362*	10,298 to 19,126
8c. Loss of eyesight total blindness	190,840	138,632	119,796*	40,984 to 54,645
9. Deafness	61,069 to 76,336	81,314	86,689*	20,492 to 27,322
10. RSI	–	12,441	–	5,464 to 8,197

** Doesn't include interest.*

Injury	*Portugal GBP 1= 332.91 PTE*	*Scotland*	*Spain GBP 1= 276.29 ESP*	*Sweden GBP 1= 15.3 SEK*
1. Instant death	–	–	See notes on pain and suffering awards for Spain	–
2. Burns A. Face B. Face (no scars) C. Body	 3,004 3,004 3,004	 30,000 15,000 30,000		1,961 to 5,882
3. Quadriplegia	24,031	130,000		47,124
4. Paraplegia		115,000		38,562
5a. Brain damage (moderate)		90,000		22,222
5b. Brain damage with motor deficiency		115,000		30,915
6a. Amputation of leg above the knee	15,019 to 18,022	55,000		16,275
6b. Amputation of leg below the knee		50,000		10,523
7a. Amputation of arm above the elbow		60,000		18,758
7b. Amputation of arm below elbow		59,000		21,908
8a. Loss of eyesight – one eye without cosmetic disability	15,019	20,000		5,229
8b. Loss of eyesight – one eye with cosmetic disability		30,000		
8c. Loss of eyesight total blindness	24,031	100,000		41,634
9. Deafness	21,027	24,000		21,242
10. RSI	3,004	7,200		2,288 to 10,327

Bloc Graphs, Pain and Suffering Awards: EU Countries

Table 1. Schedule A

Doctor, man, 40, married, 2 dependent children – burns; GBP

Ireland	45,802 to 64,885
England & Wales	A; 55,000 B; 45,000 C; 35,000
Germany	15,385 to 30,769
Belgium	28,418
Scotland	A;25,000 B;12,000 C; 25,000
Luxembourg	22,370
Italy	10,954
The Netherlands	9,563
Austria	4,814 to 8,753
Finland	A;7,372 B;7,372 C;3,733
France	5,510
Denmark	5,497
Greece	3,534 to 5,302
Sweden	980 to 4,575
Portugal	3,004

Table 2. Schedule A

Doctor, man, 40, married, 2 dependent children – quadriplegia; GBP

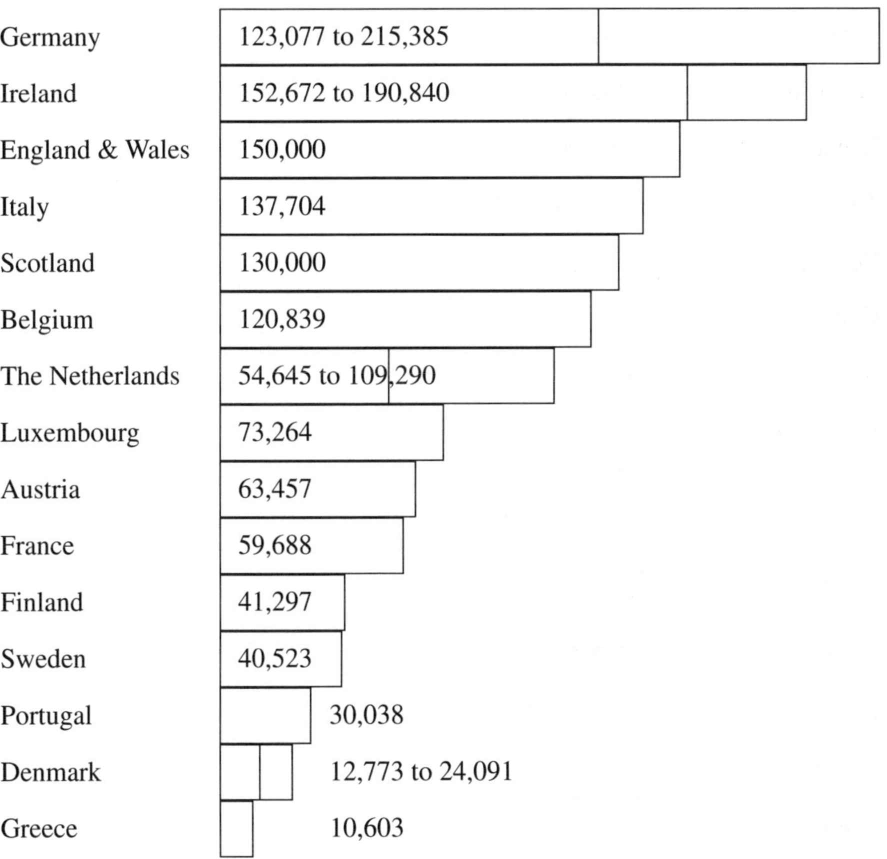

Table 3. Schedule A

Doctor, man, 40, married, 2 dependent children – paraplegia; GBP

Country	Award (GBP)
Ireland	114,504 to 152,672
Scotland	115,000
England & Wales	110,000
The Netherlands	54,645 to 109,290
Belgium	97,078
Germany	61,538 to 92,308
Italy	90,784
Luxembourg	55,070
Austria	45,952
France	45,914
Finland	41,297
Sweden	33,007
Portugal	30,038
Denmark	12,773 to 24,091
Greece	8,836

Table 4. Schedule A

Doctor, man, 40, married, 2 dependent children – brain damage (moderate); GBP

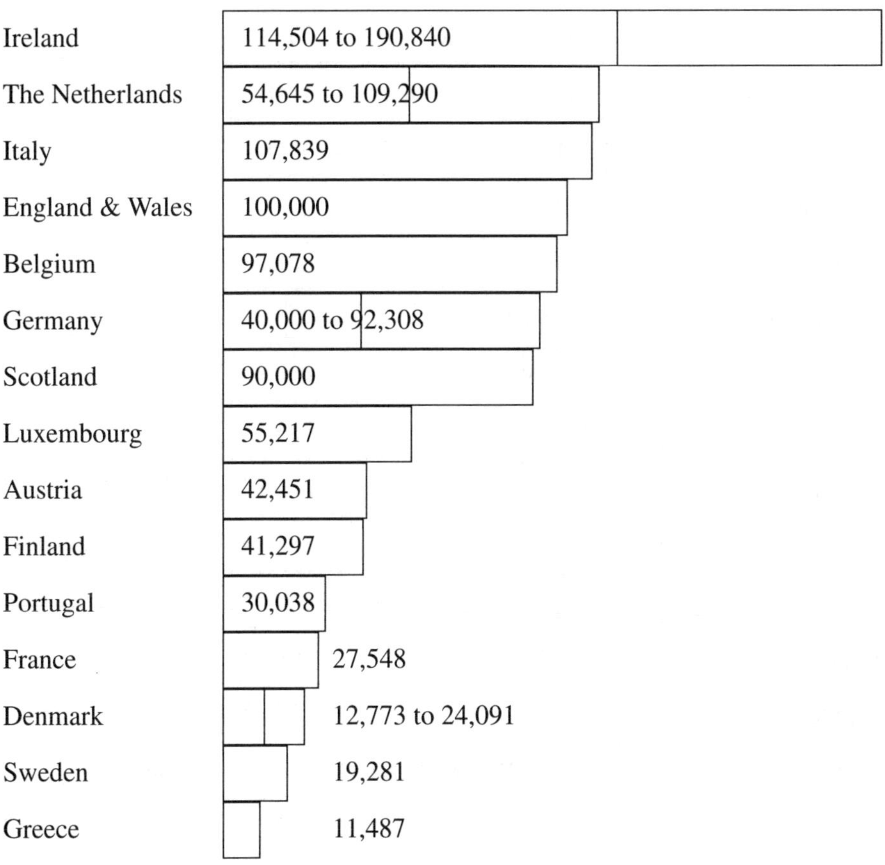

Table 5. Schedule A

Doctor, man, 40, married, 2 dependent children – brain damage (motor deficiency); GBP

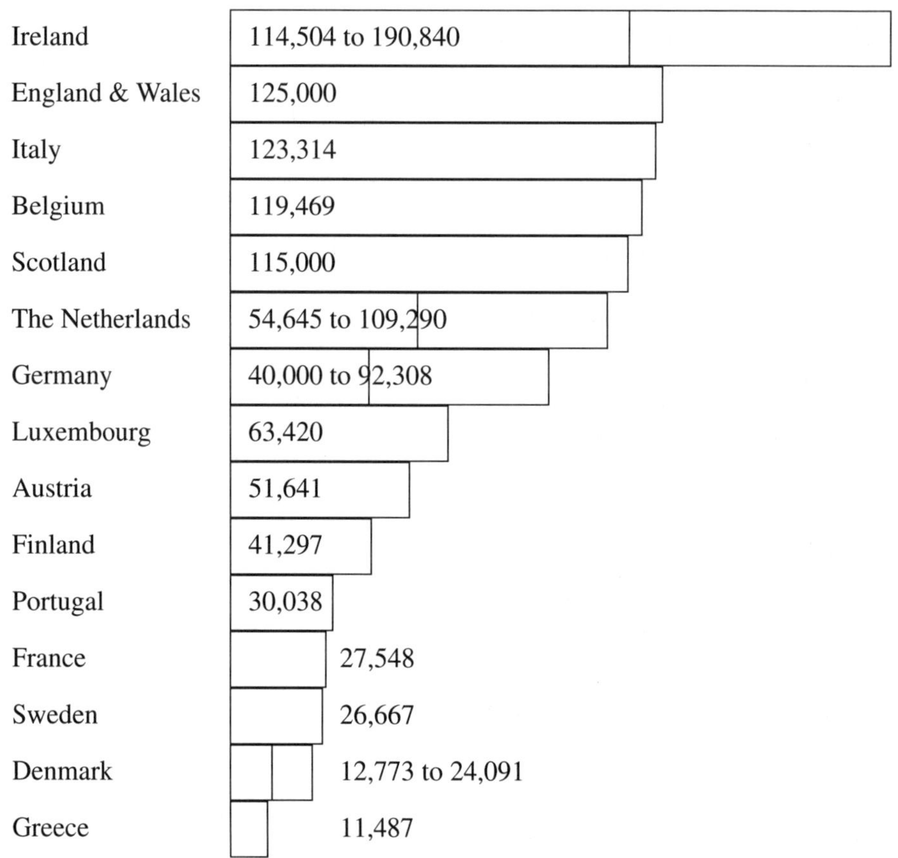

Table 6. Schedule A

Doctor, man, 40, married, 2 dependent children – amputation above knee; GBP

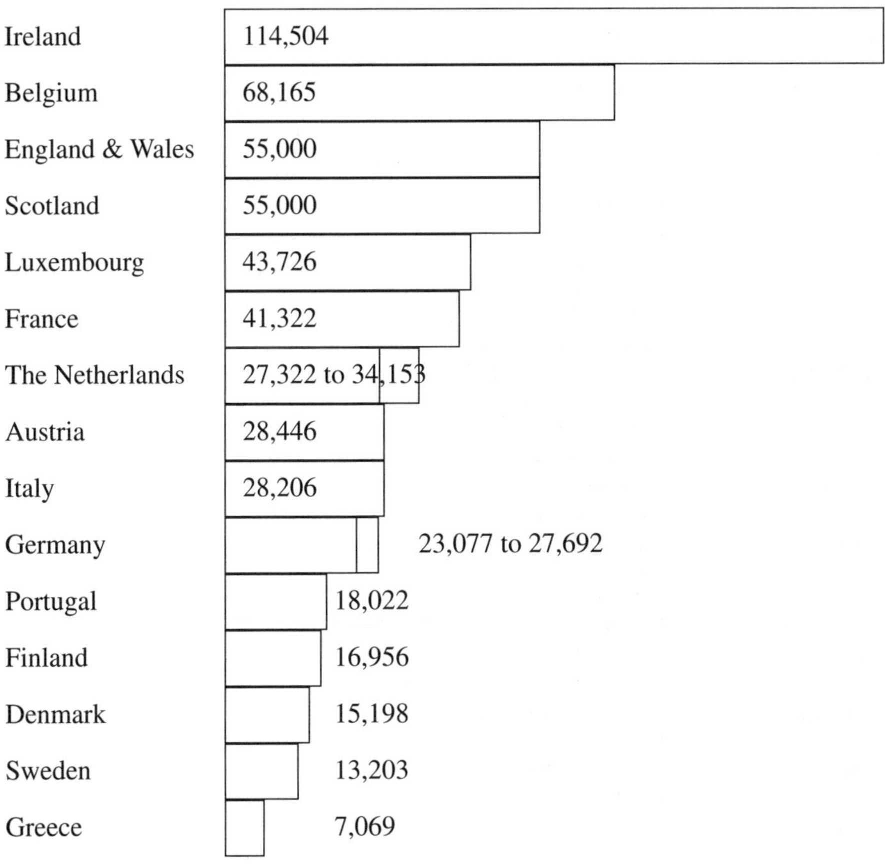

Table 7. Schedule A

Doctor, man, 40, married, 2 dependent children – amputation of leg below knee; GBP

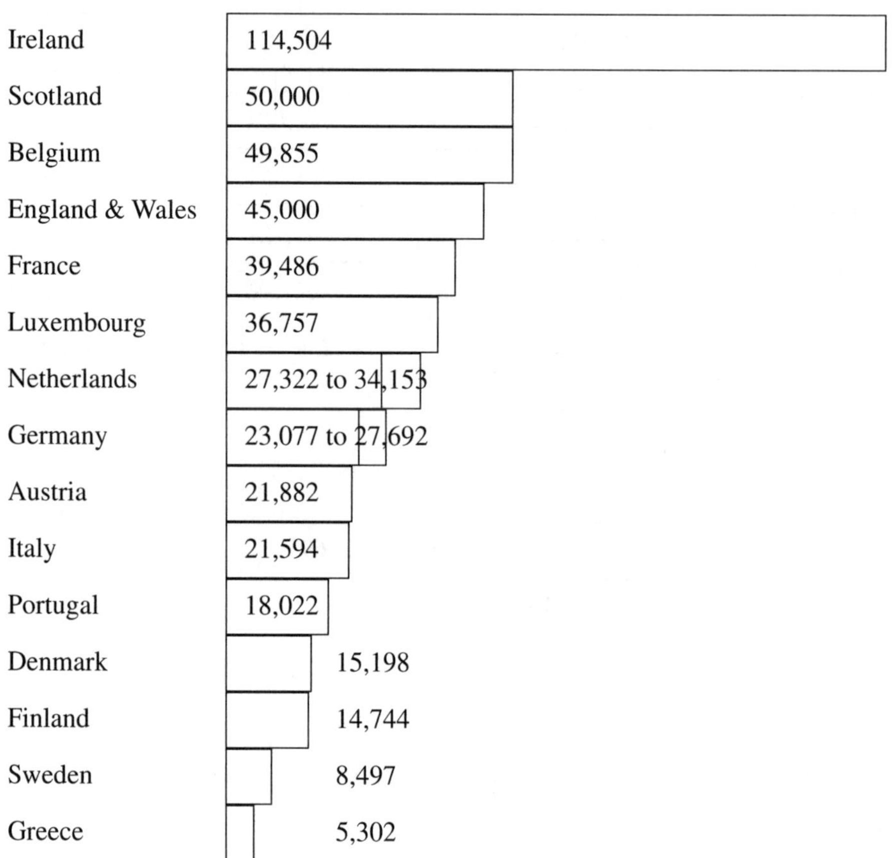

Table 8. Schedule A

Doctor, man, 40, married, 2 dependent children – amputation of arm above the elbow; GBP

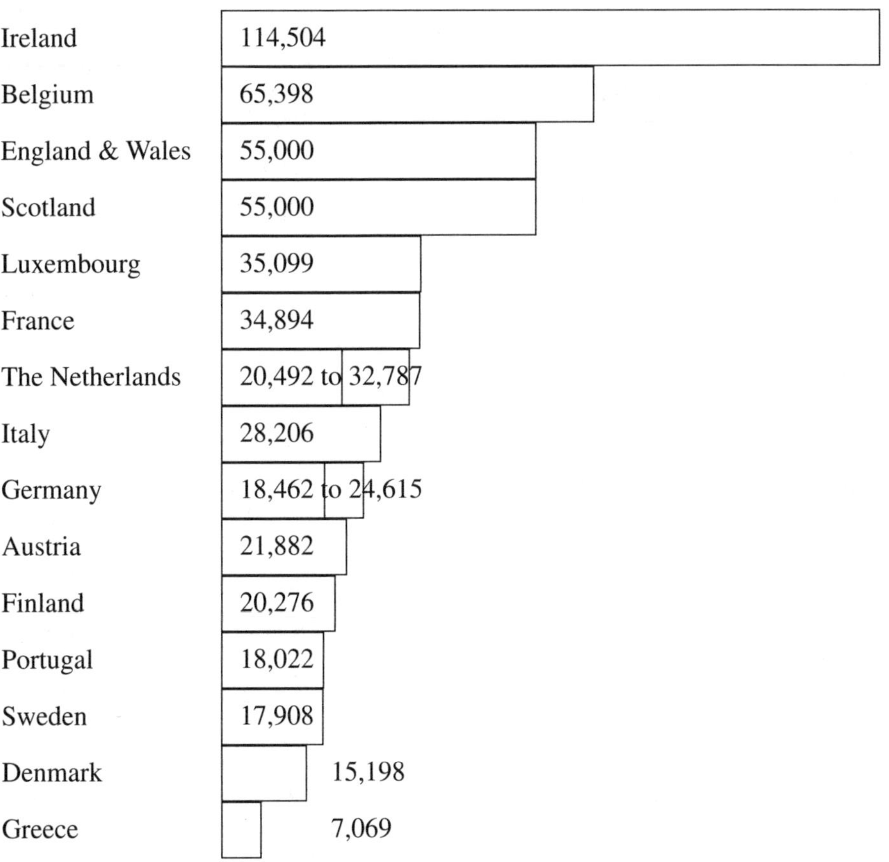

Table 9. Schedule A

Doctor, man, 40, married, 2 dependent children – amputation of of arm below the elbow; GBP

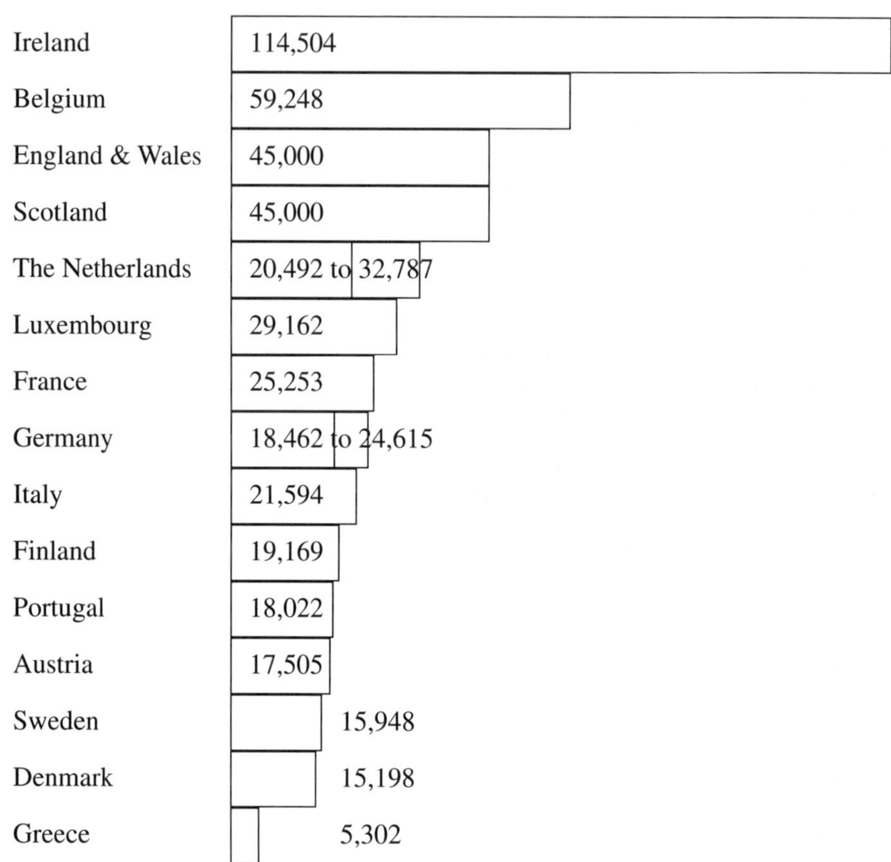

Table 10. Schedule A

Doctor, man, 40, married, 2 dependent children – loss of eye without cosmetic injury; GBP

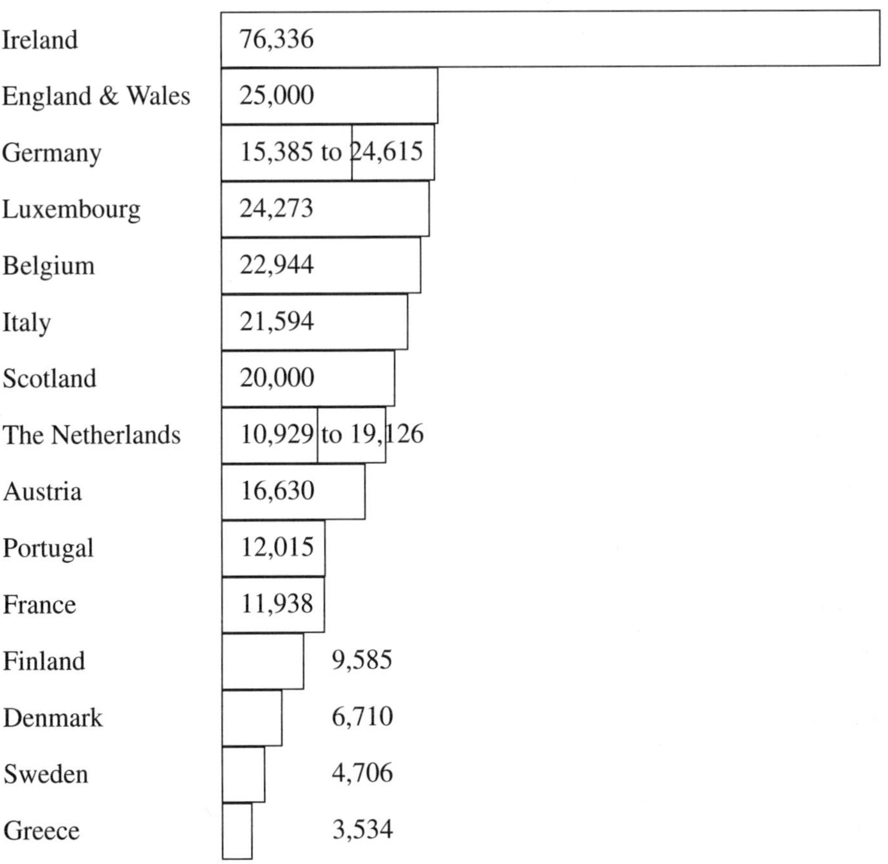

Table 11. Schedule A

Doctor, man, 40, married, 2 dependent children – loss of eye with cosmetic injury; GBP

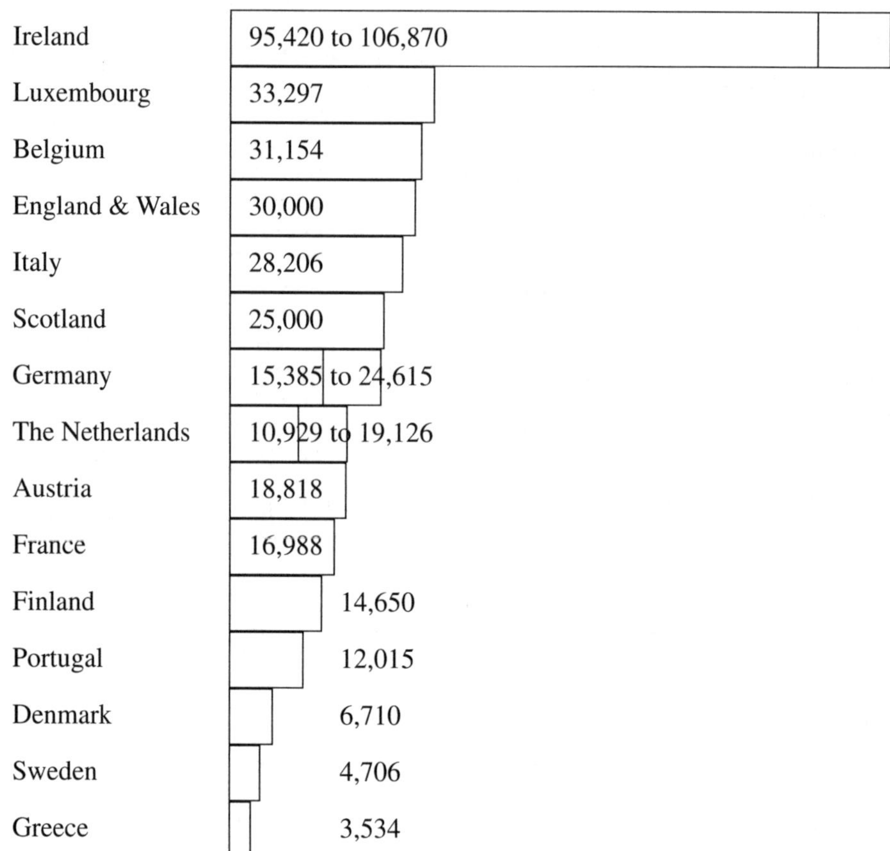

Table 12. Schedule A

Doctor, man, 40, married, 2 dependent children – loss of eyesight – total blindness; GBP

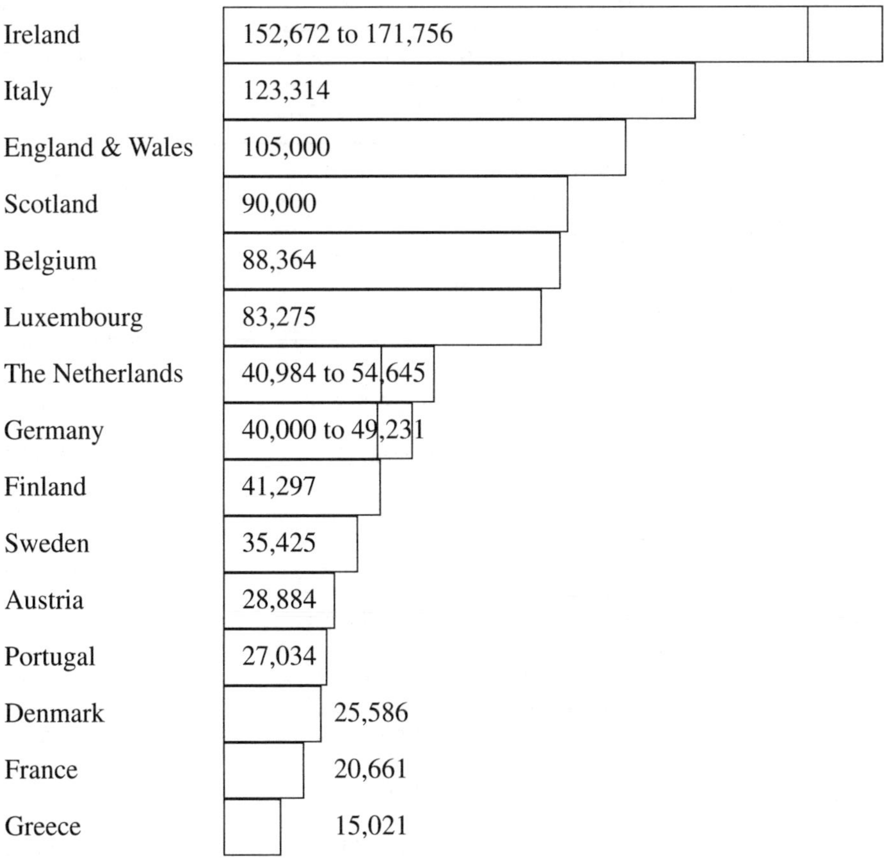

Table 13. Schedule A

Doctor, man, 40, married, 2 dependent children – deafness; GBP

Country	GBP
Luxembourg	86,197
Ireland	57,252 to 76,336
Italy	72,329
Belgium	69,931
England & Wales	47,500
The Netherlands	20,492 to 27,322
Germany	21,538 to 23,077
Finland	21,382
Portugal	21,027
France	18,825
Austria	18,818
Sweden	18,301
Scotland	18,000
Denmark	15,198
Greece	5,302

Table 14. Schedule A

Doctor, man, 40, married, 2 dependent children – RSI; GBP

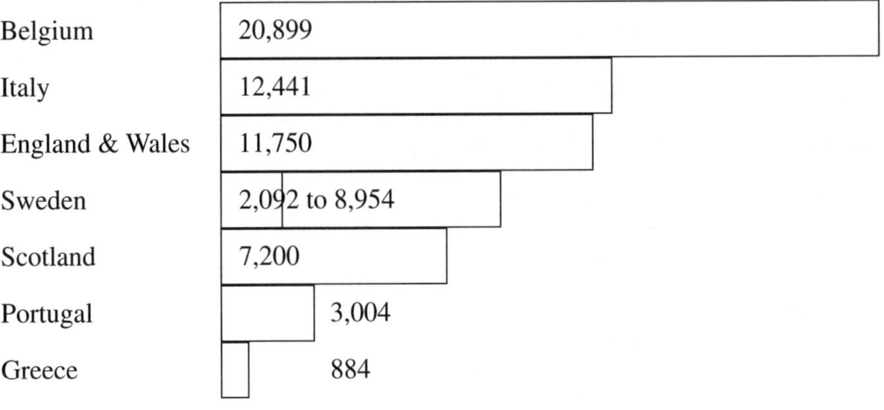

Table 15. Schedule B

Legal secretary, woman, 20, single – Burns; GBP

Country	GBP
Ireland	61,069 to 83,969
England & Wales	A; 55,000 B; 45,000 C; 35,000
Germany	15,385 to 30,769
Scotland	15,000 to 30,000
Belgium	29,910
Luxembourg	23,190
Italy	12,314
Austria	5,689 to 10,066
The Netherlands	9,563
France	6,887 to 8,264
Finland	4,300 to 8,223
Sweden	1,961 to 5,882
Denmark	5,093
Portugal	3,004
Greece	1,767 to 2,121

Table 16. Schedule B

Legal secretary, woman, 20, single – quadriplegia; GBP

Country	GBP
Ireland	190,840
Italy	154,810
Germany	92,308 to 153,846
England & Wales	150,000
Belgium	132,027
Scotland	130,000
The Netherlands	54,645 to 109,290
Luxembourg	93,119
Austria	67,834
France	59,688
Finland	49,807
Sweden	47,124
Denmark	12,773 to 25,586
Portugal	24,031
Greece	10,063

Table 17. Schedule B

Legal secretary, woman, 20, single – paraplegia; GBP

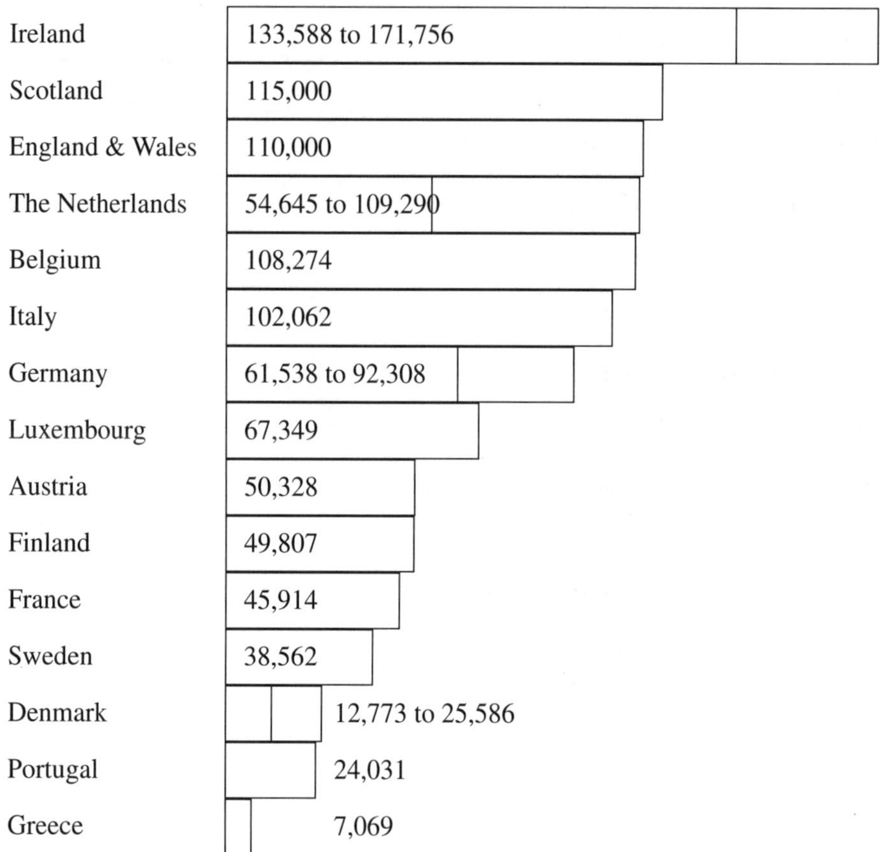

Table 18. Schedule B

Legal secretary, woman, 20, single – brain damage (moderate); GBP

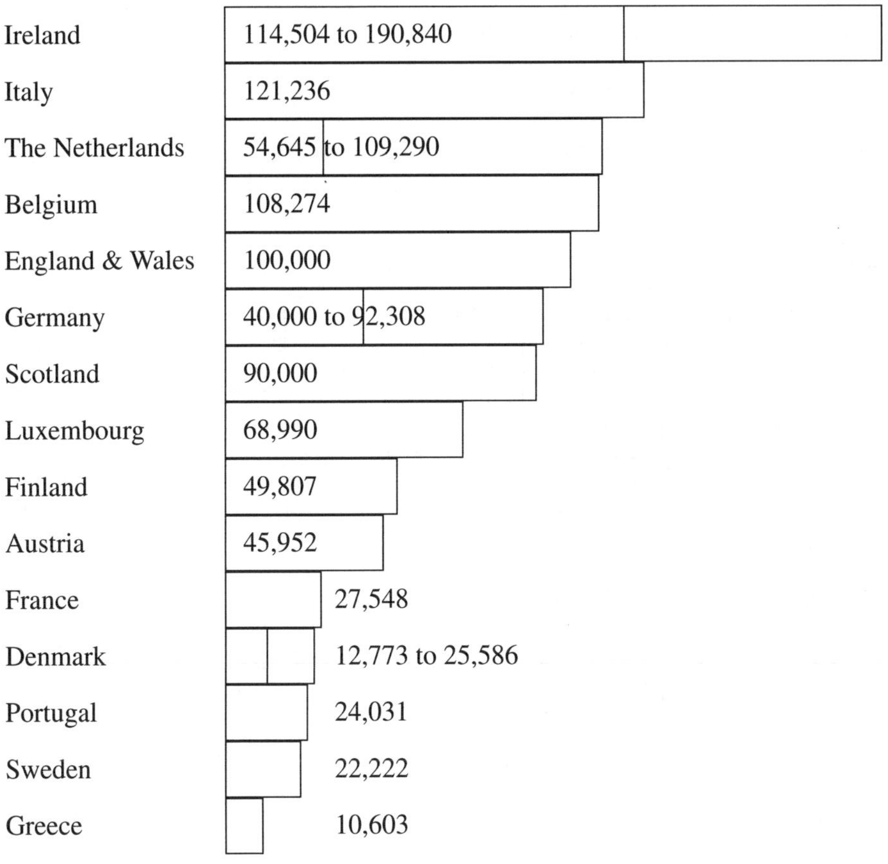

Table 19. Schedule B

Legal secretary, woman, 20, single – brain damage (motor deficiency); GBP

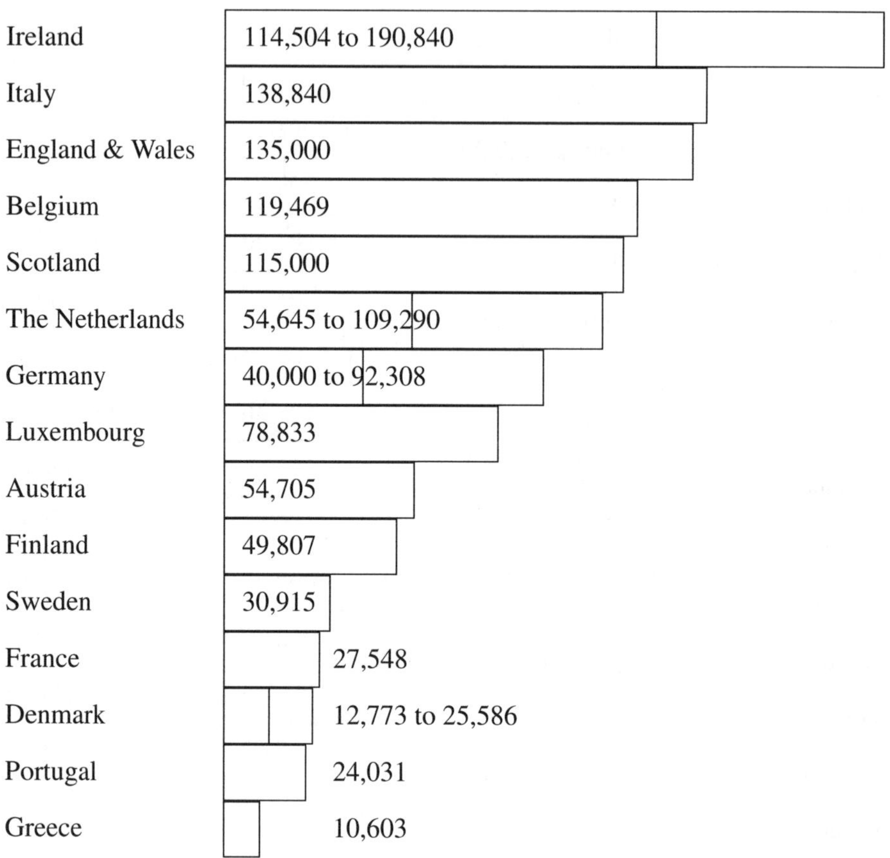

Table 20. Schedule B

Legal secretary, woman, 20, single – amputation of leg above the knee; GBP

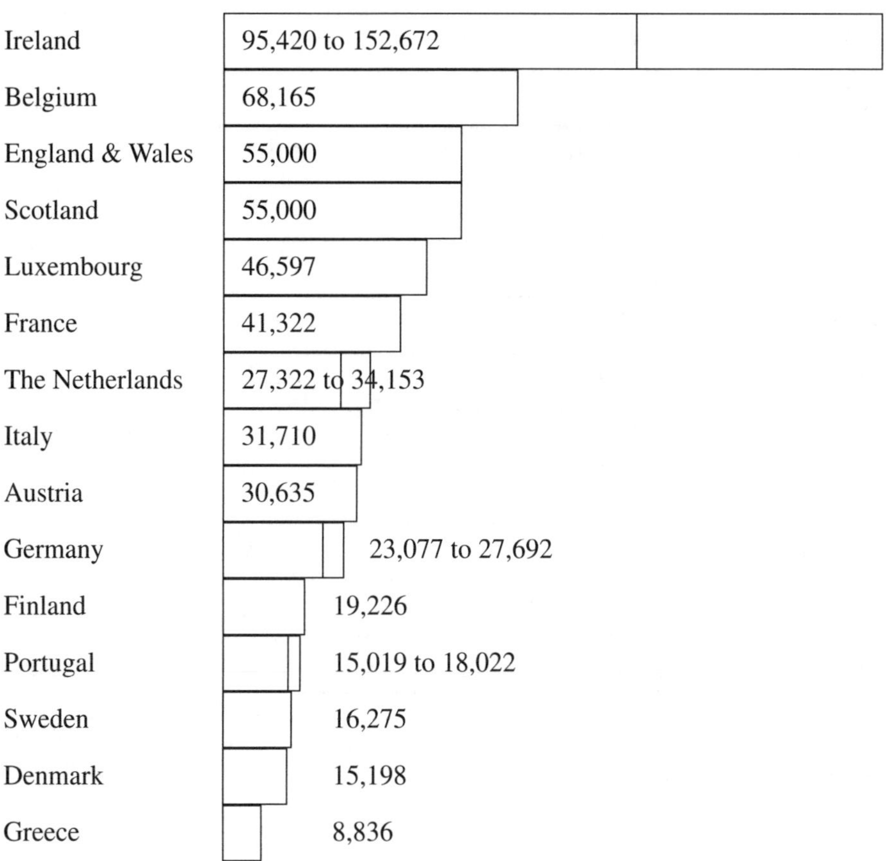

Table 21. Schedule B

Legal secretary, woman, 20, single – amputation of leg below the knee; GBP

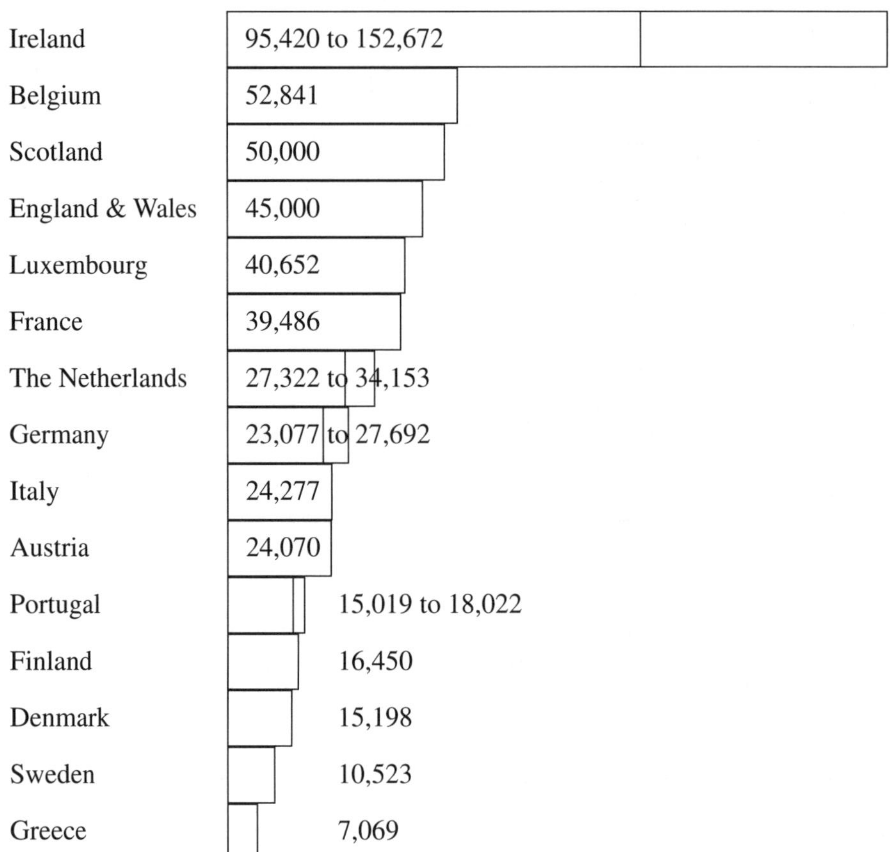

Table 22. Schedule B

Legal secretary, woman, 20, single – amputation of arm above the elbow; GBP

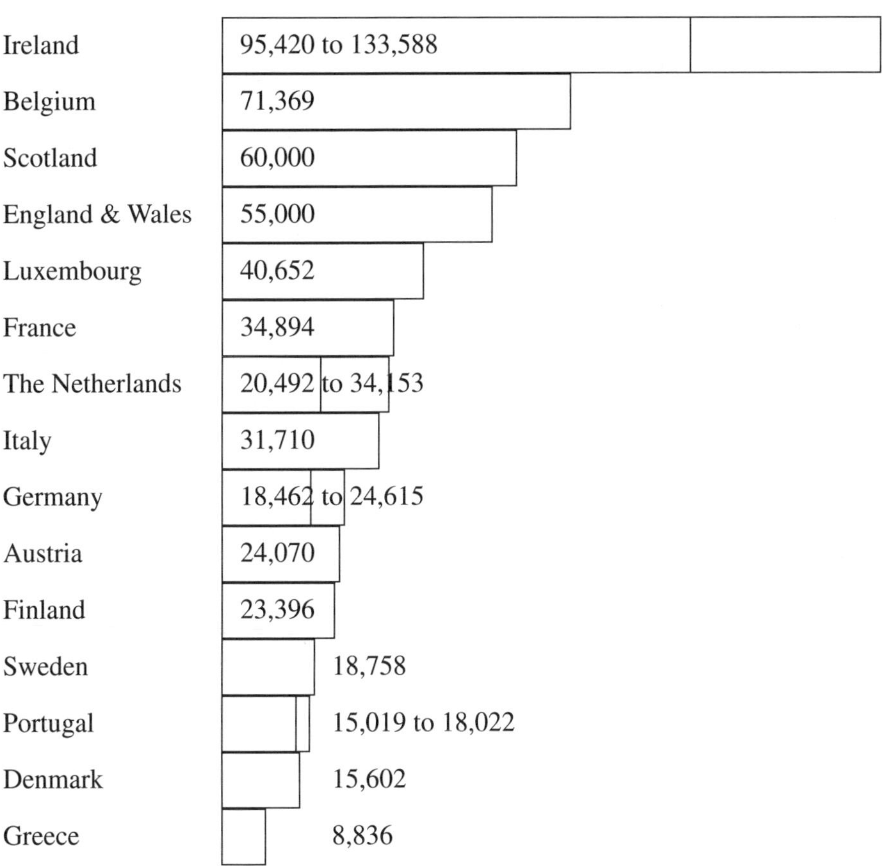

Table 23. Schedule B

Legal secretary, woman, 20, single – amputation of arm below the elbow; GBP

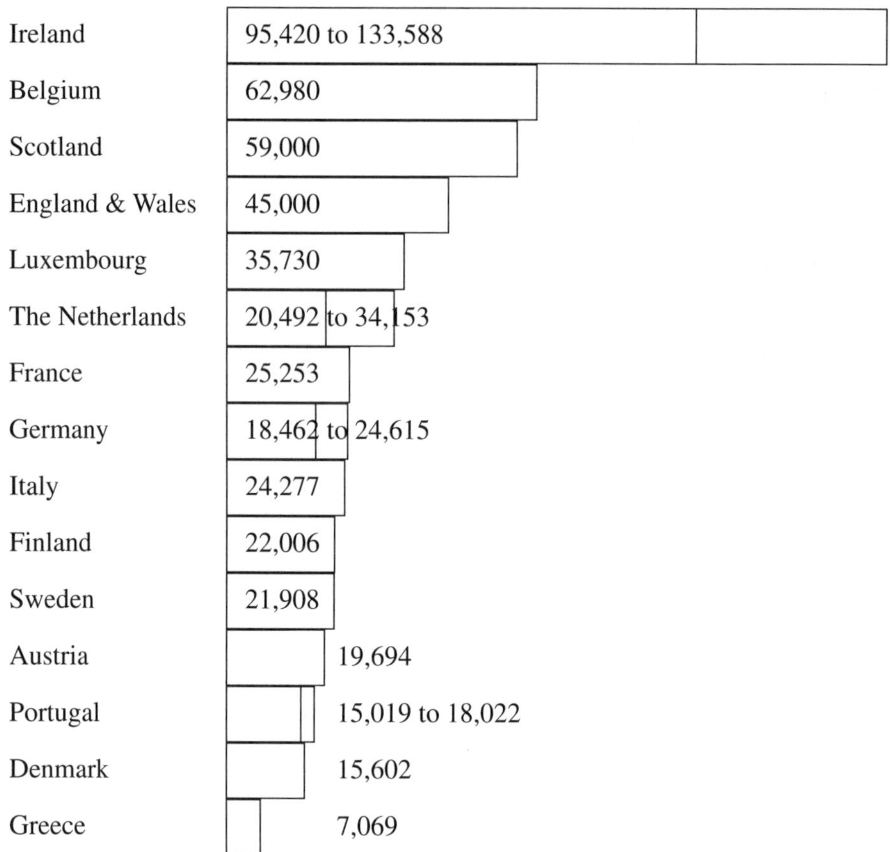

Table 24. Schedule B

Legal secretary, woman, 20, single – loss of one eye without cosmetic injury; GBP

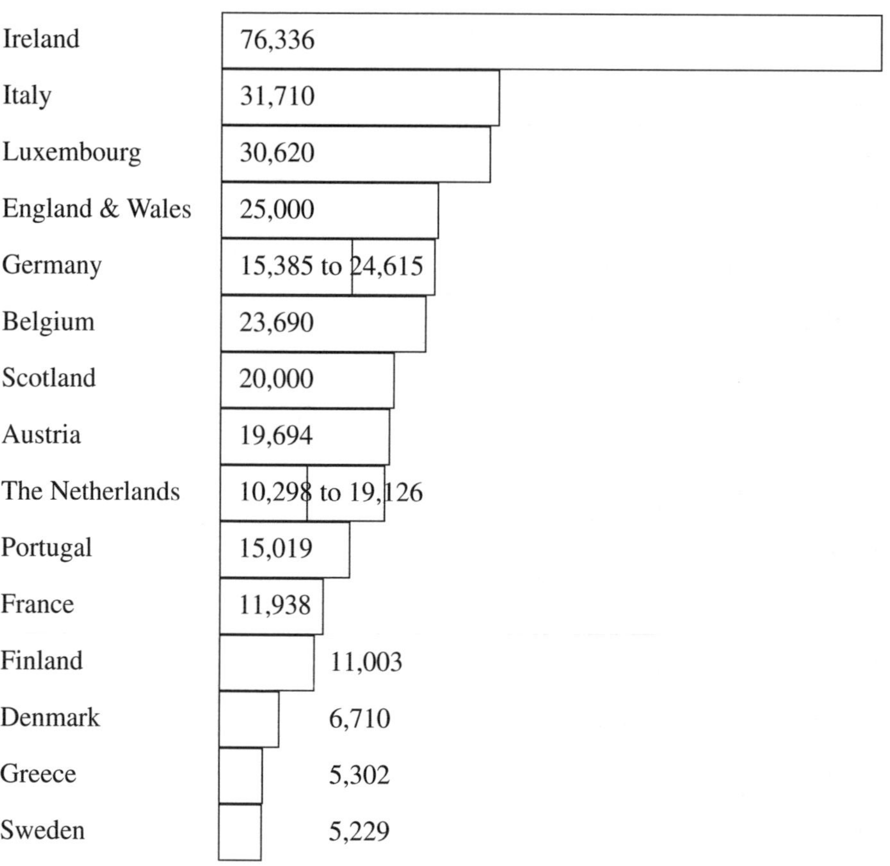

Table 25. Schedule B

Legal secretary, woman, 20, single – loss of one eye with cosmetic injury; GBP

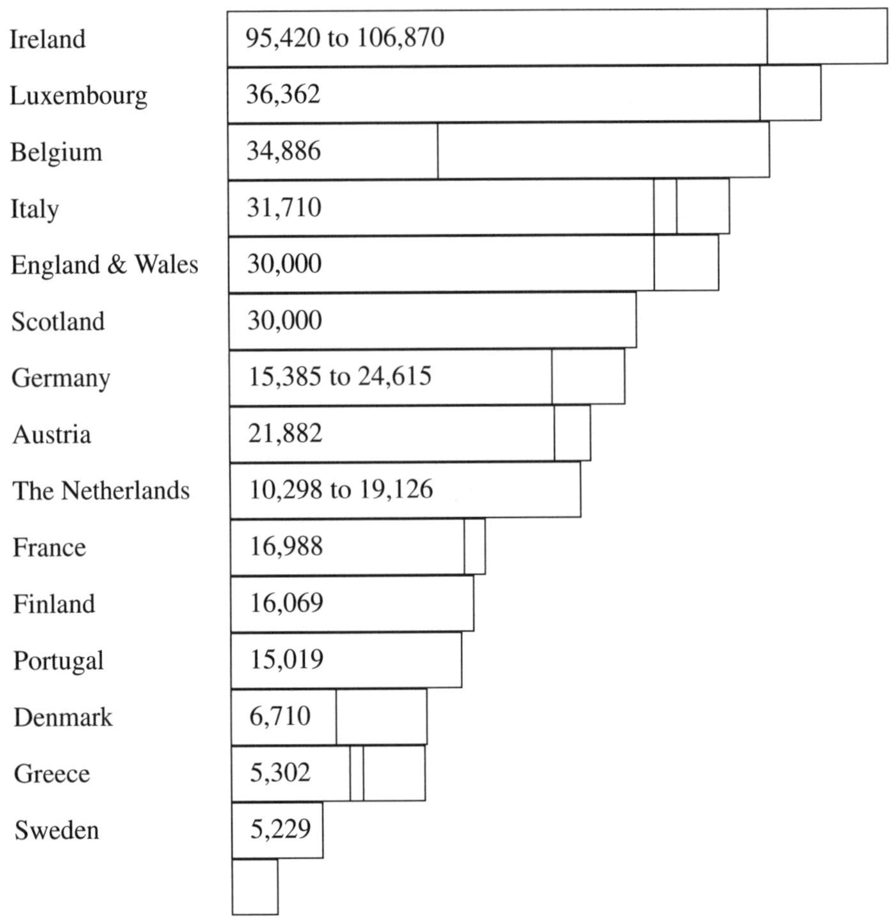

Country	Award (GBP)
Ireland	95,420 to 106,870
Luxembourg	36,362
Belgium	34,886
Italy	31,710
England & Wales	30,000
Scotland	30,000
Germany	15,385 to 24,615
Austria	21,882
The Netherlands	10,298 to 19,126
France	16,988
Finland	16,069
Portugal	15,019
Denmark	6,710
Greece	5,302
Sweden	5,229

Table 26. Schedule B

Legal secretary, woman, 20, single – loss of eyesight, total blindness; GBP

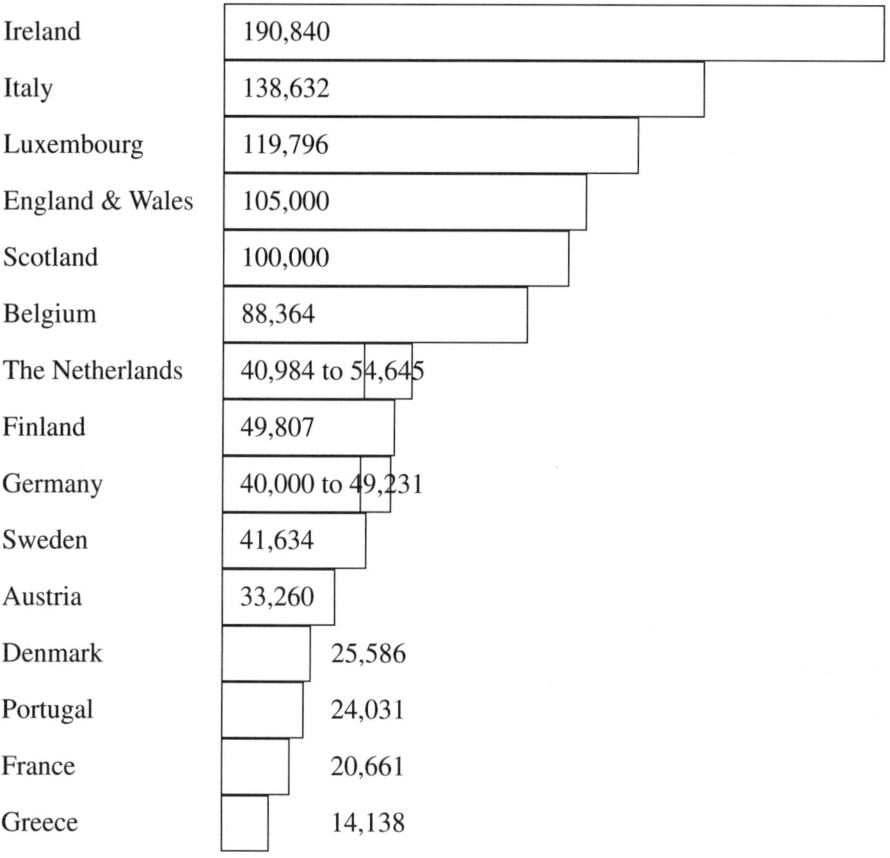

Table 27. Schedule B

Legal secretary, woman, 20, single – deafness; GBP

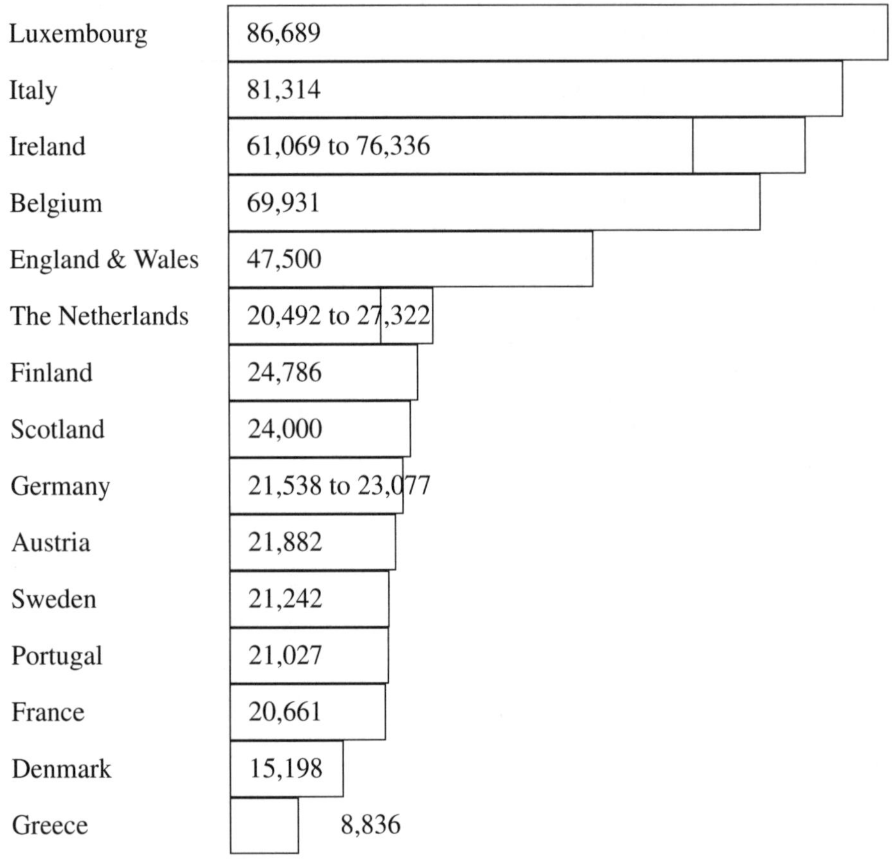

Table 28. Schedule B

Legal secretary, woman, 20, single – RSI; GBP

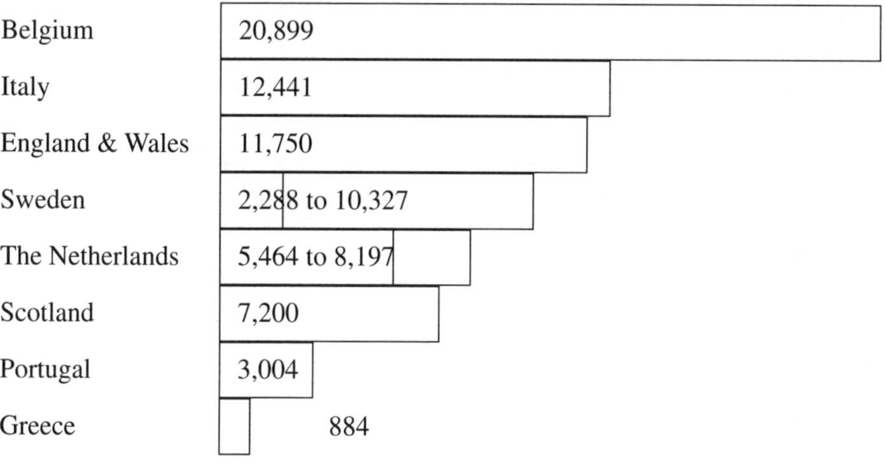

BEREAVEMENT DAMAGES

Table 1. Schedule A

Doctor, man, 40, married, 2 dependent children – instant death; GBP

Italy	367,209
Scotland	35,175
Luxembourg	32,438
France	24,334
Switzerland	19,762
Belgium	19,294
Greece	18,768
Ireland	15,267
Portugal	15,019
England & Wales	9,031
Austria	None
Denmark	None
Finland	None
Germany	None
Iceland	None
Liechtenstein	None
The Netherlands	None
Norway	None
Spain	No figures available
Sweden	None

Table 2. Schedule B

Legal secretary, woman, 20, single – instant death; GBP

Italy	133,136
Switzerland	Up to 27,668
France	27, 548
Belgium	16,495
Ireland	15,267
Portugal	15,019
Luxembourg	6,432
Greece	4,489
Scotland	4,080
Austria	None
Denmark	None
England & Wales	None
Finland	None
Germany	None
Iceland	None
Liechtenstein	None
The Netherlands	None
Norway	None
Spain	No figures available
Sweden	None

TOTAL COMPENSATION: EFTA COUNTRIES

Table 1. Schedule A

Doctor, man, 40, married, 2 dependent children; currency at 4 July 2001

Injury	*Iceland GBP 1= 145.08 ISK*	*Liechtenstein GBP 1= 2.53 CHF*	*Norway GBP 1= 13.19 NOK*	*Switzerland GBP 1= 2.53 CHF*
1. Instant death	141,301*	466,529	87,748	506,275
2. Burns				
A. Face	35,842*	53,915	36,892	83,004
B. Face (no scars)	35,842*	–	36,892	–
C. Body	35,842*	29,231	36,892	–
3. Quadriplegia	445,961*	518,035	264,329	944,664
4. Paraplegia	329,473* to 445,961*	278,126	247,521	936,759
5a. Brain damage (moderate)	128,205* to 445,961*	228,433	255,527	–
5b. Brain damage with motor deficiency		244,944	264,329	936,759
6a. Amputation of leg above the knee	288,806*	98,519	45,694	256,917
6b. Amputation of leg below the knee	207,472*	84,986	40,887	256,917
7a. Amputation of arm above the elbow	329,473*	120,171	45,694	430,830
7b. Amputation of arm below elbow	288,806*	112,053	40,887	430,830
8a. Loss of eyesight – one eye without cosmetic disability	107,527*	44,551	9,606	79,051
8b. Loss of eyesight – one eye with cosmetic disability	128,205*	69,559	9,606	79,051
8c. Loss of eyesight total blindness	445,961*	207,592	265,869	942,737
9. Deafness	41,356* to 268,817*	128,725	106,263	729,249
10. RSI	74,442* to 128,205*	–	82,623	90,513

Table 2. Schedule B

Legal secretary, woman, 20, single; currency at 4 July 2001

Injury	*Iceland GBP 1= 145.08 ISK*	*Liechtenstein GBP 1= 2.53 CHF*	*Norway GBP 1= 13.19 NOK*	*Switzerland GBP 1= 2.53 CHF*
1. Instant death	2,068*	2,708	2,312	2,372
2. Burns A. Face B. Face (no scars) C. Body	19,300* 19,300* 19,300*	15,427 – 25,767	12,434 12,434 12,434	32,411 – –
3. Quadriplegia	270,885*	230,599	136,748	449,802
4. Paraplegia	194,376* to 270,885*	203,965	116,627	303,360
5a. Brain damage (moderate)	71,685* to 270,885*	143,447	126,604	–
5b. Brain damage with motor deficiency		159,416	136,748	449,802
6a. Amputation of leg above the knee	168,872*	83,146	22,571	139,921
6b. Amputation of leg below the knee	119,934*	69,613	17,044	139,921
7a. Amputation of arm above the elbow	194,376*	72,319	22,571	232,806
7b. Amputation of arm below elbow	168,872*	64,199	17,044	232,806
8a. Loss of eyesight – one eye without cosmetic disability	59,278*	33,454	11,069	53,755
8b. Loss of eyesight – one eye with cosmetic disability	71,685*	43,577	11,069	53,755
8c. Loss of eyesight total blindness	270,885*	123,690	136,748	449,802
9. Deafness	26,192* to 157,155*	55,106	77,074	266,166
10. RSI	42,735* to 71,685*	–	61,729	41,423

* *Deduct welfare state benefits and add interest. See notes on Iceland.*

BLOC GRAPHS, TOTAL COMPENSATION: EFTA COUNTRIES

Table 1. Schedule A

Doctor, man, 40, married, 2 dependent children – instant death; GBP

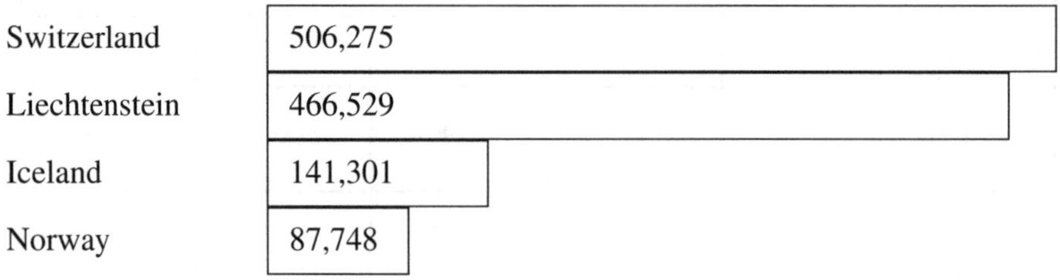

Country	GBP
Switzerland	506,275
Liechtenstein	466,529
Iceland	141,301
Norway	87,748

Table 2. Schedule A

Doctor, man, 40, married, 2 dependent children – burns; GBP

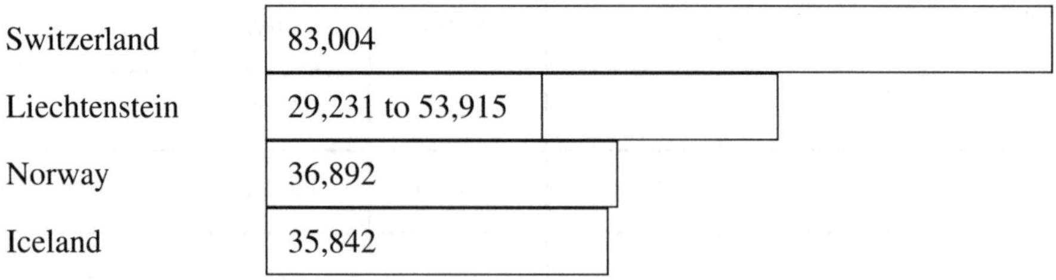

Country	GBP
Switzerland	83,004
Liechtenstein	29,231 to 53,915
Norway	36,892
Iceland	35,842

Table 3. Schedule A

Doctor, man, 40, married, 2 dependent children – quadriplegia; GBP

Country	GBP
Switzerland	944,664
Liechtenstein	518,035
Iceland	445,961
Norway	264,329

Table 4. Schedule A

Doctor, man, 40, married, 2 dependent children – brain damage (moderate); GBP

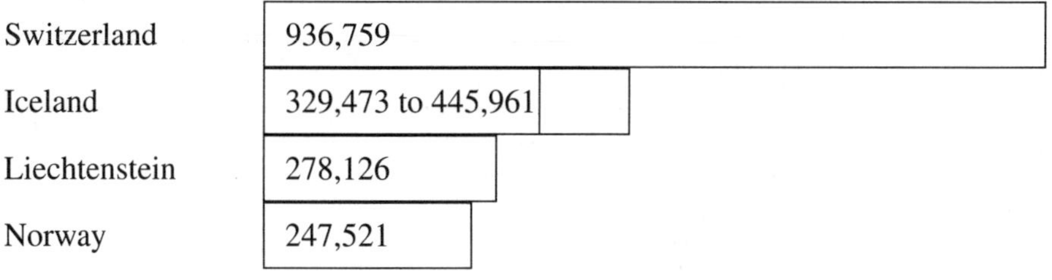

Table 5. Schedule A

Doctor, man, 40, married, 2 dependent children – brain damage (moderate); GBP

Country	GBP
Switzerland	Unavailable
Iceland	128,205 to 445,961
Norway	255,527
Liechtenstein	228,433

Table 6. Schedule A

Doctor, man, 40, married, 2 dependent children – brain damage (motor deficiency); GBP

Country	GBP
Switzerland	936,759
Iceland	128,205 to 445,961
Norway	264,329
Liechtenstein	244,944

Table 7. Schedule A

Doctor, man, 40, married, 2 dependent children – amputation of leg above the knee; GBP

Country	GBP
Iceland	288,806
Switzerland	256,917
Liechtenstein	98,519
Norway	45,694

Table 8. Schedule A

Doctor, man, 40, married, 2 dependent children – amputation of leg below the knee; GBP

Country	GBP
Switzerland	256,917
Iceland	207,472
Liechtenstein	84,986
Norway	40,887

Table 9. Schedule A

Doctor, man, 40, married, 2 dependent children – amputation of arm above the elbow; GBP

Country	GBP
Switzerland	480,830
Iceland	329,473
Liechtenstein	120,171
Norway	45,694

Table 10. Schedule A

Doctor, man, 40, married, 2 dependent children – amputation of arm below the elbow; GBP

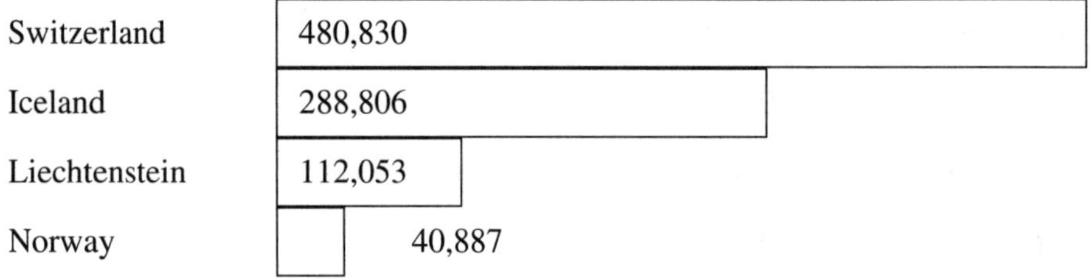

Table 11. Schedule A

Doctor, man, 40, married, 2 dependent children – loss of one eye without cosmetic injury; GBP

Country	GBP
Iceland	107,527
Switzerland	79,051
Liechtenstein	44,551
Norway	9,606

Table 12. Schedule A

Doctor, man, 40, married, 2 dependent children – loss of one eye with cosmetic injury; GBP

Country	GBP
Iceland	128,205
Switzerland	79,051
Liechtenstein	69,559
Norway	9,606

Table 13. Schedule A

Doctor, man, 40, married, 2 dependent children – loss of eyesight, total blindness; GBP

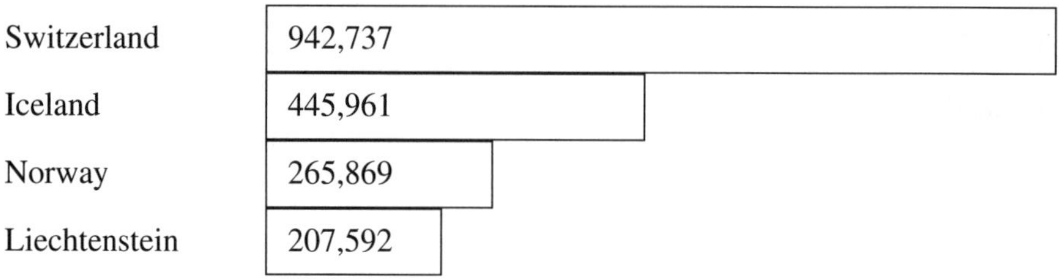

Country	GBP
Switzerland	942,737
Iceland	445,961
Norway	265,869
Liechtenstein	207,592

Table 14. Schedule A

Doctor, man, 40, married, 2 dependent children – deafness; GBP

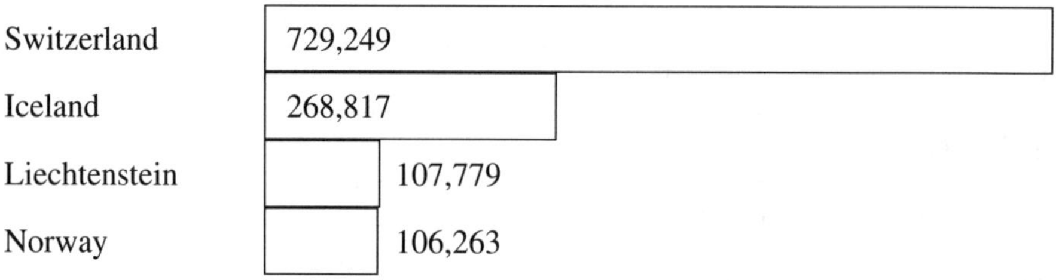

Country	GBP
Switzerland	729,249
Iceland	268,817
Liechtenstein	107,779
Norway	106,263

Table 15. Schedule A

Doctor, man, 40, married, 2 dependent children – RSI; GBP

Country	GBP
Liechtenstein	Unavailable
Iceland	74,442 to 128,205
Switzerland	90,513
Norway	82,623

Table 16. Schedule B

Legal secretary, woman, 20, single – instant death; GBP

Country	GBP
Liechtenstein	2,708
Switzerland	2,372
Norway	2,312
Iceland	2,068

Table 17. Schedule B

Legal secretary, woman, 20, single – burns; GBP

Country	GBP
Switzerland	32,411
Liechtenstein	15,427 to 25,767
Iceland	19,300
Norway	12,434

Table 18. Schedule B

Legal secretary, woman, 20, single – quadriplegia; GBP

Country	GBP
Switzerland	449,802
Iceland	270,885
Liechtenstein	230,599
Norway	136,748

Table 19. Schedule B

Legal secretary, woman, 20, single – paraplegia; GBP

Country	GBP
Switzerland	303,360
Iceland	194,376 to 270,885
Liechtenstein	203,965
Norway	116,627

Table 20. Schedule B

Legal secretary, woman, 20, single – brain damage (moderate); GBP

Country	GBP
Switzerland	Unavailable
Iceland	71,685 to 270,885
Liechtenstein	143,447
Norway	126,604

Table 21. Schedule B

Legal secretary, woman, 20, single – brain damage (motor deficiency); GBP

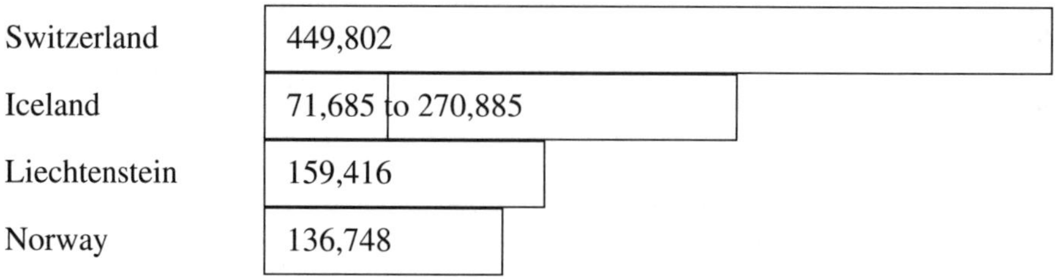

Country	GBP
Switzerland	449,802
Iceland	71,685 to 270,885
Liechtenstein	159,416
Norway	136,748

Table 22. Schedule B

Legal secretary, woman, 20, single – amputation of leg above the knee; GBP

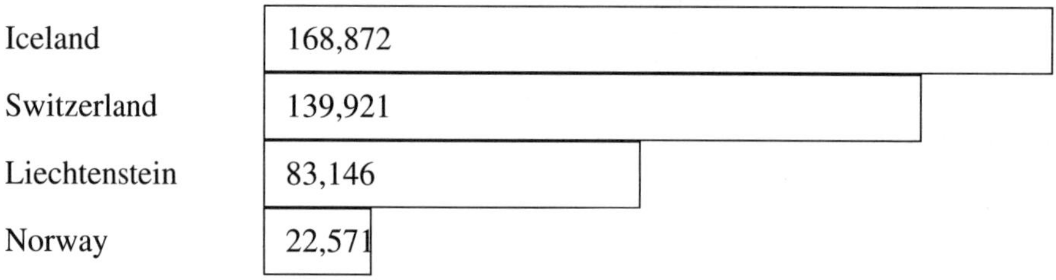

Country	GBP
Iceland	168,872
Switzerland	139,921
Liechtenstein	83,146
Norway	22,571

Table 23. Schedule B

Legal secretary, woman, 20, single – amputation of leg below the knee; GBP

Table 24. Schedule B

Legal secretary, woman, 20, single – amputation of arm above the elbow; GBP

Switzerland	232,806
Iceland	194,376
Liechtenstein	72,319
Norway	22,571

Table 25. Schedule B

Legal secretary, woman, 20, single – amputation of arm below the elbow; GBP

Country	GBP
Switzerland	232,806
Iceland	168,872
Liechtenstein	64,199
Norway	17,044

Table 26. Schedule B

Legal secretary, woman, 20, single – loss of one eye without cosmetic injury; GBP

Country	GBP
Iceland	59,278
Switzerland	53,755
Liechtenstein	33,454
Norway	11,069

Table 27. Schedule B

Legal secretary, woman, 20, single – loss of one eye with cosmetic injury; GBP

Country	GBP
Iceland	71,685
Switzerland	53,755
Liechtenstein	43,577
Norway	11,069

Table 28. Schedule B

Legal secretary, woman, 20, single – loss of eyesight, total blindness; GBP

Country	GBP
Switzerland	449,802
Iceland	270,885
Norway	136,748
Liechtenstein	123,690

Table 29. Schedule B

Legal secretary, woman, 20, single – deafness; GBP

Country	GBP
Switzerland	266,166
Iceland	26,192 to 157,155
Norway	77,074
Liechtenstein	55,106

Table 30. Schedule B

Legal secretary, woman, 20, single – RSI; GBP

Country	GBP
Liechtenstein	Unavailable
Iceland	42,735 to 71,685
Norway	61,729
Switzerland	41,423

PAIN AND SUFFERING COMPENSATION: EFTA COUNTRIES

Table 1. Schedule A

Doctor, man, 40, married, 2 dependent children; currency at 4 July 2001

Injury	*Iceland GBP 1= 145.08 ISK*	*Liechtenstein GBP 1= 2.53 CHF*	*Norway GBP 1= 13.19 NOK*	*Switzerland GBP 1= 2.53 CHF*
1. Instant death	–	–	–	–
2. Burns A. Face B. Face (no scars) C. Body	10,339* 10,339* 10,339*	10,827 – 5,955	5,610 5,610 5610	3,953 – –
3. Quadriplegia	49,628*	78,491	50,432	39,526+
4. Paraplegia	49,628*	56,838	33,623	35,573
5a. Brain damage (moderate)	18,610* to 49,628*	52,508	41,630	–
5b. Brain damage with motor deficiency		63,875	50,432	35,573+
6a. Amputation of leg above the knee	22,057*	35,185	14,412	19,763+
6b. Amputation of leg below the knee	15,164*	27,066	9,606	
7a. Amputation of arm above the elbow	26,192*	27,066	14,412	19,763
7b. Amputation of arm below elbow	22,057*	21,656	9,606	
8a. Loss of eyesight – one eye without cosmetic disability	7,582*	20,570	9,606	39,526
8b. Loss of eyesight – one eye with cosmetic disability	9,650*	23,277	9,606	
8c. Loss of eyesight total blindness	49,268*	35,727	50,432	39,526
9. Deafness	20,678*	23,277	20,015	25,691
10. RSI	5,514* to 9,650*	–	5,610	9,882

Table 2. Schedule B

Legal secretary, woman, 20, single; currency at 4 July 2001

Injury	*Iceland GBP 1= 145.08 ISK*	*Liechtenstein GBP 1= 2.53 CHF*	*Norway GBP 1= 13.19 NOK*	*Switzerland GBP 1= 2.53 CHF*
1. Instant death	–	–	–	–
2. Burns A. Face B. Face (no scars) C. Body	 10,339* 10,339* 10,339*	 12,450 – 7,037	 6,459 6,459 6,459	 5,929 – –
3. Quadriplegia	49,628*	83,903	58,089	39,526+
4. Paraplegia	49,628*	62,251	38,726	39,526+
5a. Brain damage (moderate)	18,610* to 49,628*	55,888	47,945	–
5b. Brain damage with motor deficiency		67,664	58,089	39,526+
6a. Amputation of leg above the knee	22,057*	37,892	16,596	11,858 to 19,763
6b. Amputation of leg below the knee	15,164*	29,772	11,069	
7a. Amputation of arm above the elbow	26,192*	29,772	16,596	19,763+
7b. Amputation of arm below elbow	22,057*	24,360	11,069	
8a. Loss of eyesight – one eye without cosmetic disability	7,582*	24,360	11,069	39,526
8b. Loss of eyesight – one eye with cosmetic disability	9,650*	27,066	11,069	
8c. Loss of eyesight total blindness	49,628*	41,140	58,089	39,526
9. Deafness	20,678*	27,066	23,055	19,763 to 31,620
10. RSI	5,514* to 9,650*	–	6,459	5,877

* *Add interest. See notes on Iceland.*

Bloc Graphs, Pain and Suffering Awards: EFTA Countries

Table 1. Schedule A

Doctor, man, 40, married, 2 dependent children – burns; GBP

Country	GBP
Liechtenstein	5,955 to 10,827
Iceland	10,339
Norway	5,610
Switzerland	3,953

Table 2. Schedule A

Doctor, man, 40, married, 2 dependent children – quadriplegia; GBP

Country	GBP
Liechtenstein	78,491
Norway	50,432
Iceland	49,628
Switzerland	39,526

Table 3. Schedule A

Doctor, man, 40, married, 2 dependent children – paraplegia; GBP

Country	GBP
Liechtenstein	56,838
Iceland	49,628
Norway	33,623
Switzerland	33,573

Table 4. Schedule A

Doctor, man, 40, married, 2 dependent children – brain damage (moderate); GBP

Country	GBP
Switzerland	Unavailable
Liechtenstein	52,508
Iceland	18,610 to 49,628
Norway	41,630

Table 5. Schedule A

Doctor, man, 40, married, 2 dependent children – brain damage (motor deficiency); GBP

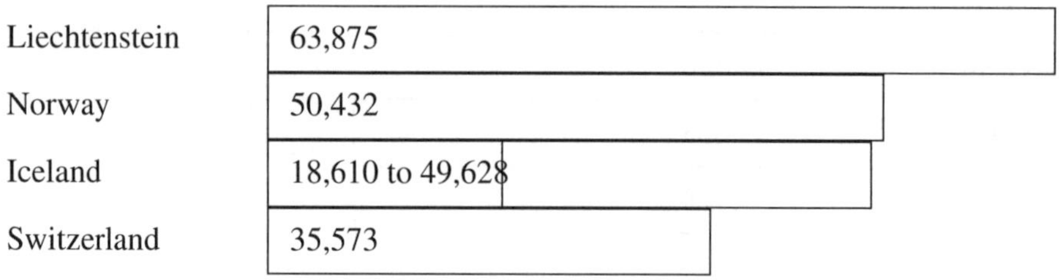

Country	GBP
Liechtenstein	63,875
Norway	50,432
Iceland	18,610 to 49,628
Switzerland	35,573

Table 6. Schedule A

Doctor, man, 40, married, 2 dependent children – amputation of leg above the knee; GBP

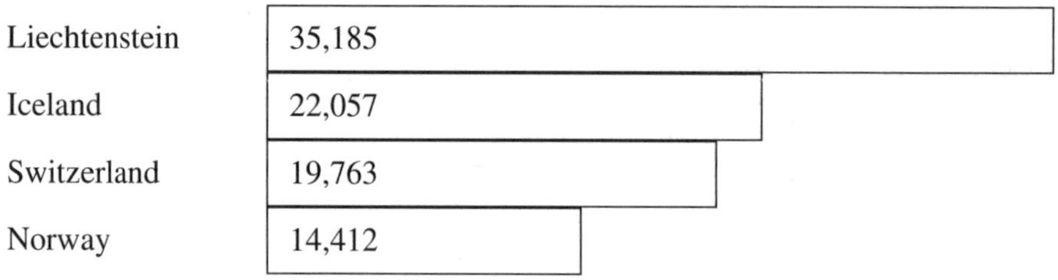

Country	GBP
Liechtenstein	35,185
Iceland	22,057
Switzerland	19,763
Norway	14,412

Table 7. Schedule A

Doctor, man, 40, married, 2 dependent children – amputation of leg below the knee; GBP

Country	GBP
Liechtenstein	27,066
Switzerland	19,763
Iceland	15,164
Norway	9,606

Table 8. Schedule A

Doctor, man, 40, married, 2 dependent children – amputation of arm above the elbow; GBP

Country	GBP
Liechtenstein	27,066
Iceland	26,192
Switzerland	19,763
Norway	14,412

Table 9. Schedule A

Doctor, man, 40, married, 2 dependent children – amputation of arm below the elbow; GBP

Country	GBP
Iceland	22,057
Liechtenstein	21,656
Switzerland	19,763
Norway	9,606

Table 10. Schedule A

Doctor, man, 40, married, 2 dependent children – loss of one eye without cosmetic injury; GBP

Country	GBP
Switzerland	39,526
Liechtenstein	20,570
Norway	9,606
Iceland	7,582

Table 11. Schedule A

Doctor, man, 40, married, 2 dependent children – loss of one eye with cosmetic injury; GBP

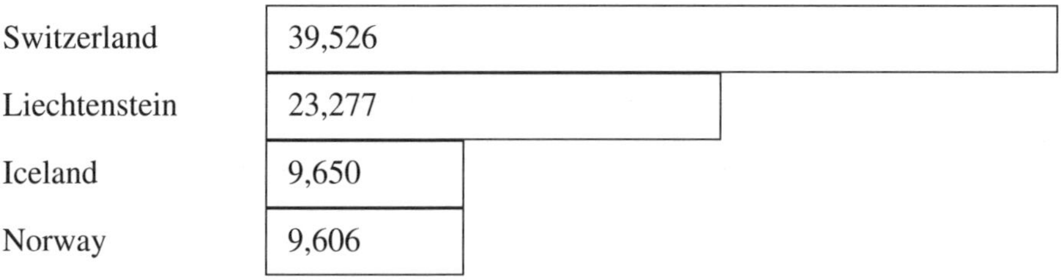

Country	GBP
Switzerland	39,526
Liechtenstein	23,277
Iceland	9,650
Norway	9,606

Table 12. Schedule A

Doctor, man, 40, married, 2 dependent children – loss of eyesight, total blindness; GBP

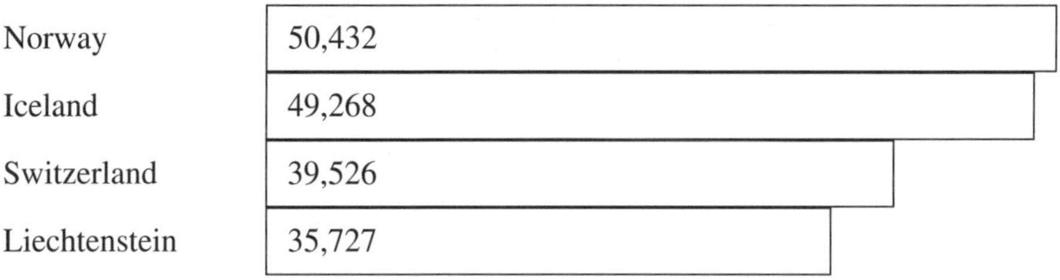

Country	GBP
Norway	50,432
Iceland	49,268
Switzerland	39,526
Liechtenstein	35,727

Table 13. Schedule A

Doctor, man, 40, married, 2 dependent children – deafness; GBP

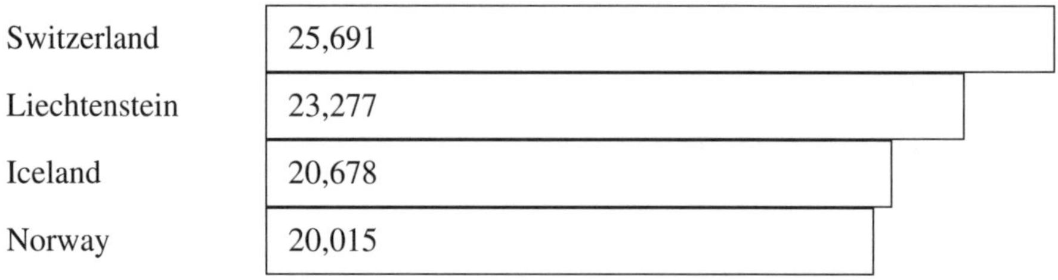

Country	GBP
Switzerland	25,691
Liechtenstein	23,277
Iceland	20,678
Norway	20,015

Table 14. Schedule A

Doctor, man, 40, married, 2 dependent children – RSI; GBP

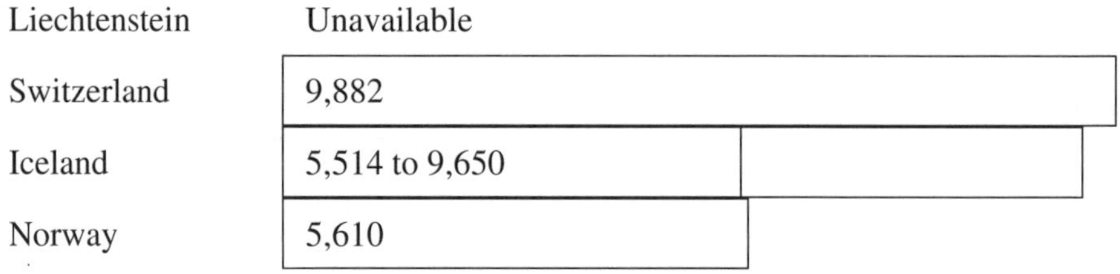

Country	GBP
Liechtenstein	Unavailable
Switzerland	9,882
Iceland	5,514 to 9,650
Norway	5,610

Table 15. Schedule B

Legal secretary, woman, 20, single – burns; GBP

Country	GBP
Liechtenstein	7,037 to 12,450
Iceland	10,339
Norway	6,459
Switzerland	5,929

Table 16. Schedule B

Legal secretary, woman, 20, single – quadriplegia; GBP

Country	GBP
Liechtenstein	83,903
Norway	58,089
Iceland	49,628
Switzerland	39,526+

Table 17. Schedule B

Legal secretary, woman, 20, single – paraplegia; GBP

Country	GBP
Liechtenstein	62,251
Iceland	49,628
Switzerland	39,526+
Norway	38,726

Table 18. Schedule B

Legal secretary, woman, 20, single – brain damage (moderate); GBP

Country	GBP
Switzerland	Unavailable
Liechtenstein	55,888
Iceland	18,610 to 49,628
Norway	47,945

Table 19. Schedule B

Legal secretary, woman, 20, single – brain damage (motor deficiency); GBP

Liechtenstein	67,664
Norway	58,089
Iceland	18,610 to 49,628
Switzerland	39,526

Table 20. Schedule B

Legal secretary, woman, 20, single – amputation of leg above the knee; GBP

Liechtenstein	37,892
Iceland	22,057
Switzerland	11,858 to 19,763
Norway	16,596

Table 21. Schedule B

Legal secretary, woman, 20, single – amputation of leg below the knee; GBP

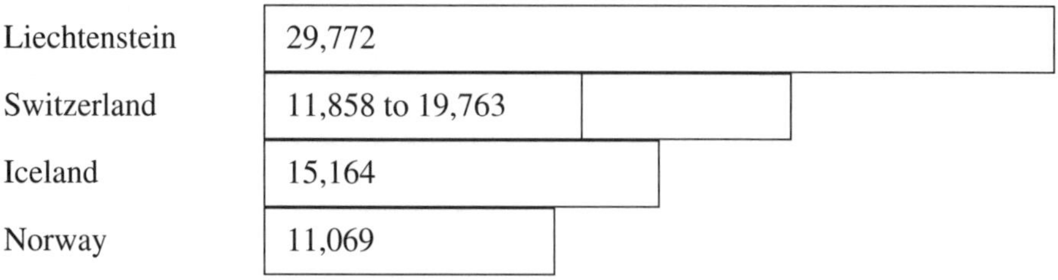

Country	GBP
Liechtenstein	29,772
Switzerland	11,858 to 19,763
Iceland	15,164
Norway	11,069

Table 22. Schedule B

Legal secretary, woman, 20, single – amputation of arm above the elbow; GBP

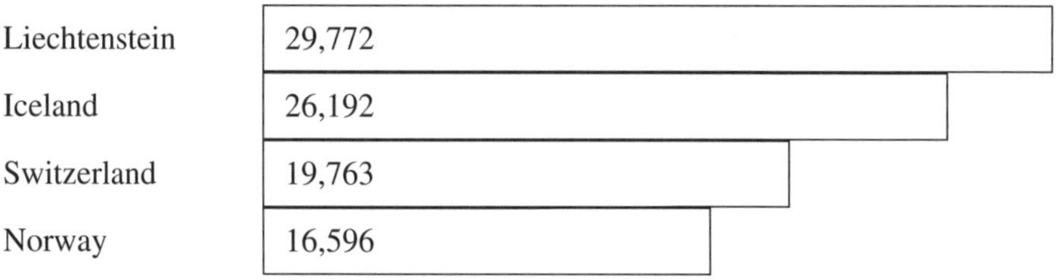

Country	GBP
Liechtenstein	29,772
Iceland	26,192
Switzerland	19,763
Norway	16,596

Table 23. Schedule B

Legal secretary, woman, 20, single – amputation of arm below the elbow; GBP

Country	GBP
Liechtenstein	24,360
Iceland	22,057
Switzerland	19,763
Norway	11,069

Table 24. Schedule B

Legal secretary, woman, 20, single – loss of one eye without cosmetic injury; GBP

Country	GBP
Switzerland	39,526
Liechtenstein	24,360
Norway	11,069
Iceland	7,582

Table 25. Schedule B

Legal secretary, woman, 20, single – loss of one eye with cosmetic injury; GBP

Country	GBP
Switzerland	39,526
Liechtenstein	27,066
Norway	11,069
Iceland	9,650

Table 26. Schedule B

Legal secretary, woman, 20, single – loss of eyesight, total blindness; GBP

Country	GBP
Norway	58,089
Iceland	49,628
Liechtenstein	41,140
Switzerland	39,526

Table 27. Schedule B

Legal secretary, woman, 20, single, deafness; GBP

Switzerland	19,763 to 31,620
Liechtenstein	27,066
Norway	23,055
Iceland	20,678

Table 28. Schedule B

Legal secretary, woman, 20, single, RSI; GBP

Liechtenstein	Unavailable
Iceland	5,514 to 9,650
Norway	6,459
Switzerland	5,877

Comments and Recommendations

Repetitive strain injury and Upper Limb Disorders (ULDs)

In our second edition (1994) we reported on a new trend in England and Wales – claims in respect of repetitive strain injury (RSI) and for the first time, included RSI as a case study. This form of claim was then virtually unknown to most of our European correspondents. We reported on claims made in the UK by office workers who alleged that the repetitive action of striking keys on a keyboard caused an upper limb disorder (ULD) entitling them to social security benefits and compensation from their employers.

In 1994, the medical profession (and judicial opinion) was divided as to whether such repetitive action could cause a physical injury. Some medical experts were suggesting that RSI claimants were converting psychological fears for example, concerns regarding the use of new technology into perceived but not clinically detectable pain in the upper limbs. The medical experts did accept that some jobs involving traction of the upper limbs such as plucking poultry could cause physical injury to the limbs, muscles and tendons.

"RSI" is now a recognised claim in a number of EU countries surveyed: Belgium, Italy, Sweden, Scotland, Greece, the Netherlands and Portugal and in a number of the EFTA states: Iceland, Norway and Switzerland.

Claims in respect of "RSI" continue to be made in England although this term is imprecise and can be misleading.

Work related upper limb disorders (WRULDs) cover a range of musculoskeletal (MSD) disorders which are now said to be the most common form of work related ill-health problems in England. ULDs generally affect the upper limb or neck areas of the body and these injuries include:

- Tenosynovitis – inflammation of the tendon sheath.
- Tendonitis – inflammation of a tendon
- Epicondylitis – inflammation of the tendons where they attach to the bones at the elbow.
- Carpal Tunnel Syndrome – a condition which develops when the median nerve is compressed within the carpal tunnel.
- Cubital Tunnel Syndrome – involves compression of the ulnar nerve where it passes the elbow point near the "funny bone".

- Thoracic Outlet Syndrome – affects the nerves and blood vessels of the neck and shoulder.

Medical experts now agree that ULDs can be caused by a variety of factors including repetitive tasks and overworking. Occupations with the highest annual rates of ULDs include road construction and maintenance workers, assemblers/line workers, computer data processing operators, typists and word processor operators.

In *Smith v. Baker and McKenzie [1994 C.L.Y 1662 & 1994 WL 1061509],* a legal secretary who was diagnosed with tenosynovitis successfully claimed that this was a work related repetitive strain injury. The total amount awarded by the court was GBP 35,313 (USD 49,671 and EUR 58,627[1]) on April 11 1994. In *McPherson v. Camden LBC (unreported, 1999)* damages in the amount of GBP 98,194 (USD 138,120 and EUR 163,022) were awarded to an employee whose RSI was caused by the use of a keyboard at work which did not meet the standards set by the relevant health and safety regulations. In *Conaty v. Barclays Bank plc (unreported, May 25 2000)* damages in the sum of GBP 243,792 (USD 342,918 and EUR 404,743) were awarded to an employee who suffered an injury while working as a cashier for Barclays Bank.

The condition has become a European issue and November 2000, the European Agency for Health and Safety at Work published responses to the green paper: "People First, Living and Working in the Information Society, (24 September 1997)" which refers in particular to injuries such as RSI and stress.

A subsequent survey in 2000 by the European Agency for Safety & Health at Work on Repetitive Strain Injuries,[2] revealed that compensation for "RSI" is recognised in six Member States: Denmark, Ireland, Italy, the Netherlands, Spain and the UK. However, with the exception of the UK, claims against the employer are rare. One reason for this may be differences in the various social security/insurance system. Ireland, Denmark and the Netherlands have reported only a few RSI cases, although the Dutch expect that the number of cases will rise in view of trades union support for claims.

1 The figures in brackets in this section refer to conversion rates based on the exchange rate on 4 July 2001 unless otherwise stated (GBP 1 = USD 1.4066 = EUR 1.6602.)

2 European Agency for Safety and Health at Work: "Repetitive Strain Injuries in the Member States of the European Union: The results of an information request", 2000. Please note: As there is no common terminology, RSI is referred to as a concept in a wide sense, including the concepts of: stress as the cause of a disease, the region of the body which is affected, the disease itself and the reference to structures involved.

In the Netherlands, a recent study by the National Health Council found that between 20% and 40% of the Dutch working population suffer from RSI -related problems. RSI is sometimes associated with the increased use of technology and "Nintendo thumb", is a form of RSI that has become a problem among computer-crazy children, as a Dutch newspaper reported in February 2001.[3]

In the United States, it has been reported that twelve US property/casualty insurers have filed a law suit asking the courts to review a new ergonomic standard designed to protect US workers from work related RSI. This follows claims made by US businesses that the new Occupational Safety and Health Administration (OSHA) ergonomic standard (in effect since January 2001) will drive many employers out of business. The new OSHA compensation scheme provides for mandatory payments for medical treatment and lost wages for qualifying musculoskeletal disorders. The OSHA estimated that firms will spend approximately USD 4.2 billion (about GBP 2.99 billion and EUR 4.96 billion) per year to implement the scheme.

Conditional Fee Agreements

Since the second edition there have been changes to the way in which personal injury claims are funded. In the UK Conditional Fee Agreements (CFA) have become a familiar feature. The aim of these changes was to ensure greater access to justice CFAs are existent in England & Wales and Scotland.

Conditional Fee Agreements were first introduced by the Courts and Legal Services Act 1990 and have been extended to cover personal injury cases since 1995. Civil legal aid has been abolished for personal injury claims with only limited exceptions (clinical negligence claims and claims involving a public interest element). The CFA is based on the principle that if the case is won, the lawyer has the right to charge an additional success fee as a percentage of his profit costs (referred to as an "uplift").

Since the introduction of the Collective Conditional Fee Regulations in 2000, insurers, commercial organisations and trade unions, are able to enter into collective CFAs with their lawyers. The purpose of introducing collective CFAs was to

3 "Kids' RSI is a matter of time, experts warn", Het Financieele Dagblad, 28/02/01, an article by Christine Lucassen

reduce the cost of pursuing or defending separate individual cases by simplifying the CFA process.

Another new feature in personal injury litigation is After-The-Event (ATE) insurance policies, which enable a party to purchase insurance after the incident from which the action arises. In the event that the party taking out the policy loses their case, the Insurer pays their opponents costs. The extent to which their own costs are covered depends on the kind of policy taken out and can cover all of their own solicitors' and counsels' fees.

Under the Access to Justice Act 1999, which has been in force since April 2000, success fees and paid insurance premiums can be recovered from the other side if the claim succeeds. A limit of 100% has been set on the level of the uplift.

In the leading case on these funding changes, *Callery v Gray,* the claim arose out of a personal injury claim that settled pre-action. The Court of Appeal held that this road traffic accident claim was a "straightforward" case and the costs of both the CFA and the ATE insurance premium were recoverable from the defendant. The maximum uplift in similar claims was set by the Court of Appeal at 20%.

CFAs have now even been expanded beyond personal injury litigation and can even be used in commercial litigation.[4]

Greece is the only other European country which allows CFAs and contingency fees are permitted in connection with any litigation case, provided that they do not exceed 20% of the amount of damages claimed or recovered.[5] However, it may be a matter of time before other European countries adopt similar procedures.

Pain and suffering awards

As reported in our previous editions, a comparison of the principles upon which our surveyed countries award damages for the pain and suffering of the injury itself (commonly termed "non-economic loss"), rather than its measurable financial consequences, continues to show some marked differences.

Pain and suffering awards still vary widely across Europe from GBP 215,000[6] (USD 302,419 and EUR 356,943) to nothing at all.

---

4 E.g. a current case before the High Court, *Arkin v Borchard and others*, case 1997 Folio 956

5 *Civil Procedures in EC Countries*, by David McIntosh and Marjorie Holmes, 1991

6 German award in relation to quadriplegia

In England and Wales, laudable efforts have been made, since our first edition was published, to improve consistency in levels of awards for non-economic loss. The Judicial Studies Board *Guidelines for the Assessment of General Damages in Personal Injury Cases*[7] (2000) is now in its fifth edition. These guidelines, although not published as any form of fixed tariff have become widely accepted and are the first point of reference for both personal injury practitioners and the judiciary.

In a series of cases grouped together as *Heil v Rankin* [2001] QB 272, the Court of Appeal was asked to increase general damages in line with a Law Commission recommendation, in its report published on 20 April 1999 (Law Commission Report 257). This recommended that damages for pain and suffering in the most serious cases should be increased by up to 100% and that the higher Courts should issue guidelines to effect these changes.

The Court of Appeal, clearly concerned about the effect its decision would have on the insurance industry and the NHS decided to increase damages by one third for the more serious injuries with smaller increases for the less serious injuries. In one of the linked cases the trial Judge's award of £135,000 to a claimant suffering from cerebral palsy was increased by the Court of Appeal to £175,000, an increase of some 30%.

The Court of Appeal compared English awards to the levels of awards in other Member States of the EU and EFTA countries and, gratifyingly for the authors of this report, referred to our 2nd edition in their judgment. The Law Commission in its report had regarded England and Wales as being somewhere in the middle of the EU damages "league".

Most countries in our survey continue to disregard, in awarding damages for non-economic loss, the degree to which the defendant was at fault in causing the injury. Germany, Greece, Italy, Portugal and Norway, do however, take the degree of fault into account, and in Norway the award is additionally influenced by the defendant's ability to pay an award of compensation.

Our French correspondent has reported that there have been a number of significant awards in France in HIV and/or Hepatitis C cases in the past few years. In HIV cases, the average awards are around EUR 198,187 (GBP 119,376 and USD 167,914) and the highest have exceeded EUR 457,355 (GBP 275,482 and USD 387,493). The highest French award in a Hepatitis C case is EUR 304,904 (GBP

7 Guidelines for the assessment of general damages in personal injury cases, 5th edition 2000, Judicial Studies Board

183,655 and USD 258,329.) In similar cases in England, damages of up to GBP 230,000 (USD 323,518 and EUR 381,846) have been awarded.

Our German correspondent advised us that compensation awards for pain and suffering continue to increase only very slowly. In March 2001, a road accident victim was awarded EUR 510,830 (GBP 307,692 and USD 432,800) for pain and suffering by a court in Munich.[8] The sum was awarded partly in the form of a lump sum of EUR 383123 (GBP 230,799 and USD 324,642) with a further monthly payment of EUR 766 (GBP 462 and USD 650) for life.

In Greece, pain and suffering awards have increased considerably, even ignoring currency fluctuations of 34% since 1994. The award for pain and suffering made to a widow in respect of the instant death of her husband, a doctor, aged 40 with 2 dependent children has risen from 400,000 GRD (GBP 1,270 from the rates at the time of the 2nd edition) in the previous edition to GRD 3,000,000 (GBP 5,302, USD 7,457 and EUR 8,802) plus interest, a nominal increase of GRD 2,600,000 (GBP 4,595, USD 6,463 and EUR 7,629).

In the Netherlands, Marinus Mac Lean referred us to the largest damages awarded ever made by the Courts: EUR 136,082 (GBP 81,967 and USD 115,295) to a patient infected with HIV through the negligence of a hospital. Our correspondent explained that he expects future awards for very serious injuries to increase gradually.

Our Austrian correspondent, Ivo Greiter, reported on the comparatively low awards for pain and suffering, which are confirmed by our study. The highest award for pain and suffering was made by the Austrian Supreme Court in a ruling of 1997 (6 Ob 2394/96 v). The amount was ATS 1,750,000 (GBP 76,586, USD 107,726 and EUR 127,149) awarded to a minor who sustained brain damage as a result of medical negligence.

Since the second edition (1994) we have still not detected any narrowing of the divergence in the levels of awards made across the EU. Unacceptable lack of conformity remains. Although currency fluctuations provide some explanation for the changes we note in the main text, the underlying trend seems to lead away from any growing consistency in awards.

The Republic of Ireland, England & Wales, together with Italy top what ought not to be a league table for pain and suffering awards whilst Portugal, Greece, Sweden and Finland are at the bottom of the scale. Whilst Greece remains near the bottom in terms of awards they are increasing significantly by comparison to other jurisdictions previously in a similar position.

---

8 Landgericht München I, Az 19 08647/00 or Deutsches Autorecht 2001/368

In claims involving fatal injuries, only certain jurisdictions allow the surviving spouse and/or dependants to make a claim for damages. In the Republic of Ireland, there is a claim for mental distress, which is recognised as an injury. Italian law has recently been amended to allow awards to dependents such as "the trauma of facing death", which was not previously compensatable. The award is made to the surviving relatives. We find the same situation in Austria, where an award of compensation for the emotional suffering of children, who were present when their mother was seriously injured and as a result of the accident were separated from their mother for a long period, was made by the Austrian Supreme Court in a judgment in 1994.[9] The German Courts similarly award compensation for "shock" to relatives in respect of their own, and not the victims' trauma.

In England, in a recent out of court settlement, a woman who suffered from post traumatic stress disorder (PTSD) after witnessing her mentally ill brother stab their mother to death received GBP 550,000 (USD 773,630 and EUR 913,110) for mental trauma from the South London and Maudsley NHS Trust who admitted liability for their lack of care. This settlement is believed to be the highest payment to date for psychiatric injury.

Non-Financial compensation

In 2001, the British National Health Service (NHS) reportedly paid out GBP 400 million (about USD 563 million and EUR 664 million) in compensation and lawyers' fees for clinical negligence claims. This led to an announcement by Alan Milburn, the Health Secretary, in July 2001, that the NHS may provide "no-fault compensation" in cases of injuries sustained as a result of clinical negligence which the government believes may save time and costs in achieving settlements. This would encourage a more open system by not blaming staff. 'Fixed tariff schemes' for victims of medical negligence are expected to be proposed in the NHS White Paper later this year.

While patients will retain the right to sue the NHS if, for example, the offered settlements are insufficient, the British Government believes that most people will prefer the speed and certainty of fixed payments. Courts will be expected to take into account NHS offers to provide non-financial compensation, such as the provision of nursing care when calculating damages and, therefore to refuse to award multi-million-pound sums to cover private nursing.

9 Decision of July 16, 1994 (2ob 45/93 AS 30,000)

We have not come across similar proposals elsewhere in Europe.

Foreign Sickness Treatment and Reimbursement

In two recent judgments of the European Court, *Vanbraekel v Alliance Nationale des Mutualites Chretiennes*[10] and *BSM Geraets-Smits v Stichting Ziekenfonds VGZ*,[11] dealing with reimbursement for sickness treatment abroad, the Court held that in the absence of harmonisation at Community level, Member States were free to determine the conditions for entitlement to benefits as long as they are in line with Community law. The requirement for patients to obtain prior authorisation before medical costs incurred in another Member State are reimbursed may however constitute a barrier to the free movement of services which would not be acceptable under European law.

In *Smits* the Court decided that patients have the right to be referred for treatment elsewhere in the EU if they could not receive the same or equally effective treatment without "undue delay" at home. Shortly after this decision, the Department of Health stated that the Government could no longer deny UK patients the opportunity of being treated abroad as the NHS had already started to "purchase" operations in private hospitals within the UK to reduce the waiting lists for certain treatments in NHS hospitals. The first NHS patients have now been sent to French hospitals, which appears to have been a success.

However, the Government has not yet addressed an issue which arises when patients treated abroad are negligently treated: current rules in the UK provide that legal aid is only available to claimants who are "injured" in the UK.

A further issue is who the claimants should sue: the NHS which referred the patient to another jurisdiction, or the treating hospital. At what level should damages be awarded: according to UK law or the law of the country in which treatment is provided?

---

10 Referral of a Belgian court re the question of reimbursement of medical treatment after a Belgian national was refused authorisation from her sickness insurance fund to under go surgery in France – *ECJ C 368/98*

11 In this case, a Dutch national went to a specialist clinic in Germany to undergo treatment – *ECJ C 157/99* Preliminary ruling 11 July 2000

Bereavement – moral damages – loss of society

Compensation for grief and the loss of a loved one is given to the relatives of a deceased victim in 10 out of the 16 EU jurisdictions in our survey (including Great Britain as two distinct jurisdictions England and Wales and Scotland). Our Austrian correspondent advised us that in general damages for emotional suffering can only be claimed by those who actually suffer a physical injury. However, the Austrian Supreme Court, in a recent judgment,[12] for the first time awarded compensation for the extreme suffering of close relatives.

As we reported in our second edition, Denmark, Germany, the Netherlands, Finland and Sweden make no such award, and it is perhaps notable that all five of those countries have predominantly Protestant histories. Germany and the Netherlands do however recognise that a claimant who suffers psychiatric damage on witnessing the death of his or her spouse or child is entitled to claim compensation and similar claims made by varying categories of shocked witnesses are recognised either expressly or by implication in other European countries. A recent ruling of the Amsterdam Court of Justice recognised this head of damage.

The basis of the award, its amount, and even its name vary between countries. In England and Wales the award is made in respect of "bereavement damages". The widow of a married man is now entitled to a fixed sum of GBP 10,000 (USD 14,066 and EUR 16,602 from 1 April 2002[13] (increased by legislation from the GBP 3,500 (USD 4,923 and 5,811) current at the time our first edition 1991 was published to GBP 7,500 (USD 10,550 and EUR 12,452) until 31 March 2002). In contrast the parents of an unmarried 20 year old woman have no entitlement to claim bereavement damages. In Scotland, the award is described as "loss of society", the amount is discretionary and the sum of GBP 2,000 (USD 2,813 and EUR 3,320) would probably be awarded to each surviving parent in the case of the 20 year old unmarried woman, regardless of whether she was in any way maintaining her parents(s) financially at the time of her death. In some of the other EU countries, e.g. Greece, relatives more remote than spouses, parents and children can claim a similar form of award.

Of the EFTA countries, Switzerland and Liechtenstein award some element of bereavement damages as a separate head of compensation, but Liechtenstein

---

12 Austrian Supreme Court, decision of May 16, 2001 (2 ob 84/01 v)

13 The figures used in the Country section is £7,500 because the question of comparison were carried out in 2000

restricts the award to claims arising out of death in road traffic accidents. Whilst funeral expenses are recoverable, in one Swiss case a further sum was awarded to a claimant to buy a black dress to wear at the funeral, but a claim for expenses in connection with the maintenance of the grave was denied. Iceland makes no separate award for bereavement, but includes a sum for that loss in the overall combined payment for dependency and bereavement. Our Icelandic correspondents estimate that around 10% of the lump sum award consists of bereavement compensation.

Structured settlements

In our second edition in 1994, we reported that the payment of compensation by annuity over time, rather than as a single lump sum at the date of trial or settlement was growing in popularity in England and Wales. This trend has not continued. Only around one hundred very seriously injured people in England and Wales now receive part of their compensation by way of a structured settlement. By comparison, in the United States structured settlements are increasingly popular. In 1998, around 50,000 compensation claims were settled using this mechanism.

It is noteworthy that legislative changes in England & Wales prohibit the imposition of structured settlements without the consent of the parties (Finance Acts 1995 and 1996). This need for consent may account for the low take up of these settlements and there is a debate in England as to whether the courts should be given the power to impose structured compensation against a claimant's wishes to have the damages paid as an immediate lump sum. In March 2000, the Lord Chancellor's department published a consultation paper asking whether structured settlements are a real alternative to traditional lump sum payments and whether they should be imposed by the courts. The answer is interesting for NHS and Health Authority cases, as in the recent case of *Clegg v Burnley, Pendle & Rossendale Health Authority*, the defendant Health Authority refused to agree to payment in the form of a structured sum.

In England & Wales structured settlements are made on a 'top-down' basis, which means that a lump sum is agreed, and then the viability of a structured settlement using the capital sum available is investigated.

The alternatives are known as "bottom-up" or "with profits"schemes, in which by evaluating the needs of the claimant on an annual basis, a capital sum is arrived at. This fund will not provide for future uncertainties as once a settlement is agreed, the payments cannot be changed and this is viewed as the main disadvantage of the structured settlement in its traditional form. There are now two different forms of "with-profits" structured settlements available; one provides for income growth in line with inflation, the other provides for income growth in line with average earnings.

There is a misconception among lawyers that the structured settlement is a creature of the United States legal system, emerging in California in the mid-1970s in response to the growing number of litigated claims. The concept of compensation by regular income over a long period following trial is much older and almost certainly originates on the mainland of Europe. Several EU states recognise (and some impose) structured compensation in one form or another, and have done so for many years.

France leads the EU in structuring compensation in the great majority of serious cases. Under German civil law, loss of earnings and/or increased requirements as a consequence of injury, must, in principle, be compensated in the form of a pension. It is, nevertheless, very common for insurance companies to seek settlements in which the victim is offered a single lump sum payment, the aim of which is to provide compensation for his future loss of earnings from the capital and accruing interest. Out-of-court settlements in Germany tend to result in single lump sum payments rather than annuity-tied receipts. The same situation applies in Switzerland.

In Austria, the loss of income claim, including future loss can be paid by either a lump sum award or monthly payments. The monthly payment system is preferred as it can be adapted to economic and personal development. Finland and Sweden also provide for an annuity-based method of compensating future loss of earnings.

Greece has no formal system for structuring awards, but settlements are often agreed on the basis of instalment payments without the need to impose any sophisticated scheme on the parties. The Greek Civil Code provides for damages payable to the relatives of a deceased for loss of support. Damages payable to an injured party are paid in monthly instalments and not in a lump sum save in exceptional cases.

The Belgian and Luxembourg Courts have the power to structure compensation awards but annuities are still unpopular with claimants and tend to be imposed in cases in which the injured person's life expectancy is low.

Spain is moving toward acceptance of structured compensation in serious cases, usually in the form of an immediate lump sum payment of 20% of the assessed damages together with an annuity for the remainder.

In our second edition we reported that efforts to introduce structured compensation to the Republic of Ireland were unsuccessful, although our Irish correspondents reported that it was only a matter of time before they would gain acceptance.

However, at the time of this third edition structured settlements are still not a popular feature in Ireland.

Provisional Damages

Some countries (including England and Wales) provide for provisional damages awards if the claimant's condition is likely to deteriorate in the future. In Scotland, for instance, provisional damages have been awarded in claims involving head injuries where there is a risk of epilepsy developing. Provisional damages awards are commonly made in asbestos related disease claims in Scotland and in England and Wales where there is a future risk of asbestos-related cancer.

Jury trial

Of all of the EU and EFTA jurisdictions we surveyed, Scotland alone allows for personal injury claims to be tried by a lay jury. As acceptance of jury trials is increasing, our Scottish correspondent expects that this will lead to a harmonisation of judge and jury awards, almost inevitably upwards.

Both the Republic of Ireland and Northern Ireland allowed jury trial of personal injury claims until 1988. The abolition there of jury trial was expected to stabilise levels of awards of compensation and to reduce the rate at which they were increasing. This has not been the case and Katherine Delahunt confirms that Irish judges are as generous with their awards if not more generous than before (but awards in some countries such as Italy have increased more).

No jury has tried a personal injury claim in England and Wales (save for certain claims arising from deliberate assault and false imprisonment) for over 35 years. An unsuccessful attempt was made during 1991 to revive jury trial of personal injury claims in the English courts. The Court of Appeal ruled in *H. v. Ministry of Defence* [1991] 2 A11 ER 834 that even where the injuries involved were exceptional (the plaintiff was a young unmarried man who suffered surgical amputation of his penis), the interests of justice in maintaining consistency of awards required that the trial be held before a judge alone.

Claimants' income and standard of living

Gross and net incomes, and standards of living generally, vary from country to country within the EU and EFTA. The levels of awards reported by our correspondents must be viewed in the context of their domestic "value".

One would expect the differing tax regimes throughout the EU and EFTA to be reflected in some correlation of levels of personal injury compensation and indeed tax rates in Scandinavia are very much higher than in most other countries included in our survey. Tax differentials and tax allowances alone cannot, however, explain why in general Scandinavian awards are so much lower than elsewhere. Other factors play a part, among them the generosity of state-funded (and tax levied) social security benefits which top up payments of damages, and restrictions on levels of compensation. In Denmark alone among our surveyed countries, a statutory cap on loss of earnings claims acts to depress levels of awards: the deemed maximum annual income upon which loss of earnings can be compensated is fixed at DKK 550,000 (GBP 44,462, USD 62,541 and EUR 73,816). Any earnings above that level are not compensated.

Medical expenses

There are some marked differences between our surveyed countries in the principles of recoverability of medical expenses made necessary by a compensatable injury.

Medical expenses are not recoverable as an item of compensation in Denmark, Iceland or Norway, since in those countries private medical care is virtually unknown and the cost of treatment is almost always paid by the social security system and not by the claimant.

Germany and the Netherlands do not normally allow claimants to recover these expenses. Those countries' legal systems assume that injured claimants will not themselves have had to pay for treatment but will instead have benefited from private health care arrangements and that health care insurers will recover their outlay directly from the insurers of the defendant responsible for causing the injury. In Germany, for instance, it is estimated that over 95 percent of the population has permanent health insurance of one form or another. In order to ensure the closest sensible comparison between surveyed countries, we have included in our

German study some notional medical expenses (based on British medical expenses which are likely to be typical) only for the more serious injuries.[14]

Social security benefits

The level and scope of social security provisions in Europe is generally high, but differs between the Member States.

The correlation between payments, benefits and levels of compensation is interesting. In Denmark for instance levels of benefit are high but so are levels of payment into the system made by protected persons through their own and government contributions, as distinct from their employers' contributions. Awards of compensation are comparatively low despite the high standard of living.

Social security benefits in Germany, Luxemburg and The Netherlands are higher than those in Denmark, yet levels of compensation for injury are also higher, when one might expect them to be lower so as to reflect the generous level of state benefits. Part of the explanation for the inconsistency lies in the extensive and complex rules of subrogation which apply, particularly in Germany, to allow recoupment of benefits paid to injured people. Our Dutch correspondents advise that awards of compensation have risen to offset falls in the real value of social security benefits.

In the Netherlands, our correspondent advised us that levels of social security benefits have declined and, as a direct result, claims for loss of income against a liable party are on the increase.

There is little if any correlation between levels of benefit and levels of compensation in the other countries surveyed. Greece, Portugal and Spain have comparatively meagre levels of benefit, but awards of damages are also low compared to the rest of Europe. The Republic of Ireland pays quite low levels of benefit but awards high levels of damages.

Social security contributions are particularly high in France, Germany, and the Netherlands, where they account for over 68% of total funding. At the other end of the scale, Denmark and Ireland finance their social security systems mainly through taxes, which account for a 60% +share of funding. Sweden and the UK are

---

14 These injuries are numbered 3 – 8c. in the tables

also heavily dependent on general government contributions: 48% and 49.5% respectively.[15]

The actuarial approach

Many of the countries surveyed recognise the value of actuarial evidence in making fair and, as far as is achievable accurate predictions of future financial losses and in particular the cost of future medical and nursing care. In some countries the courts use published actuarial tables, Belgium and Switzerland among them. In others, the Republic of Ireland being the most prominent example, the basis of the calculation is not standardised and actuaries are involved in assessing future loss in each individual case as it arises.

In our second edition we reported that the Courts of England and Wales were slow to accept the value of actuarial assessment.

The situation has now changed and the use of actuarial tables is provided for in the Damages Act 1996. The Ogden Tables, which were first produced by a working party of lawyers and actuaries in 1984 are now in their fourth edition. The tables are very detailed in the information they contain. They give guidance in relation to many contingencies and are now heavily relied upon by judges in the absence of any contrary actuarial evidence. The Tables are used in virtually all personal injury cases with a future loss element. The Tables suggest a "discount for contingencies" in calculating future loss which is very much smaller than that previously made by the judges.

Our Scottish correspondents have advised us that the use of the Ogden Tables in personal injury claims was initially met with resistance by the courts. However, since the House of Lords' Wells & Wells ruling in 1998 (which held that actuarial tables should provide the starting point when selecting a multiplier for a future loss claim) actuarial tables are more widely accepted in Scotland.

Our Swiss correspondent informed us that actuarial tables are popular there and that the Swiss courts apply actuarial tables prepared by Stauffer/Schaetzle, which are based on statistical material, when evaluating life expectancy and the average periods of professional activity.

---

15 Source of information: Europe in Figures, 5th edition 2000, Eurostat

Punitive Damages

Unlike the situation in the United States, damages which are intended to punish the defendant for his actions rather than compensate the injured party for his actual loss, are rarely, if ever, awarded in the civil courts of our surveyed countries. In England and Wales (but not Scotland) an award of "exemplary damages" may be made if the claimant can prove that the case falls within one of two limited categories laid down by the House of Lords in *Rookes v Barnard* [1964] AC 1120 and applied by the Court of Appeal in *AB v South West Water Services* [1992] 4 All ER 574. These categories are in summary:

1. Where there has been oppressive, arbitrary or unconstitutional action by the servants of the government; or
2. Where the defendant's conduct has been calculated by him to make a profit for himself which may well exceed the compensation payable to the injured party.

It has never been decided definitely in England whether exemplary or punitive damages lie in an action for personal injuries, but in principle the possibility of their being given in such a claim is recognised by the judgment in *AB v. South West Water [1993] QB 507,* a claim arising out of contamination of a water supply and the alleged conduct of the defendants in telling their consumers that the water was safe to drink when in fact it was far from being of wholesome quality. The victims of this alleged misconduct failed in their claim for exemplary damages since they could bring their case within either of the *Rookes v Barnard* "categories".

In England the Law Commission published a report on punitive damages (15/12/1997) following consultation. The report made various recommendations including that punitive damages should be available for most torts. The UK Government has not legislated to introduce these recommendations and in a debate in the House of Commons on 9/11/1999, suggested that "some further judicial development of the law in this area might help clarify the issues". '

Mercedes Pallares from our Madrid office has advised us that in Spain there is a form of "punitive" interest for delayed payment of compensation, which is payable following three months after the date of the accident. In practice, the majority of insurers deposit in Court the minimum amount three months after the date of the accident, to avoid facing huge interest payments for delay. Spain has introduced a special rate of 20% payable by insurance companies in motor cases. In France, a special rule applies only where insurance companies are involved on behalf of Defendants in road traffic cases. An insurance company can be required to pay double interest, if in the Court's view, the company should have settled the case before the Court action.[16]

The position of the EU and national governments

In publishing our first edition in 1991, we intended not only to assist practitioners and insurers to understand the discrepancies in personal injury compensation which apply in Europe, but also to stimulate interest among European lawmakers to grasp the opportunity to move swiftly toward uniformity and harmonisation of concepts of liability and quantum in Member States of the EU.

Our recommendation that the EU should inquire into and report on the discrimination against nationals resulting from disparity in levels of personal injury compensation has not been taken up by the Commission and there is still wide disparity in compensation awards across Europe. Nevertheless our first edition appeared to be widely welcomed and to have had some impact on national governments. For example, the Irish Government referred to it in its review of capping awards in Ireland.

Some national governments have passed new legislation to reduce a few of the anomalies we highlighted in 1990. The Law Commission of England and Wales has begun to publish its provisional findings on levels of damages, structured compensation and actuarial evidence. But this is not enough. What we continue to call for is European Commission led initiatives.

Article 12 of the Treaty establishing the European Community (EC Treaty) prohibits discrimination within the Community against any of its citizens on the basis of nationality, and the very existence of the Court of Justice and the European Court of Human Rights is proof positive that justice is neither the exclusive nor even the predominant concern of domestic governments who subscribe to the principles of the European Community. Many of the measures adopted by the EC to harmonise the laws of Member States in the pursuit of common denominators of consumer protection are justice related and yet justice in the levels of personal injury awards has been left to the discretion of Members States which is why the amounts recoverable are still a lottery depending upon where the claims are made and not, as ought to be the case, the nature of injuries.

---

16 Civil Procedures in EC Countries, by David McIntosh and Marjorie Holmes, 1991

Astonishingly given the principle of Article 12 EC Treaty back in 1992, Karl van Miert, the Commissioner then responsible for Consumer Affairs, told the Wall Street Journal (Europe) in relation to levels of damages awarded by judges in domestic courts throughout the EU that: "The Community considers justice to be mainly the responsibility of individual member states".

In preparing the third edition of this book, we again contacted the European Commission to draw their attention to the need for harmonisation in relation to personal injury awards. We were referred to the framework of the follow-up application of the liability Directive.[17] The Commission told us the level of awards made in personal injury claims in Member States and the impact on the internal market would be a part of their analysis. In their conclusion to their report, the Commission state that, at present, "no assessment is possible as to the real impact of the co-existence of national laws transposing the directive with other liability systems" and therefore, the Commission is planning to initiate a survey in relation to how the different national systems diverge from each other, eg. in relation to products and damages covered, and inter alia, levels of damages awarded. At the date of going to press, our research has revealed that the Commission have allocated funds for a research project on EU law systems which will involve a comparison of personal injury law and litigation.

This limited activity contrasts with the Commission's concern to extend legal aid to all civil disputes involving cross-border litigation. So it does not seem to consider the funding of litigation to be "mainly the responsibility of individual Member State".

The recent introduction of the Euro (in twelve of the 15 Member States of the EU only, as the UK, Denmark and Sweden have decided not to participate in monetary union at this stage) will, by making the discrepancies even more obvious have an enormous effect on harmonising the levels of awards in Europe. The Euro may also have an impact on the levels of awards in general. We are convinced that the Euro will promote harmonisation as it will lead to an easier comparison between levels of awards in the Member States. The recent judgment by the European Court of Justice *BSM Geraets-Smits v Stichting Ziekenfonds VGZ* (see above Foreign Sickness Treatment and Reimbursement) in which it was held that patients have the right to be referred for medical treatment elsewhere in the EU if they can not receive the same or equally effective treatment without "undue delay"

---

17 Report from the Commission on the Application of Directive 85/374 on Liability for Defective products, Brussels 31 January 2001

at home may also help to level out the huge discrepancies in awards as insurance companies will need to plan and reserve on a "Europe-wide" basis.

Following the review of International Aviation Conventions after the World Trade Centre disaster, the European Commission have intervened. Rather than leave this issue to Member States, they have put forward a proposal to bring in compulsory minimum insurance for all carriers and operators flying within the European Union. This includes a proposal that the carrier be insured for 250,000 SDRS (186,846€, £112,544, US$158,304, ISDR = 0.747385€) per passenger for death or personal injury. Whilst this is aimed at creating a level playing field for carriers, it will inevitably have a knock on affect on personal injury awards.

Public opinion and the increase of the levels of awards

The figures given in the Bloc Graphs illustrate that the levels of awards do not simply increase in line with inflation. An interesting feature is that the compensation payments made in mass tort or disaster will have a knock-on effect on the levels of awards made in the more routine personal injury claims. For this reason it is worth reviewing some of the large accidents that have occurred since our last edition, and the consequent effect on levels of awards generally.

In the Air France-Concorde settlement reached in May 2001 by the relatives of the 75 Germans citizens who were killed in the crash and Air France (although in total 113 people lost their lives in this accident) the threat of a trial in the US is reported to have led to a compensation award of between USD 100 million and USD 125 million (about GBP 71-89 million and EUR 118-148 million). Although the Air France Concorde carried only one American passenger and crashed outside Paris, the claimants' lawyers filed their suit in the US. They argued that the Concorde plane was bound for the US on the first leg of a Caribbean cruise vacation and therefore the case "belonged" to the US courts. In view of this "risk" of the case being dealt with by a US court, the damages award was closer to the US concept of compensation than the German or French levels. Air France paid far more in compensation than they would have had the claim been litigated in a European court.

The Kaprun alpine railway accident of 11 November 2000, in which 155 people died when the cable cars they were travelling in caught fire, led to a lawsuit in the US State of New York, although most of the passengers were Austrian and only 3 were US American. The victims of the railway disaster filed the lawsuit in the US, accusing Siemens, the German technology group and its Austrian subsidiary of negligence. The victims are said to have demanded hundreds of millions of US dollars in compensation. Press reports indicate that US$ 550-620million (about GBP 391-440 million and EUR 649-732 million) is being claimed in damages for the 155 victims. The case has not been settled yet.

Following a cable car accident near Cavalese, Italy, on 3 February 1998, the relatives of each victim were paid damages of USD 2 million (about GBP 1.42 million and EUR 2.36 million) in total. The only surviving victim received ITL 1,500 million (GBP 466,528, USD 656,218 and EUR 774,530). The families of all 20 people killed when a Marine jet crashed into an Italian ski gondola accepted settlements of the equivalent of nearly GBP 2 million (about USD 2.81 million and EUR 3.32 million) per victim. These payments are governed by the accord covering civil and criminal legal activities of NATO troops in foreign countries. Under the accord, the host country pays 25% of the damages while the country responsible for the accident pays the remaining 75%. The victims filed a lawsuit in the US State of Virginia although a federal judge in Greenville ruled that they could not seek compensation in the US because of the Status of Forces Agreement which governs the activities of NATO troops in foreign countries.

The Mont Blanc tunnel fire, in which 41 people died in March 1999, resulted in many death and injury claims which at the date of this publication going to print have not been settled. The Italian lawyer acting on behalf of the insurer of the lorry which caused the fire advised us that settlement discussions are still ongoing between the assumed liable parties and the victims' lawyers under the French Government's supervision. It was initially reported that the appropriate level of compensation would be decided under French, rather than Italian, law as it had been established that the fire started in the French part of the tunnel. However, Italian awards in fatal cases, depending on the personal status of the victim, are 3-4 times higher than the equivalent French awards and the victims are reluctant to accept that French law only is applicable. Although personal injury awards in France are generally accepted as being lower than in Italy due to a differing "national regime", an accident such as this highlights that an Italian is "worth" more in financial terms than a Frenchman where both die in the same accident which is unacceptable.

Whilst there is a general lack of public interest in inter-country comparisons (except on the part of those who suffer an injury), there is massive public interest in the large awards made in multiple claim cases. What is missing is widespread appreciation of the plight of those who are involved in un-newsworthy claims and who receive far too little in compensation.

Asbestos

In the UK claims related to asbestos are increasing and insurance companies are raising their reserves in respect of these claims which generally relate to exposure decades ago (the incubation period for the asbestos related cancer, mesothelioma, is up to 40 years.) Fewer "traditional" claims from the lagging industries are reported but there are more so called "third generation" claims from shop-fitters, electricians and workers who handled asbestos containing products. A report from the TUC (the UK Trades Union Congress, representing the vast majority of organized workers), dated April 2000, reported that there were 18,000 deaths in the previous four years as a result of working with asbestos. The report estimated that by 2020, up to 10,000 people per annum will die of asbestos-related illnesses. Because of the exorbitant US awards which have had to be met by European Insurer some have become bankrupt (like many of their Insureds) and many future claimants will not be compensated.

Strict liability schemes

In each of the 20 jurisdictions we surveyed for this edition there are fault-based liability systems and some jurisdictions impose a system of "strict liability". In this context it is important to consider the impact of the European Product Liability Directive (Directive 85/374/EEC) on the different liability regimes across Europe. The Directive was adopted in 1985 and attempted to introduce a regime of strict liability for injury arising from a defect in a product across Europe, although the Directive did not impose standardisation of the quantum of awards. One area in which the application of the Directive varies from country to country relates to the development risks defence. This defence enables a producer or manufacturer to argue that the state of scientific knowledge at the time the product was put on the market was such that the defect could not be identified. A recent Commission report that looked at the impact of the Directive highlighted how the defence is applied across the European Union. In Finland and Luxembourg it is not available to the producers of any type of product, whilst in Spain it cannot be used by food producers or pharmaceutical companies and in France it is not available for products derived from body parts. The report concluded that as a result of this fragmented approach there was insufficient information to show whether or not the Directive has made an impact on the underlying legal system in each country.

However a recent decision in the UK courts indicates that interpretation of the Directive may become more uniform as its provisions are more strictly interpreted.

In *A v the National Blood Authority* 117 claimants were infected with Hepatitis C virus from blood transfusions they received during the course of clinical treatment between 1 March 1988 and September 1991. The claimants' case was that they were entitled to recover damages even though the Hepatitis C virus had not been identified at the time some of them were infected and that no screening test for the virus had been available for many of them. The case was finally decided on a strict interpretation of the Articles of the Directive.

Article 6 of the Directive provides that a product is defective if it does not provide the safety that persons are entitled to expect generally. The Judge in the case ruled that this was an objective test that could be assessed by the Court as the informed representative of the public at large. The Judge concluded that the public had a legitimate expectation that the blood transfused to them would be 100% safe and would not infect them with Hepatitis C. The Judge rejected the argument that, as blood was a natural product which carried with it an inherent risk of being infected by the virus, it was sufficient that the medical profession knew of the risk.

The development risk defence, as provided for under Article 7(e) of the Directive, was used by the defendant in this case. In considering their arguments the Judge rejected the defendant's contention that the development risks defence related to the discovery of the defect in the product, rather than the product's manufacture. He concluded that as soon as the risk of infection was known, the defence was no longer available, even if the risk in a particular product could not be avoided.

In this case the Directive was interpreted in its purist form. It was held that the purpose of the Directive was to make it easier for injured consumers to recover damages. In applying the Directive in a purposive way the UK court has demonstrated that the strict liability regime is very strict indeed.

Another example of the principle of "liability with no fault" are the tobacco cases in the various Member States. In Sweden, on the basis of liability without fault, compensation was claimed from the Swedish tobacco company Swedish Match for the damage caused to the claimants' health because of lack of information on the risks of smoking, and in particular in relation to the risk of cancer. The case was however, rejected by a court in Stockholm in 1997. On appeal, the Swedish Supreme Court referred the case back on a point of procedure. The tobacco company, considered the case was politically motivated. Two similar cases were lodged against SEITA in France in 1996 for failure to provide information on the dangers of smoking Gauloises cigarettes. Invoking the manufacturer's liability without fault, the victims claimed damages and interest of FRF 2,668,090 (GBP

245,004, USD 344,623 and EUR 406,756) and FRF 1,158,499 (GBP 106,382, USD 149,637 and EUR 176,615) respectively.[18]

In Germany haemophiliacs were infected with the HIV virus by contaminated blood products during the period of 1980 to 1993 and a compensation fund was established.[19] Several Member States (Germany, France, Denmark, UK, Sweden, Italy, Finland and Austria) have adopted new legislation in recent years under which schemes administered by governments provide compensation payments to victims of vaccine-related injuries.[20]

Summary of additional recommendations

In our first edition we made five principal recommendations:

- Inquiry by the EU into the discrimination against nationals resulting from disparity in levels of personal injury compensation.
- Consideration of a single scale of compensation for pain and suffering (that is, for "non-economic" loss) to be adopted throughout Europe, taking the ECU (Euro) as the standard unit of currency.
- Consideration of a single scale of compensation for the estate of a deceased person who suffered instantaneous death to be adopted throughout Europe.
- Production of guidelines for the judges of national courts to follow in assessing levels of damages, as a step towards harmonising levels of awards within European countries before harmonising such levels between those countries.
- The piloting of a scheme of no fault compensation for the UK, with appropriate caps on levels of awards, running in tandem with the current tort system

The first three of our recommendations have been disregarded; the fourth partially met by reference to judicial guidelines and to the Ogden tables in England and

18 See Le Monde 20, 27 and 28 December; source: "Green paper on liability for defective products", European Commission, 28 July 1999

19 BGBl. I 1995, 972

20 Source: Report from the European Commission on the application of Directive 85/374 on liability for defective products – 31 January 2001

Wales. The fifth has also been partially met by the proposal for a limited "no fault" regime in respect of medical negligence cases.

We nevertheless offer these recommendations in full and call for urgent adoption.

In our related publication "Civil Procedures in EC Countries"[21] we recommended that Judges should be interchanged between Member States in an advisory capacity at appellant level. This recommendation has not been universally adopted. However, there has been some interchange. Training of Judges on European wide initiatives such as Human Rights is now more commonplace. We are aware of the English judiciary and an English Judge advising the Czech Republic which has applied to join the EU on changes to their civil procedures. Finally, the Commission have allocated funds of 100,000 euros in 2002, for the purpose of training national Judges in EC Competition Law. This is a move in the right direction which will be we hope extended to other areas of law.

[21] Civil Procedures in EC Countries, by David McIntosh and Marjorie Holmes, 1991

EU COUNTRIES*

* Because of the number of jurisdictions involved in this comparative report, changes in law in the 20 jurisdictions after January 2001 have not been incorporated.

AUSTRIA

Dr Ivo Greiter

Introduction*

In Austria, compensation for pain and suffering is rather low in comparison to most of the western European states. The highest amounts for pain and suffering are given for paraplegia or decerebration syndrome (persistent vegetative state).

The largest award paid in respect of pain and suffering (as of October 10, 2001) was made by the Supreme Court on February 13, 1997 (6 Ob 2394/96v). The award was 1.750.000 Austrian Schillings (£76,586) to a minor who, because of a serious lack of oxygen during his birth, suffered irreparable brain damage that led to near immobility.

Liability is established mainly through the General Civil Code of Austria (*Allgemeines Buergerliches Gesetzbuch, ABGB*). Additionally, various provisions of the Railway and Motor Vehicle Liability Law (*Eisenbahn-Kraftfahrzeug-Haftpflichtgesetz, RKHG*) can form the basis for tort claims. Article 1295 of the General Civil Code of Austria applies in general cases, while the Railway and Motor Vehicle Liability Law is more limited in scope and contains a strict liability provision. As such, it places a higher degree of responsibility upon the tortfeasor. Generally the tortfeasor (*Schädiger*) has to pay for the cost for medical treatment (*Heilungskosten*). Should there be different possibilities for medical treatment the claimant has the right to proceed within his normal standard of living. For example, if this corresponds to his normal living standard the claimant can elect to stay in hospital in a first class ward. The claimant can still claim the costs of medical treatment, even when the medical treatment was not successful, if the medical treatment was objectively reasonable. When calculating the amount of compensation, the claimant must deduct an amount equivalent to what he saves in his housekeeping costs during his stay in hospital.

Problems which may arise concerning the costs of medical treatment are sometimes due to the fact that, in most cases, the claimant receives social insurance payments. Under Austrian law the claim of the injured person is transferred by force of law to the Austrian social insurance (*Übergang der Ersatzansprüche*).

Generally the tortfeasor must also compensate the claimant for any loss of income (*Verdienstentgang*) including future loss (*zukünftiger Verdienstentgang*). This can be paid as a lump sum or in the form of a monthly payment. The monthly payment award can be adapted to actual economic and personal development. Normally, the monthly payment is given as long as the claimant is incapable of earning his living (*Erwerbsunfähigkeit*).

There is also a claim for loss of profit (*Gewinnentgang*) if the claimant cannot conclude a favourable bargain due to his injuries, e.g. if he cannot, take possession of a farm which was intended for him. Loss of profit is only paid if gross negligence (*große Fahrlässigkeit*) or intent to injure (*Verletzungsvorsatz*) on the side of the tortfeasor is given.

Compensation for pain and suffering (*Schmerzensgeld*) is given to compensate physical pain (*körperliche Schmerzen*) and as a compensation if the claimant becomes crippled or disfigured. The calculation of compensation for pain and suffering includes the nature and intensity of the injury [and pain] duration of inability to earn a living, etc. Pain is usually broken down into four categories, in which damages are awarded for each day that each type of pain is suffered as follows:

Table 1

	ATS
For light pain:	1,000 to 1,500 daily (£44-£66)
For moderate pain:	1,500 to 2,500 daily (£66-£88)
For strong pain:	2,000 to 4,200 daily (£88-£184)
For very strong pain:	3,000 to 4,900 daily (£132-£214)

These figures are current guidelines only as at February 1999 and differ from court to court.

Emotional suffering (*seelische Schmerzen*) can only be claimed by those who actually suffered a physical injury. Emotional suffering includes: inability to procreate, lasting decrease in ability to earn a living, impediment to the enjoyment of life's pleasures, feelings of listlessness.

Compensation for the emotional suffering of children, who were present when their mother was seriously injured and as a result of the accident were separate from their mother for a long period of time, was accepted for the first time by the Supreme Court in its decision of July 16, 1994 (2ob 45/93 ATS30,000 – around £1,313) and in a subsequent decision on December 21, 1995 (2 ob 99/94

ATS200,000 – around £8,753) but only because the accident caused deep emotional injury such that the children required medical treatment.

Further, compensation for the extreme suffering of close relatives (nahe Angehörige) without the relatives requiring medical care as a result of the loss of the relatives was, for the first time, allowed by the Supreme Court in its decision of May 16, 2001 (2 ob 84/01v); however only when the injury was caused by intention (Vorsatz) or gross negligence (grobe Fahrlässigkeit) of the tortfeasor. If there is only slight negligence (leichte Fahrlässigkeit) or strict liability (Gefährdungshaftung, also ohne Fährlässigkeit) no compensation is granted.

In addition to suffering due to disfigurement, Austrian law also recognises that such disfigurement may hinder a person's chances in later life (*Verhinderung des besseren Fortkommens*). This type of award takes into account, for example, the decreased chance of marriage for a young person who suffers an injury which results in disfigurement.

The highest compensation award made in respect of disfigurement (as at September 1, 1999) was made by the Court of Appeal (OLG) Vienna in its judgment of November 11, 1996 (12 R 89/96g) and amounted to 400,000 Austrian Schillings (£17,505.)

To prevent prescription (or the claim being time barred) the claimant has first to seek a declaratory judgment (*Feststellungsklage*) concerning future damages. Judgment declares that the tortfeasor is liable towards the claimant for all future results of the injury for a period of 30 years. The claimant can then claim all costs including the cost of future operations, the cost of therapy and devices including artificial limbs etc when these costs are occasioned by the injury. If certain determined preconditions exist, it is also possible, via declaratory judgment, to receive compensation for future pain and suffering.

With regard to Schedules A and B, the following should be noted:

All figures given in the calculation are estimated figures, as compensation awards will not always correspond to the cases described in this summary, as it is seldom the case that, in a traffic accident, a claimant only has one specific injury, e.g. loss of one eye and no further injuries.

Figures for medical expenses are calculated on the basis of the cost of a standard hospital bed in Austria, which is between ATS 2,000 and 5,000 (£88-£219.) In Vienna, prices are higher. A bed in the *Allgemeines Krankenhaus,* Vienna would cost approximately up to ATS 10,000 (£438) per day.

These figures are given as lump sums and if the claimant has to stay in hospital for a long period of time (e.g. in the intensive ward), then the cost may be much higher. Furthermore, these figures do not include further costs if for example the claimant has to stay in hospital for plastic surgery due to the injury.

The duration of a stay in hospital is estimated, as this would depend on the individual injury and the claimant's individual circumstances.

The figures for miscellaneous losses are also provided as an estimate. The actual figures are dependent on the individual situation, e.g. travel costs for visitors, specialist's costs, phone calls, wheelchair, etc.

The maintenance claim of the dependent wife and children is calculated on what was legally due and what was really given. So far as Austrian social insurance laws are applied, it is normally the case that payments in the form of a widow's or an orphan's pension are paid by the insurance company. A pension awarded to the widow will normally expire on remarriage.

In the application of Austrian social insurance law to the case of a claimant who suffers loss of earnings, it is the duty of the employer to continue to pay the injured person's salary for the for a specific period of time, normally up to a minimum of twelve weeks. After that it is normally the case that the injured person receives payments from social insurance or, under certain circumstances, from pension insurance. Normally, such payments will be deducted from the compensation award. This is usually the case where the injured person is unable to resume his previous employment and receives payments from an insurance company.

Lastly the figures concerning pain and suffering also in respect of disfigurement compensation are only average amounts made by assessments. There are variations according to the individual circumstance of each claim and due to the different judgments given by the Austrian courts.

Table 2. Schedule A

Claimant:	Man
Age:	40
Status:	Married – 2 dependent children aged 5 and 7
Occupation:	Doctor
Income:	ATS 700,000 p.a.
Settlement:	Three years after accident

If compensation is to be paid in the form of a monthly pension, then this income is usually subject to Austrian income tax. If compensation is paid in the form of a lump sum, then generally this payment is not subject to tax.

In addition to compensation, monthly interest of 4% p.a. can be demanded by the claimant. The following example is based on the assumption that no payments are made by social insurance, etc. If they are, then in most cases they have to be deducted from the amount calculated.

1. Instant Death		ATS
a) Funeral expenses		60,000
b) Wife's dependence (calculated according to her husband's salary	700,000	
Net income of husband	280,000	
Deduct fixed costs of the whole family (40%)	420,000	
27% dependence for wife	113,400	
Half fixed costs of the 40%	140,000	
In addition dependence for wife p.a.	253,400	
Maintenance until settlement after 3 years		760,200
Future loss of maintenance yearly ATS 253,400		
c) Children' dependence:		
First child, 5 years	60,000	
Dependence p.a	70,000	
Fixed costs quarter p.a.	130,000	
Maintenance until settlement after 3 years		
Future loss of maintenance yearly ATS 130,000 until new assessment		
Second child, 7 years old	66,000	
Dependence p.a	70,000	
Fixed costs quaerter p.a.	136,000	
Maintenance until settlement after 3 years		
Future loss of maintenance yearly ATS 136,000 until new assessment		408,000

d) Bereavement (emotional suffering) (see introduction)	–
TOTAL AWARD	**1,618,200**

2a. Burns (10-15%)

Assume that claimant is able to resume his employment six months after the accident

a) Medical expenses: stay in hospital: 10 days	40,000
b) Loss of income until consolidation after six months	350,000
c) Miscellaneous losses (travel costs for visitors, specialist's costs, phone calls, etc	40,000
d) Pain and suffering	80,000
Disfigurement compensation	30,000
	540,000

2b. Burns (20%)

Assume that claimant is able to resume his employment six months after the accident

a) Medical expenses: stay in hospital: 14 days	56,000
b) Loss of income until consolidation after 1 year	700,000
c) Miscellaneous losses	40,000
d) Pain and suffering	150,000
Disfigurement compensation	50,000
	996,000

3. Quadriplegia

a) Medical expenses: stay in hospital including a stay in a rehabilitation centre 12 months (365 days X AtS 4,000 per day)	1,460,000
b) Loss of income until settlement after 3 years Future loss of income yearly ATS 700,000 until new assessment	2,100,000
c) Miscellaneous losses (e.g. wheelchair, running expenses, etc.)	200,000
d) Pain and suffering	1,200,000
Disfigurement compensation	250,000
e) Prospective medical assistance (if the costs are not paid by the claimant's social insurance) but normally only up to the costs of a nursing home: until settlement after 3 years, rest of 24 months at ATS 25,000 per month	600,000
TOTAL AWARD	**5,810,000**

4. Paraplegia

a) Medical expenses: stay in hospital including a stay in a rehabilitation centre 6 months	730,000
b) Loss of income until settlement after 3 years Future loss of income yearly ATS 700,000 until new assessment	2,100,000
c) Miscellaneous losses (e.g. modifying home, wheelchair, special equipment, etc.)	700,000
d) Pain and suffering	850,000
Disfigurement compensation	200,000
e) Prospective medical assistance in the form of half time medical assistance (if these costs are not paid by the claimant's social insurance) –	

	nurse: until settlement after 3 years, rest of 30 months at ATS 18,600 per month	558,000
	TOTAL AWARD	**5,138,000**

5a. Brain Damage

a)	Medical expenses: stay in hospital 2 months	240,000
b)	Loss of income until settlement after 3 years Future loss of income yearly ATS 700,000 until new assessment	2,100,000
c)	Miscellaneous losses	60,000
d)	Pain and suffering	850,000
	Disfigurement compensation	120,000
e)	Prospective medical assistance (if the costs are not paid by the claimant's social insurance) but normally only up to the costs of a nursing home: until settlement after 3 years, rest of 34 months at ATS 25,000 per month	850,000
	TOTAL AWARD	**4,220,000**

5b. Brain damage (90%)

a)	Medical expenses: stay in hospital 3 months	360,000
b)	Loss of income until settlement after 3 years Future loss of income yearly ATS 700,000 until new assessment	2,100,000
c)	Miscellaneous losses	60,000
d)	Pain and suffering	1,000,000
	Disfigurement compensation	180,000
e)	Prospective medical assistance (if the costs are not paid by the claimant's social insurance) but normally only up to the costs of a nursing	

home: until settlement after 3 years, rest of 33 months at ATS 25,000 per month	825,000
TOTAL AWARD	**4,525,000**

6a. Amputation of leg above knee

Assume that claimant is able to resume his employment one year after accident

a)	Medical expenses: stay in hospital 20 days	80,000
b)	Loss of income until settlement after 1 year	700,000
c)	Miscellaneous losses (artificial limb, special equipment, e.g. costs of automatic driving gear for a car, etc.)	300,000
d)	Pain and suffering	450,000
	Disfigurement compensation	200,000
e)	Prospective medical expenses and prospective costs (if these costs are not paid by the claimant's social insurance), costs of therapeutics etc.: until settlement after 3 years ATS 25,000 per year	90,000
	TOTAL AWARD	**1,820,000**

6b. Amputation of leg below knee

Assume that claimant is able to resume his employment one year after accident

a)	Medical expenses: stay in hospital 20 days	80,000
b)	Loss of income until settlement after 1 year	700,000
c)	Miscellaneous losses (artificial limb, special equipment, e.g. costs of automatic driving gear for a car, etc.)	200,000
d)	Pain and suffering	350,000
	Disfigurement compensation	150,000

e) Prospective medical expenses and prospective costs (if these costs are not paid by the claimant's social insurance), costs of therapeutics etc.: until settlement after 3 years ATS 30,000 per year	90,000
TOTAL AWARD	**1,570,000**

7a. Amputation of arm above the elbow

Assume that claimant is able to resume his employment but only takes up light duties one year after accident at ATS 350,000 salary net p.a.

a) Medical expenses: stay in hospital 20 days	80,000
b) Loss of income until consolidation after 1 year	700,000
c) Future loss of income until settlement after 3 years, rest of 2 years	700,000
d) Miscellaneous losses (artificial limb, special equipment, etc.)	150,000
e) Pain and suffering	300,000
Disfigurement compensation	200,000
f) Prospective medical expenses and prospective costs (if these costs are not paid by the claimant's social insurance), costs of therapeutics etc.: until settlement after 3 years ATS 30,000 per year	90,000
TOTAL AWARD	**2,220,000**

7b. Amputation of arm below the elbow

Assume that claimant is able to resume his employment, but only takes up light duties one year after accident at ATS 350,000 salary net p.a.

a) Medical expenses: stay in hospital 20 days	80,000
b) Loss of income until consolidation after 1 year	700,000
Future loss of income until settlement after 3 years, rest of 2 years	700,000

c) Miscellaneous losses (artificial limb, special equipment, etc.)	100,000
d) Pain and suffering	250,000
Disfigurement compensation	150,000
e) Prospective medical expenses and prospective costs (if these costs are not paid by the claimant's social insurance), costs of therapeutics etc.: until settlement after 3 years ATS 30,000 per year	90,000
TOTAL AWARD	**2,070,000**

8a. Loss of eyesight – one eye without cosmetic disability

Assume that claimant is able to resume his employment six months after accident

a) Medical expenses: stay in hospital 12 days	48,000
b) Loss of income until settlement after six months	350,000
c) Miscellaneous losses	30,000
d) Pain and suffering	300,000
Disfigurement compensation	80,000
e) Prospective medical expenses (if these costs are not paid by the claimant's social insurance): until settlement after 3 years ATS 5,000 per year	15,000
TOTAL AWARD	**823,000**

8b. Loss of eyesight – one eye with cosmetic disability

Assume that claimant is able to resume his employment one year after accident

a) Medical expenses: stay in hospital 20 days	80,000
b) Loss of income until settlement after 1 year	700,000
c) Miscellaneous losses	60,000

d) Pain and suffering Disfigurement compensation	350,000 80,000
e) Prospective medical expenses (if these costs are not paid by the claimant's social insurance), cost of therapeutics etc.: until settlement after 3 years ATS 5,000 per year	15,000
TOTAL AWARD	**1,285,000**

8c. Loss of eyesight – total blindness

Assume that claimant is unable to resume employment

a) Medical expenses: stay in hospital 30 days	120,000
b) Loss of income until settlement after 3 years Future loss of income yearly ATS 700,000 until new assessment	2,100,000
c) Miscellaneous losses	80,000
d) Pain and suffering	500,000
Disfigurement compensation	160,000
e) Prospective medical expenses and prospective costs (if these costs are not paid by the claimant's social insurance), cost of therapeutics etc.: until settlement after 3 years, rest of 35 months, ATS 25,000 per month	875,000
TOTAL AWARD	**3,835,000**

9a. Deafness – (total)

Assume that claimant is able to resume his employment, but only takes up light duties one year after accident at ATS 210,000 salary net p.a.

a) Medical expenses: stay in hospital 12 days	48,000

b)	Loss of income until consolidation after 1 year	700,000
	Future loss of income until settlement after 3 years, rest of 2 years	980,000
c)	Miscellaneous losses (special equipment)	100,000
d)	Pain and suffering	350,000
	disfigurement compensation	80,000
e)	Prospective medical expenses and prospective costs (if these costs are not paid by the claimant's social insurance), costs of therapeutics etc.: until settlement after 3 years, ATS 40,000 per year	120,000
	TOTAL AWARD	**2,378,000**

Table 3. Schedule B

Claimant:	Woman
Age:	20
Status:	Single
Occupation:	Legal Secretary
Income:	ATS 150,000
Trial:	Three years after accident

If compensation is to be paid in the form of a monthly pension, then this income is usually subject to Austrian income tax. If the compensation is to be paid in the form of a lump sum, then normally no tax is paid.

In addition to compensation, monthly interest of 4% p.a. can be demanded. The example is based on the assumption that no payments are made by social insurance, etc. If they are made, then in most cases they have to be deducted from the amount calculated

1. Instant Death

a) Funeral expenses	50,000
b) Maintenance: nothing	
c) Bereavement (emotional suffering): see introduction	
TOTAL AWARD	**50,000**

2a. Burns (10-15%)

Assume, that claimant is able to resume his employment six months after the accident

a) Medical expenses: stay in hospital: 10 days	40,000
b) Loss of income until consolidation after six months	75,000
c) Miscellaneous losses (travel costs for visitors, specialist's costs, phone calls, etc)	40,000
d) Pain and suffering	80,000
Disfigurement compensation	50,000
TOTAL AWARD	**285,000**

2b. Burns (20%)

Assume, that claimant is able to resume his employment six months after the accident

a) Medical expenses: stay in hospital: 14 days	56,000
b) Loss of income until consolidation after 1 year	150,000
c) Miscellaneous losses	40,000
d) Pain and suffering	150,000
Disfigurement compensation	80,000
	476,000

3. Quadriplegia

a) Medical expenses: stay in hospital including a stay in a rehabilitation centre 12 months (365 days x ATS 4,000 per day)	1,460,000
b) Loss of income until settlement after 3 years Future loss of income yearly ATS 150,000 until new assessment	450,000
c) Miscellaneous losses (e.g. wheelchair, running expenses, etc.)	200,000
d) Pain and suffering	1,200,000
Disfigurement compensation	350,000
e) Prospective medical assistance (if the costs are not paid by the claimant's social insurance) but normally only up to the costs of a nursing home: until settlement after 3 years, rest of 24 months at ATS 25,000 per month	600,000
TOTAL AWARD	**4,260,000**

4. Paraplegia

a) Medical expenses: stay in hospital including a stay in a rehabilitation centre 6 months	730,000
b) Loss of income until settlement after 3 years Future loss of income yearly ATS 150,000 until new assessment	450,000
c) Miscellaneous losses (eg. modifying home, wheelchair, special equipment, etc)	700,000
d) Pain and suffering	850,000
Disfigurement Compensation	300,000
e) Prospective medical assistance in the form of half time medical assistance (if these costs are not paid by the claimant's social	

	insurance) – nurse: until settlement after 3 years, rest of 30 months at ATS 18,600 per month	558,000
f)	Household help: until settlement after 3 years, rest of 30 months, 2 hours daily at ATS 6,000 per month	180,000
	TOTAL AWARD	**3,768,000**

5a. Brain Damage (80%)

a)	Medical expenses: stay in hospital 2 months	240,000
b)	Loss of income until settlement after 3 years Future loss of income yearly ATS 150,000 until new assessment	450,000
c)	Miscellaneous losses	60,000
d)	Pain and suffering Disfigurement compensation	850,000 200,000
e)	Prospective medical assistance (if the costs are not paid by the claimant's social insurance) but normally only up to the costs of a nursing home: until settlement after 3 years, rest of 34 months at ATS 25,000 per month	850,000
	TOTAL AWARD	**2,650,000**

5b. Brain damage (90%)

a)	Medical expenses: stay in hospital 3 months	360,000
b)	Loss of income until settlement after 3 years Future loss of income yearly ATS 150,000 until new assessment	450,000
c)	Miscellaneous losses	60,000

d) Pain and suffering Disfigurement compensation	1,000,000 250,000
e) Prospective medical assistance (if the costs are not paid by the claimant's social insurance) but normally only up to the costs of a nursing home: until settlement after 3 years, rest of 33 months at ATS 25,000 per month	825,000
TOTAL AWARD	**2,945,000**

6a. Amputation of leg above knee

Assume that claimant is able to resume his employment one year after accident

a) Medical expenses: stay in hospital 20 days	80,000
b) Loss of income until settlement after 1 year	150,000
c) Miscellaneous losses (artificial limb, special equipment, eg. costs of automatic driving gear for a car, etc.)	300,000
d) Pain and suffering Disfigurement Compensation	450,000 250,000
e) Prospective medical expenses and prospective costs (if these costs are not paid by the claimant's social insurance), costs of therapeutics etc.: until settlement after 3 years ATS 30,000 per year	90,000
f) Household help: until settlement after 3 years, 2 hours daily at ATS 6,000 per month	216,000
TOTAL AWARD	**1,536,000**

6b. Amputation of leg below knee

Assume that claimant is able to resume his employment one year after accident

a)	Medical expenses: stay in hospital 20 days	80,000
b)	Loss of income until settlement after 1 year	150,000
c)	Miscellaneous losses (artificial limb, special equipment, e.g. costs of automatic driving gear for a car, etc.)	200,000
d)	Pain and suffering	350,000
	Disfigurement compensation	200,000
e)	Prospective medical expenses and prospective costs (if these costs are not paid by the claimant's social insurance), costs of therapeutics etc.: until settlement after 3 years ATS 30,000 per year	90,000
f)	Household help: until settlement after 3 years, 2 hours daily at ATS 6,000 per month	216,000
	TOTAL AWARD	**1,286,000**

7a. Amputation of arm above the elbow

Assume that claimant is able to resume his employment but only takes up light duties one year after accident at ATS 100,000 salary net p.a.

a)	Medical expenses: stay in hospital 20 days	80,000
b)	Loss of income until consolidation after 1 year	150,000
c)	Future loss of income until settlement after 3 years, rest of 2 year	100,000
d)	Miscellaneous losses (artificial limb, special equipment, etc.)	150,000
e)	Pain and suffering	300,000
	Disfigurement compensation	250,000
f)	Prospective medical expenses and prospective costs (if these costs are not paid by the claimant's social insurance), costs of	

therapeutics etc.: until settlement after
3 years ATS 30,000 per year 90,000

g) Household help: until settlement after
3 years, 2 hours daily at ATS 6,000 per month 216,000

TOTAL AWARD **1,336,000**

7b. Amputation of arm below the elbow

Assume that claimant is able to resume his employment, but only takes up light duties one year after accident at ATS 100,000 salary net p.a.

a) Medical expenses: stay in hospital 20 days 80,000

b) Loss of income until consolidation after 1 year 150,000
Future loss of income until settlement
after 3 years, rest of 2 years 100,000

c) Miscellaneous losses (artificial limb, special equipment, etc.) 100,000

d) Pain and suffering 250,000
Disfigurement compensation 200,000

e) Prospective medical expenses and prospective costs (if these costs are not paid by the claimant's social insurance), costs of therapeutics etc.: until settlement after 3 years ATS 30,000 per year 90,000

f) Household help: until settlement after
3 years, 2 hours daily at ATS 6,000 per month 216,000

TOTAL AWARD **1,186,000**

8a. Loss of eyesight – one eye without cosmetic disability

Assume that claimant is able to resume his employment six months after accident

a) Medical expenses: stay in hospital 12 days 48,000

b) Loss of income until consolidation after six months 75,000

c) Miscellaneous losses	30,000
d) Pain and suffering Disfigurement compensation	300,000 150,000
e) Prospective medical expenses (if these costs are not paid by the claimant's social insurance): until settlement after 3 years ATS 5,000 per year	15,000
TOTAL AWARD	**618,000**

8b. Loss of eyesight – one eye with cosmetic disability

Assume that claimant is able to resume his employment one year after accident

a) Medical expenses: stay in hospital 20 days	80,000
b) Loss of income until consolidation after 1 year	150,000
c) Miscellaneous losses	60,000
d) Pain and suffering Disfigurement compensation	350,000 150,000
e) Prospective medical expenses (if these costs are not paid by the claimant's social insurance), costs of therapeutics etc.: until settlement after 3 years ATS 5,000 per year	15,000
TOTAL AWARD	**805,000**

8c. Loss of eyesight – total blindness

Assume that claimant is unable to resume employment

a) Medical expenses: stay in hospital 30 days	120,000
b) Loss of income until settlement after 3 years Future loss of income yearly ATS 150,000 until new assessment	450,000
c) Miscellaneous losses	80,000

d) Pain and suffering	500,000
Disfigurement compensation	260,000
e) Prospective medical expenses and prospective costs (if these costs are not paid by the claimant's social insurance), costs of therapeutics etc.: until settlement after 3 years, rest of 35 months, ATS 25,000 per month	875,000
TOTAL AWARD	**2,285,000**

9a. Deafness – (total)

Assume that claimant is able to resume his employment, but only takes up light duties one year after accident at ATS 100,000 salary net p.a.

a) Medical expenses: stay in hospital 12 days	48,000
b) Loss of income until consolidation after 1 year	150,000
Future loss of income until settlement after 3 years, rest of 2 years	100,000
c) Miscellaneous losses (special equipment etc.)	100,000
d) Pain and suffering	350,000
Disfigurement compensation	150,000
e) Prospective medical expenses and prospective costs (if these costs are not paid by the claimant's social insurance), costs of therapeutics etc.: until settlement after 3 years ATS 40,000 per year	120,000
TOTAL AWARD	**1,018,000**

BELGIUM

Roger O. Dalcq and Daniel de Callatay

Introduction

1. In Belgium there is no statute governing compensation awards in personal injury claims (this section of law). Damages are based purely on previous case law of facts.

The Belgian Courts have full discretion in relation to quantum and they are not bound by previous case law. The (abundant) case law is considered by the parties and by the Court as guidance in each case. There is also an indicatory table periodically restated by judges but without any binding force. This table provides some indication of the awards made by the courts and can be useful for the purposes of settlements.

The most important criteria to be taken into account when awarding damages in Belgium are:

- age;
- past and future medical costs;
- income at the moment of the accident;
- future disability;
- material damages (such as possible modification of the house);
- the existence of any dependents;
- "non-economic" damages such as: suffering (pretium doloris), aesthetic injury, moral suffering due to death or loss of related people, the loss of sexual capacity, …

2. Interest is usually calculated at a rate of 7% but reduced to 5% for the damage indexed or re-evaluated at the date of the trial. Interest is calculated from the date of injury or from the [date costs are incurred] payment date of fees. Interest is not awarded on any compensation for future prejudice.

3. In Belgian litigation there is only limited application of the principle '*loser bears winner's costs*'. In fact, the loser will only pay court related costs such as costs related to the service of the Writ and the costs of instructing a medical expert – if these costs are awarded by the Court. However, the loser does not reimburse the successful claimant in respect of his legal costs irrespective of the outcome of the case, each party bears its own legal costs.

4. There are further procedural distinctions as follows:

a) all road traffic litigation including criminal pursuits proceedings for infringing the Highway Code, victims' compensation, litigation between the insurers is within the exclusive jurisdiction of the police court with an appeal to the first jurisdiction court;

b) pedestrians, cyclists and passengers who are injured in a road traffic accident are always indemnified, except in cases of "inexcusable fault" on the part of the injured person. Compensation is paid by the relevant insurer;

c) in non-road traffic accident claims, if the injury is a result of a criminal offence (assault and battery or wilful homicide or manslaughter), the victim can join in the criminal prosecution by the public prosecutor in the criminal court or alternatively, bring proceedings in the civil courts, e.g. on medical liability matters;

5. The awards are indicated in Belgian Francs. On the date of writing this text a pound is equal to BEF 63 and one dollar is equal to BEF 39. The Euro currency is equal to BEF 40.3399.

6. The economic injuries are calculated in principle on a net basis, i.e. after taxes and social insurance contributions have been paid.) Compensation for the loss of "chargeable" income (normally professional income) is also claimed.

Table 1. Schedule A

Claimant:	Man
Age:	40
Status:	Married – 2 dependent children aged 5 and 7
Occupation:	Doctor
Income:	BEF 1.800.000 net p.a.
Trial	2.5 years after date of accident

1. Instant death

BEF

There is no 'statutory bereavement' in Belgium but an indemnity for 'moral damage' to very near relatives in case of death and for the victim in other claims.

A. For the widow

	BEF
a) Funeral expenses: refund reasonable expenses including repatriation expenses if death (or a burial) has taken place in foreign country: on average[1]	150.000
b) Moral damage for the loss of a husband (or of a cohabitant companion)	350.000 – 500.000
c) Material or pecuniary damage	
– net value of income	1.800.000
– deceased own expenditures: ± 25% if the widow has no professional income	– 450.000
	1.350.000
Loss of income to date of trial	
2,5 years x 1.350.000	3.375.000

1 The expenses must be justified by proof. If the breadwinner would have normally survived the victim then only the expenses anticipated will be taken into account.

d) Future loss age of the deceased at the date of trial 42 years: probable survival to 65 years to capital at 4% annuities[2] 1.350.000 x 14,37362	19.404.38

On the contrary if the widow has a free income of 1.200.000 the calculation will be as follows:

House income: 1.800.000 + 1.200.000 =	3.000.000
Personal care of the deceased: 25% =	750.000
Widow injury: 1.800.000 – 750.000 =	1.050.000
e) Interest 2.5 years at 7% on 5.000.000 on items (a) and (b)	87.500
1.25 (= an average) years at 7% on 3.375.000	295.312
Total interest	382.812
Total damage	**23.662.199**

B. For the children

a) Moral damage for the loss of their father: to 3000.000 for each of them x 2	600.000
b) Interest 2.5 years at 7% on item (a)	105.000
Total damage	**705.000**
TOTAL AWARD: 23.662.199 + 705.000	**24.367.19**

2 The "professional life" of a doctor can last up to 70 years.

2. Burns (A, B, C)

Assume that claimant is able to resume losses two years after accident

a)	Loss of income 2 years x 1.800.000[3]	3.600.000
b)	Medical expenses and miscellaneous losses to date of trial – from 200.000 to 2.000.000	1.000.000
c)	Moral damage to date of trial 90 days hospitalisation x 1.250	112.500
	640 days without hospitalisation x 800	512.000
	182.5 days without hospitalisation x 800 x 20%	29.200
		653.700
d)	Interest 1.25 years at 7% on 4.453.700	389.699
e)	Future moral and material damage assume there is no more loss of income 20 x 50.000	1.000.000
f)	Aesthetic injury (for loss of looks)[4]	250.000
	TOTAL AWARD	**6.893.399**

---

3 This point is of general application to all loss of income awards; if the victim receives welfare these payments will be subtracted from the award but the paying party (or his insurer) will have to reimburse these benefits to the State. [For the liable party there is therefore no difference.]

4 The damage for loss of looks is very hard to assess. It depends on the following four factors:

(1) importance of the prejudice, whereby a scale from 1 to 7 is used;

(2) the sex of the victim, whereby women generally get more "préjudice esthétique" than men;

(3) the age of the person; and

(4) whether the person is married or not (a single person not being able [is assumed to be unable] to marry because of loss of looks.)

In general terms, the scale is following:

(1) insignificant loss: BEF 10.000 to 30.000

3. Quadriplegia

a) Loss of income to date of trial	
2.5 years x 1.800.000	4.500.000
b) Cost of nursing care/medical expenses to date of trial One year hospitalisation	3.000.000
One and a half years at home	2.700.000
c) Cost of modifying home and special equipment, say	1.400.000
d) Moral damage until date of trial 365 days hospitalisation x 1.500	547.500
547 days without hospitalisation x 1.000	547.000
e) Interest 1.25 years at 7% on items (a), (b), (c) and (d) on 12.694.500	1.110.769
f) Future loss of income[5] 42.5 years old at date of trial, assume retirement at 65 years coefficient to capitalise at 4% annuities = 14.37362	25.872.51
g) Future costs of nursing (life expectancy at 42 is 33.49 more years) coefficient to capitalised at 4% annuities = 17.82317.823 x 1.800.000	32.081.400
h) Future moral damage[6] 100 x 50.000	5.000.000

---

(2) very light loss: BEF 30.000 to 60.000

(3) light loss: BEF 60.000 to 90.000

(4) average loss: BEF 90.000 to 250.000

(5) serious loss: BEF 250.000 to 400.000

(6) very serious loss: BEF 400.000 to 1.000.000

(7) extremely serious loss: more than BEF 1.000.000.

5 This type of injury may be compensated by a payment of a monthly indexed rent.

6 Idem note 5 (or by capitalisation of monthly rent).

i) Aesthetic injury	500.000
j) Sexual injury	1.500.000
k) Repercussion injury for the wife	500.000
Repercussion injury for the children 2 x 250.000	500.000
TOTAL AWARD	**79.759.185**

4. Paraplegia

a) Loss of income to date of trial 2.5 years x 1.800.000	4.500.000
b) Cost of nursing and medical to date of trial	
One year hospitalisation	3.000.000
One year and a half at home	1.800.000
c) Cost of modifying home and special equipment	± 1.400.000
d) Moral damage until date of trial	
365 days hospitalisation x 1.250	456.250
547 days without hospitalisation x 1.000	547.000
e) Interest 1.25 years at 7% on 11.703.250	1.024.035
f) Future loss of income 70.100 x 14.37362 x 1.800.000	18.110.761
g) Estimated future costs of nursing care Medical expenses 75.000 x 12 x 17.823	16.040.700
h) Future moral damage	3.500.000
i) Aesthetic injury	500.000
j) Sexual injury	1.500.000
k) Repercussion injury for the wife	500.000
l) Repercussion injury for the children 2 x 250.00	500.000
TOTAL AWARD	**53.378.746**

5a. Brain damage

a) Loss of income to date of trial 2.5 years x 1.800.000	4.500.000
b) Cost of nursing/medical care One year hospitalisation One year and a half at home	 3.000.000 500.000
c) Cost of modifying home and special equipment	±500.000
d) Moral damage until trial (same as for paraplegia)[7] 456.250 x 547.000	1.003.250
e) Interest 1.25 years at 7% on 9.503.250	831.534
f) Future loss of income 80.100 x 14.37362 x 1.800.000	20.698.013
g) Estimated future costs of nursing care Medical expenses 180.000 x 17.823	3.208.140
h) Future moral damage	4.000.000
i) Aesthetic injury	300.000
j) Sexual injury	1.500.000
k) Repercussion injury for the wife	500.000
l) Repercussion injury for the children 2 x 250.000	500.000
TOTAL AWARD	**41.040.937**

5b. Brain damage with motor deficiency

a) Loss of income to date of trial 2.5 years x 1.800.000	4.500.000
b) Cost of nursing care/medical expenses to date of trial	5.000.000
c) Cost of modifying home equipment	± 1.400.000

7 The amount of the moral injury could be discussed if the victim is not conscious of his/her state.

d) Moral damage until trial (same as for preceding case & note 7)	1.003.250
e) Interest 1.25 years at 7% on 11.903.250	1.041.534
f) Future loss of income (assuming he can still earn 10% of his former income) 90.100 x 14.37262 x 1.800.000	23.283.644
g) Estimated future costs of nursing 200.000 x 12 x 17.823	42.774.200
h) Future moral damage 90 x 50.000	4.500.000
i) Aesthetic injury	1.000.000
j) Sexual injury	1.500.000
k) Repercussion injury for wife	500.000
l) Repercussion injury for the children 2 x 250.00	500.000
TOTAL AWARD	**87.003.628**

6a. Amputation of leg above knee

Assume claimant able to resume his employment 1.5 years after accident

a) Loss of income 1.5 years x 1.800.000	2.700.000
b) Medical expenses and miscellaneous losses to date of trial	1.000.000
c) Moral damage until date of trial	
60 days hospitalisation x 1.250	75.000
487 days without hospitalisation x 1.000	487.000
365 days without hospitalisation x 70% x 800	204.400
	766.400
d) Interest 1.25 years at 7% on 4.466 on items (a), (b), (c)	390.810

e) Future material damage[8] 1.800.000 x 70.100 x 14.37362	18.110.761
f) Future moral damage 40.000 x 70	2.800.000
g) Aesthetic injury	1.000.000
TOTAL AWARD	**26.767.971**

6b. Amputation of leg below knee

a) Loss of income (same as preceding case)	2.700.000
b) Medical expenses and miscellaneous losses to date of trial	900.000
c) Moral damage until trial	
60 days hospitalisation x 1.250	75.000
487 days without hospitalisation x 800	389.600
365 days without hospitalisation at 60% x 800	175.200
	639.800
d) Interest 1.25 years at 7% on 4.239.800 on items (a), (b), (c)	370.982
e) Future moral damage 40.000 x 60	2.400.000
f) Future material damage 1.800.000 x 60% x 14.37362	15.523.509
g) Aesthetic injury	300.000
TOTAL AWARD	**22.834.291**

8 When the victim is able to carry out his/her professional activity and to keep his/her income despite the incapacity, the material damage award is evaluated by application of the incapacity percentage to the incomes which appreciably reduces the amount of the indemnity.

7a. Amputation of arm above elbow

Assume claimant not able to resume employment but takes up light duties 1.5 years after accident but assume he earns 600.000 from his new income

a) Loss of income	
1.5 years x 1.800.000	2.700.000
1 year x 1.200.000	1.200.000
	3.900.000
b) Medical expenses and miscellaneous losses to date of trial	1.000.000
c) Moral damage until trial	
60 days hospitalisation x 1.250	75.000
487 days without hospitalisation x 1.000	487.000
365 days without hospitalisation at 75% x 800	219.000
	781.000
d) Interest 1.25 years at 7% on 5.681.000 on items (a), (b), (c)	497.087
e) Future loss of earnings 14.37362 x 1.200.000	17.248.344
f) Future moral damage 40.000 x 75	3.000.000
g) Aesthetic injury	600.000
TOTAL AWARD	**27.026.431**

7b. Amputation of arm below the elbow

a) Loss of income (same as in preceding case)	3.900.000
b) Medical expenses and miscellaneous losses to date of trial	1.000.000

c) Moral damage until trial	
60 days hospitalisation x 1.250	75.000
487 days without hospitalisation x 800	389.600
	204.400
	669.000
d) Interest 1.25 years at 7% on 5.681.000 on items (a), (b), (c)	497.087
e) Future loss of earnings 14.37362 x 1.200.000	17.248.344
f) Future moral damage 40.000 x 75	2.8000.000
g) Aesthetic injury	500.000
TOTAL AWARD	**26.604.631**

8a. Loss of eyesight – one eye without cosmetic disability

Assume claimant able to resume his employment one year after the accident

a) Loss of income 1 year x 1.800.000	1.800.000
b) Medical expenses and miscellaneous loss to date of trial	150.000
c) Moral damage until trial	
30 days hospitalisation x 1.250	37.500
335 days without hospitalisation x 800	268.000
548 days without hospitalisation at 30% x 800	131.520
	437.020
d) Interest 1.25 years at 7% on 2.387.020 on items (a), (b), (c)	208.864
e) Future loss of earnings 14.37362 x 1.800.000 x 30%	7.761.755
f) Future moral damage 30.000 x 30	900.000

g) Aesthetic injury	200.000
TOTAL AWARD	**11.457.639**

8b. Loss of eyesight – one eye with cosmetic disability

The same as precedent case except 'aesthetic injury'	750.000

8c. Total blindness

a) Loss of income until trial 2.5 years x 1.800.000	4.500.000
b) Cost of care and medical expenses	1.000.000
c) Moral damage 30 days hospitalisation x 1.250 882 days without hospitalisation at 1000	 37.500 882.000
	919.500
d) Interest 1.25 years at 7% on 6.419.500 on items (a), (b), (c)	561.706
e) Future loss of income 14.37362 x 1.800.000	25.872.516
f) Future moral damage (including aesthetic injury) 50.000 x 100	5.000.000
g) Future cost of assistance 365.000 x 17.823	6.505.395
TOTAL AWARD	**44.359.117**

9. Deafness

Assume claimant able to resume employment of 1.5 years after accident at 1.250.000 BEF/year.

a) Loss of income until trial	
1.5 years x 1.800.000	2.700.000
1 year x 1.800.000 – 1.250.000	550.000
	3.250.000
b) Medical expenses and miscellaneous losses too date of trial	400.000
c) Moral Damage	
30 days hospitalisation x 1.250	37.500
517 days without hospitalisation x 800 x 100%	413.600
365 days without hospitalization 8080 x 80%	233.600
	684.700
d) Interest 1.25 years at 7% on 4.334.700 on items (a), (b), (c)	379.286
e) Future loss of income	
14.37362 x 550.000	7.905.491
f) Future moral damage 50.000 x 80	4.000.000
g) Future cost of assistance	
365 x 500 x 17.823	3.252.697
TOTAL AWARD	**19.872.174**

10. Repetitive strain injury – persistent pain and stiffness

Assume claimant unable to resume his employment as surgeon and taking up light duties six months after sustaining injury. Suppose income new job at 600.000

a) Loss of income	
0.5 years x 1.800.000	900.000
2 years x 1.200.000	2.400.000
	3.300.000
b) Medical expenses and miscellaneous losses to date of trial	300.000

c) Moral damage to date of trial (no hospitalisation)	
182 days at 800 x 100%	145.600
730 days at 800 x 35%	204.400
	350.000
d) Interest 1.25 years at 7% on 3.950.000 on items (a), (b), (c)	345.625
e) Future loss of earnings[5] 14.37362 x 1.200.000	17.248.344
f) Future moral damage 30.000 x 35	1.050.000
TOTAL AWARD	**22.593.969**

Table 2. Schedule B

Claimant:	Woman
Age:	20
Status:	Single
Occupation:	Legal Secretary
Income:	BEF. 500.000 net p.a. increasing to 750.000 by age 30 and to BEF 875.000 net by age 40
Trial:	2.5 years after date of accident

1. Instantaneous death

a) Funeral expenses[1]	150.000
b) Moral damage of the father and mother 300.000 each[9]	600.000

9 This amount will in practice fluctuate according to:
(a) how many children they have;
(b) the tragic circumstances;
(c) whether the child was still living with its parents.

c) Material damage to date of trial and thereafter, depending on whether she was the income earner for somebody else; if this is so then damage will be calculated to the moment on which the dependent person becomes self-supporting	pro memoria
d) Interest 2.5 years at 7% on 750.000 on items (a) and (b) + moral damage for brother or sister where applicable: + 100.000 p.p. when living together, or + 60.000 when not living together + moral damage for grandparents: + 100.000 p.p. when living together or + 50.000 when not living together	131.250

2. Burns (A, B, C)

Assume claimant able to resume her employment two years after accident

a) Loss of income 2 years x 500.000	1.000.000
b) Medical expenses and miscellaneous losses to date of trial	1.000.000
c) Moral damage to date of trial 90 days hospitalisation x 1.250	112.500
640 days without hospitalisation x 800	512.000
182.5 days without hospitalisation 800 x 20/100	29.200
	653.700
d) Interest 1.25 years at 7% on 2.653.700	232.198
e) Future moral and material damage (effort to work at 100% with 20% disability) 20 x 50.000	1.000.000
f) Aesthetic injury (for loss of looks)[4]	350.000
TOTAL AWARD	**4.235.898**

3. Quadriplegia

a) Loss of income to date of trial 2.5 years x 500.000	1.250.000
b) Cost of nursing care/medical expenses to date of trial	
One year hospitalisation	3.000.000
One year and a half at home	2.700.000
c) Cost of modifying home and special equipment, say	1.400.000
d) Moral damage until date of trial	
365 days hospitalisation x 1.500	547.500
547 days without hospitalisation x 1.000	547.000
	1.094.500
e) Interest 1.25 years at 7% on items (a), (b), (c) and (d) on 9.444.500	826.393
f) Future loss of income	
22.5 years old at date of trial, assume retirement at 65 years income 500.000 from 22 to 30 income 750.000 from 30 to 40 income 875.000 from 40 to 65 coefficients to capitalise at 4% at 22 years 20.39647 at 30 years 18.60856 at 40 years 15.48250 value of one BEF to be paid after interest at 4% 8 years (22.30) 0.73069 18 years (22.40) 0.49363	
Loss of income	
500.000 x 20.39647	10.198.235
250.000 x 18.60856 x 0.73069	3.399.272
125.000 x 15.48240 x 0.49363	955.322
	14.552.829
g) Future cost of nursing (life expectancy at 22 is 58.62 more years) coefficient to capitalise at 4% annuities = 22.48693	
22.48693 x 1.800.000	40.476.474

h) Future moral damage 100 x 50.000	5.000.000
i) Aesthetic injury	750.000
j) Sexual injury	2.000.000
TOTAL AWARD	**73.050.196**

4. Paraplegia

a) Loss of income to date of trial 2.5 years x 500.000	1.250.000
b) Cost of nursing and medical to date of trial One year hospitalisation One year and a half at home	 3.000.000 1.800.000
c) Cost of modifying home and special equipment	± 1.400.000
d) Moral damage until date of trial 365 days hospitalisation x 1.250 547 days without hospitalisation x 1.000	 456.250 547.000
	1.003.250
e) Interest 1.25 years at 7% on 8.453.250	739.659
f) Future loss of income 70/100 x 14.552.829[10]	10.186.980
g) Estimated future loss of nursing care Medical expenses 75.000 x 12 x 22.48693	20.238.237
h) Future moral damage	3.500.000
i) Aesthetic injury	750.000
j) Sexual injury	2.000.000
TOTAL AWARD	**45.868.126**

10 See the detail of this award for the quadriplegia.

5a. Brain damage

a) Loss of income to date of trial 2.5 years x 500.000	1.250.000
b) Cost of nursing/medical care One year hospitalisation One year and a half at home	 3.000.000 500.000
c) Cost of modifying home and special equipment	± 500.000
d) Moral damage until trial (same as for paraplegia) 457.250 + 547.000	
e) Interest 1.25 years at 7% on 6.253.250	547.159
f) Future loss of income 80% x 14.552.829	11.642.263
g) Estimated future costs of nursing care Medical expenses 180.000 x 22.48693	4.047.647
h) Future moral damage	4.000.000
i) Aesthetic injury	300.000
j) Sexual injury	1.500.000
TOTAL AWARD	**28.290.319**

5b. Brain damage with motor deficiency

a) Loss of income to trial	
2.5 year x 500.000	1.250.000
b) Cost of nursing care/medical expenses to date of trial	5.000.000
c) Cost of modifying home equipment	± 1.400.000
d) Moral damage until trial (same as for preceding case & note 7)	1.003.350
e) Interest 1.25 years at 7% on 8.653.250	757.159

f) Future loss of income (assuming she can still earn 10% of her former income) Total loss of income (see quadriplegia) 10% x 20.39647 x 500.000		 14.552.829 – 1.019.823
		13.533.006
g) Estimated future cost of nursing 200.000 x 12 x 22.48693	53.968.632	
h) Future moral damage 90 x 50.000	4.500.000	
i) Aesthetic injury	1.000.000	
j) Sexual injury	1.500.000	
TOTAL AWARD		**83.912.047**

6a. Amputation of leg above knee

Assume claimant able to result her employment 1.5 years after accident

a) Loss of income 1.5 years x 500.00	 750.000
b) Medical expenses and miscellaneous losses to date of trial	 1.000.000
c) Moral damage until date of trial 60 days hospitalisation x 1.250 487 days without hospitalisation x 1.000 365 days without hospitalisation 70% x 800	 75.000 487.000 204.400
	766.400
d) Future material damage 500.000 x 70/100 x 20.39647	 7.138.764
e) Future moral damage 40.000 x 70	 2.800.000
f) Aesthetic injury	1.000.000
TOTAL AWARD	**13.675.349**

6b. Amputation of leg below knee

a) Loss of income (same as preceding case)	750.000
b) Medical expenses and miscellaneous losses to date of trial	900.000
c) Moral damage until trial	
60 days hospitalisation x 1.250	75.000
487 days without hospitalisation x 800	389.600
365 days without hospitalisation 60% x 800	175.200
	639.800
d) Interest 1.25 years at 7% on 2.289.800 on items (a), (b), (c)	200.357
e) Future moral damage 40.000 x 60	2.400.000
f) Future material damage 500.000 x 60% x 20.39647	6.118.941
g) Aesthetic injury	500.000
TOTAL AWARD	**11.509.098**

7a. Amputation of arm above elbow

Assume claimant not able to resume employment but takes up light duties 1.5 years after accident with income of 200.000 from her new income

a) Loss of income	
1.5 years x 500.000	750.000
1 year x 300.000	300.000
	1.050.000
b) Medical expenses and miscellaneous losses to date of trial	1.000.000
c) Moral damage until trial	
60 days hospitalisation x 1.250	75.000
487 days without hospitalisation x 1.000	487.000
365 days without hospitalisation 75% x 800	219.000

	781.000
d) Interest 1.25 years at 7% on 2.831.000 on items (a), (b), (c)	247.712
e) Future loss of earnings	
Total loss of income (see quadriplegia)	14.552.829
20.39647 x 200.000	– 4.079.294
	10.473.535
f) Future moral damage	
40.00 x 75	3.000.000
g) Aesthetic injury	1.000.000
TOTAL AWARD	**17.552.247**

7b. Amputation of arm below elbow

a) Loss of income (same as preceding case)	1.050.000
b) Medical expenses and miscellaneous losses to date of trial	1.000.000
c) Moral damage until trial	
60 days hospitalisation x 1.250	75.000
487 days without hospitalisation x 800	389.600
365 days without hospitalisation 70% x 800	204.400
	669.000
d) Interest 1.25 years at 7% on 2.719.000 on items (a), (b), (c)	237.912
e) Future loss of earnings (same as preceding case)	10.473.535
f) Future moral damage	
40.000 x 70	2.800.000
g) Aesthetic injury	750.000
TOTAL AWARD	**16.980.447**

8a. Loss of eyesight – one eye without cosmetic disability

Assume claimant able to resume her employment one year after the accident

a) Loss of income 1 year x 500.000	500.000
b) Medical expenses and miscellaneous losses to date of trial	150.000
c) Moral damage	
30 days hospitalisation x 1.250	37.500
335 days without hospitalisation x 800	268.000
548 days without hospitalisation 30% x 800	131.520
	437.020
d) Interest 1.25 years at 7% on 1.087.020 on items (a, (b), (c)	95.114
e) Future loss of earnings 20.39647 x 500.000 x 30%	3.059.470
f) Future moral damage 30.000 x 30	900.00
g) Aesthetic injury	250.000
TOTAL AWARD	**5.391.604**

8b. Loss of eyesight – one eye with cosmetic disability

The same as precedent case except 'aesthetic injury'	1.000.000

8c. Total blindness

a) Loss of income until trial	1.250.000
b) Cost of care and medical expenses	1.000.000
c) Moral damage	
30 days hospitalisation x 1.250	37.500
882 days without hospitalisation 1.000	882.000
	919.500

d) Interest 1.25 years at 7% on 3.169.500 on items (a), (b), (c)	277.331
e) Future loss of income	14.552.829
f) Future moral damage (including aesthetic injury) 365.000 x 22.48693	5.000.000
g) Future cost of assistance 365.000 x 22.48693	8.207.729
TOTAL AWARD	**31.207.389**

9. Deafness

Assume claimant able to resume employment 1.5 years after accident at 200.000

a) Loss of income	
1.5 years x 500.000	750.000
1 year x 500.000 – 200.000	300.000
	1.050.000
b) Medical expenses and miscellaneous losses to date of trial	400.000
c) Moral damage	
30 days hospitalisation x 1.250	37.500
517 days without hospitalisation x 800 x 100%	413.600
365 days without hospitalisation x 800 x 80%	233.600
	684.700
d) Interest 1.25 years at 7% on 2.134.700 on items (a), (b), (c)	186.786
e) Future loss of income	
Total loss of income (see quadriplegia)	14.552.829
20.39647 x 200.000	– 4.079.294
	10.473.535
f) Future moral damage 50.000 x 80	4.000.000

g) Future cost of assistance 365 x 500 x 22.48693	4.103.864
TOTAL AWARD	**20.898.885**

10. Repetitive strain injury – persistent pain and stiffness

Assume claimant unable to resume her employment as legal secretary and taking up light duties six months after sustaining injury. Suppose that she earns 200.000 for her new job

a) Loss of income until trial	
0.5 years x 500.000	250.000
2 years x 300.000	600.000
	850.000
b) Medical expenses and miscellaneous losses to date of trial	300.000
c) Moral damage to date of trial (no hospitalisation)	
182 days at 800 x 100%	145.600
730 days at 800 x 35%	204.400
	350.000
d) Interest 1.25 years at 7% on 1.500.000 on items (a), (b), (c)	131.250
e) Future loss of earnings	
Total loss of income (see quadriplegia)	14.552.829
20.39647 x 200.000	– 4.079.294
	10.473.535
f) Future moral damage 30.000 x 35	1.050.000
TOTAL AWARD	**13.154.785**

DENMARK

Jorgen Rasch

Introduction

The first edition of this report disclosed that the level of compensation in Denmark was amongst the lowest in Europe and has resulted in queries as to why a highly developed country like Denmark accepts such a level of settlement.

To enlighten the reader I will give a brief summary of the background. In socio-political theory there are two main areas of accident compensation law i.e. systems of compensation which primarily cover certain groups of accidents and are financed by others, other than the victims. One type of accident compensation consists of damages paid by the tortfeasor or his liability insurance company, the other type is workers compensation insurance. Other accident compensation schemes are being developed, such as compensation for vaccine damage, criminal injuries and the effects of medical maltreatment.

In Denmark the social security system covers all social contingencies such as accidents, sickness, old age and unemployment and is mainly financed out of general taxation revenue. In addition, private insurance and pension schemes are available for those who wish to secure a supplement to social benefits.

The question arises whether accident compensation should be integrated in the overall social contingencies or should be based on law and may be supplemented with rules of strict "enterprise liability". New Zealand decided to discard accident compensation for the benefit of a general social accidents insurance scheme. Denmark chose a "middle of the road" approach on this issue – as in many other jurisdictions – when introducing the 1989 Liability Compensation Act according to which the following elements of compensation are available.

Social security benefits

Social security benefits are available for temporary loss of income (minor injuries) and loss of future income (serious injuries). Temporary loss of income benefit, in the form of sick pay or sickness benefit, is paid by employers during the first five weeks of incapacity and thereafter by the local authorities. Loss of future income is awarded in cases where the claimant suffers a permanent reduction in his earning capacity of at least 50% and will consist of sick pay or sickness benefits and disablement pension and to a lesser extent, welfare benefits which are subject to a means test. This system favours employees, who will receive nearly full indemnification, whereas self-employed persons, housewives and students will not receive any kind of sickness benefit unless they have a private scheme. They will however, receive some welfare benefits.

Compensation for certain types of injury

1. New legislation provides for compensation in the event that a patient suffers injury following vaccination. The level of compensation follows the 1989 Liability Compensation Act.
2. Legislation also provides for compensation for criminal injuries. In addition to compensation for bodily injuries – which are compensated in accordance with the 1989 Act – the act gives guidelines for compensation in respect of non-economic loss.
3. We have recently seen a new trend in claims in the form of Post Incident Traumatic Disease. The most recent judgment (award) stated the disability at 50% or equivalent to the loss of all fingers on the left hand.

Compensation following catastrophes

The shipping industry in Scandinavia have seen three major casualties with loss of life, bodily injury and Post Incident Traumatic Disease which gave rise to compensation above the normal level. These compensation awards were not the result of decisions by the courts, but were the result of settlement agreements reached between lawyers representing the dependants of the deceased and the injured and the liability insurers of the ship owners.

Workers' compensation

Workers' compensation benefits cover only permanent economic and non-economic losses caused by work-related accidents and for the most part these benefits have relevance only in cases involving serious injuries.

Who will claim damages

A study carried out in April 1974 – March 1975 of injured persons admitted to four Danish hospitals and diagnosed with some traumatic bodily harm according to the WHO classification (a total of some 7,500 persons) revealed that 85% never made a claim for damages. The reason given was mainly that no one was at fault, ignorance of liability and a general reluctance to sue for damages. Only about 3% of the injured persons sought advice from a qualified lawyer.

Amount of damages

Of the injured persons who recovered damages, 30% were compensated for non-economic loss only. For short-term incapacity (less than two months) the share was 43%. A total of 60% recovered less than DKK 10,000 and 75% less than DKK 25,000 (£808-£2,020). The low rate of compensation for injured persons with large economic losses is not difficult to explain. These losses are mostly permanent losses of income which are recovered under both the social security system and tort law.

Settling of claims

The study showed that more than 70% of the claims were settled out of court with a tendency that minor injuries were settled to a greater extent than serious injuries. There does no seem to be a nuisance value settlement level.

Type of disputes

The most frequent cause of dispute is the issue of contributory negligence and only rarely is the actual assessment of damage the sole cause of dispute. Of compensation claims, 47% of the amounts of damages were not dealt with by the courts, especially claims for damages for non-economic losses. It seems that most injured persons accept the amounts of damages offered by the tortfeasor's liability insurance company.

Payment of compensation

The study further shows that in cases settled out of court, almost 40% of the damages were paid within six months after the accident occurred whereas settlement in court cases within the same period amounted to less than 20%. Compensation of more than DKK 50,000 (£4,040) was rarely paid within one year after the accident occurred and most often later than two years after the accident occurred.

Who paid the damages

Only 3% of the total damages were paid by the tortfeasor alone; the rest was paid by liability insurers.

Voluntary first party benefit

Voluntary first party benefit which includes benefits from accident insurance or other kinds of insurance taken out by the injured person, benefits from private pensions schemes and other kinds of private assistance (family members, trade unions, charitable institutions) were received by about 10% of the injured persons in the study mentioned above.

Total compensation for personal injury

The study revealed that social security benefits amounted to 61% of the total compensation award; workers' compensation benefits 16%, damages 10% and voluntary benefits 13%. As can be seen from these figures, the system of tort law is the least important system for receiving compensation.

The Liability Compensation Act 1989

The Act has very detailed provisions for compensation of non-economic loss and compensation for disability. The extent of any disability is established by a government body *(Arbejdsskadestyrelsen)*, which also establishes the degree of disability for the purpose of workers' compensation. According to the Act the party paying social benefits, including [even if] the employer, has no recourse against the tortfeasor.

There is provision for compensation to be reduced or even cease in the event that it is unreasonably burdensome for the tortfeasor.

Summary

As can be seen from the study the various social benefits compensate the injured person to a large extent. Only a limited number of injured persons will claim damages and only a minority of this number will seek qualified legal assistance. Most claims are settled out of court and, if the matter is taken to court, the amount of compensation is rarely at issue.

This state of affairs is no doubt the result of the private economy in a social welfare state where the high level of taxation (68% income tax for income above about DKK 250,000, (£20,200) 25% VAT and 200% tax on cars) is compensated by a social security system which will enable any injured person to continue living in nearly the same lifestyle as before the accident occurred.

Note

These figures do not include any payment for medical expenses, as in Denmark all such expenses are paid by the National Health Service. In my opinion, Danish courts would be reluctant to award medical expenses in cases where an injured person has chosen a private hospital rather than a hospital in the state system.

Table 1

Total paralysis of plexus brachialis – right arm	60%
Total paralysis of plexus brachialis – left arm	65%
Total paralysis of nervus femuarlis – legs	20%
Ischiadiscus parese	up to 50%

In my summary I have used the same level of disablement/injury for permanent injury compensation and damages. Case studies show that the percentage of damages (loss of future income) is a little less (10%) than the permanent injury compensation.

The level of compensation shown in the following schedules are based on the annual regulation of the 1989 Act for the year 2001, and an increase in the annual incomes of 10%.

Table 2. Schedule A

Claimant:	Man
Age:	40
Status:	Married – 2 dependent children aged 5 and 7
Occupation:	Doctor
Annual Income:	DKK 400,000 (above average) Gross (DKK265,000 net)

1. Instant Death	DKK
Funeral expenses	max 21,000
Dependent wife and children have separate claims	
Wife: 30% of total disablement compensation	
(annual income x 6)	720,000
Child 5 years; 13 years at 8,213 = 100%	213,538
Child 7 years: 11 years at 8,213 = 100%	180,686
Total award	**1,135,224**
TOTAL AWARD YEAR 2000	**1,370,000**

2. Burns (A, B, C)

No permanent disablement	
Severe scars	
Pain and suffering	
DKK 140 per day confined to bed	
DKK 70 per day not confined to bed	
Max (at court's discretion over DKK 22,000 approx)	38,000
Loss of income 2 x 400,000	800,000
Less daily benefits (no recourse)	270,000
	530,000
Permanent injury compensation (estimated) Medical expenses will be paid by the NHS with no recourse	30,000
Total award	**598,000**
TOTAL AWARD YEAR 2000	**649,000**

3-5b. Brain damage

Paraplegia/paralysis, 50% disablement	
Pain and suffering	38,000
Permanent injury compensation	120,000
Damages, annual income 6 x 50%	1,200,000
Net loss of income until state of disablement established, say 1 year	265,000
Total award	**1,623,000**
TOTAL AWARD YEAR 2000	**1,836,000**

Quadriplegia/paralysis – 120% disablement

Pain and suffering	38,000
Permanent injury compensation	260,000
Damages, annual income 6 x 120%	2,880,000
Net loss of income 1 year	265,000
Total award	**3,444,3000**
TOTAL AWARD YEAR 2000	**3,924,500**

6a-6b. Amputation of leg and 9. Deafness

65% disablement/injury	
Pain and suffering	38,000
Permanent injury compensation	150,000
Damages, annual income 6 x 65%	1,560,000
Net loss of income 1 year	265,000
Total award	**2,013,000**
TOTAL AWARD YEAR 2000	**2,283,600**

7a.-7b. Amputation of right arm

70% disablement/injury	
Pain and suffering	38,000
Permanent injury compensation	150,000
Damages, annual income 6 x 70%	1,680,000
Net loss of income 1 year	265,000
Total award	**2,133,000**

TOTAL AWARD YEAR 2000	**2,432,000**

8a.-8b. Loss of eyesight – one eye

20% disablement/injury	
Pain and suffering	38,000
Permanent injury compensation	45,000
Damages, annual income 6 x 20%	480,000
Net loss of income 6 months	132,200
Total award	**695,000**
TOTAL AWARD YEAR 2000	**791,000**

8c. Total blindness

100% disablement/injury	
Maximum compensation	
Pain and suffering	38,000
Maximum permanent injury compensation	278,500
Max damages, 300,000 x 6 x 100%	2,400,000
Net loss of income 2.5 years	662,500
Total award	**3,339,000**
TOTAL AWARD YEAR 2000	**3,270,500**

9. Deafness

See 6a.-6b. above

TOTAL AWARD YEAR 2000	**2,283,600**

Note

Compensation and damages will be awarded according to the rates applicable at the date of the judgment. Minimum and maximum rates will be adjusted yearly based on the consumer price index. Interest will be payable at the rate of 13% per year from the time of the accident until the date of payment (part payment is advisable).

Recoverable court costs about 1% of the amount claimed.

Recoverable attorneys fees are set by the courts according to rates approved by the Danish Bar Association, e.g. judgment DKK 1,000,000 – fee 52,000; judgment DKK 3,000,000 – fee 125,000.

Table 3. Schedule B

Claimant:	Woman
Age:	20
Status	Single – no dependants
Occupation :	Legal Secretary
Annual income :	:DKK 240,000 gross (DKK 144,000 net)

1. Instant death

Funeral expenses	max 21,000
TOTAL AWARD YEAR 2000	**26,000**

No further compensation

Note

If the deceased was living with someone and had an established relationship (common household and economy), compensation may be awarded if the relationship lasted for more than 2 years. Case law has accepted a relationship after 3 years but not after 1.5 years. Also homosexual partnerships are accepted even if the relationship has not been registered (as a marriage).

Other injuries are compensated as in Schedule A save for loss of income, i.e. disablement is established by a government body, the Social Security Benefits Directorate (*Arbejdsskadestyrelsen*).

Some examples of levels used:

Table 4

Loss of second finger (no permanent injury compensation)	10%
Amputation of arm above elbow	60-65%
Amputation of arm below elbow	55-60%
Loss of lower leg (good functioning of prosthesis)	30%
Loss of lower leg (bad functioning of prosthesis)	35-40%
DAC calculate on basis of above:)	

Table 5

2. Burns (A, B, C)		
Pain and suffering		38,000
Loss of income		
2 x 240,000	480,000	
Less daily benefits 40% (no recourse)	192,000	
		288,000
Permanent injury compensation		351,000
TOTAL AWARD YEAR 2000		**391,000**

3. and 5. Quadriplegia and brain damage

120% disablement

Pain and suffering	38,000
Permanent injury compensation	278,500
Damages annual income 6 x 120%	1,728,000
Loss of income 1 year 240,000 less 40%	144,000
Total award	**2,188,500**
TOTAL AWARD YEAR 2000	**2,515,700**

4. Paraplegia

50% disablement

Pain and suffering	38,000
Permanent injury compensation	278,500
Damages annual income 6 x 50%	720,00
Loss of income 1 year 240,000 less 40%	144,000
Total award	**1,180,500**
TOTAL AWARD YEAR 2000	**1,200,000**

3.-5b. Brain damage

Paraplegia/paralysis, 50% disablement

Pain and suffering	38,000
Permanent injury compensation	120,000
Damages annual income 6 x 50%	720,400

Loss of income until state of disablement established, say 1 year	144,000
Total award	**1,022,000**
TOTAL AWARD YEAR 2000	**1,200,400**

Quadriplegia/paralysis, 120% disablement

Pain and suffering	38,000
Permanent injury compensation	278,00
Damages annual income 6 x 120%	1,728,000
Net loss of income 1 year	144,000
Total award	**2,118,500**
TOTAL AWARD YEAR 2000	**2,515,700**

6a – 6b. Amputation of leg and 9. Deafness

65% disablement/injury

Pain and suffering	38,000
Permanent injury compensation	150,000
Damages annual income 6 x 65%	93,600
Net loss of income, 1 year	144,000
Total award	**1,268,000**
TOTAL AWARD YEAR 2000	**1,455,600**

7a – 7b. Amputation of right arm

70% disablement/injury

Pain and suffering	38,000
Permanent injury compensation	155,000
Damages annual income 6 x 70%	1,008,000
Net loss of income, 1 year	144,000
Total award	**1,345,000**
TOTAL AWARD YEAR 2000	**1,552,000**

8a – 8b. Loss of eyesight – one eye

20% disablement/injury

Pain and suffering	38,000
Permanent injury compensation	45,000
Damages annual income 6 x 20%	288,000
Net loss of income, 6 months	72,000
Total award	**433,000**
TOTAL AWARD YEAR 2000	**508,800**

8c. Loss of eyesight – Total blindness

100% disablement/injury

Maximum compensation	38,000
Pain and suffering	278,500
Max. permanent injury compensation	1,440,000

Max. damages, 200,000 x 6 x 100%	360,000
2.5 years net loss of income	360,000
Total award	**2,116,500**
TOTAL AWARD YEAR 2000	**2,112,500**

9. Deafness

See 6a. - 6b. above

TOTAL AWARD YEAR 2001	**1,455,600**

ENGLAND AND WALES

Malcolm Henké

Calculation of damages

1. How do lawyers calculate the likely quantum of damages in personal injury cases?

The lawyer needs in particular the following information and evidence:

a) The claimant's date of birth, sex and marital status;

b) The claimant's pre accident state of health, activities, interests and responsibilities;

c) Medical reports detailing the cause, progress and prognosis of the injury;

d) Details of the claimant's employment and of his pre accident gross and net earnings;

e) Details of the gross and net earnings lost by the claimant to the date of calculation;

f) The security of the claimant's pre-accident employment (if any);

g) The likely future earnings and earning capacity of the claimant;

h) The cost of past and the likely cost of future medical treatment, nursing care and other assistance or special equipment made reasonably necessary by the injury;

i) Benefits and other monies paid to the claimant by the State or by others as a consequence of the injuries;

j) The defendant's prospects of obtaining some reduction in the claim because the claimant was partly responsible for his own injury.

With this information and evidence, the lawyer then calculates the likely value of the award under each of the following heads of damage:

a) Pain, suffering and loss of amenity (general damages) – past and future non pecuniary loss;

b) Special Damage (pecuniary loss to the date of calculation) including loss of earnings, medical expenses, etc;

c) Interest to the date of calculation;

d) Loss of future earnings;

e) cost of future care, treatment, equipment and associated expense.

The Calculation

The calculations have an air of unreality about them, so of necessity we have to make certain assumptions. Ordinarily each case will be calculated on its actual pecuniary elements.

Multipliers

In order to calculate future loss (whether loss of earnings or the cost of services and/or equipment) the Courts adopt what is traditionally known as the multiplier/ multiplicand approach. The multiplicand is the annual figure which represents the claimant's loss. That figure is then multiplied by the number of years purchase (the multiplier) necessary to allow the claimant's multiplicand requirement to be achieved by a combination of investment income and asset disposal during the life time of the accrued loss. The ultimate aim is to ensure that the fund awarded provides an annual income equal to that which would have been achieved had the loss not occurred.

Traditionally, multipliers were based on a loose interpretation of actuarial tables published by the Government's Actuary Department. Following the House of Lords decision in *Wells v Wells* (and others) (1998) the Courts are now encouraged to rely upon published actuarial tables for personal injury and fatal accident act cases (the so called Ogden Tables) which set out in tabular form appropriate multipliers for lost earnings, life time expenses, pension losses and payments for terms certain. Following the decision in Wells there are now no maximum multipliers applied. The multipliers vary as a result of the discount rate adopted in calculation thereof, which rate reflects investment return on primarily index linked Government stock. In reaching their decision in Wells their Lordships brought to an end the premise that a claimant should adopt the policy of a prudent investor. Those who had suffered injury resulting in long term loss were deemed "special case" and thus were entitled to adopt a more conservative investment policy leading by implication to a lower discount rate and to higher multipliers. The arguments in relation to the multiplicand multiplier approach continue to be debated.

The multiplicand/multiplier approach varies in respect of personal injury claims and Fatal Accidents Act actions. In the former, the multiplier is calculated from the date of settlement or trial, in respect of the latter the multiplier is calculated from the date of death.

Smith and Manchester/Loss of Congenial Employment

No allowance is made in the attached examples for the above heads of damage. Such awards vary wildly and are dependent upon the nature of the claimant's employment, the area in which he resides, his age and a variety of other factors. It is extremely aware for either award to exceed twice the annual salary of the claimant.

Assessing damages for pain and suffering

Assessing damages for pain and suffering is a notoriously difficult exercise, and has resulted in inconsistencies in the amounts awarded. We have seen a trend towards harmonisation in recent years. The Judicial Studies Board now publish "Guidelines for the Assessment of General Damages in Personal Injury Cases" which is the first point of reference for personal injury practitioners and for the judiciary. This publication has been endorsed by two Masters of the Rolls and is now in its fourth edition. The guidelines are submitted free to all judges involved in personal injury litigation.

Although these guidelines are the definitive reference point damages awarded for pain, suffering and loss of amenity are expected to increase substantially following the recommendations of the Law Commission in report No 257 . In that consultation document the Law Commission debated the current level of awards provided in personal injury actions and decided that such damages should be increased by between 50% and 100% during the course of the next three years. The Law Commission went so far as to indicate that such increased should be volunteered by the Courts but if that progression failed, then appropriate law should be passed. This increase in general damages has long been expected, the profession generally accepting that such awards have fallen below the general public expectation of fair compensation.

English law denies a claim for damages for pain, suffering and loss of amenity where death occurs instantaneously.

Damages for bereavement (payable to surviving spouses or parents of children under the age of 18) are fixed by statute at GBP 7,500.

Interest

Interest on bereavement damages, funeral expenses and expended loss accrues at the full short term investment account rate currently 7%. Interest on accruing special damage (lost earnings) accrues at half short term investment account rate currently 3.5%.

Interest on general damages accrues at 2% per annum. It is generally assumed that damages of pain, suffering and loss of amenity are index linked by way of increasing awards and thus entitlement to interest is a minimal one.

Offset of Welfare Benefits

In order to avoid the pitfall of double recovery, the law has traditionally allowed for the offsetting of welfare benefits paid to a claimant. Historically Section 2 of the Law Reform (Personal Injuries) Act 1948 provided for a 50% offset of most (but not all) welfare benefits. This provision was replaced by Section 22 of the Social Security Act 1989, as amended, which provides for the deduction of welfare benefits in full from payments of compensation from the 3 September 1990 to injury occurring on or after the 1 January 1999. The benefits are deducted from compensation paid by the defendant and reimbursed to the Department of Social Security.

The Act was further amended by the introduction of the Social Security (recovery of benefits) Act 1997 which removed the exemption previously allowed for small claims (of below £2,500) and further introduced ring fencing to ensure the benefits were deducted only on a like for like basis for those heads of damage claimed within the action. The rationale behind the amendment to the Act was to prevent the claimant suffering a generalised deduction for heads of damage for which he pursued no claim.

The Act provides a list of those benefits which are deductible . In short the Act operates thus :

a) Compensation Payments
   (i) The defendant deducts an amount equivalent to the relevant benefit paid or to be paid to the claimant over the relevant period on a like for like basis;

(ii) The relevant period begins on the day after the accident or injury occurs and ends five years later on or when the final compensation payment is made whichever is the earlier;

(iii) The defendant pays the net compensation to the claimant, together with a Certificate of Refundable Benefit and within 14 days pays to the Department of Social Security a sum equivalent to that deducted.

Payments made under the Fatal Accidents Act are excluded from the scheme.

Bereavement Damages

Bereavement damages included are £7,500 as of 2000 increased since first edition. As of 1 April 2002 increased to £10,000 but only £7,580 included as comparison in year 2000.

Table 1. Schedule A

Claimant :	Man
Age :	40
Status :	Married (Children 5 and 7
Occupation :	Doctor
Income :	GBP 36,000 pa net
Trial :	2.5 years post accident

1. Instant death		GBP
a) (i) Statutory bereavement damages		7,500
(ii) Funeral expenses		1,250
b) Dependency claim 75% of 36,000 pa net	27,000	
c) Value of lost services (pa) (DIY/gardening etc)	3,000	
d) Loss to date of trial		75,000
e) Interest on (a) 7% x 2.5 years		1,531
Interest on (b) and (c) 3.5% x 2.5 years		5,250
f) Future dependency 14.5 years @ 30,000 pa		435,000
TOTAL AWARD		**525,531**

2. Burns		
General Damages		55,000
Assume return to work after 2 years		
a) Loss of earnings 2 x 36,000	72,000	
Less deductible benefits, say	15,000	
		57,000

b) Miscellaneous losses, say		5,000
c) Interest on general damages 2% x 1.5 years		1,650
d) Interest on (a) 3.5% x 2.5 years		4,987
e) Interest on (b) 7% x 2.5 years		875
TOTAL AWARD		**124,512**

2. Burns (B)

General Damages		45,000
Assume return to work after 2 years		
a) Loss of earnings 2 x 36,000	72,000	
Less deductible benefits, say	15,000	
		57,000
b) Miscellaneous losses, say		5,000
c) Interest on general damages 2% x 1.5 years		1,350
d) Interest on (a) 3.5% x 2.5 years		4,987
e) Interest on (b) 7% x 2.5 years		875
TOTAL AWARD		**114,212**

2. Burns (C)

	General Damages		35,000
	Assume return to work after 2 years		
a)	Loss of earnings 2 x 36,000	72,000	
	Less deductible benefits, say	15,000	
			57,000
b)	Miscellaneous losses, say		5,000
c)	Interest on general damages 2% x 1.5 years		1,050
d)	Interest on (a) 3.5% x 2.5 years		4,987
e)	Interest on (b) 7% x 2.5 years		875
	TOTAL AWARD		**103,912**

3. Quadriplegia

	General damages		150,000
a)	Loss of earnings to trial 2.5 x 36,000pa	90,000	
	Less deductible benefits, say	25,000	
			65,000
b)	Care to date 2 x 50,000pa		100,000
c)	Hospital charges		10,000
d)	Lost services (DIY etc) 2.5 x 2,250		5,625
e)	Housing/aids equipment		25,000

f)	Miscellaneous expenses to date 2 x 25,000		62,500
g)	Interest on general damages 2% x 1.5 years		4,500
h)	Interest on (a) 3.5% x 2.5		5,687
i)	Interest on (b) to (f) 7% x 2.5		35,546
j)	Future loss of earnings (42.5 at trial – retirement at age 65) 16 x 36,000		576,000
k)	Future care 20.5 x 50,000		1,025,000
l)	Lost services 20.5 x 2,250		46,125
m)	Holiday costs 20.5 x 1,500		30,750
n)	Transport 20.5 x 2,500		51,250
o)	Housing adaptation		100,000
p)	Aids and equipment		75,000
q)	Investment fees		50,000
	TOTAL AWARD		**2,417,983**

4. Paraplegia

	General damages		110,000
a)	Loss of earnings to trial 2.5 x 36,000pa	90,000	
	Less deductible benefits, say	25,000	

Less sedentary income 1 year post accident @ 5,000pa	7,500	
		57,500
b) Care to date 2 x 10,000pa		20,000
c) Hospital charges		10,000
d) Lost services 2.5 x 2,250		5,625
e) Housing/aids equipment		50,000
f) Miscellaneous expenses to date		25,000
g) Interest on general damages 2% x 1.5 years		3,300
h) Interest on (a) 3.5% x 2.5		5,031
i) Interest on (c) to (f) 7% x 2.5		15,859
j) Future loss of earnings 16 x 31,000		496,000
k) Future care 15 x 5,000 5.5 x 25,000		 75,000 137,500
l) Holiday costs 20.5 x 1,500		30,750
m) Transport 20.5 x 1,500		30,750
n) Housing adaptations		100,000
o) Aids and equipment		50,000
p) Investment fees		25,000
TOTAL AWARD		**1,247,315**

5. Brain Damage

Moderate brain damage

	General damages		100,000
a)	Loss of earnings to trial 2.5 x 36,000pa	90,000	
	Less deductible benefits, say	25,000	
			65,000
b)	Care to date 2 x 10,000pa		25,000
c)	Hospital charges		10,000
d)	Lost services (DIY etc) 2.5 x 2,250		5,625
e)	Aids/equipment/miscellaneous		25,000
f)	Interest on general damages 2% x 1.5 years		3,000
g)	Interest on (a) 3.5% x 2.5		5,687
h)	Interest on (b) to (e) 7% x 2.5		11,484
i)	Future loss of earnings 16 x 36,000		576,000
j)	Future care 20.5 x 5,000		102,500
k)	Lost services 20.5 x 2,250		46,125
l)	Holiday costs 20.5 x 1,500		30,750
m)	Transport 20.5 x 2,500		51,250
n)	Aids and equipment		50,000
p)	Investment fees		25,000
	TOTAL AWARD		**1,132,421**

5. Moderately severe brain damage (B)

	General damages		125,000
a)	Loss of earnings to trial 2.5 x 36,000pa	90,000	

Less deductible benefits, say	25,000	
		65,000
b) Care to date 2 x 40,000pa		80,000
c) Hospital charges		10,000
d) Lost services (DIY etc) 2.5 x 2,250		5,625
e) Aids and equipment		25,000
f) Interest on general damages 2% x 1.5 years		3,750
g) Interest on (a) 3.5% x 2.5		5,687
h) Interest on (b) to (e) 7% x 2.5		21,109
i) Future loss of earnings 16 x 36,000		576,000
j) Future care 20.5 x 40,000		820,000
k) Lost services 20.5 x 2,250		46,125
l) Holiday costs 20.5 x 1,500		30,750
m) Transport 20.5 x 2,500		51,250
n) Aids and equipment		25,000
p) Investment fees		45,000
TOTAL AWARD		**1,935,296**

6. Amputation of leg above knee (A)

	General damages	55,000	
	Assume return to work after 1.5 years		
a)	Loss of earnings 1.5 x 36,000	54,000	
	Less deductible benefits, say	15,000	
			39,000
b)	Miscellaneous losses		1,500
c)	Lost services 2.5 x 2,250		5,625
d)	Interest on general damages 2% x 1.5		1,650
e)	Interest on (a) 3.5% x 2.5		3,412
f)	Interest on (b) and (c) 7% x 2.5 years		1,246
g)	Lost services 20.5 x 2,250		45,000
h)	Transport		10,000
i)	Prosthetics		100,000
	TOTAL AWARD		**287,433**

6. Amputation of leg below knee (B)

	General damages		45,000
	Assume return to work after 1.5 years		
a)	Loss of earnings 1.5 x 36,000	54,000	
	Less deductible benefits, say	15,000	
			39,000

b) Miscellaneous losses		1,500
c) Lost services 2.5 x 2,250		5,625
d) Interest on general damages 2% x 1.5		1,350
e) Interest on (a) 3.5% x 2.5		3,412
f) Interest on (b) and (c) 7% x 2.5 years		1,246
g) Lost services 20.5 x 2,250		45,000
h) Transport		10,000
i) Prosthetics		75,000
TOTAL AWARD		**227,133**

7. Amputation of arm above elbow (A)

General damages	55,000	
Light duties after 1.5 years		
a) Loss of earnings 1.5 x 36,000 + 1 year partial loss	 54,000 26,000	
	80,000	
Less deductible benefits, say	10,000	
		70,000
b) Miscellaneous losses		1,500
c) Lost services 2.5 x 2,250		5,625
d) Interest on general damages 2% x 1.5		1,650

e) Interest on (a) 3.5% x 2.5		6,125
f) Interest on (b) and (c) 7% x 2.5 years		1,246
g) Future loss of earnings 16 x 26,000		416,000
h) Lost services 20.5 x 2,250		45,000
i) Prosthetics		100,000
j) Aids and equipment		15,000
k) Transport		10,000
TOTAL AWARD		**727,146**

7. Amputation of arm below elbow (B)

General damages		45,000
Light duties after 1.5 years		
a) Loss of earnings 1.5 x 36,000	54,000	
+ 1 year partial loss	26,000	
	80,000	
Less deductible benefits, say	10,000	
		70,000
b) Miscellaneous losses		1,500
c) Lost services 2.5 x 2,250		5,625
d) Interest on general damages 2% x 1.5		1,350
e) Interest on (a) 3.5% x 2.5		6,125

f)	Interest on (b) and (c) 7% x 2.5 years		1,246
g)	Future loss of earnings 16 x 26,000		416,000
h)	Lost services 20.5 x 2,250		45,000
i)	Prosthetics		75,000
j)	Aids and equipment		10,000
k)	Transport		10,000
	TOTAL AWARD		**686,846**

8. Loss of eyesight – one eye without cosmetic disability (A)

	General damages		25,000
	Return to work after 1 year		
a)	Loss of earnings 1.5 x 36,000	36,000	
	Less deductible benefits, say	10,000	
			26,000
b)	Miscellaneous losses		1,500
c)	Interest on general damages 2% x 1.5		750
d)	Interest on (a) 3.5% x 2.5		2,275
e)	Interest on (b) 7% x 2.5 years		262
	TOTAL AWARD		**55,787**

8. Loss of eye sight – one eye with cosmetic disability (B)

	General damages		30,000
	Return to work after 1 year		
a)	Loss of earnings 1 x 36,000	36,000	
	Less deductible benefits, say	10,000	
			26,000
b)	Miscellaneous losses		1,500
c)	Interest on general damages 2% x 1.5		900
d)	Interest on (a) 3.5% x 2.5		2,275
e)	Interest on (b) 7% x 2.5 years		262
	TOTAL AWARD		**60,937**

8. Loss of eyesight – total blindness (C)

	General damages		105,000
	Unable to return to work		
a)	Loss of earnings to trial 2.5 x 36,000	90,000	
	Less deductible benefits, say	25,000	
			65,000
b)	Care and expenses		25,000
c)	Lost services 2.5 x 5,000		12,500
d)	Interest on general damages 2% x 1.5		3,150

e) Interest on (a) 3.5% x 2.5		5,687
f) Interest on (b) and (c) 7% x 2.5 years		6,562
g) Future loss of earnings 16 x 36,000		576,000
h) Lost services 20 x 5,000		100,000
i) Transport 20 x 5,000		100,000
j) Aids and equipment		75,000
TOTAL AWARD		**1,033,899**

9. Deafness

General damages		47,500
Return to light work		
a) Loss of earnings 1.5 x 36,000	54,000	
1 year partial loss	11,000	
	65,000	
Less deductible benefits, say	25,000	
		40,000
b) Miscellaneous losses		1,500
c) Interest on general damages 2% x 1.5		1,425
d) Interest on (a) 3.5% x 2.5		3,500
e) Interest on (b) 7% x 2.5 years		262

f)	Future loss of earnings 16 x 11,000		176,000
	TOTAL AWARD		**270,187**

10. Repetitive strain injury

	General damages		11,750
	Assume return to light duties	30,000	
a)	Loss of earnings 0.5 x 36,000 2 x partial loss	 18,000 12,000	
	Less deductible benefits, say	2,500	
			27,500
b)	Miscellaneous losses		500
c)	Lost services 2.5 x 1,500		3,750
d)	Interest on general damages 2% x 1.5		352
e)	Interest on (a) 3.5% x 2.5		2,406
f)	Interest on (b) and (c) 7% x 2.5 years		297
g)	Future loss of earnings 16 x 6,000		96,000
h)	Lost services 20 x 1,500		30,000
	TOTAL AWARD		**172,555**

Schedule B

Claimant :	Woman
Age :	20
Status :	Single
Occupation :	Legal Secretary
Income :	£10,000 pa net
Trial :	2.5 years post accident

1. Instant death

a) Funeral expenses		1,250
b) Interest 7% x 2.5		218.75
TOTAL AWARD		**1,468.75**

NB: No statutory bereavement damages payable

No dependency claim

2. Burns (A)

General Damages		55,000
Return to work 2 years post accident		
a) Loss of earnings 2 x 10,000	20,000	
Less deductible benefits, say	10,000	
		10,000
b) Miscellaneous losses, say		1,500
c) Interest on general damages 2% x 1.5 years		1,650
d) Interest on (a) 3.5% x 2.5 years		875

e) Interest on (b) 7% x 2.5 years		262
TOTAL AWARD		**69,287**

2. Burns (B)

General Damages		45,000
Return to work 2 years post accident		
a) Loss of earnings 2 x 10,000	20,000	
Less deductible benefits, say	10,000	
		10,000
b) Miscellaneous losses, say		1,500
c) Interest on general damages 2% x 1.5 years		1,350
d) Interest on (a) 3.5% x 2.5 years		875
e) Interest on (b) 7% x 2.5 years		262
TOTAL AWARD		**59,987**

2. Burns (C)

General Damages		35,000
Return to work 2 years post accident		
a) Loss of earnings 2 x 10,000	20,000	
Less deductible benefits, say	10,000	
		10,000
b) Miscellaneous losses, say		1,500

c) Interest on general damages 2% x 1.5 years		1,050
d) Interest on (a) 3.5% x 2.5 years		875
e) Interest on (b) 7% x 2.5 years		262
TOTAL AWARD		**48,687**

3. Quadriplegia

General damages		150,000
a) Loss of earnings to trial 2.5 x 36,000pa	25,000	
Less deductible benefits, say	15,000	
		10,000
b) Care to date 2 x 50,000pa		100,000
c) Hospital charges		10,000
d) Housing/aids/equipment		25,000
e) Miscellaneous expenses to date 2 x 25,000		62,500
f) Interest on general damages 2% x 1.5 years		4,500
g) Interest on (a) 3.5% x 2.5		875
h) Interest on (b) to (e) 7% x 2.5		34,562
i) Future loss of earnings (allowing for chance of childbirth) 20 x 10,000		200,000
j) Future care 27.5 x 50,000		1,375,000

k) Holidays 27.5 x 1,500		41,250
l) Transport 27.5 x 2,500		68,750
m) Housing adaptation		100,000
n) Aids and equipment		75,000
o) Investment fees		50,000
TOTAL AWARD		**2,307,437**

4. Paraplegia

General damages		110,000
a) Loss of earnings to trial 2.5 x 10,000pa	25,000	
Less deductible benefits on a like for like basis, say	10,000	
Less sedentary income 1 year post accident @ 5,000pa	7,500	
		7,500
b) Care to date 2 x 20,000pa		50,000
c) Statutory hospital charges		10,000
d) Aids and equipment		25,000
e) Miscellaneous expenses to date 2.5 x 10,000		25,000
f) Interest on general damages 1.5 x 2% x 110,000		3,300
g) Interest on (a) 2.5% x 3.5 x 7,500		656
h) Interest on (b) to (e) 2.5 x 7% x 110,000		19,250

i) Future loss of earnings 20 x 10,000		200,000
j) Future care 20 x 25,000 7 x 45,000		500,000 350,000
k) Holiday costs 27 x 1,500		40,500
l) Transport 27 x 1,500		40,500
m) Housing costs adaptations		100,000
n) Aids and equipment		50,000
o) Investment fees		25,000
TOTAL AWARD		**1,556,706**

5. Brain Damage (A)

Moderate brain damage		
General damages		100,000
a) Loss of earnings to trial 2.5 x 10,000pa	25,000	
Less deductible benefits, say	15,000	
		10,000
b) Care to date 2 x 20,000pa		50,000
c) Hospital charges		10,000
d) Aids and equipment		10,000
e) Interest on general damages 2% x 1.5 years		3,000
f) Interest on (a) 3.5% x 2.5		875
g) Interest on (b – e) 7% x 2.5		12,250

h) Future loss of earnings 20 x 10,000		200,000
i) Future care 27 years x 7,500		202,500
j) Holiday costs 27 x 1,500		40,500
k) Transport 27 x 2,500		67,500
l) Aids and equipment		50,000
m) Investment fees		25,000
TOTAL AWARD		**781,625**

5. Brain Damage (B)

Moderately severe		
General damages		135,000
a) Loss of earnings to trial 2.5 x 10,000pa	25,000	
Less deductible benefits, say	15,000	
		10,000
b) Care to date 2 x 40,000pa		80,000
c) Hospital charges		10,000
d) Aids and equipment		10,000
e) Interest on general damages 2% x 1.5 years		4,050
f) Interest on (a) 3.5% x 2.5		875
g) Interest on (b – d) 7% x 2.5		17,500
h) Future loss of earnings 20 x 10,000		200,000

i) Future care 27 years x 50,000		1,350,000
j) Holiday costs 27 x 1,500		40,500
k) Transport 27 x 2,500		67,500
l) Aids and equipment		50,000
m) Investment fees		45,000
TOTAL AWARD		**2,020,425**

6. Amputation of leg above knee (A)

General damages		55,000
a) Loss of earnings to trial 2.5 x 10,000	15,000	
Less deductible benefits, say	10,000	
		5,000
b) Miscellaneous losses		1,500
c) Interest on general damages 2% x 1.5 years		1,650
d) Interest on (a) 3.5% x 2.5		437
e) Interest on (b) 7% x 2.5		262
f) Transport		10,000
g) Prosthetics		100,000
h) Care 27 x 2,500		67,500
i) Aids and equipment		25,000
TOTAL AWARD		**266,349**

6. Amputation of leg below knee (B)

General damages		45,000
Assume return to work after 1.5 years		
a) Loss of earnings to trial 1.5 x 10,000	15,000	
Less deductible benefits, say	10,000	
		5,000
b) Miscellaneous losses		1,500
c) Interest on general damages 2% x 1.5 years		1,350
d) Interest on (a) 3.5% x 2.5		437
e) Interest on (b) 7% x 2.5		262
f) Household care 27 x 1,500		40,500
g) Prosthetics		75,000
TOTAL AWARD		**169,049**

7. Amputation of arm above elbow (A)

Moderate brain damage		
General damages		55,000
a) Loss of earnings to trial 2.5 x 10,000pa	25,000	
Less partial earnings	4,000	
	21,000	
Less deductible benefits, say	10,000	
		11,000
b) Miscellaneous losses		1,500

c)	Care and assistance to date 2.5 x 1,500		3,750
d)	Interest on general damages 2% x 1.5		1,650
e)	Interest on (a) 3.5% x 2.5		962
f)	Interest on (b and e) 7% x 2.5		918
g)	Future loss of earnings 20 x 6,000		120,000
h)	Future care 27 years x 1,500		40,500
i)	Prosthetics		100,000
j)	Aids and equipment		15,000
k)	Transport		10,000
	TOTAL AWARD		**360,280**

7. Amputation of arm below elbow (B)

	General damages		45,000
a)	Loss of earnings to trial 2.5 x 10,000	25,000	
	Less partial earnings	4,000	
		21,000	
	Less deductible benefits, say	10,000	
			11,000
b)	Miscellaneous expenses		1,500
c)	Interest on general damages 2% x 1.5		1,350
d)	Interest on (a) 3.5% x 2.5		962

e) Interest on (b) 7% x 2.5		262
f) Future loss of earnings 20 x 4,000		80,000
g) Future care 27 years x 1,000		27,000
h) Prosthetics		75,000
i) Aids and equipment		10,000
j) Transport		10,000
TOTAL AWARD		**262,074**

8. Loss of eyesight – one eye without cosmetic disability (A)

General damages		25,000
Return to work after 1 year		
a) Loss of earnings 1 x 10,000	10,000	
Less deductible benefits, say	5,000	
		5,000
b) Miscellaneous losses		1,500
c) Interest on general damages 2% x 1.5		750
d) Interest on (a) 3.5% x 2.5		437
e) Interest on (b) 7% x 2.5		262
TOTAL AWARD		**32,949**

8. Loss of eyesight – one eye with cosmetic disability (B)

	General damages		30,000
	Return to work after 1 year		
a)	Loss of earnings 1 x 10,000	10,000	
	Less deductible benefits, say	5,000	
			5,000
b)	Miscellaneous losses		1,500
c)	Interest on general damages 2% x 1.5		900
d)	Interest on (a) 3.5% x 2.5		437
e)	Interest on (b) 7% x 2.5		262
	TOTAL AWARD		**38,099**

8. Loss of eyesight – Total Blindness (C)

	General damages		105,000
	Unable to return to work		
a)	Loss of earnings to trial 2.5 x 10,000	25,000	
	Less deductible benefits, say	15,000	
			10,000
b)	Care and expenses		25,000
c)	Interest on general damages 2% x 1.5		3,150
d)	Interest on (a) 3.5% x 2.5		875

e)	Interest on (b) 7% x 2.5		4,375
f)	Future loss of earnings 20 x 10,000		200,000
g)	Transport 27 x 5,000		135,000
h)	Aids and equipment		75,000
i)	Care and assistance 27 x 1,500		40,500
	TOTAL AWARD		**598,900**

9. Deafness (Total)

	General damages		47,500
a)	Loss of earnings to trial 2.5 x 10,000	25,000	
	Less partial earnings	6,000	
		19,000	
	Less deductible benefits, say	10,000	
			9,000
b)	Miscellaneous losses		1,500
c)	Interest on general damages 2% x 1.5		1,425
d)	Interest on (a) 3.5% x 2.5		787
e)	Interest on (b) 7% x 2.5		262
f)	Future loss of earnings 20 x 4,000		80,000
	TOTAL AWARD		**140,474**

10. Repetitive Strain Injury

Persistent Pain and stiffness		
General damages		11,750
Assume return to light duties		
a) Loss of earnings 0.5 x 10,000	5,000	
2 x partial loss	8,000	
	13,000	
Less deductible benefits, say	4,500	
		8,500
b) Miscellaneous losses		500
c) Interest on general damages 2% x 1.5		352
d) Interest on (a) 3.5% x 2.5		743
e) Interest on (b) 7% x 2.5		87
f) Future loss of earnings 20 x 4,000		80,000
TOTAL AWARD		**101,932**

STRESS SCHEDULE

Fiona Gill

Stress in the workplace

Since the second edition of our book was published in 1994, "stress" in the workplace has become an important issue. The European Foundation's Working Conditions survey[1] found that "stress" is "one of the most common work-related health problems with backache (reported by 33% of respondents), muscular pains in the neck and shoulders (23%) and overall fatigue (23%.) 28% of respondents claimed to suffer from "stress".

In the UK a recent report from the Trades Union Congress reported that work related stress claims increased twelve fold in 2001, with 6428 new cases reported compared to only 516 cases in 2000. Despite the increased number of stress claims, the TUC reported that the number of new personal injury claims supported by unions was slightly down compared to the previous year. However, a recent decision of the Court of Appeal in *Terence Sutherland v. Penelope Hatton* and three other cases set new guidelines for employers. At the time of going to print, *Hatton* is on appeal at the House of Lords. A Schedule in relation to stress claims in England and Wales can be found below.

The word "stress" is capable of several interpretations. In this report, we intend to refer to "occupational stress" as an aversive characteristic of the work environment and its consequences and to distinguish it from, for example, the psychological shock caused by witnessing a relative suffer injury (this category of loss is dealt with under bereavement and moral damages/loss of society). Lord Read's interpretation in *Rorrison v. West Lothian College (1999 CT of SESS)* of stress was:

> adverse pressures of the work environment so great as to be likely to cause a pathological reaction.

---

1 European Foundation for the Improvement of living and Working Conditions: "Ten years of working conditions in the European Union", 2000

Having reviewed the House of Lords pronouncement on psychiatric damage in *Frost v. Chief Constable of Yorkshire*, he stated:

> I can find nothing in these matters (or elsewhere in the pursuer's pleadings) which, if proved, could establish that Andrews and Henning ought to have foreseen that the pursuer was under a material risk of sustaining a psychiatric disorder in consequence of their behaviour towards her. They might have foreseen that she would at times be unsatisfied, frustrated, embarrassed and upset, but that is a far cry from suffering a psychiatric disorder. Many if not all employees are liable to suffer those emotions and others mentioned in the present case such as stress, anxiety, loss of confidence and low mood. To suffer such emotions from time to time, not least because of problems at work, is a normal part of human existence. It is only if they are liable to be suffered to such a pathological degree as to constitute a psychiatric disorder that a duty of care to protect against them can arise.

The Health and Safety Commission which is part of the UK Government published a Code of Practice[2], on 25 June 2001 which defines stress as: "the reaction people have to excessive pressures or other types of demand placed on them". According to the Code, an employer's first objective should be to prevent work related stress completely. Employers are under a duty to reduce stress to the lowest level reasonably practicable and have a corresponding duty to mitigate the consequences of any remaining stress. The HSE identify problems that can lead to stress ("stressors") which include "lack of communication and consultation".

The first significant stress claim in the UK was *Walker and Northumberland County Council*. This case was the primary point of reference for UK practitioners until the recent decision in *Sutherland v. Hatton*. Mr Walker was a social worker who suffered a nervous breakdown which he said was due to his inability to manage his work load which included cases involving child abuse. He recovered sufficiently from this first breakdown to return to work and his employers promised assistance which did not materialise. Mr Walker then suffered a second breakdown and sued his employers. The Judge found for Mr Walker who recovered GBP 175,000 (USD 246,155 and EUR 290,535) in an out of court settlement.

---

2 This has been published recently as: "Tackling work-related stress – a manager's guide to improving and maintaining employee health and well-being"

Sutherland v. Hatton involved four appeals to the Court of Appeal which were all heard together. In each case the lower court had awarded damages for stress-induced psychiatric injury. Three of the four claimants lost on appeal to the Court of Appeal. The case has clarified the law on stress claims and the Judgment includes a series of observations about both liability and quantum which are fundamental to any assessment of damages for psychiatric injury.

In short, an employer is entitled to assume that his employee can withstand the normal pressure of the job unless he or she is shown to be vulnerable to psychiatric injury. The employer can take at face value what the employee tells him about his health and has a duty to take steps only when the indications of impending harm to the employee's health are plain. One of the *Sutherland* claimants succeeded – she worked as an administrative assistant and the lower court awarded her GBP 157,541 (USD 221,597 and EUR 261,550) made up of

- GBP 22,500 (USD 31,649 and EUR 37,355) general damages and interest of £1,300
- GBP 38,921 (USD 54,746 and EUR 64,617) past earnings loss and expenses including interest
- GBP 94,820 (USD 133,374 and EUR157,420) future loss

However, the Court of Appeal made observations to the effect that the trial Judge's award in this case should not be taken as any guidance for future similar claims.

Stress is also becoming a European issue and a recent Opinion of the Economic and Social Committee stated that work related stress is seen as one of the new health risks which will result in increased costs both to employers and society at large. The Committee's opinion is that while worker's perceptions of risks to their health and safety due to occupational activities had improved in the period 1990-2000, an increasing proportion of workers are reporting work related health problems. Musculoskeletal disorders and overall fatigue are on the increase whereas stress remains at the same levels as in an earlier survey in 1995.

A report by the International Labour Organisation which covers Germany, Poland, the UK, Finland and the USA revealed that as many as one in 10 office workers in those countries suffer from depression, anxiety, stress or burnout. Stress at work is now the second most disabling illness for workers after heart disease, according to the survey. Stress related illnesses are the main cause of workers claiming disability pensions in Finland. A German survey reported that depression accounted for almost seven percent of early retirements while stress-related incapacity lasts 2.5 times longer than incapacity due to other illnesses. In the EU, the treatment costs of such illnesses amounts to 3-4% of GDP.

In the Netherlands, no distinction is made between disability caused by work or otherwise, the person injured will still receive work-related invalidity benefits. Dutch legislation has responded to the high number of invalidity claims by addressing the issue of workplace stress, and legislation there specifically allows for work design programmes as a means of preventing and managing such stress.

Our Italian correspondent, Alessandro Giorgetti has advised us that stress as defined in the above sense is not known in Italy. He referred to the phenomenon of "mobbing", a term used in Italy to describe any discrimination at work in relation to religion, race, sex or politics. "Mobbing" is defined as having a certain intention to harm somebody and voluntarily causing emotional stress but not physical harm.

Schedule A

Claimant : Man

Age : 40

1. Stress / Psychiatric Damage: Moderately severe

	General damages		28,500
	Assume claimant is able to resume his employment two years after the accident		
a)	Loss of income 2 years x £36,000	72,000	
	Less		
	Deduct all welfare state benefits received and receivable within 2.5 years of accident say, £10,000	10,000	
			62,000
b)	Miscellaneous losses, say		1,500
c)	Interest on damages for injury 1.5 years x 2% = 3% of £57,500		1,725
d)	Interest on items (a) and (b) 12.81% (2.5 years x 5.125%) of £63,500		8,135.94
	TOTAL AWARD		**101,860.94**

2. Stress / Psychiatric Damage: Moderate

General damages		9,500
Assume claimant is able to resume his employment two years after the accident		
a) Loss of income 2 years x £36,000	72,000	
less		
Deduct all welfare state benefits received and receivable within 2.5 years of accident say, £10,000	10,000	
		62,000
b) Miscellaneous losses, say		1,500
c) Interest on damages for injury 1.5 years x 2% = 3% of £9,500		285
d) Interest on items (a) and (b) 12.81% (2.5 years x 5.125%) of £63,500		8,135.94
TOTAL AWARD		**81,420.94**

3. Stress / Psychiatric Damage: Minor

General damages		3,000
Assume claimant is able to resume his employment two years after the accident		
a) Loss of income 2 years x £36,000	72,000	
less		
Deduct all welfare state benefits received and receivable within 2.5 years of accident say, £10,000	10,000	
		62,000
b) Miscellaneous losses, say		1,500

c) Interest on damages for injury 1.5 years x 2% = 3% of £3,000		90
d) Interest on items (a) and (b) 12.81% (2.5 years x 5.125%) of £63,500		8,135.94
TOTAL AWARD		**74,725.94**

Schedule B

Claimant : Woman

Age : 20

1. Stress / Psychiatric Damage: Moderately severe

General damages		28,500
Assume claimant is able to resume her employment two years after the accident		
a) Loss of income 2 years x £10,000		
less	20,000	
Deduct all welfare state benefits received and receivable within 2.5 years of accident say, £10,000	10,000	
		10,000
b) Miscellaneous losses, say		1,500
c) Interest on damages for injury 1.5 years x 2% = 3% of £57,500		1,725
d) Interest on items (a) and (b) 12.81% (2.5 years x 5.125%) of £11,500		1,473.44
TOTAL AWARD		**43,198.44**

2. Stress / Psychiatric Damage: Moderate

	General damages		9,500
	Assume claimant is able to resume her employment two years after the accident		
a)	Loss of income 2 years x £10,000	20,000	
	less		
	Deduct all welfare state benefits received and receivable within 2.5 years of accident say, £10,000	10,000	
			10,000
b)	Miscellaneous losses, say	1,500	
c)	Interest on damages for injury 1.5 years x 2% = 3% of £9,500	285	
d)	Interest on items (a) and (b) 12.81% (2.5 years x 5.125%) of £11,500	1,473.44	
	TOTAL AWARD		**22,758.44**

3. Stress / Psychiatric Damage: Minor

	General damages		3,000
	Assume claimant is able to resume her employment two years after the accident		
a)	Loss of income 2 years x £10,000		
	less	20,000	
	Deduct all welfare state benefits received and receivable within 2.5 years of accident say, £10,000	10,000	
			10,000
b)	Miscellaneous losses, say		1,500

c) Interest on damages for injury 1.5 years x 2% = 3% of £3,000	90
d) Interest on items (a) and (b) 12.81% (2.5 years x 5.125%) of £11,500	1,473.44
TOTAL AWARD	**16,063.44**

FINLAND

Henrik Lagenskiold

Introduction

1. Instant death

Funeral expenses

Road Traffic insurance compensates funeral expenses (coffin, grave, gravestone, catering, death notice and travelling expenses, etc.) to a reasonable amount , considering living conditions and the customs of the domicile of the deceased. This insurance will only compensate expenses which are not otherwise compensated.

Family pension

Entitled to compensation:

a) spouse, the children of the deceased (including unborn children) and adopted children;

b) children living in the home of and care of deceased and the widow/widower;

c) other person who has taken care of by the deceased either by agreement or by court order;

d) cohabitor, when cohabitors have been living together at the time of the accident and when cohabitors have a mutual or acknowledged child, or when the cohabitors have made a mutual maintenance allowance agreement, or when the cohabitors have been previously married to one another or when they have been living together in a marriage-like relationship continuously during at least three (3) years.

Compensation:

Spouse	60% of the income
Spouse and 1 child	65% of the income
Spouse and 2 children	70% of the income
Spouse and 3 children	75% of the income
Spouse and more than 3 children	75% of the income
1 orphan	50% of the income
2 orphans	60% of the income
3 orphans	65% of the income
more than 3 orphans	70% of the income

When both spouse and children receive compensation, two shares are for the spouse and one share for the children.

When compensation is received only by orphans, the compensation amount is divided equally between the children.

2. Pain and suffering

Injuries, where pain and suffering is compensated are classified in three categories:

- A light injuries
- B minor injuries
- C severe injuries

Compensation for pain and suffering

Category A		No compensation
Category B		1,000 – 15,000
	B1 minor injuries	1,000 – 5,000
	B2 more severe than minor injuries	5,000 – 15,000
Category C		15,000 –
	C1 severe injuries	15,000 – 40,000
	C2 very severe injuries	40,000 – 80,000
	C3 exceptionally severe injuries	80,000 –

Permanent defect and handicap

Compensation is usually paid as a lump sum, but may be paid continually; for example, if the injured is exceptionally severely handicapped. Compensation for permanent defect and handicap is not payable if the consequences of the accident are only cosmetic. Permanent cosmetic defect, however, is compensated.

Compensation paid as lump sum

If the injured is under 18 at the time of the accident, the minimum amount he can receive is 7,000 FIM. When over 18, the minimum amount is 14,000 FIM

The injuries are classified in 20 categories:

Table 1

Category	*Age under 18*	*Age 18 +*
1.	7000	14,000
2.	14,000	28,000
3.	21,000	42,000
4.	28,000	56,000
5.	35,000	70,000
6.	42,000	84,000
7.	49,000	98,000
8.	56,000	112,000
9.	63,000	126,000
10.	70,000	140,000
11.	77,000	154,000
12.	84,000	168,000
13.	91,000	182,000
14.	98,000	196,000
15.	105,000	210,000
16.	112,000	246,000
17.	119,000	285,000
18.	126,000	327,000
19.	133,000	372,400
20.	140,000	420,000

When determining the category of injury, only the nature of the injury is considered – no other circumstances, such as the injured person's occupation, will be taken into account.

Thereafter, the occupation of the injured person is taken into consideration. If he is not able to return to his former work, but has to take up a new occupation, the compensation amount may be multiplied by the factor 1.1-2.0. depending on the new occupation. The factor will not be used where the new occupation is "more profitable".

When determining the amount of compensation the injured person's hobbies is also considered e.g., if the injured person is a sportsman, decreasing results are considered. The amount may then be multiplied by the factor 1.1-1.5.

If compensation has already been paid for permanent defect and handicap and the injury later proves to be more severe, the compensation may be increased to correspond to the new category of injury.

The disability percentage is determined by a physician and the injury category is determined by medical examination. The disability percentage is determined by the injury category. For category 1, the injury percentage is 5%. The principle is that 5% is added for each further category of injury. For category 5, for example, the disability percentage would be 25%.

2. Loss of income

Loss of income is determined by the annual income of the injured person. The decrease in annual income caused by the injury is compensated in full. The amount of compensation is not determined by the degree of disability, the actual loss of income is decisive. The principle is to compensate for the total, actual loss of income.

When the state of injury is permanent, the injured person will not receive compensation for loss of income any more, but will receive a disability pension instead. The disability pension will be the same amount as the compensation for loss of income. It constitutes a continued compensation for the decrease in earnings. When the injured person reaches retirement age he receives 60% of his annual income.

Loss of income must be added to Schedules A and B: it is calculated according to the principles presented above.

3. Nursing allowance

Nursing allowance is not included in the figures below in Schedules A and B. In addition to direct medical costs, the injured person will also receive a nursing allowance. The allowance is paid as long as he is helpless. Injured persons are classified in four different categories, as follows:-

1. Injured persons who are bedridden and in need of help with normal everyday routines including those with very severe brain damage.
2. Injured persons who to a large extent are in need of other people's help and assistance, for example, those with severe brain damage.
3. Injured persons who need a wheelchair.
4. Injured persons in continuous need of help with certain everyday routines.

Table 2

Category	*Nursing allowance FIM/day*
1.	121
2.	96.80
3.	66.55
4.	36.30

Table 3. Schedule A

Claimant:	Male
Age:	40
Status:	Married – 2 dependent children aged 5 and 7
Occupation:	Doctor
Income:	300,000 FIM

1. Instant death	FIM
a) Funeral expenses	Reasonable
b) Family pension, 70% income	210,000
TOTAL AWARD	**210,000**

2a. Burns, face, 15-20%	
a) Pain and suffering (range 15,000 – 40,000 FIM)	40,000
b) Permanent defect and handicap, category 3, 42,000 FIM 42,000 – (40 – 18)% x 42,000 =	32,760
TOTAL AWARD	**72,760**

2b. Minor burns to other parts of the body	
a) Pain and suffering (range 5,000 – 15,000 FIM)	15,000
b) Permanent defect and handicap, category 2, 28,000 – (40 – 18)% x 28,000 =	21,840
TOTAL AWARD	**36,840**

3. Quadriplegia, 100%

a) Pain and suffering	80,000
b) Permanent defect and handicap, category 20, 420,000 FIM 420,000 – (40 – 18)% x 420,000 =	327,600
TOTAL AWARD	**407,600**

4. Paraplegia, 70%

a) Pain and suffering	80,000
b) Permanent defect and handicap, categories 16-20, 246,000 – 420,000 FIM 420,000 – (40 – 18)% x 420,000 =	327,600
TOTAL AWARD	**407,600**

5a. Brain damage, 80%

a) Pain and suffering (range 40,000 – 80,000)	80,000
b) Permanent defect and handicap, categories 16-20, 246,000 – 420,000 FIM 420,000 – (40 – 18)% x 420,000 =	327,600
TOTAL AWARD	**407,600**

5b. Brain damage, 90%

a) Pain and suffering	80,000
b) Permanent defect and handicap, category 20, 420,000 FIM 420,000 – (40 – 18)% x 420,000 =	327,000
TOTAL AWARD	**407,600**

6a. Amputation of leg above knee, 40%

a) Pain and suffering (range 40,000 – 80,000)	80,000
b) Permanent defect and handicap, about category 8, 112,00 112,000 – (40 – 18)% x 420,000 =	87,360
TOTAL AWARD	**167,360**

6b. Amputation of leg below knee, 30%

a) Pain and suffering (range 40,000 – 80,000	80,000
b) Permanent defect and handicap, category 6, 84,000 84,000 – (40 – 18)% x 84,000 =	65,520
TOTAL AWARD	**145,520**

7a. Amputation of arm above elbow, 55%

a) Pain and suffering (range 40,000 – 80,000)	80,000
b) Permanent defect and handicap, category 11, 154,000 154,000 – (40 – 18)% x 154,000 =	120,120
TOTAL AWARD	**200,120**

7b. Amputation of arm below elbow, 50%

a) Pain and suffering (range 40,000 – 80,000)	80,000
b) Permanent defect and handicap, category 5, 70,000 70,000 – (40 – 18)% x 70,000 =	109,200
TOTAL AWARD	**189,200**

8a. Loss of eyesight, one eye, 25%

a) Pain and suffering (range 15,000 – 40,000)	40,000
b) Permanent defect and handicap, category 5, 70,000 70,000 – (20 – 18)% x 70,000	54,600
TOTAL AWARD	**94,600**

8b. Loss of eyesight, one eye, 25% with cosmetic damage

a) Pain and suffering (range 15,000 – 40,000)	40,000
b) Permanent defect and handicap, category 5, 70,000 70,000 – (40 – 18)% x 70,000	54,600
c) Cosmetic damage (range 25,000 – 50,000)	50,000
TOTAL AWARD	**144,600**

8c. Total blindness, 100%

a) Pain and suffering (range 80,000)	80,000
b) Permanent defect and handicap, category 20, 420,000 420,000 – (40 – 18)% x 420,000 =	327,600
TOTAL AWARD	**407.600**

9. Deafness, 50%

a) Pain and suffering (range 40,000 – 80,000)	80,000
b) Permanent defect and handicap, categories about 10 – 12, 140,000 168,000 168,000 – (40 – 18)% x 168 x 168,000 =	131,040
TOTAL AWARD	**211,040**

Table 4. Schedule B

Claimant:	Woman
Age:	20
Status:	Single
Occupation:	Legal Secretary
Income:	100,000 FIM

1. Instant death

a) Funeral expenses	Reasonable
TOTAL AWARD	**Reasonable**

2a. Burns, face, 15-20%

a) Pain and suffering (range 15,000 – 40,000)	40,000
b) Permanent defect and handicap, category 3, 42,000 42,000 – (20 – 18)% x 42,000 =	41,160
TOTAL AWARD	**81,160**

2b. Minor burns to other parts of the body

a) Pain and suffering (range 5,000 – 15,000)	15,000
b) Permanent defect and handicap, category 2, 28,000 28,000 – (20 – 18)% x 28,000 =	27,440
TOTAL AWARD	**42,440**

3. Quadriplegia, 100%

a) Pain and suffering (range 80,000 –)	80,000
b) Permanent defect and handicap, category 20, 420,000 420,000 – (20 – 18)% x 420,000 =	411,600
TOTAL AWARD	**491,600**

4. Paraplegia, 70%

a) Pain and suffering (range 80,000 –)	80,000
b) Permanent defect and handicap, categories 16-20, 246,000 – 420,000 FIM 420,000 – (20 – 18)% x 420,000 =	411,600
TOTAL AWARD	**491,600**

5a. Brain damage, 80%

a) Pain and suffering (range 40,000 – 80,000)	80,000
b) Permanent defect and handicap, categories 16-20, 246,000 – 420,000 FIM 420,000 – (20 – 18)% x 420,000 =	411,600
TOTAL AWARD	**491,600**

5b. Brain damage, 90%

a) Pain and suffering (range 80,000 –)	80,000
b) Permanent defect and handicap, category 20, 420,000 FIM 420,000 – (20 – 18)% x 420,000 =	411,600
TOTAL AWARD	**491,600**

6a. Amputation of leg above knee, 40%

a) Pain and suffering (range 40,000 – 80,000)	80,000
b) Permanent defect and handicap, about category 8, 112,00 112,000 – (20 – 18)% x 420,000 =	109,760
TOTAL AWARD	**189,760**

6b. Amputation of leg below knee, 30%

a) Pain and suffering (range 40,000 – 80,000	80,000
b) Permanent defect and handicap, category 6, 84,000 84,000 – (20 – 18)% x 84,000 =	82,320
TOTAL AWARD	**162,360**

7a. Amputation of arm above elbow, 55%

a) (Pain and suffering (range 40,000 – 80,000)	80,000
b) Permanent defect and handicap, category 11, 154,000 154,000 – (40 – 18)% x 154,000 =	150,920
TOTAL AWARD	**230,920**

7b. Amputation of arm below elbow, 50%

a) Pain and suffering (range 40,000 – 80,000)	80,000
b) Permanent defect and handicap, category 10, 140,000 70,000 – (40 – 18)% x 70,000 =	137,200
TOTAL AWARD	**217,200**

8a. Loss of eyesight, one eye, 25%

a) Pain and suffering (range 15,000 – 40,000)	40,000
b) Permanent defect and handicap, category 5, 70,000 70,000 – (20 – 18)% x 70,000	68,600
TOTAL AWARD	**108,600**

8b. Loss of eyesight, one eye, 25% with cosmetic damage

a) Pain and suffering (range 15,000 – 40,000)	40,000
b) Permanent defect and handicap, category 5, 70,000 70,000 – (20 – 18)% x 70,000	68,600
c) Cosmetic damage (range 25,000 – 50,000)	50,000
TOTAL AWARD	**158,600**

8c. Total blindness, 100%

a) Pain and suffering (range 80,000 –)	80,000
b) Permanent defect and handicap, category 20, 420,000 420,000 – (20 – 18)% x 420,000 =	411,600
TOTAL AWARD	**491.600**

9. Deafness, 50%

a) Pain and suffering (range 40,000 – 80,000)	80,000
b) Permanent defect and handicap, categories about 10 – 12, 140,000 – 168,000 168,000 – (20 – 18)% x 168 x 168,000 =	164,640
TOTAL AWARD	**244,640**

FRANCE

Gérard Honig

Introduction

Our English colleagues point out that our calculations have an air of unreality because we have had to make certain assumptions. An actual claim would be calculated on its pecuniary elements.

We would add that:

(1) the amount of compensation awarded even in similar claims will vary from court to court since the judges are, in principle, free to determine the amount that they consider sufficient;

(2) as far as the category "special damages" (Part A) is concerned, the figures have to be increased by roughly 3.4% which corresponds to the inflation rate between 1994 and 1999;

(3) the method of calculating compensation differs from country to country.

We shall summarise below the principles of valuation and compensation as they exist in France. As a general rule, an insured party is entitled to full compensation for any kind of personal injury he or she sustained. The amount of damages is always determined on the date of consolidation of the injuries (i.e. the date on which the permanent extent of the injury can be definitely ascertained).

Compensation, awards are calculated as follows.

Special Damages

Special damages are known as *incapacité totale temporaire* or ITT for short (total temporary invalidity) and cover:

(1) Medical expenses until consolidation.

(2) Actual pecuniary loss (ITT) which corresponds to a general indemnity paid to the injured party to compensate from the date of the accident to the date of consolidation of the injuries in respect of the temporary invalidity suffered as a result of the accident.

The figures will differ depending on the type of injury and the length of the disability or invalidity period (loss of income until employment is resumed.)

General Damages

1. Prospective pecuniary loss

Future or prospective pecuniary loss is, known in French law as incapacité partielle permanente or IPP for short (partial permanent incapacity). The amount of damages awarded in this category is not easy to evaluate. Generally, after medical examination, a percentage of IPP is determined and, on that basis, damages are awarded (a medical expert appointed by the court determines the percentage of IPP).

IPP is calculated as follows: the value of what is called the "point" (i.e. a certain amount of money is given according to the age of the injured person at the time of consolidation and the IPP rate) is multiplied by the IPP. For example:

Point = 8,000 x IPP 15 = 120,000

2. Non pecuniary loss

a) Pretium doloris (pain and suffering)

Pretium doloris literally means the "price of pain" and damages are awarded in respect of pain and suffering

b) Loss of leisure (prejudice d'agrément)

This category is relevant to damages payable to the injured party as compensation for the impossibility of pursuing the leisure activities he or she used to practice. A person, for example, who can no longer practice his favourite sport, as a consequence of the accident, is entitled to damages to this category. In determining the amount of damages the Court will take into account, the importance the injured party attached to the particular leisure activity and the regularity with which it is practiced.

c) Aesthetic injury

When, as a consequence of the accident, the injured party's physical appearance has been altered, he or she is entitled to damages in this category. Once again, the amount of compensation will depend on what sort of aesthetic injury the 40 year old man and the 20 year old woman have sustained and where the injuries are situated (for example, burns on the face will obviously attract a larger amount than burns on the foot).

d) Impairment of sexual performance

This injury, is compensatable/indemnifiable, depending on the degree of the sexual impediment.

Table 1. Schedule A

Claimant :	Man
Age :	40
Status :	Married, 2 dependent children aged 5 and 7
Occupation :	Doctor
Income :	FRF 350,000 pa

1. Instant Death	FRF
a) Funeral expenses	25,000
b) Wife's dependency (calculated according to her husband's salary)	1,742,440
c) Children's dependency	1,306,830
d) Bereavement	
1. Wife	115,000
2. Children	150,000
TOTAL AWARD	**3,339,270**

2a. Burns (15%)

A. Special damages (ITT)	
a) Medical expenses until consolidation	275,000
b) Miscellaneous	
c) Actual pecuniary loss until consolidation (assume that claimant is able to resume his employment 1.8 years after the accident)	648,000
B. General damages	
a) Prospective pecuniary loss (IPP 15%)	97,380
b) Non pecuniary loss pain and suffering aesthetical injury	35,000
c) Prospective medical expenses	20,000
TOTAL AWARD	**1,075,380**

2b. Burns (20%)

A. Special damages (ITT)	
a) Medical expenses until consolidation	405,000
b) Miscellaneous	
c) Actual pecuniary loss until consolidation (assume that claimant is able to resume his employment 1.8 years after the accident)	648,000
B. General damages	
a) Prospective pecuniary loss (IPP 15%)	129,840
b) Non pecuniary loss pain and suffering aesthetical injury	35,000
c) Prospective medical expenses	25,000
TOTAL AWARD	**1,242,840**

2. Quadriplegia

A. Special damages (ITT)

a) Medical expenses until consolidation	750,000
b) Miscellaneous (modifying home and special equipment)	320,000
c) Actual pecuniary loss until consolidation	825,000
d) Interest payable on pre-trial pecuniary loss	161,287

B. General damages

a) Prospective pecuniary loss (IPP 100%)	1,728,000
b) Non pecuniary loss	
pain and suffering	200,000
aesthetical injury	150,000
loss of leisure	300,000
c) Prospective medical expenses (medical assistance 24 hours a day)	6,720,000
TOTAL AWARD	**11,154,287**

3. Paraplegia

A. Special damages (ITT)

a) Medical expenses until consolidation	575,000
b) Miscellaneous (modifying home and special equipment)	320,000
c) Actual pecuniary loss until consolidation	825,000

B. General damages

a) Prospective pecuniary loss	1,211,600
b) Non pecuniary loss	
pain and suffering	150,000

aesthetical injury	150,000
loss of leisure	200,000
c) Prospective medical expenses (half-time assistance)	3,360,000
TOTAL AWARD	**6,791,600**

5a. Brain damage

A. Special damages (ITT)

a) Medical expenses until consolidation	575,000
b) Miscellaneous	
c) Actual pecuniary loss until consolidation	825,000

B. General damages

a) Prospective pecuniary loss (IPP 80%)	1,211,600
b) Non pecuniary loss	
pain and suffering	100,000
aesthetical injury	
loss of leisure	200,000
c) Prospective medical expenses	6,720,000
TOTAL AWARD	**9,631,600**

5b. Brain damage with motor deficiency

A. Special damages (ITT)

a) Medical expenses until consolidation	575,000
b) Miscellaneous	
c) Actual pecuniary loss until consolidation	825,000

B. General damages

a) Prospective pecuniary loss	1,476,720

b) Non pecuniary loss	
pain and suffering	100,000
aesthetical injury	
loss of leisure	200,000
c) Prospective medical expenses	6,720,000
TOTAL AWARD	**9,896,720**

6a. Amputation of leg above knee

A. Special damages (ITT)	
a) Medical expenses until consolidation	300,000
b) Miscellaneous	
c) Actual pecuniary loss until consolidation (assume claimant is able to resume his employment 1.25 years after the accident)	477,000
B. General damages	
a) Prospective pecuniary loss (IPP 60%)	770,340
b) Non pecuniary loss	
pain and suffering	150,000
aesthetical injury	200,000
loss of leisure	100,000
c) Prospective medical expenses (artificial prosthetic limb)	100,000
TOTAL AWARD	**2,097,340**

6b. Amputation of leg below knee

A. Special damages (ITT)	
a) Medical expenses until consolidation	230,000

b) Miscellaneous	
c) Actual pecuniary loss until consolidation	477,000
B. General damages	
a) Prospective pecuniary loss (IPP 45%)	500,000
b) Non pecuniary loss	
pain and suffering	150,000
aesthetical injury	200,000
loss of leisure	80,000
c) Prospective medical expenses (medical prosthetics limb)	150,000
TOTAL AWARD	**1,737,000**

7a. Amputation of arm above elbow

A. Special damages (ITT)	
a) Medical expenses until consolidation	160,000
b) Miscellaneous (modifying home and special equipment)	
c) Actual pecuniary loss until consolidation (assume claimant is able to resume his employment 1.9 years after accident)	689,000
B. General damages	
a) Prospective pecuniary loss (IPP 60%)	770,340
b) Non pecuniary loss	
pain and suffering	150,000
aesthetical injury	150,000
loss of leisure	80,000
c) Prospective medical expenses (artificial prosthetics limb)	150,000
TOTAL AWARD	**2,149,340**

7b. Amputation of arm below the elbow

A. Special damages (ITT)	
a) Medical expenses until consolidation	150,000
b) Miscellaneous	
c) Actual pecuniary loss until consolidation	689,000
B. General damages	
a) Prospective pecuniary loss (IPP 50%)	579,850
b) Non pecuniary loss	
pain and suffering	100,000
aesthetical injury	125,000
loss of leisure	50,000
c) Prospective medical expenses	150,000
TOTAL AWARD	**1,843,850**

8a. Loss of eyesight – one eye without cosmetic disability

A. Special damages (ITT)	
a) Medical expenses until consolidation	130,000
b) Miscellaneous	
c) Actual pecuniary loss until consolidation	150,000
B. General damages	
a) Prospective pecuniary loss (IPP 25%)	205,000
b) Non pecuniary loss	
pain and suffering	80,000
aesthetical injury	50,000
c) Prospective medical expenses	
TOTAL AWARD	**615,000**

8b. Loss of eyesight – one eye with cosmetic disability

A. Special damages (ITT)	
a) Medical expenses until consolidation	190,500
b) Miscellaneous	
c) Actual pecuniary loss until consolidation	312,000
B. General damages	
a) Prospective pecuniary loss (IPP 25%)	205,000
b) Non pecuniary loss	
pain and suffering	85,000
aesthetical injury	100,000
plus professional incidence	
c) Prospective medical expenses	110,000
TOTAL AWARD	**1,025,500**

8c Loss of eyesight – Total blindness

A. Special damages (ITT)	
a) Medical expenses until consolidation	457,500
b) Miscellaneous	175,000
c) Actual pecuniary loss until consolidation	825,000
B. General damages	
a) Prospective pecuniary loss (IPP 85%)	1,333,820
b) Non pecuniary loss	
pain and suffering	125,000
aesthetical injury	100,000
plus professional incidence	350,000
c) Prospective medical expenses	
TOTAL AWARD	**3,366,320**

9. Deafness (total)

General damages (IPP 80%)	1,211,600
Prospective pecuniary loss	
Pretium dolori	20,000 – 25,000*
Loss of leisure (*prejudice d'agrément*)	180,000
TOTAL AWARD	**1,411,600 – 1,416,600**

*It depends on the number of operations the person has undergone; in some cases the pretium doloris can be nil if there is no operation at all.

Table 2. Schedule B

Claimant :	Woman
Age :	20
Status :	Single
Occupation :	Legal Secretary
Income :	FRF 100,000 pa

1. Instant Death

a) Funeral expenses	25,000
b) Bereavement	
1. Parents (assuming both father and mother are alive)	220,000
2. Relatives (assuming the deceased had one brother and one sister (40,000 each))	80,000
TOTAL AWARD	**325,000**

2a. Burns (15%)

A. Special damages (ITT)

a) Medical expenses	275,000
b) Miscellaneous	162,000
c) Actual pecuniary loss	

B. General damages

a) Prospective pecuniary loss (IPP 15%)	104,730
b) Non pecuniary loss	
pain and suffering	40,000
aesthetical injury	35,000
c) Prospective medical expenses	
TOTAL AWARD	**616,730**

2b. Burns (20%)

A. Special damages (ITT)

a) Medical expenses	405,000
b) Miscellaneous	162,000
c) Actual pecuniary loss	

B. General damages

a) Prospective pecuniary loss (IPP 15%)	162,230
b) Non pecuniary loss	
pain and suffering	45,000
aesthetic injury	45,000
c) Prospective medical expenses	
TOTAL AWARD	**814,320**

3. Quadriplegia

A. Special damages (ITT)

a) Medical expenses until consolidation	750,000
b) Miscellaneous (modifying home and special equipment)	320,000
c) Actual pecuniary loss until consolidation	206,250

A. General damages

a) Prospective pecuniary loss (IPP 100%)	1,976,800
b) Non pecuniary loss	
pain and suffering	200,000
aesthetical injury	150,000
loss of leisure	300,000
c) Prospective medical expenses (medical assistance 24 hours a day)	6,720,000
TOTAL AWARD	**10,623,050**

4. Paraplegia (80%)

A. Special damages (ITT)

a) Medical expenses until consolidation	575,000
b) Miscellaneous (modifying home and special equipment)	320,000
c) Actual pecuniary loss until consolidation	166,250

A. General damages

a) Prospective pecuniary loss (IPP)	1,388,000
b) Non pecuniary loss	
pain and suffering	150,000
aesthetical injury	150,000
loss of leisure	200,000

c) Prospective medical expenses (half-time assistance)	3,360,000
TOTAL AWARD	**6,309,250**

5a. Brain damage (80%)

A. Special damages (ITT)

a) Medical expenses until consolidation	575,000
b) Miscellaneous	
c) Actual pecuniary loss until consolidation	206,250

B. General damages

a) Prospective pecuniary loss (IPP 80%)	1,388,000
b) Non pecuniary loss	
pain and suffering	100,000
aesthetical injury	
loss of leisure	200,000
c) Prospective medical expenses	6,720,000
TOTAL AWARD	**9,189,250**

5b. Brain damage (90%)

A. Special damages (ITT)

a) Medical expenses until consolidation	575,000
b) Miscellaneous	
c) Actual pecuniary loss until consolidation	206,250

B. General damages

a) Prospective pecuniary loss (IPP)	1,696,770

b) Non pecuniary loss	
pain and suffering	100,000
aesthetical injury	
loss of leisure	200,000
c) Prospective medical expenses	6,720,000
TOTAL AWARD	**9,498,020**

6a. Amputation of leg above knee

A. Special damages (ITT)

a) Medical expenses until consolidation	300,000
b) Miscellaneous	
c) Actual pecuniary loss until consolidation	119,000

B. General damages

a) Prospective pecuniary loss (IPP 60%)	885,780
b) Non pecuniary loss	
pain and suffering	150,000
aesthetical injury	200,000
loss of leisure	100,000
c) Prospective medical expenses	100,000
TOTAL AWARD	**1,854,500**

6b. Amputation of leg below knee

A. Special damages (ITT)

a) Medical expenses until consolidation	230,000
b) Miscellaneous	
c) Actual pecuniary loss until consolidation	119,250

B. General damages

a) Prospective pecuniary loss (IPP 45%)	570,195
b) Non pecuniary loss	
pain and suffering	150,000
aesthetical injury	200,000
loss of leisure	80,000
c) Prospective medical expenses	100,000
TOTAL AWARD	**1,449,445**

7a. Amputation of arm above elbow

A. Special damages (ITT)

a) Medical expenses until consolidation	160,000
b) Miscellaneous	
c) Actual pecuniary loss until consolidation	151,250

B. General damages

a) Prospective pecuniary loss (IPP 60%)	885,780
b) Non pecuniary loss	
pain and suffering	150,000
aesthetical injury	150,000
loss of leisure	80,000
c) Prospective medical expenses (artificial prosthetics limb)	150,000
TOTAL AWARD	**1,727,030**

7b. Amputation of arm below the elbow

A. Special damages (ITT)

a) Medical expenses until consolidation	150,000

b) Miscellaneous	
c) Actual pecuniary loss until consolidation	151,250
B. General damages	
a) Prospective pecuniary loss (IPP 50%)	662,450
b) Non pecuniary loss	
pain and suffering	100,000
aesthetical injury	125,000
loss of leisure	50,000
c) Prospective medical expenses	150,000
TOTAL AWARD	**1,388,700**

8a. Loss of eyesight – one eye without cosmetic disability

A. Special damages (ITT)	
a) Medical expenses until consolidation	130,000
b) Miscellaneous	
c) Actual pecuniary loss until consolidation	78,000
B. General damages	
a) Prospective pecuniary loss (IPP 25%)	226,075
b) Non pecuniary loss	
pain and suffering	80,000
aesthetical injury	50,000
c) Prospective medical expenses	
TOTAL AWARD	**564,075**

8b. Loss of eyesight – one eye with cosmetic disability

A. Special damages (ITT)	
a) Medical expenses until consolidation	190,500
b) Miscellaneous	
c) Actual pecuniary loss until consolidation	78,000
B. General damages	
a) Prospective pecuniary loss (IPP 25%)	226,075
b) Non pecuniary loss	
pain and suffering	85,000
aesthetical injury	100,000
plus professional incidence	110,000
c) Prospective medical expenses	
TOTAL AWARD	**789,575**

8c. Loss of eyesight – total blindness

A. Special damages (ITT)	
a) Medical expenses until consolidation	457,500
b) Miscellaneous	175,000
c) Actual pecuniary loss until consolidation	206,250
B. General damages	
a) Prospective pecuniary loss (IPP 85%)	1,530,170
b) Non pecuniary loss	
pain and suffering	125,000
aesthetical injury	100,000
plus professional incidence	350,000
c) Prospective medical expenses	
TOTAL AWARD	**2,943,920**

9. Deafness (total)

General damages (IPP 80%)	1,388,000
Prospective pecuniary loss	
Pretium doloris (pain and suffering)	20,000 – 25,000
Loss of leisure (*prejudice d'agrément*)	200,000
TOTAL AWARD	**1,608,000-1,613,000**

GERMANY

Johannes Wuppermann

Introduction

Under German law, a claim for compensation in respect of personal injury could until now succeed, only if the liable party could be proved to have been negligent. It has always been possible to make a claim in respect of loss of earning capacity, even where the negligence of the liable party is not proved, if the facts meet the requirements for strict liability. These circumstances are provided for, inter alia, in the laws on road traffic, railway and air travel where it is sufficient for a personal injury to have been caused by "the operation of" one of these means of transport (operational hazards). Until now, this type of owner's liability did not apply to the owner of a motor vehicle, if the driver had taken every possible care, according to the circumstances (circumstances beyond a person's control).

In future, a basis for a claim for compensation in the event of strict liability will also exist, if the injured party suffers "serious long-term injury" (article 253 para. 2 German Civil Code).The obligation to indemnify arising out of strict liability will then only be excluded if the accident was caused by force majeure (article 7 para. 2 Road Traffic Law).

In addition, upper limits for liability in the event of death or injury are established by statute in respect of road traffic accidents. Liability insurance in excess of the statutory amounts is offered by the insurance companies in this respect on a voluntary basis.

Compensation amounts continue to increase only slowly in Germany. Nevertheless, there have now been nine cases (these awards do not include medical expenses as those are dealt with directly by insurance companies) in which compensation of DEM 500,000 (£153,846) or more was awarded. There are only two decisions in which the awards were higher: in one case, in 1998, a 54-year-old woman was awarded DEM 600,000 (£184,615) compensation for medical malpractice after an operation on her spine resulted in paraplegia and other impairments. In this case, what is known as a non-material reservation was made in favour of the victim, which means that if a further belated claim should arise after the judicial hearing, the victim may sue for additional compensation.

In the second case, in 1995, a 6-year-old girl was awarded not only compensation of DEM 700,000 (£215,385), but also a monthly pension of DEM 750 (£231) as a result of paraplegia with almost total inability to breathe spontaneously. If capitalised, the pension would equate to a total award of DEM 871,000 (£268,000.)

Since 1990, compensation claims have been inheritable. This means that claims do not have to be made "against the clock". Legal precedent has acknowledged that delayed settlement of compensation will justify a supplementary award in the evaluation of the compensation amount. Incidentally, compensation payments are not subject to tax, in the same way as loss of subsistence.

In addition to the net damages, the paying party is required to pay the social security contributions which the victim will have to pay in order to be able to secure his old age. The paying party is also required to pay income tax on the damages which would have been charged to the victim.

Funeral expenses appropriate to the social status of the victim are also compensatable.

Under German procedural law, the losing party is liable for all the costs of the proceedings, including the fees of the other party's lawyers. In a claim for compensation for pain and suffering, the claimant may seek "an appropriate indemnity at the discretion of the Court". It need then only be determined what level of payment the claimant deems appropriate. This type of application can reduce the risk of being required to pay part of the costs of proceedings because the claim in respect of pain and suffering was too high.

Bereavement

A claim on the part of survivors has not yet been regulated by German law. So-called compensation for shock is only acknowledged by case law, if the immediate experience of an accident, particularly the serious injury of a close relative, results in an actual detriment to health which far exceeds the shock which every person experiences and must come to terms with as a consequence of the news of the death of a relative in the course of his life. In a case in which parents lost their three children in an accident caused by a third party, the Court in Nuremberg awarded the Father DEM 60,000 (£18,462) and the Mother DEM 30,000 (£9,231) for pain and suffering. The Father had to undergo psychiatric treatment for nine years after the accident, and was permanently unable to work. The Mother had to restrict her employment to a considerable degree, particularly because she had to care for her husband and after her employment was terminated by her employer, she lost contact with the outside world to a considerable extent.

Settlement of claims/adjustment

In Germany, loss of earnings and/or increased requirements resulting from injuries must, in principle, be compensated by a pension (article 843 para.1 Civil Code).

However, it is quite usual for the insurance companies to seek settlements in which the victim is offered a single payment, the aim of which is to put the victim in a position to obtain compensation for his future loss of earnings from the capital and interest accruing.

Calculation of the settlement amount is based on capitalisation tables with an appropriate deduction of unaccrued interest of between 5% and 5.5%. Loss of earnings are calculated to the 65th birthday for both men and women.

In the event that a victim's relatives are entitled to claim compensation for loss of maintenance after his death, capitalisation of the monthly damages may not be based on the period to the 65th birthday alone, but must take into account the life expectancy of the surviving spouse and the likelihood of re-marriage. Appropriate capitalisation tables are available for both circumstances. Surviving children may claim a maintenance allowance until completion of their school or university education.

Table 1. Schedule A

Claimant:	Man
Age:	40
Status:	Married, 2 dependent children aged 5 and 7
Occupation:	Doctor
Income:	DEM 100,000 net p.a.
Settlement:	2.5 years after accident

1. Instant death		DEM
a) Claim for funeral expenses		10,000
Interest on funeral expenses (2.5 years at 6%[1])		1,500
b) Dependent wife and children would have separate claims for loss of maintenance		
Benefits payable by third persons (e.g. social security, insures, relatives) are not deductible		
Net income	100,000	
Deduct: fixed costs[2]	30,000	
	70,000	
1. Wife 30%[3]	21,000	
At half fixed costs[4]	15,000	
	36,000	

---

1 Rate of interest according to the personal credit terms of the victim, at least 4% p.a. Interest on loss of earnings is calculated at 6% until date of settlement in all sample cases.

2 Income not used for maintenance must be deducted.

3 This distribution has been developed by case law.

4 Fixed costs must be proved individually. The Courts do not accept statistical material.

Maintenance until settlement		90,000
Interest on maintenance until settlement (6.0%p.a.)		6,750
Future loss of maintenance about factor 15.0[5]		540,000
2. Children (15% each)	10,500	
At quarter fixed cost each	7,500	
	18,000	
Maintenance until settlement for both children		90,000
Interest on maintenance until settlement (6.0% p.a.)		6,750
Future loss of maintenance		
5-27[6] years, about factor 13.0[7]		234,000
7-27 years, about factor 12.0		216,000
		1,319,000

2. Burns

Assume that the claimant is able to resume his employment two years after accident

a) Monetary losses

1. Medical expenses[8]	
2. Loss of income until settlement	250,000
Interest on loss of income until settlement	18,750

5 According to capitalisation tables for so-called "joined pensions" for married couples of the same age.

6 Completion of university education; factor 9.5 or 8.5 until 18th birthday.

7 According to capitalisation table for a pension which is payable monthly.

8 It is not possible to provide details here, because of the lack of reliable figures. The costs incurred are settled directly by the insurance companies, and are therefore not subject of court proceedings.

	3. Miscellaneous losses[9]	100,000
b)	Non material losses, i.e. pain and suffering	50,000 – 100,000

3. Quadriplegia

a)	Monetary losses	
	1. Medical expenses	
	2. Loss of income until settlement	250,000
	Interest on loss of income until settlement	18,750
	Future loss of income (assume retirement at 65) about factor 13.5[10]	1,350,000
	3. Miscellaneous losses	200,000
b)	Pain and suffering	400,000 – 700,000

4. Paraplegia

a)	Monetary losses; see 3 above	
b)	Pain and suffering	200,000 – 300,000

5. Brain damage

a)	Monetary losses; see 3 above	
b)	Pain and suffering	130,000 – 300,000

6. Amputation of leg

Assume that claimant is unable to resume his employment 1.5 years after accident

9 This includes all additional costs incurred as a result of the injury, the amount given here is an unreliable assumption.

10 According to capitalisation table, annuity for men up to their 65th year (mortality table 1995/97).

a) Monetary losses	
1. Medical expenses	
2. Loss of income until settlement	150,000
Interest on loss of income until settlement	15,750
3. Miscellaneous losses	15,000
b) Pain and suffering	75,000 – 90,000

7. Amputation of arm

Assume that claimant is unable to resume his employment but takes up light duties 1.5 years after accident at DEM 60,000 net p.a.

a) Monetary losses	
1. Medical expenses	
2. Loss of income until settlement	190,000
Interest on loss of income until settlement	17,000
Future loss of income (assume retirement at 65) about factor 13.5[11]	540,000
3. Miscellaneous losses	50,000
b) Pain and suffering	60,000 – 80,000

8a. and 8b. Loss of eyesight – one eye

Assume that claimant is able to resume his employment one year after accident

a) Monetary losses	
1. Medical expenses	
2. Loss of income	100,000
Interest on loss of income until settlement	12,000
b) Pain and suffering	50,000 – 80,000

---

11 According to capitalisation table, annuity for men up to their 65th year (mortality table 1995/97).

8c. Loss of eyesight – total blindness

Assume that claimant is unable to resume his employment

a) Monetary losses	
1. Medical expenses	
2. Loss of income, see 3 above	
Miscellaneous losses	100,000
b) Pain and suffering	130,000 – 160,000

9. Deafness (total)

Assume that claimant is unable to resume his employment but takes up light duties 1.5 years after accident at DM 60,000 net p.a.

a) Monetary losses	
1. Medical expenses	
2. Loss of income	190,000
Interest on loss of income until settlement	17,000
Future loss of income (assume retirement at 65, about factor 13.0[12]	520,000
3. Miscellaneous losses	50,000
b) Pain and suffering	70,000 – 75,000

12 According to capitalisation table, annuity for men up to their 65th year (mortality table 1995/97).

Table 2. Schedule B

Claimant:	Woman
Age:	20
Status:	Single
Occupation:	Legal Secretary
Income:	DEM 25,000 net p.a. increasing to DEM 35,000 net p.a. by age 30 and DEM 40,000 net p.a. by age 40
Settlement:	2.5 years after accident

1. Instant death	DEM
a) Funeral expenses	7,500
Interest on funeral expenses (2.5 years at 6%)	1,500
b) Loss of maintenance	none

2. Burns

Assume that the claimant is able to resume her employment two years after accident

a) Monetary losses	
1. Medical expenses	
2. Loss of income until settlement	50,000
Interest on loss of income until settlement	4,500
3. Miscellaneous losses	100,000
b) Non material losses, i.e. pain and suffering	50,000 – 100,000

3. Quadriplegia

a) Monetary losses	
1. Medical expenses	
2. Loss of income	62,500

Interest on loss of income until settlement		4,700
Future loss of income (assume retirement at 65) 25,000 about factor 6.5[13] 35,000 about factor 7.8 x factor 0.599486[14] 40,000 about factor 13.8[15]	 162,500 163,660 552,000	
		878,160
3. Miscellaneous losses		200,000
b) Pain and suffering		300,000 – 500,000

4. Paraplegia

Assume income earned in sedentary job 1.5 years after accident at 15,000 p.a.

a) Monetary losses		
1. Medical expenses	—	
2. Loss of income	47,500	
Interest on loss of income until settlement	4,238	
Future loss of income (assume retirement at 65) 10,000 about factor 6.8[16] 20,000 about factor 7.8 x factor 0.599486[17] 25,000 about factor 13.8[18]	 68,000 93,520 345,000	
		506,520

13 According to capitalisation table, annuity to 65th year - women (mortality table 1995/97)

14 According to table for deduction of unaccrued interest for capital cash value at an interest rate of 5.25% for 10 years.

15 According to capitalisation table, annuity to 65th year - women (mortality table 1995/97).

16 See footnote 13 for 8.5 years.

17 See footnote 14.

18 See footnote 15.

Miscellaneous losses	200,000
b) Pain and suffering	200,000 – 300,000

5. Brain damage

a) Monetary losses; see 3 above	1,145,360
b) Pain and suffering	130,000 – 300,000

6. Amputation of leg

Assume that claimant is able to resume her employment 1.5 years after accident

a) Monetary losses	
1. Medical expenses	
2. Loss of income	37,500
Interest on loss of income until settlement	3,938
b) Pain and suffering	75,000 – 90,000

7. Amputation of arm

Assume that claimant is unable to resume her employment but takes up light duties 1.5 years after accident at DM 15,000 net p.a., DM 25,000 net p.a. by age 30 and DM 50,000 net p.a. by age 40[19]

a) Monetary losses	
1. Medical expenses	
2. Loss of income until settlement	47,500
Interest on loss of income until settlement	4,238

19 The income commencing in the 40th year of life exceeds the damage occurring previously, so that there is no further loss of income to be compensated.

Future loss of income (assume retirement at 65)		
10,000 about factor 6.8[20]	68,000	
10,000 about factor 7.8 x factor 0.599486[21]	46,760	
3. Miscellaneous losses		50,000
b) Pain and suffering		60,000 – 80,000

8a. and 8b. Loss of eyesight – one eye

Assume that claimant is able to resume her employment one year after accident

a) Monetary losses	
1. Medical expenses	
2. Loss of income	250,000
Interest on loss of income until settlement	3,000
b) Pain and suffering	50,000 – 80,000

8c. Loss of eyesight – total blindness

Assume that claimant is unable to resume her employment

a) Monetary losses	
1. Medical expenses	
2. Loss of income, see 3 above	
Miscellaneous losses	100,000
b) Pain and suffering	130,000 – 160,000

20 See footnote 13 for 8.5 years.

21 See footnote 14.

9. Deafness (total)

Assume that claimant is unable to resume her employment but takes up light duties 1.5 years after accident at DM 15,000 net p.a., DM 25,000 net p.a. by age 30, and DM 30,000 net p.a. by age 40

a) Monetary losses		
1. Medical expenses		
2. Loss of income		47,500
Interest on loss of income until settlement		4,238
Future loss of income (assume retirement at 65)		
10,000 about factor 6.8[22]	68,000	
10,000 about factor 7.8 x factor 0.599486[23]	46,760	
3. Miscellaneous losses		50,000
b) Pain and suffering		70,000 – 75,000

22 See footnote 13 for 8.5 years.

23 See footnote 14.

GREECE

E. Tsouroulis, N. Domvros and D. G. Rediadis

Introduction

Under Greek law the party who has culpably (whether intentionally or negligently) injured another party is liable to pay damages. The injured person is entitled to claim the amount of pecuniary loss which he proves he has sustained as well as that which he is likely to suffer in the future, and for pain and suffering.

In the case of death, the culpable party must also pay funeral expenses. Furthermore, in the case of death he must pay any medical expenses incurred by the victim as a result of the injuries which led to his death.

As regards pain and suffering the quantum of damages is in the discretion of the courts and depends on various relevant factors, such as the degree of fault, the financial and social position of the parties, the gravity of the particular circumstances of the incident, etc. Where the victim has died, the persons entitled to recover are the members of his family, i.e. the surviving spouse, the children, grandchildren, parents, grandparents and brothers and sisters of the deceased, but cousins are excluded. In cases of sexual impairment, damages for pain and suffering are payable both to the victim and to the spouse. In recent years the quantum of damages for pain and suffering awarded by the courts has increased considerably.

Under Greek law there is no deceased estate as such. The deceased's heirs step into his shoes under the Law of Succession (whether the deceased is testate or intestate).

In the hypothetical cases under consideration, the rights of the claimants are not based on inheritance but are direct claims arising from the death/injury of the two hypothetical victims.

Under specific provision of the Greek Civil Code damages payable to the relatives of the deceased for loss of support, as well as damages payable to an injured party, are paid in monthly instalments and not in a lump sum save in exceptional cases. In the latter event the current state of the law is that the amount payable in a lump sum is the total of the monthly instalments, but, according to a better view not often adopted by our courts, the lump sum is a figure arrived at by taking into account the interest which can be earned if the money is invested. In this latter (rather complicated) method of calculation the amount payable would, in fact, be much less than the total monthly instalments.

The legal rate of interest in Greece stands today at 18% p.a. which generally speaking is payable either from the date of the event which gave rise to the claim or from the date of service of the writ.

In our schedules no provision has been made for nursing and medical expenses in respect of cases involving less serious injuries.

It has been assumed that there is no upper limit applicable to awards. Road traffic accidents are covered by separate legislation providing for strict-blameless-liability [strict (no fault) liability] covered by compulsory insurance. An insurer's liability is limited to the sums agreed to in the insurance policy, for which there is a minimum provision of GRD 165 million in respect of death and personal injury claims.

It is important to stress that damages in respect of death or personal injury are recoverable irrespective of and in addition to any other lump sum compensation or pension fund payments received under social security schemes or private insurance arrangements made by the victim [and/or by his dependents] or of the other beneficiaries of such damages.

Table 1. Schedule A

Claimant:	Man
Age :	40
Status :	Married, 2 dependent children aged 5 and 7
Occupation :	Doctor
Income :	GRD 7,200,000 net p.a.
Trial:	2.5 years after accident
Service of Writ :	One year after accident

1. Instant death		GRD
a) Pain and suffering		
Widow	3,000,000	
Children x 2 @ 3,000,000	6,000,000	
Funeral expenses	700,000	
		9,700,000
b) Wife and children's dependence		
Net value of income	7,200,000	
Deduct		
Deceased's own expenditure (25%)	1,800,000	
Add		
Value of services provided by deceased (eg house maintenance, gardening, etc now has to be paid for)	500,000	
Total annual dependence	**5,900,000**	
Dependence divided 50% to wife 2,950,000 x 25 years	73,750,000	
Child 'A' 25% 1,475,000 x 11 years – ie up to age of majority of 18	16,225,000	
Child 'B' 25% 1,475,000 x 13 years	19,175,000	
		109,150,000

c) Interest on accumulated dependence, pain and suffering and funeral expenses up to time of trial 15,600,000 at 18% pa x 1.5 years		4,212,000
TOTAL AWARD		***123,062,000**

* *Plus* interest at 18% p.a. on any single monthly instalment to be added for the time between date when each one is due until date of settlement, for items under (b) above

2. Burns (A, B, C)

Disability percentage: 15%

a) Pain and suffering		2,000,000
b) Pecuniary claims: Assume that the claimant is able to resume his employment two years after the accident		
i) loss of income 2 years at 7,200,000	14,400,000	
23 years (i.e. until retirement age 65) 7,200,000 x 15%	24,840,000	
ii) miscellaneous losses say 20,000 per month for the first two years	480,000	
		40,720,000
c) Interest on accumulated pain and suffering, loss of income and miscellaneous losses for the period of the litigation: 9,440,000 at 18% p.a. x 1.5 years		2,548,800
TOTAL AWARD		***45,268,800**

* *Plus* interest at 18% p.a. on any single monthly instalment to be added for the time between date when each one is due until date of settlement, for items (b) (i) and (ii), above

Disability percentage: 20%

a) Pain and suffering		3,000,000

b) Pecuniary claims:
Assume that the claimant is able to resume his employment two years after the accident

i) loss of income 2 years at 7,200,000	14,400,000	
23 years at 7,200,000 x 20%	33,120,000	
ii) miscellaneous losses say 30,000 per month for the first two years	720,000	
		48,240,000
c) Interest on accumulated pain and suffering, loss of income and miscellaneous losses for the period of the litigation: 10,560,000 at 18% p.a. x 1.5 years		2,851,200
TOTAL AWARD		***54,091,200**

* *Plus* interest at 18% p.a. on any single monthly instalment to be added for the time between date when each one is due until date of settlement, for items (b) (i) and (ii), above.

3. Quadriplegia

Disability percentage: 100%

a) Pain and suffering		6,000,000
b) Pecuniary claims:		
i) loss of income 25 years at 7,200,000	216,000,000	
ii) cost of nursing care/medical expenses from date of accident to retirement age 65 years 25 years at 6,000,000	150,000,000	
iii) value of services provided by claimant which now have to be paid for 25 years at 500,000	12,500,000	
iv) cost of modifying home	3,200,000	
		381,700,000

c) Interest on accumulated pain and suffering, loss of income, nursing care and medical expenses, etc for the period of the litigation: 22,400,000 at 18% p.a. x 1.5 years		6,048,000
TOTAL AWARD		***393,748,000**

* *Plus* interest at 18% p.a. on any single monthly instalment to be added for the time between date when each one is due until date of settlement, for items (b) (i) (ii) and (iii), above.

4. Paraplegia

Disability percentage: 70%

a) Pain and suffering		5,000,000
b) Pecuniary claims:		
i) loss of income 25 years at 7,200,000 (assume that the claimant is able to resume his employment 1.5 years after the accident):		
1.5 years at 7,200,000	10,800,000	
23.5 years at 7,200,000 x 70%	118,440,000	
ii) nursing care/medical expenses		
1.5 years at 5,000,000	7,500,000	
23.5 years at 1,000,000	23,500,000	
iii) value of services provided by claimant which now have to be paid for 25 years at 300,000	7,500,000	
iv) special equipment	1,000,000	
		168,740,000
c) Interest on accumulated pain and suffering, loss of income, nursing care and medical expenses, etc. for the period of the litigation: 18,500,000 at 18% p.a. x 1.5 years		4,955,000
TOTAL AWARD		***178,735,000**

* *Plus* interest at 18% p.a. on any single monthly instalment to be added for the time between date when each one is due until date of settlement, for items (b) (i) (ii) and (iii), above.

5a. and 5b. Brain damage

Disability percentage: 80%

a) Pain and suffering		6,500,000
b) Pecuniary claims:		
i) loss of income (assume that the claimant is able to resume employment 6 months after the accident)		
0.5 years at 7,200,000	3,600,000	
24.5 years at 7,200,000 x 80%	141,120,000	
ii) nursing care/medical expenses		
0.5 years at 4,000,000	2,000,000	
24.5 years at 1,500,000	36,750,000	
iii) value of services provided by claimant which now have to be paid for		
25 years at 300,000	7,500,000	
iv) special equipment	1,000,000	
		191,970,000
c) Interest on accumulated pain and suffering, loss of income, nursing care and medical expenses, etc. for the period of the litigation: 16,030,000 at 18% p.a. x 1.5 years		4,328,100
TOTAL AWARD		***202,798,100**

* *Plus* interest at 18% p.a. on any single monthly instalment to be added for the time between date when each one is due until date of settlement, for items (b) (i), (ii) and (iii), above.

6a. and 7a. Amputation of leg above knee and arm above elbow

Disability percentage: 35%

a) Pain and suffering		4,000,000
b) Pecuniary claims:		
i) loss of income (assume that the claimant is able to resume employment 1.5 years after the accident)		
1.5 years at 7,200,000	10,800,000	
23.5 years at 7,200,000 x 35%	59,220,000	
ii) miscellaneous losses (including special conversion of car)	1,000,000	
iii) nursing care/medical treatment expenses 1.5 years at 600,000	900,000	
iv) value of services provided by claimant which now have to be paid for 1.5 years at 300,000	450,000	
		72,370,000
c) Interest on accumulated pain and suffering, loss of income, nursing care and medical expenses, etc. for the period of the litigation: 13,100,000 at 18% p.a. x 1.5 years		3,537,000
TOTAL AWARD		***79,907,000**

* *Plus* interest at 18% p.a. on any single monthly instalment to be added for the time between date when each one is due until date of settlement, for items (b) (i), (iii) and (iv), above.

6b. and 7b. Amputation of leg below knee and arm below elbow

Disability percentage: 30%

a) Pain and suffering		3,000,000
b) Pecuniary claims:		
i) loss of income (assume claimant is able to resume employment for 1.5 years		

after the accident)		
1.5 years at 7,200,000	10,800,000	
23.5 years at 7,200,000 x 30%	50,760,000	
ii) miscellaneous losses (including special conversion of car)	1,000,000	
iii) nursing care/medical treatment expenses 1.5 years at 600,000	900,000	
iv) value of services provided by claimant which now have to be paid for 1.5 years at 300,000	450,000	
		63,910,000
c) Interest on accumulated pain and suffering, loss of income, nursing care and medical expenses, etc. for the period of the litigation: 12,100,000 at 18% p.a. x 1.5 years		3,267,000
TOTAL AWARD		***70,177,000**

* *Plus* interest at 18% p.a. on any single monthly instalment to be added for the time between date when each one is due until date of settlement, for items (b) (i), (iii) and (iv), above.

8a. and 8b. Loss of eyesight – one eye

Disability percentage: 30%

a) Pain and suffering		2,000,000
b) Pecuniary claims:		
i) loss of income (assume claimant is able to resume employment one year after the accident)		
1 year at 7,200,000	7,200,000	
24 years 7,200,000 x 30%	51,840,000	
ii) miscellaneous losses	500,000	
iii) medical treatment expenses	500,000	
		60,040,000

c) Interest on accumulated pain and suffering, loss of income and medical treatment expenses, etc. for the period of the litigation: 10,200,000 at 18% p.a. x 1.5 years		2,754,000
TOTAL AWARD		***64,794,000**

* *Plus* interest at 18% p.a. on any single monthly instalment to be added for the time between date when each one is due until date of settlement, for items (b) (i), above.

8c. Loss of eyesight – total blindness

Disability percentage: 100%

a) Pain and suffering		8,500,000
b) Pecuniary claims:		
i) loss of income 25 years at 7,200,000	180,000,000	
ii) medical expenses and nursing care first 2.5 years at 1,200,000 remaining 22.5 years at 360,000	 3,000,000 8,100,000	
iii) replacement aids	1,000,000	
iv) value of services provided by claimant which now have to be paid for 25 years at 400,000	10,000,000	
		202,100,000
c) Interest on accumulated pain and suffering, loss of income, nursing care and medical expenses, etc. for the period of the litigation: 18,300,000 at 18% p.a. x 1.5 years		4,941,000
TOTAL AWARD		***215,541,000**

* *Plus* interest at 18% p.a. on any single monthly instalment to be added for the time between date when each one is due until date of settlement, for items (b) (i), (ii) and (iv), above.

9. Deafness (total)

Disability percentage: 50%

a) Pain and suffering		3,000,000
b) Pecuniary claims:		
i) loss of income (assume claimant unable to resume previous employment, but takes on lighter duties 1.5 years after the accident)		
1.5 years at 7,200,000	10,800,000	
23.5 years at 7,200,000 x 50%	84,600,000	
ii) miscellaneous expenses	1,000,000	
		96,400,000
c) Interest on accumulated pain and suffering, loss of income and miscellaneous losses for the period of the litigation: 11,200,000 at 18% p.a. x 1.5 years		3,024,000
TOTAL AWARD		***102,424,000**

* *Plus* interest at 18% p.a. on any single monthly instalment to be added for the time between date when each one is due until date of settlement, for items (b) (i), above.

10. Repetitive strain injury – Persistent pain and stiffness of wrist

Disability percentage: 20%

a) Pain and suffering		500,000
b) Pecuniary claims:		
i) loss of income (assume claimant unable to resume previous employment, but takes on lighter duties six months after the accident)		
0.5 years at 7,200,000	3,600,000	
24.5 years at 7,200,000 x 20%	35,280,000	
ii) miscellaneous expenses	100,000	
		38,980,000

c) Interest on accumulated pain and suffering, loss of income and miscellaneous losses for the period of the litigation: 4,920,000 at 18% p.a. x 1.5 year		1,328,400
TOTAL AWARD		***40,808,400**

* *Plus* interest at 18% p.a. on any single monthly instalment to be added for the time between date when each one is due until date of settlement, for items (b) (i), above.

Table 2. Schedule B

Claimant:	Woman
Age:	20
Status:	Single
Occupation:	Legal Secretary
Income:	GRD. 2,500,000 p.a.
Trial:	2.5 years after accident
Service of writ:	One year after accident

1. Instant death

a) Pain and suffering paid to parents 2 x 1,000,000	2,000,000	
Funeral expenses	800,000	
		2,800,000
b) Parents' dependence: – from age 25-30 at 500,000 p.a.	2,500,000	
– from age 30-35 at 600,000 p.a	3,000,000	
		5,500,000

c) Interest on accumulated pain and suffering, dependence and funeral expenses up to time of trial 3,300,000 at 18% p.a. x 1.5 years		891,000
TOTAL AWARD		***9,191,000**

* *Plus* interest at 18% p.a. on any single monthly instalment to be added for the time between date when each one is due until date of settlement, for items under (b) above.

2. Burns (A, B, C)

Disability percentage: 15%

a) Pain and suffering		1,000,000
b) Pecuniary claims:		
Assume that the claimant is able to resume employment two years after the accident		
i) loss of income (assume that disability affects the victim and 5 x 15%)		
2 years at 2,500,000	5,000,000	
5 years at 2,500,000 x 15%	1,875,000	
		6,875,000
ii) miscellaneous losses say 20,000 per month for the first two years		480,000
c) Interest on accumulated pain and suffering, loss of income and miscellaneous losses for the period of the litigation: 3,740,000 at 18% p.a. x 1.5 years		1,009,800
TOTAL AWARD		***9,364,800**

* *Plus* interest at 18% p.a. on any single monthly instalment to be added for the time between date when each one is due until date of settlement, for items (b) (i) and (ii), above.

Disability percentage: 20%

a) Pain and suffering		1,200,000
b) Pecuniary claims: (assume that the claimant is able to resume employment two years after the accident)		
i) loss of income (assume that disability affects the victim for 7 years (2 x 100% and 5 x 20%)		
2 years at 2,500,000	5,000,000	
5 years at 2,500,000 x 20%	2,500,000	
		7,500,000
ii) miscellaneous losses say 20,000 per month for the first two years		480,000
c) Interest on accumulated pain and suffering, loss of income and miscellaneous losses for the period of the litigation: 3,940,000 at 18% p.a. x 1.5 years		1,063,800
TOTAL AWARD		***10,243,800**

* *Plus* interest at 18% p.a. on any single monthly instalment to be added for the time between date when each one is due until date of settlement, for items (b) (i) and (ii), above.

3. Quadriplegia

Disability percentage: 100%

a) Pain and suffering		6,000,000
b) Pecuniary claims:		
i) loss of income 45 years at 2,500,000	112,500,000	
ii) cost of nursing care/medical expenses from date of accident to retirement age 65 years 45 years at 4,500,000	202,500,000	

iii) cost of modifying home and special equipment, say	3,000,000	
		318,000,000
c) Interest on accumulated pain and suffering, loss of income, nursing care and medical expenses, etc. for the period of the litigation: 11,500,000 at 18% p.a. x 1.5 years		3,105,000
TOTAL AWARD		***327,105,000**

* *Plus* interest at 18% p.a. on any single monthly instalment to be added for the time between date when each one is due until date of settlement, for items (b) (i) (ii) and (iii), above.

4. Paraplegia

Disability percentage: 70%

a) Pain and suffering		4,000,000
b) Pecuniary claims:		
i) loss of income (assume that the claimant is able to resume employment 1.5 years after the accident):		
1.5 years at 2,500,000	3,750,000	
43.5 years at 2,500,000 x 70%	76,125,000	
ii) nursing care/medical expenses		
1.5 years at 2,000,000	3,000,000	
43.5 years at 1,000,000	43,500,000	
iii) modifying home/special equipment	1,000,000	
		127,375,000
c) Interest on accumulated pain and suffering, loss of income, nursing care and medical expenses, etc. for the period of the litigation: 9,500,000 at 18% p.a. x 1.5 years		2,565,000
TOTAL AWARD		***133,940,000**

* *Plus* interest at 18% p.a. on any single monthly instalment to be added for the time between date when each one is due until date of settlement, for items (b) (i) (ii) and (iii), above.

5a. and 5b. Brain damage

Disability percentage: 80%

a) Pain and suffering		6,000,000
b) Pecuniary claims:		
i) loss of income (assume that claimant is able to resume employment 6 months after the accident)		
0.5 years at 2,500,000	1,250,000	
44.5 years at 2,500,000 x 80%	89,000,000	
ii) nursing care/medical expenses		
0.5 years at 3,500,000	1,750,000	
44.5 years at 1,400,000	62,300,000	
iii) cost of special equipment	1,000,000	
		155,300,000
c) Interest on accumulated pain and suffering, loss of income, nursing care and medical expenses, etc. for the period of the litigation: 9,500,000 at 18% p.a. x 1.5 years		2,565,000
TOTAL AWARD		***163,865,000**

* *Plus* interest at 18% p.a. on any single monthly instalment to be added for the time between date when each one is due until date of settlement, for items (b) (i), (ii) and (iii), above.

6a. and 7a. Amputation of leg above knee and arm above elbow

Disability percentage: 35%

a) Pain and suffering	5,000,000

b) Pecuniary claims:

i) loss of income (assume that the claimant is able to resume employment 1.5 years after the accident)		
1.5 years at 2,500,000	3,750,000	
43.5 years at 2,500,000 x 35%	38,062,500	
ii) miscellaneous losses (including special conversion of car)	1,000,000	
iii) nursing care/medical treatment expenses 1.5 years at 600,000	900,000	
		43,712,500
c) Interest on accumulated pain and suffering, loss of income, nursing care and medical expenses, etc. for the period of the litigation: 9,400,000 at 18% p.a. x 1.5 years		2,538,000
TOTAL AWARD		***51,250,500**

* *Plus* interest at 18% p.a. on any single monthly instalment to be added for the time between date when each one is due until date of settlement, for items (b) (i), (ii) and (iii), above.

6b. and 7b. Amputation of leg below knee and arm below elbow

Disability percentage: 30%

a) Pain and suffering		4,000,000
b) Pecuniary claims:		
i) loss of income (assume claimant is able to resume employment for 1.5 years after the accident)		
1.5 years at 2,500,000	3,750,000	
43.5 years at 2,500,000 x 30%	32,625,000	
ii) miscellaneous losses (including special conversion of car)	1,000,000	

iii) nursing care/medical treatment expenses 1.5 years at 600,000	900,000	
		38,275,000
c) Interest on accumulated pain and suffering, loss of income, nursing care and medical expenses, etc. for the period of the litigation: 8,100,000 at 18% p.a. x 1.5 years		2,187,000
TOTAL AWARD		***44,462,000**

* *Plus* interest at 18% p.a. on any single monthly instalment to be added for the time between date when each one is due until date of settlement, for items (b) (i) and (iii), above.

8a. and 8b. Loss of eyesight – one eye

Disability percentage: 30%

a) Pain and suffering		3,000,000
b) Pecuniary claims:		
i) loss of income (assume claimant is able to resume employment one year after the accident) 1 year at 2,500,000	2,500,000	
44 years 2,500,000 x 30%	33,000,000	
ii) miscellaneous losses	500,000	
iii) medical treatment expenses	500,000	
		36,500,000
c) Interest on accumulated pain and suffering, loss of income and medical treatment expenses, etc. for the period of the litigation: 6,500,000 at 18% p.a. x 1.5 years		1,755,000
TOTAL AWARD		***41,255,000**

* *Plus* interest at 18% p.a. on any single monthly instalment to be added for the time between date when each one is due until date of settlement, for items (b) (i) and (ii), above.

8c. Loss of eyesight – total blindness

Disability percentage: 100%

a) Pain and suffering		8,000,000
b) Pecuniary claims:		
i) loss of income 45 years at 2,500,000	112,500,000	
ii) nursing care and medical expenses first 2.5 years at 1,200,000 remaining 42.5 years at 360,000	 3,000,000 15,300,000	
iii) replacement aids	1,000,000	
		131,800,000
c) Interest on accumulated pain and suffering, loss of income, nursing care and medical expenses, etc. for the period of the litigation: 12,700,000 at 18% p.a. x 1.5 years		3,429,000
TOTAL AWARD		***143,229,000**

* *Plus* interest at 18% p.a. on any single monthly instalment to be added for the time between date when each one is due until date of settlement, for items (b) (i), (ii) and (iii), above.

9. Deafness (total)

Disability percentage: 50%

a) Pain and suffering		5,000,000
b) Pecuniary claims:		
i) loss of income (assume claimant unable to resume previous employment, but takes on lighter duties 1.5 years after the accident) 1.5 years at 2,500,000 43.5 years at 2,500,000 x 50%	 3,750,000 54,375,000	
ii) miscellaneous expenses	1,000,000	
		59,125,000

c) Interest on accumulated pain and suffering, loss of income and miscellaneous losses for the period of litigation: 8,500,000 at 18% p.a. x 1.5 years		2,295,000
TOTAL AWARD		***66,420,000**

* *Plus* interest at 18% p.a. on any single monthly instalment to be added for the time between date when each one is due until date of settlement, for items (b) (i), above.

10. Repetitive strain injury – Persistent pain and stiffness of wrist

Disability percentage: 20%

a) Pain and suffering		500,000
b) Pecuniary claims:		
i) loss of income (assume claimant unable to resume previous employment, but takes on lighter duties six months after the accident)		
0.5 years at 2,500,000	1,250,000	
44.5 years at 2,500,000 x 20%	22,250,000	
ii) miscellaneous expenses	100,000	
		23,600,000
c) Interest on accumulated pain and suffering, loss of income and miscellaneous losses for the period of the litigation: 2,350,000 at 18% p.a. x 1.5 years		634,500
TOTAL AWARD		***24,734,500**

* *Plus* interest at 18% p.a. on any single monthly instalment to be added for the time between date when each one is due until date of settlement, for items (b) (i), above.

IRELAND

Katherine Delahunt, Frank Beatty and Joseph G. Byrne

Introduction

Personal Injury Litigation in the Republic of Ireland is perceived to be closer to the United States than the UK as overall awards and the pain and suffering element therein are much likely to be higher in Ireland than in other EU and EFTA Countries.

The Irish Legal System is a Common Law System with a split legal profession involving Solicitors and Barristers, both strands of the profession have full access to all Courts but apart from routine motions and the like cases in the higher courts tend to be conducted by Barristers. In Ireland, extensive use is now made of pre-trial settlement meetings which in very many cases lead to an early settlement thereby reducing not only legal fees but other professional fees that are incurred. A "door of the Court settlement" is another prominent feature in claims settlement and on any given day one could well find the majority if not all of the listed cases being settled in this fashion. This latter type settlement will not however reduce costs incurred.

Some of the differences between Ireland and the U.K. are as follows:

1. Statutory Bereavement damages in Ireland which are governed by the Civil Liability Act 1996 allow for an award of "tear money" of up to IEP 20,000.
2. When awarding future loss of earnings in an action a Court can allow for inflation and also discount the future loss on the basis that no-one is guaranteed a job for life.
3. It is unusual to award interest on any pre-trial losses.

There are three Courts of first instance to hear Personal Injury claims:

1. District Court: Claims up to IEP 5,0002.
2. Circuit Court: Claims between IEP 5,000 – 30,000

3. High Court: Claims over IEP 30,000

The Supreme Court deals with appeals from the High Court on points of law.

General

As outlined, damages in Ireland for personal injuries have always appeared high in comparison to the rest of Europe. It was thought with the abolition of Juries some twelve years ago that awards would decrease but this has not been the case and Judges have been as generous with their awards if not more generous than before. As there are no specific guidelines on which awards are based sometimes Judges are criticised for being unpredictable with some seen to be more generous towards Plaintiffs than others but in fact it is possible to advise Litigants on the general average. The different attitude taken by Judges has recently come to the fore in Army Deafness cases. This area has received significant judicial attention in recent years and because of noticeable differences in awards for seemingly the same levels of deafness the Government brought in the Civil Liability (Assessment of Hearing Injuries) Act, 1998. A formula known as the Green Book Formula was introduced and immediately challenged. The High Court held that this formula was limited as it only accounted for loss of hearing at the date of the trial and did not address the potential for future loss. The Supreme Court has over-ruled this and laid down a specific formula for calculation of general damages for hearing loss into the future.

Heads of Damages

Damages in Ireland are awarded for non-pecuniary loss, pain, suffering, loss of amenity and for loss of enjoyment of life resulting from a disability. These are usually described as general damages. Pecuniary loss both past and future is described as special damages.

General Damages

There is no specific cap on the amount of general damages that can be awarded however the Supreme Court has laid down by way of precedent, guidelines for the

High Court to follow. The first of these cases was *Sinnott v Quinnsworth & another in 1984* where the maximum level of general damages was capped at IEP 150,000. Over the years this has been gradually eroded and in the case of *Paula Kealy v the Minister for Health,* the President of the High Court Morris J. held that the Sinnott case was decided at a time of depression when interest rates were high and incomes relative to the present day small and an award of IEP 250,000 was made. These were so to speak catastrophic type cases. Recently the Supreme Court in the case of *Ramos v Kapitaen Manfred Draxl Schiffahrts GmbH*, [unreported] reduced an award for general damages from IEP 250,000 to 150,000 and the Chief Justice advised he was being generous even in this. The injuries received by the Plaintiff were life threatening but he had recovered well and therefore the Supreme Court held that the High Court was wrong in assessing the injuries in the same way as one would a catastrophic case.

In assessing general damages the following will be considered by a Judge:

1. The severity of the injury on a scale of injuries i.e. from catastrophic downwards;
2. The age of the Plaintiff. Obviously a serious injury to a younger person will attract higher damages than a similar injury to an older person;
3. The occupation of the Plaintiff;
4. The sex of the Plaintiff. For example severe scarring will merit a higher award for a female than a male;
5. The nature, location and duration of the injury.

Special Damages

Special damages are the out of pocket expenses of the Plaintiff that is the actual financial loss suffered and this is normally divided into two:

a) Past loss i.e. expenses to the date of the trial;

b) Future loss i.e. estimated anticipated loss of the Plaintiff and this is often calculated with the help of an Actuary. For example in a serious injury case one could take into account [as per the schedule attached herewith] accommodation, aids and appliances, special car, care costs, loss of vocational opportunity and so on. The Supreme Court in the case of *Reddy v Bates* 1984 ILRM 197 has stated that in assessing the amount to award for future loss of earnings etc; actuarial figures are to be used only as a guideline and the Court will have to consider evidence relating to risk to employment, redundancy illness, marriage prospects etc.

Fatal Injuries

The Civil Liability Act 1961 as amended allows the dependants of a person whose death was caused by a wrongful act to make a claim for damages up to IEP 20,000. These damages are known as "tear money". The word dependant is defined as a spouse, grandparent, step-parent, child, grandchild, step-child, brother, sister, half brother or half sister of the deceased. A person who was not the deceased's spouse but had been living with the deceased for a period of not less than three years and/ or a person who was dependant even though there was a decree of divorce. This is in effect a claim for mental distress, which is a recognised injury in this jurisdiction and the authority of *Jarvis & Swan Tours Limited* 1973 IQB233 has been accepted by the Irish Courts.

In assessing these damages a Judge may not take account of any sum payable under a contract of insurance or any pension or gratuity to which the deceased was entitled.

Medical Treatment

Private Health Insurance Companies will request a plaintiff to insert, as part of the claim, the amount paid out by the Insurers on their behalf. In road traffic accidents a Health Board is required to charge an injured person for services and this is also included in the claim. This relates to road traffic accidents only and is presently the subject matter of High Court proceedings to assess what level of payment should be claimed.

Welfare Benefits

Self-employed taxpayers are unlikely to receive Social Welfare benefits under existing legislation however for people entitled, the Social Welfare Consolidation Act 1981 allows for a deduction of disability benefit and invalidity pension which have accrued or will probably accrue as a result of the accident.

Impact of Taxation on Damages

Section 5 of the Finance Act provides that a plaintiff who is permanently and totally physically or mentally incapacitated and incapable of looking after himself then that plaintiff is not liable for tax on the investment income that he or she will receive from the investment of his or her damages. It is important to note however that this section is confined to a Plaintiff who is "permanently incapacitated".

Future Developments

Disquiet has been expressed at all levels including Government, Employers Associates and the Insurance Industry at the amount of general damages awarded. As a result certain types of cases and in particular actions arising for the decimination of infected blood plasma are now being dealt with through a Tribunal which has the power to award damages, future loss and a punitive sum against the State. A claimant has always had the constitutional right to have their case dealt with by a Court but the Tribunal has proved to be expeditious and cost effective. It is envisaged that the Army deafness cases will also be heard by a Tribunal in the future as legislation is enacted. Many commentators believe arising from this, and subject to constitutional restrictions, unique to Ireland, the future for Personal Injury Actions may be to have all cases dealt with in the first instance by a Tribunal with an appeal to the Court.

Table 1. Schedule A

Claimant :	Man
Age :	40
Status :	Married, 2 dependent children aged 5 & 7
Occupation :	Doctor
Income :	IEP 50,000 net p.a.
Trial :	2.5 years after accident

1. Instant Death		IEP
(a) Funeral Expenses		2,000
(b) Bereavement damages		20,000
(c) Wife & children's dependency		
Net value of income	50,000 p.a.	
Less – Deceased's expenditure (20%)	10,000 p.a.	
Net loss	40,000 p.a.	
Plus – Value of Deceased's services	1,000 p.a.	
Total Loss	41,000 p.a.	
Multiplier 19 years		
Value of Loss: 41,000 x 19		779,000
TOTAL AWARD		**801,000**

The accelerated value of deductible assets passing to the dependants is deducted from the above amount. Deductible assets are exclusive of the family residence and the proceeds of life assurance policies on the life of the deceased.

Any gratuity or pension paid to the Plaintiff as a result of her husband's death is non-deductible under Section 50 Civil Liability Act 1961.

2. Burns (A)

General damages	75,000 – 85,000
Assume that claimant is able to resume his employment two years after the accident	
(a) Loss of income 2 years x 50,000	100,000
(b) Miscellaneous losses, say	10,000
TOTAL AWARD	**185,000 – 195,000**

2. Burns (B)

General damages	60,000
Assume that claimant is able to resume his employment two years after the accident	
(a) Loss of income 2 years x 50,000	100,000
(b) Miscellaneous losses, say	10,000
TOTAL AWARD	**170,000**

2. Burns (C)

General damages	60,000
Assume that claimant is able to resume his employment two years after the accident	
(a) Loss of income 2 years x 50,000	100,000
(b) Miscellaneous losses, say	10,000
TOTAL AWARD	**170,000**

3. Quadriplegia

General damages	200,000 – 250,000
Pecuniary claims:	
(a) Loss of income to trial 2.5 years at 50,000	125,000
(b) Cost of nursing care/medical expenses to date of trial	125,000
(c) Value of services provided by claimant (which now have to be paid for) 2.5 years x 1,000	2,500
(d) Cost of modifying home and special equipment, say	40,000
(e) Future loss of income (42.5 years old at date of trial – retirement at 65) and life expectation of 20 years	600,000
(f) Future cost of nursing care/medical expenses/aids 13 years at 50,000 p.a.	650,000
(g) Future cost of household services provided by the Claimant 13 years at 1,000 p.a.	13,000
TOTAL AWARD	**1,755,500- 1,805,500**

4. Paraplegia

General damages		150,000 – 200,000
Pecuniary claims:		
(a) Loss of income to trial 2.5 years at 50,000	125,000	
Less		
income earned in sedentary work commenced 1 year after the accident, say	6,000	
		119,000
(b) Cost of nursing care/medical expenses/aids to date of trial, say		30,000

(c) Value of services provided by claimant for 2.5 years x 1,000		2,500
(d) Cost of modifying house		7,000
(e) Future loss of income (42.5 years old at date of trial – retirement age at 65 and normal life expectation net loss 50,000) less 6,000 per annum sedentary employed 14 years of 44,000		616,000
(f) Future care of nursing care/medical expenses /aids 18 years x 20,000		360,000
Future cost of household services provided by the claimant 18 years at 1,000		18,000
TOTAL AWARD		**1,302,500 – 1,352,500**

5. Brain damage

General damages		150,000 – 250,000
Pecuniary claims:		
(a) Loss of income to trial 2.5 years at 50,000		125,000
(b) Cost of nursing care/medical expenses/aids to date of trial, say		15,000
(c) Value of services provided by claimant for 2.5 years x 1,000		2,500
(d) Cost of special equipment		15,000
(e) Future loss of income (42.5 years old at date of trial – retirement age at 65 and normal life expectation net loss	50,000	
Less	2,500	
sheltered employment 14 years x 47,500		665,000
(f) Future care of nursing care/medical expenses /aids 18 years x 6,000		108,000

(g) Future cost of household services provided by the claimant 18 years at 1,000	18,000
TOTAL AWARD	**1,098,500-1,198,500**

5b. Brain damage with motor deficiency

General damages	200,000 – 250,000
Pecuniary claims:	
(a) Loss of income to trial 2.5 years at 50,000	125,000
(b) Cost of nursing care/medical expenses/aids to date of trial, say	15,000
(c) Value of services provided by claimant for 2.5 years x 1,000	2,500
(d) Cost of special equipment	15,000
(e) Future loss of income (42.5 years old at date of trial – retirement age at 65) life expectation of 20 years 12 years x 50,000	600,000
(f) Future care of nursing care/medical expenses /aids 13 years x 60,000	780,000
(g) Future cost of household services provided by the claimant 13 years at 1,000	13,000
TOTAL AWARD	**1,750,500-1,800,500**

6. Amputation of leg above knee

General damages	150,000	
Assume claimant able to resume his employment two years after the accident		
(a) Loss of income		100,000

(b) Miscellaneous losses including nursing care and prostheses	10,000
(c) Value of services provided by claimant now paid for 2.5 years x 1,000	2,500
(d) Future cost of household services provided by claimant 22 years at 1,000	22,000
(e) Future prostheses at 2,500 every 3 years 8 years at 2,500	20,000
TOTAL AWARD	**304,500**

6b. Amputation of leg below the knee

General damages	150,000
Assume claimant able to resume his employment 1.5 years after the accident	
(a) Loss of income 1.5 years at 50,000	75,000
(b) Miscellaneous losses	7,500
(c) Value of services provided by claimant now paid for at 2.5 years x 1,000	2,500
(d) Future cost of household services provided by claimant 22 years at 1,000	22,000
(e) Future prostheses at 1,600 every 3 years 8 years at 1,600	12,800
TOTAL AWARD	**269,800**

7a. Amputation of arm above elbow

General damages	150,000
Claimant not able to resume employment but takes up light duties 1.5 years after accident	

(a) Loss of income	125,000	
Less 1 years light work earnings	28,000	
		97,000
(b) Miscellaneous losses		5,000
(c) Prostheses to the date of the trial		3,000
(d) Services provided by claimant 2.5 years x 1,000		2,500
(e) Future loss of earnings to age 65 17 years at 22,000		374,000
(f) Future cost of household services provided by the claimant 22 years at 1,000		22,000
(g) Future prostheses at 1,750 every 3 years 8 years at 1,750		14,000
TOTAL AWARD		**667,500**

7b. Amputation of arm below elbow

General damages		150,000
Claimant not able to resume employment but takes up light duties 1.5 years after accident		
Pecuniary claims:		
(a) Loss of income	125,000	
Less 1 year's light work earnings	28,000	
		97,000
(b) Miscellaneous losses		5,000
(c) Prostheses to the date of the trial		3,000
(d) Services provided by claimant 2.5 years x 1,000		2,500
(e) Future loss of earnings to age 65 17 years at 22,000		374,000

(f) Future cost of household services provided by the claimant 22 years at 1,000	22,000
(g) Future prostheses at 1,050 every 3 years 8 years at 1,050	8,400
TOTAL AWARD	**661,900**

8a. Loss of eyesight – one eye without cosmetic disability

General damages	100,000
Assume that claimant is able to resume his employment one year after the accident	
(a) Loss of income 1 year	50,000
(b) Miscellaneous losses	2,500
TOTAL AWARD	**152,500**

8b. Loss of eyesight – one eye with cosmetic disability

General damages	125,000 – 140,000
Assume that claimant is able to resume his employment one year after the accident	
Pecuniary claims	
(a) Loss of income 1 year	50,000
(b) Miscellaneous losses	5,000
TOTAL AWARD	**180,000 – 195,000**

8c. Loss of eyesight – total blindness

General damages	200,000 – 225,000
Assume that claimant is unable to resume his employment	
Pecuniary claims	
(a) Loss of income to trial	125,000
(b) Cost of care and medical expenses	15,000
(c) Future loss of earnings to age 65 14 years at 50,000	700,000
(d) Future costs of services 18 years at 1,000	18,000
TOTAL AWARD	**1,058,000-1,083,000**

9. Deafness

General damages	75,000 – 100,000
Assume that claimant is unable to resume employment	
Pecuniary claims	
(a) Loss of income 2.5 years	125,000
(b) Miscellaneous expenses	5,000
(c) Future loss of income: Assume claimant capable of administrative work post-trial salary at 25,000	
Multiplier 14 years x 25,000	350,000
TOTAL AWARD	**580,000 – 605,000**

Table 2. Schedule B

Claimant:	Woman
Age:	20
Status:	Single
Occupation:	Legal Secretary
Income:	8,500 net p.a.
Trial:	2.5 years after accident.

1. Instant Death

(a) Funeral Expenses		2,500
(b) Bereavement damages		20,000
TOTAL AWARD		**22,500**

2. Burns (A)

General damages		110,000
Assume that claimant is able to resume her employment two years after the accident		
(a) Loss of income 2 years x 8,500	17,000	
Less		
Deduct welfare state benefits in full, say	2,300	
		14,700
(b) Miscellaneous losses, say		10,000
TOTAL AWARD		**134,700**

2. Burns (B)

General damages		100,000
Assume that claimant is able to resume her employment two years after the accident		
(a) Loss of income 2 years x 8,500	17,000	
Less		
Deduct welfare state benefits in full, say	2,300	
		14,700
(b) Miscellaneous losses, say		3,000
TOTAL AWARD		**117,700**

2. Burns (C)

General damages		80,000 – 90,000
Assume that claimant is able to resume her employment two years after the accident		
(a) Loss of income 2 years x 8,500	17,000	
Less		
Deduct welfare state benefits in full, say	2,300	
		14,700
(b) Miscellaneous losses, say		3,000
TOTAL AWARD		**97,700 – 107,700**

3. Quadriplegia

General damages		250,000
Pecuniary claims:		
(a) Loss of income to trial 2.5 years at 8,500	21,250	
Less		
Deduct welfare state benefits in full, say	10,000	
		11,250
(b) Cost of nursing care/medical expenses to date 2.5 years x 25,000		62,500
(c) Cost of modifying home and special equipment, say		25,000
Future loss of income (22.5 years old at date of trial – retirement at 65 and life expectancy of 35 years)		190,000
(e) Future cost of nursing care/medical expenses 18 years at 50,000		900,000
TOTAL AWARD		**1,438,750**

4. Paraplegia

General damages		175,000 – 225,000
Pecuniary claims:		
(a) Loss of income to trial 2.5 years at 8,500	21,250	
Less		
Deduct welfare state benefits in full, say	10,000	
Less		
income earned in sedentary work commenced 2 years after the accident, say	4,000	
		7,250
(b) Cost of medical expenses etc to date of trial		30,000

(c) Cost of modifying home		7,000
(d) Future loss of income allowing for the income earned in sedentary employment (4,000 p.a.)		132,000
(e) Future cost of nursing care/medical expenses/aids 22 years at 20,000		440,000
TOTAL AWARD		**791,250 – 841,250**

5a. Brain damage

General damages		150,000 – 200,000
Pecuniary claims:		
(a) Loss of income to trial 2.5 years at 8,500	21,250	
less welfare benefits in full, say	11,000	
		10,250
(b) Cost of medical care to date		10,000
(c) Cost of modifying home and special equipment		15,000
(d) Future loss of income (22.5 years old at date of trial – retirement age at 65 and normal life expectation) allowing for 2,500 from sheltered employment		162,000
(e) Future cost of nursing care/medical expenses/aids 22 years x 6,000		132,000
TOTAL AWARD		**479,250 – 529,250**

5b Brain damage with motor deficiency

General damages		200,000 – 250,000
Pecuniary claims:		
(a) Loss of income to trial 2.5 years at 8,500	21,250	

Less		
Deduct welfare benefits in full, say	11,000	
		10,250
(b) Cost of nursing care/medical expenses/aids to date of trial of trial 2.5 years x 30,000		75,000
(c) Cost of modifying home with special equipment		25,000
(d) Future loss of income (22.5 years old at date of trial – retirement age at 65) life expectation of 35 years		190,000
(e) Future cost of nursing care/medical expenses /aids 18 years x 60,000		1,080,000
TOTAL AWARD		**1,580,250 – 1,630,250**

6a. Amputation of leg above knee

General damages		200,000
Assume claimant able to resume her employment two years after the accident		
(a) Loss of income to date of trial	21,250	
Less		
Deduct welfare state benefits in full, say	11,000	
		10,250
(b) Miscellaneous losses including nursing care and prostheses		10,000
(c) Future prostheses at 2,500 every 3 years: 9 years at 2,500 per annum		22,500
TOTAL AWARD		**242,750**

6b. Amputation of leg below the knee

General damages		125,000 – 150,000
Assume claimant able to resume her employment 1.5 years after the accident		
(a) Loss of income 1.5 years at 8,500	12,750	
Less		
Deduct welfare state benefits in full, say	5,500	
		7,250
(b) Miscellaneous losses		7,500
(c) Future prostheses at 1,600 every 3 years 9 years at 1,600		14,400
TOTAL AWARD		**154,150 – 179,150**

7a. Amputation of arm above elbow

General damages		150,000 – 175,000
Claimant not able to resume employment		
(a) Loss of income 2.5 years x 8,500	21,250	
Less		
Deduct state benefits in full, say	11,000	
		10,250
(b) Miscellaneous losses including prostheses to date of trial		8,000
(c) Future loss of earnings to age 65		210,000
(d) Future prostheses at 1,750 every 3 years 8 years at 1,750 per annum		14,000
TOTAL AWARD		**392,225 – 417,250**

7b. Amputation of arm below elbow

General damages		125,000 – 140,000
Claimant not able to resume her employment		
(a) Loss of income 2.5 years at 8,500	21,250	
Less		
Deduct welfare state benefits in full	10,000	
		10,250
(b) Miscellaneous losses		6,000
(c) Future loss of earnings to age 65		210,000
(d) Future prostheses at 1,050 every 3 years 8 years x 1,050 per annum		8,400
TOTAL AWARD		**359,650 – 374,650**

8a. Loss of eyesight – one eye without cosmetic disability

General damages		100,000
(a) Loss of income 1 year at 8,500	8,500	
Less		
social welfare	4,000	
		4,500
(b) Miscellaneous losses		2,500
TOTAL AWARD		**107,000**

8b. Loss of eyesight – one eye with cosmetic disability

General damages		125,000-140,000
Assume that claimant is able to resume her employment one year after the accident		
(a) Loss of income 1 year	8,500	
Less		
social welfare benefits	4,000	
		4,500
(b) Miscellaneous losses	2,500	
TOTAL AWARD		**132,000 – 147,000**

8c. Loss of eyesight – total blindness

General damages		250,000
Assume claimant unable to resume employment		
(a) Loss of income 2.5 years at 8,500	21,250	
Less		
social welfare benefits	12,000	
		9,250
(b) Cost of care and medical expenses/aids		10,000
(c) Future loss of earnings to age 65 (life expectation 35 years)		190,000
TOTAL AWARD		**459,250**

9. Deafness

General damages		80,000 – 100,000
Pecuniary claims		
(a) Loss of income 2.5 years to date of trial	21,250	

Less		
social welfare benefits	11,000	
		10,250
(b) Miscellaneous expenses		5,000
(c) Future loss of income (22.5 years old at date of trial – assume retirement at 65 and life expectancy of 35 years		190,000
TOTAL AWARD		**285,250 – 305,250**

ITALY

Avv. A. Giorgetti

Introduction

The Italian system for compensating personal injuries is based on the assumption that each and every loss arising from a crime/wrongful act must be indemnified where supported by adequate evidence (see articles 2043, 1223, 1224, *2059* and 2697 of the Italian Civil Code). Originally the making of an award in these circumstances only took into consideration the income and the percentage of permanent disability of the injured person. This was seen to be inequitable and is no longer the case, other categories of damages are now included (see below) less permanent disabilities are now compensated also.

In two leading cases, the Italian Constitutional Court (C. Cost. n. 88/1979 and 184/1986) radically changed this inequitable system by recognising, in respect of fatal accidents and personal injuries, three classes of damages namely:

a) biological damages;

b) property damages;

c) moral or personal damages.

The most recent case law, moving from the so called biological damages, created a few further classes of damages including existential/hedonistic damages and biological damages payable to the bystander.

A description of the circumstances in which these damages can be awarded and how they are calculated is shown below.

Biological damages

Damages are awarded under this heading where there is a violation of the mental, psychological and physical integrity of the injured party, irrespective of the injured person's loss of income. As this head of damages was only recently created by case law there is still no well established procedure agreed upon by the Italian courts to determine the award for biological damages. Even though some of the elements that characterise such damages have been nationally recognised, there is no uniformity in the awards made.

Originally, the calculation of the award was based only on an equitable process which first endeavours to value the injured person's life before applying a multiplier that corresponds to the percentage of permanent disability. If, for example, the value of a single man aged *35* is assessed at ITL 100,000,000 and he suffered the amputation of his right arm below the elbow (an estimated 30% permanent disability) he would be likely to be entitled to an indemnity of ITL 30,000,000. In some Courts this would still be the sole criteria used to liquidate the award and the assessment of value would vary according to the following criteria:

a) age;

b) type of injury;

c) extent of permanent disability;

d) geographical location of the court.

It is notable that in the north of Italy the award is usually higher than in other parts of the peninsula. Similar considerations apply when comparing awards made in cities and those made in rural locations with some relevant exceptions like the Parma Court which supervises a very wealthy rural region.

Such an empirical way of liquidating the award for biological damage changed slightly when some Courts lead the way towards the so called Tables for the assessment of biological damage which are adjusted yearly for inflation. In this trend, initiated by Genoa and Pisa Courts, Milan Court took the lead and now its tables – better scientifically and actuarially determined – have been adopted more or less in their original form by a number of courts especially in the north of Italy. This has helped a little in providing some degree of certainty and homogeneity in the award making process and the tables are now been taken as a basis for the Government project of reform addressing and solving the problem of how biological damages should be calculated throughout Italy.

For the moment, the value of each single percentage point of permanent disability varies considerably to reflect the level and the extent of injury and suffering. At the beginning of year 2000, using the Milan Court Tables, each percentage point may range from ITL 1,700,000 to ITL 11,688,000. The calculation of the award might then be further adjusted to take into account any delays in the Court proceedings. Nevertheless awards are drastically reduced when claims are settled out of court: normally in such cases the cost of each percentage point is about 75% of the court award for the same type of damage.

It is clear that biological damage can affect the injured person's capacity to generate an income in broad and general terms but this loss of income must be proved before an award is made. Previously courts considered that, if the biological damage exceeded a predetermined percentage, normally ranging from 10% to 15%, the injured party should automatically recover a reduced percentage of the assumed loss of income, had been abandoned. Typical of this trend is the Brescia Court that assumes a loss of income for each and every personal injury that results in a permanent disability which is equal to or greater than 10/12%.

The making of an award for biological damages in the case of death had been finally resolved by the constant jurisprudence of the court of Cassation (among the most recent decision see Cass. civ., III, 10 September 1998, n.8970) in the sense that, in the event of a fatal accident, the right to an award expires in death unless a substantial period of time elapsed between the injury and the death. There are no rules at all to determine the minimum period of time between injury and death which will entitle the injured person's heirs to an award., This has been left to the courts and again the courts have not followed an established pattern.

This solution has not been satisfactory. Therefore, the first instance courts continue to raise the objection that denying a biological damage award in case of death is unconstitutional. The Constitutional Court continues to dismiss as groundless the objections raised (Const. Court, 27 October 1994, n.372, Sgrilli e others v. Colzi et others.)

On the other hand case law (Milan Court n.31.05.99 and Treviso Court 25.11.99) recognises the right for heirs to recover biological damage for the death of their loved ones, by way of construing such autonomous right as that of heirs' own biological damage consequent of the loss of companionship if it has been proved, with medical records, that the loss has affected their own psychological integrity. Usually the award made in respect of this head damage is set at half the sum that would be awarded as moral damages to the heir.

By contrast, the question of whether the courts should award biological damages in respect of a period of illness resulting in temporary disability is not debated. In fact it is now usual that, for each period of sickness resulting in temporary disability, an award is made. The Milan Tables show that such awards varying at between ITL 50,000 and ITL 100,000 for each day of total temporary disability which must be adjusted with reference to the level of pain and suffering that the injury caused to the damaged party. The greater the pain and suffering level the higher the amount awarded to the injured person.

That indemnity is awarded in addition to and independently of the biological damages assessed for permanent disability.

Bystander's Biological damages

Moving from the concept of biological damage payable to the heirs of the deceased some courts have recognised that the shock caused to a bystander by an accident, if proven by means of medical records attesting that the event has affected their psychological integrity, should also be compensatable. The level of the award and how this head of damage should be compensated is still being debated.

The existential/hedonistic damage

This is a brand new head of damage finding its roots in the award for biological damage and article 29 of the Italian Constitution.

The scholars' debate upon this recent head of damage is still ongoing but it is possible to say that the existential/hedonistic damage does cover all aspects of the life which are not strictly related to a physical/psychological injury.

A clear example might be the existential/hedonistic damage suffered by a quadriplegic, as well as by his/her family, for the continuous and intense care that such a permanent disability requires.

Due to the uncertainty of this kind of damage and the difficulties in determining the correct award the level of compensation is usually determined on an equitable base.

Property damage

This heading of damage relates to the injured party's actual loss of income and of all costs and expenses incurred as a result of the accident. Insofar as there is no evidence that the injured party suffered only a loss of income, then the indemnity awarded will be limited to biological damages. Loss of earnings is calculated by multiplying the last income of the deceased/injured party, by a predetermined "capitalisation factor"; this figure is then multiplied by the percentage of permanent disability. The making of this award would, however, be subject to a reduction of between 15 and 20% to provide for the disparity between the injured party's physical and working life.

In the event of death, the assessment of damages suffered by the dependants is not based on the deceased's income but rather on that proportion of it which was solely devoted to maintenance of the family unit. For a married man with two children, the proportion is generally 75% of his income, while for young offspring still living at home; the proportion is generally between 50 and 66%.

Notwithstanding a permanent disability affecting the injured party's earning capacity, special considerations apply in such circumstances where, outside of the injury, there is no income whatsoever; this could, for example, include housewives, students or the unemployed. In the case of housewives, the case law suggests that the assessment of damages should be based on an average housemaids' wage, calculated at the time of the accident.

In respect of students and the unemployed, however, the courts are prepared to consider the average income of the future profession (student) or the last reported income (unemployed).

If the injured party cannot prove the likelihood of a future profession or demonstrate a previous income, the court will be likely to calculate the indemnity based on the minimum "social pension" multiplied threefold.

Where personal injuries cause illness or partial and, therefore, temporary disability, it is likely that the injured party will suffer a consequential loss of earning. In these circumstances, if the injured party is employed, he will suffer no financial loss, because he or she will continue to receive the normal wages, as is provided under Italian law.

However, in respect of freelance or self-employed professional people, there is no such benefit and compensation for temporary disability is awarded.

The assessment of such damages is quite simple. The proven tax declaration of the injured party provides for the next pre-tax income of the individual. This is usually divided by 270, i.e. the average number of working days in a year, and then multiplied by the number of absent days due to sickness. The award is, however, proportionally reduced to reflect the ability of the injured party to work at any time during the period of temporary disablement.

It is usual for any award for property damages to include amongst the other heads of damages all costs and expenses that are reasonably and necessarily incurred in consequence of the accident.

Moral damages

In Italy compensation for pain and suffering is awarded in every case in which a wrongful act has been committed which is considered as such and provided for by the Italian Criminal Code. As every voluntary or negligent act causing personal injuries to or the death of a third party is considered a crime under the provision of the Criminal Code, the award for personal injuries must, [usually even if not always], take into account the element of moral damages. In fact no moral damages can be awarded in a case involving of strict liability, except if negligence or a voluntary act leading to the wrongful act is shown and proved.

Normally, moral damages are ascertained on an equitable basis varying according to the circumstances of the accident, type of injury and extent of permanent disability.

The level of moral damages awarded would be expected to rise in proportion to the extent of permanent disability and pain and suffering the injured person will face in the future. Whether aesthetic damages are considered as included in the biological damages award or part of the moral damages award is unclear, especially in such cases where the injured party is a young woman and the moral damages awarded to her are higher than those usually awarded to a man for the same type of injuries.

Moral damages are usually agreed as a lump sum; to calculate the extent of the award the courts will assess a figure somewhere between ITL 1,000,000 for a [lesser] micro-disability and ITL 400/450,000,000 for a quadriplegic.

Strict Liability

The Italian Civil Code and some legislation, i.e. DPR No. 244/88, Product Liability Act, provide for strict liability in certain circumstances. In such cases the burden of the proof is generally on the defendant and the liability exclusions are limited to proof of an act of God, and deficiencies allowed by the Act.

Article 2048 of the Civil Code provides for teachers' or parents' strict liability for the acts of their pupils or sons; article 2049 of the Civil Code provides for masters' or employers' strict liability for employees' wrongful acts; article 2050 of the Civil Code provides strict liability for damage arising from goods or animals in captivity; article 2053 of the Civil Code provides for strict liability for building collapse; and finally article 2054 of the Civil Code provides a partial strict liability in a case of damages arising from a car crash.

Compensation for monetary devaluation and interest

Although situation is improving due to the new Civil Procedural Code, it is still normal for the court proceedings and final judgment to take place long after the date of the accident. In Italy it may take three or four years before a final decision is obtained.

The injured party, therefore, is also entitled to claim for loss of "purchasing power" i.e. rising inflation or devaluation of local currency which is generally calculated by reference to an established table issued by the Central Statistical Agency, ISTAT, with reference to the so called "increment of the life cost".

[That had been completely changed when the inflation decreased to a point that the simple legal interest was exceeding such head of damage.]

Nowadays courts will not make an award including the devaluation factor unless the party has proven that in consequence of the damage he/she suffered a financial loss. A typical example of this is when a financial institution (bank, insurer or stock broker) suffers financial damage in a case and can prove that having had to divert money to remedy the damage, this resulted in further damage for loss of "purchasing power" or a "pure financial loss" which should be compensated.

On the other hand as article 1284 of the Civil Code provides that, in addition to the compensation award, the courts should also compensate the injured party by allowing interest at an established rate that is now determined year by year by the State Annual Budget Act.

For a wilful/negligent act which took place before 1 December 1990, the date on which the new rate came into force, interest is calculated at the 5% rate and afterwards at a rate of 10%; this last interest rate remained in force until the end of 1996, when the annual rate was decreased to the 5% and since 01.01.99 the annual interest rate has further gone down to 2.5%.

In either case no compensation for monetary devaluation can be awarded in addition to moral damages that are settled at the time of the judgment in current money.

The Italian social security system and its right to recover from the paying party the sums paid out in case of bodily injuries and permanent disabilities

In the case of an accident involving personal injuries different government agencies can be called on to cover medical costs, nursing care and funeral expenses on behalf of the injured party. Those agencies are entitled to be reimbursed for monies paid out only if the accident was caused wilfully or negligently. In such cases the agencies have a right of action against the culpable party.

The agencies obliged by law to anticipate these costs and expenses are:

(i) INPS or Istituto Nazionale Pensioni Sociali

This agency provides pensions and social security for disabled persons such as the blind, deaf and dumb, paraplegics, etc. irrespective of the original cause of such infirmities. If the temporary or permanent disability is the consequence of an accident then the agency has the right of subrogation against the culpable party. Such right is expressly provided by article 14 of the Act of 12 June 1984, No. 222.

(ii) INAIL or Instito Nazionale Infortuni sul Lavoro

INAIL is a special state insurer that provides social insurance for bodily injuries or diseases sustained, by any person under a contract of service or apprenticeship with an employer and which arises in the course of the employment.

When the employer's civil and/or criminal liability for the injury, or death is judicially determined, INAIL has the right to recover from the employer the amount paid to the employee or to his survivors as provided for by articles 10 and 11, D.P.R. 30 June 1965, No. 1124. in awarding pensions and indemnities to injured parties INAIL adopts larger parameters than those used by the courts in making awards in similar cases and this is often a source of controversy for the paying party and/or their insurers.

Table 1. Schedule A

Claimants :	Man
Age :	40
Status :	Married, 2 dependent children aged 5 and 7
Occupation :	Doctor
Income :	Lire 100,000,000
Trial :	2.5 years after accident occurred in June 1997

1. Instant Death		ITL
a) Damages for loss of earnings (wife and children's dependency) 75% of the annual income equal to 75,000,000, apply capitalisation factor 16.318	1,223,850,000	
Less Deduct difference between physical and working life 20%	979,080,000	
Plus Interest on principal increased by revaluation		
1.5 years x 5% = 7.5%	73,431,000	
1 year x 2.5% = 2.5%	24,477,000	
		1,076,988,000
b) Moral damages		
to wife:	590,333,334	
to each child:	295,166,667	
		1,180,666,667
TOTAL DAMAGES		**2,257,654,667**

33% to wife and the remaining 66% to children as provided by Article 581 of the Civil Code.

2a. Burns

	20% permanent disability with no loss of income	
a)	Biological damages	70,438,000
b)	Moral damages	35,000,000
c)	Aesthetical surgery and medical expenses	42,000,000
	TOTAL DAMAGES	**147,438,000**

2b. Burns

	20% permanent disability with loss of income		
a)	Biological damages		70,438,000
b)	Damages for loss of earnings (20%) = Lire 20,000,000, apply capitalisation factor 16.318	326,360,000	
	Less Deduct difference between physical and working life 20%	261,080,000	
	Plus Interest on principal increased by revaluation		
	1.5 years x 5% = 7.5%	19,581,000	
	1 year x 2.5% = 2.5%	6,527,000	
			287,188,000
c)	Moral damages		35,219,000
d)	Aesthetical surgery and medical expenses		42,000,000
	TOTAL DAMAGES		**434,845,000**

3. Quadriplegia

	100% permanent disability	
a)	Biological damages	885,500,000

b) Damages for loss of earnings (100%) Lire 100,000,000 apply capitalisation factor 16.318	1,631,800,000	
Less Deduct difference between physical and working life 20%	1,305,440,000	
Plus Interest on principal increased by revaluation		
1.5 years x 5% = 7.5%	97,908,000	
1 year x 2.5% = 2.5%	32,636,000	
		1,435,984,000
c) Moral damages		442,750,000
d) Medical costs, nursing care and special equipment		360,000,000
TOTAL DAMAGES		**3,122,234,000**

4. Paraplegia

70% permanent disability

a) Biological damages		583,786,000
b) Damages for loss of earnings (70%) Lire 70,000,000 apply capitalisation factor 16.312	1,142,260,000	
Less Deduct difference between physical and working life 20%	913,808,000	
Plus Interest on principal increased by revaluation		
1.5 years x 5% = 7.5%	68,535,600	
1 year x 2.5% = 2.5%	22,845,200	
		1,005,188,800
c) Moral damages	291,893,000	
d) Medical costs, nursing care and special equipment	250,000,000	
TOTAL DAMAGES		**2,130,867,800**

5a. Brain Damage

Severe damage, conscious but total nursing care

a) Biological damages		693,459,000
b) Damages for loss of earnings (80%) Lire 80,000,000 apply capitalisation factor 16.318	1,305,440,000	
Less Deduct difference between physical and working life 20%	1,044,352,000	
Plus Interest on principal increased by revaluation		
1.5 years x 5% = 7.5%	78,326,400	
1 year x 2.5% = 2.5%	26,108,800	
		1,148,787,200
c) Moral damages		346,729,500
d) Medical costs, nursing care and special equipment		360,000,000
TOTAL DAMAGES		**2,548,975,700**

5b. Brain damage (very severe)

a) Biological damages		792,965,000
b) Damages for loss of earnings (90%) Lire 90,000,000 apply capitalisation factor 16.318	1,468,620,000	
Less Deduct difference between physical and working life 20%	1,174,896,000	
Plus Interest on principal increased by revaluation		
1.5 years x 5% = 7.5%	88,117,200	
1 year x 2.5% = 2.5%	29,372,400	
		1,292,385,600

c) Moral damages		396,482,500
d) Medical costs, nursing care and special equipment		360,000,000
TOTAL DAMAGES		**2,841,833,100**

6a. Amputation of leg above knee

35% permanent disability

a) Biological damages		181,377,000
b) Damages for loss of earnings (35%) Lire 35,000,000 apply capitalisation factor 16.318	571,130,000	
Less Deduct difference between physical and working life 20%	456,904,000	
Plus Interest on principal increased by revaluation		
1.5 years x 5% = 7.5%	34,267,800	
1 year x 2.5% = 2.5%	11,422,600	
		502,594,400
c) Moral damages		90,688,500
d) Medical costs, nursing care and special equipment		36,000,000
TOTAL DAMAGES		**810,659,900**

6b. Amputation of leg below knee

30% permanent disability

a) Biological damages		138,863,000
b) Damages for loss of earnings (30%) Lire 30,000,000 apply capitalisation factor 16.318	489,540,000	

Less Deduct difference between physical and working life 20%	391,632,000	
Plus Interest on principal increased by revaluation		
1.5 years x 5% = 7.5%	29,372,400	
1 year x 2.5% = 2.5%	9,790,800	
		430,795,200
c) Moral damages		69,431,500
d) Medical costs, nursing care and special equipment		30,000,000
TOTAL DAMAGES		**669,089,700**

7a. Amputation of arm above the elbow

35% permanent disability

a) Biological damages		181,377,000
b) Damages for loss of earnings (35%) Lire 35,000,000 apply capitalisation factor 16.318	571,130,000	
Less Deduct difference between physical and working life 20%	456,904,000	
Plus Interest on principal increased by revaluation		
1.5 years x 5% = 7.5%		
1 year x 2.5% = 2.5%	11,422,600	
		502,594,400
c) Moral damages		90,688,500
d) Medical costs, nursing care and special equipment		36,000,000
TOTAL DAMAGES		**810,659,900**

7b. Amputation of arm below the elbow

30% permanent disability

a) Biological damages		138,863,000
b) Damages for loss of earnings (30%) Lire 30,000,000 apply capitalisation factor 16.318	489,540,000	
Less Deduct difference between physical and working life 20%	391,632,000	
Plus Interest on principal increased by revaluation		
1.5 years x 5% = 7.5%	29,372,400	
1 year x 2.5% = 2.5%	9,790,800	
		430,795,200
c) Moral damages		69,431,500
d) Medical costs, nursing care and special equipment		30,000,000
TOTAL DAMAGES		**669,089,700**

8a. Loss of eyesight – one eye without cosmetic disability

a) Biological damages		181,377,000
b) Damages for loss of earnings (35%) Lire 35,000,000 apply capitalisation factor 16.318	571,130,000	
Less Deduct difference between physical and working life 20%	456,904,000	
Plus Interest on principal increased by revaluation		
1.5 years x 5% = 7.5%	34,267,800	
1 year x 2.5% = 2.5%	11,422,600	
		502,594,400

c) Moral damages		90,688,500
d) Medical costs, nursing care and special equipment		24,000,000
TOTAL DAMAGES		**798,659,900**

8b. Loss of eyesight – one eye with cosmetic disability

a) Biological damages		181,377,000
b) Damages for loss of earnings (35%) Lire 35,000,000 apply capitalisation factor 16.318	571,130,000	
Less Deduct difference between physical and working life 20%	456,904,000	
Plus Interest on principal increased by revaluation		
1.5 years x 5% = 7.5%	34,267,800	
1 year x 2.5% = 2.5%	11,422,600	
		502,594,400
c) Moral damages		90,688,500
d) Medical costs, nursing care and special equipment		30,000,000
TOTAL DAMAGES		**804,659,900**

8c. Loss of eyesight – total blindness

Total blindness is normally regarded as a 100% disability, but in this case it has been supposed that the injured party would be able to undertake some sort of activity after he had recovered from the accident.

a) Biological damages	792,965,000

b) Damages for loss of earnings (90%) Lire 90,000,000 apply capitalisation factor 16.318	1,468,620,000	
Less Deduct difference between physical and working life 20%	1,174,896,000	
Plus Interest on principal increased by revaluation		
1.5 years x 5% = 7.5%	88,117,200	
1 year x 2.5% = 2.5%	29,372,400	
		1,292,385,600
c) Moral damages		396,482,500
d) Medical costs, nursing care and special equipment		240,000,000
TOTAL DAMAGES		**2,721,833,100**

9a. Deafness – total deafness

a) Biological damages		465,110,000
b) Damages for loss of earnings (60%) Lire 60,000,000 apply capitalisation factor 16.318	979,080,000	
Less Deduct difference between physical and working life 20%	783,264,000	
Plus Interest on principal increased by revaluation		
1.5 years x 5% = 7.5%	58,744,800	
1 year x 2.5% = 2.5%	19,581,600	
		861,590,400
c) Moral damages		232,555,000
d) Medical costs, nursing care and special equipment		30,000,000
TOTAL DAMAGES		**1,589,255,400**

9b. Deafness – non-bilateral deafness

a) Biological damages		31,637,000
b) Damages for loss of earnings (12%) Lire 12,000,000 apply capitalisation factor 16.318	195,816,000	
Less Deduct difference between physical and working life 20%	156,652,800	
Plus Interest on principal increased by revaluation		
1.5 years x 5% = 7.5%	17,748,960	
1 year x 2.5% = 2.5%	3,916,320	
		172,318,080
c) Moral damages		15,818,500
d) Medical costs, nursing care and special equipment		12,000,000
TOTAL DAMAGES		**231,773,580**

10. Repetitive strain injury

a) Moral damages	
1. Complete loss of function	70,000,000
2. Injury with significant permanent residual injury	50,000,000
3. Persistent pain and stiffness	35/40,000,000
4. If recovery is complete then the award will not be greater than:	18,000,000
a) Based on category 3 above Persistent pain and stiffness	40,000,000
b) General damages	

	Assume that claimant is unable to resume his employment as surgeon and takes on light duties after 6 months.		40,000,000
c)	Loss of income 0.5 years x 100,000,000		50,000,000
d)	Miscellaneous expenses		2,000,000
e)	Interest on damages for injury (2 years x 2.5%)		6,600,000
f)	Future loss of earnings (20%) 20,000,000 x factor of 16.318	326,360,000	
	Less Deduct difference between physical and working life 20%	261,080,000	
			261,080,000
	TOTAL DAMAGES		**399,680,000**

Table 2. Schedule B

Claimant :	Woman
Age :	20
Status :	Single
Occupation :	Legal Secretary
Income :	Lire 28,000,000
Trial :	2.5 years after accident

1. Instant Death

a)	Damages for loss of earnings (Assumed claimant would remain in the family until marriage at age 26/27: share of income devoted to the family, 50% for 6.5 years) ITL 14,000,000 x 6.5	91,000,000

b) Moral damages		
1. for the father	164,257,500	
2. for the mother	164,257,500	
3. for the brother or sister	99,550,000	
		428,065,000
c) General damages: education and maintenance costs of the daughter to the age of 20, funeral expenses, etc		48,000,000
TOTAL DAMAGES		**567,065,000**

2a. Burns

20% permanent disability with no loss of income

a) Biological damages	79,188,000
b) Moral damages	39,594,000
c) Aesthetical surgery and medical expenses	42,000,000
TOTAL DAMAGES	**160,782,000**

2b. Burns

20% permanent disability with loss of income

a) Biological damages		79,188,000
b) Damages for loss of earnings (20%) Lire 5,600,000, apply capitalisation factor 19,127	107,111,200	
Less Deduct difference between physical and working life 20%	85,688,960	
Plus Interest on principal increased by revaluation		
1.5 year x 5% = 7.5%	6,426,672	
1 year x 2.5% = 2.5%	2,142,224	

		95,257,856
c) Moral damages		39,594,000
d) Aesthetical surgery and medical expenses		42,000,000
TOTAL DAMAGES		**255,039,856**

3. Quadriplegia

a) Biological damages		995,500,000
b) Damages for loss of earnings (100%) Lire 30,000,000, apply capitalisation factor 19,127	573,810,000	
Less Deduct difference between physical and working life 20%	459,048,000	
Less Factor of accelerated receipt equal to 0.71	523,924,000	
		325,924,000
c) Moral damages		497,750,000
d) Aesthetical surgery and medical expenses		480,000,000
TOTAL DAMAGES		**2,299,174,000**

4. Paraplegia

70% permanent disability with loss of income

a) Biological damages		656,306,000
b) Damages for loss of earnings (70%) Lire 19,600,000, apply capitalisation factor 19,127	374,889,200	
Less Deduct difference between physical and working life 20%	299,911,360	

Plus Interest on principal increased by revaluation		
1.5 year x 5% = 7.5%	22,493,352	
1 year x 2.5% = 2.5%	7,497,784	
		329,902,496
c) Moral damages		328,153,000
d) Aesthetical surgery and medical expenses		252,000,000
TOTAL DAMAGES		**1,566,361,496**

5a. Brain damage

Severe damage, conscious but total nursing care

a) Biological damages		779,603,000
b) Damages for loss of earnings (80%) Lire 22,400,000, apply capitalisation factor 19,127	428,444,800	
Less Deduct difference between physical and working life 20%	342,755,840	
Plus Interest on principal increased by revaluation		
1.5 year x 5% = 7.5%	25,706,688	
1 year x 2.5% = 2.5%	8,568,896	
		377,031,424
c) Moral damages		389,801,500
d) Aesthetical surgery and medical expenses		360,000,000
TOTAL DAMAGES		**1,906,435,924**

5b. Brain damage (very severe)

a) Biological damages		891,470,000
b) Damages for loss of earnings (90%) Lire 25,200,000, apply capitalisation factor 19,127	482,000,400	
Less Deduct difference between physical and working life 20%	385,600,320	
Plus Interest on principal increased by revaluation		
1.5 year x 5% = 7.5%	28,920,024	
1 year x 2.5% = 2.5%	9,640,008	
		424,160,352
c) Moral damages		445,735,000
d) Aesthetical surgery and medical expenses		360,000,000
TOTAL DAMAGES		**2,121,365,352**

6a. Amputation of leg above knee

35% permanent disability

a) Biological damages		203,908,000
b) Damages for loss of earnings (35%) Lire 9,800,000 apply capitalisation factor 16.318	187,444,600	
Less Deduct difference between physical and working life 20%	149,955,680	
Plus Interest on principal increased by revaluation		
1.5 years x 5% = 7.5%	11,246,676	
1 year x 2.5% = 2.5%	3,748,892	
		164,951,248
c) Moral damages	101,954,000	

d) Medical costs, nursing care and special equipment		36,000,000
TOTAL DAMAGES		**506,813,248**

6b. Amputation of leg below knee

30% permanent disability

a) Biological damages		156,113,000
b) Damages for loss of earnings (30%) Lire 8,400,000 apply capitalisation factor 16.318	160,666,800	
Less Deduct difference between physical and working life 20%	128,533,440	
Plus Interest on principal increased by revaluation		
1.5 years x 5% = 7.5%	9,640,008	
1 year x 2.5% = 2.5%	3,213,336	
		141,386,784
c) Moral damages		78,056,500
d) Medical costs, nursing care and special equipment		30,000,000
TOTAL DAMAGES		**405,556,284**

7a. Amputation of arm above the elbow

35% permanent disability

a) Biological damages		203,908,000
b) Damages for loss of earnings (35%) Lire 9,800,000 apply capitalisation factor 16.318	187,444,600	

Less Deduct difference between physical and working life 20%	149,955,680	
Plus Interest on principal increased by revaluation		
1.5 years x 5% = 7.5%	11,246,676	
1 year x 2.5% = 2.5%	3,748,892	
		164,951,248
c) Moral damages		101,954,000
d) Medical costs, nursing care and special equipment		36,000,000
TOTAL DAMAGES		**506,813,248**

7b. Amputation of arm below the elbow

30% permanent disability

a) Biological damages		156,113,000
b) Damages for loss of earnings (30%) Lire 8,400,000 apply capitalisation factor 16.318	160,666,800	
Less Deduct difference between physical and working life 20%	128,533,440	
Plus Interest on principal increased by revaluation		
1.5 years x 5% = 7.5%	9,640,008	
1 year x 2.5% = 2.5%	3,213,336	
		141,386,784
c) Moral damages		78,056,500
d) Medical costs, nursing care and special equipment		30,000,000
TOTAL DAMAGES		**405,556,284**

8a. Loss of eyesight – one eye without cosmetic disability

a) Biological damages		203,908,000
b) Damages for loss of earnings (35%) Lire 9,800,000 apply capitalisation factor 16.318	187,444,600	
Less Deduct difference between physical and working life 20%	149,955,680	
Plus Interest on principal increased by revaluation		
1.5 years x 5% = 7.5%	11,246,676	
1 year x 2.5% = 2.5%	3,748,892	
		164,951,248
c) Moral damages		101,954,000
d) Medical costs, nursing care and special equipment		24,000,000
TOTAL DAMAGES		**494,813,248**

8b. Loss of eyesight – one eye with cosmetic disability

a) Biological damages	203,908,000	
b) Damages for loss of earnings (35%) Lire 9,800,000 apply capitalisation factor 16.318	187,444,600	
Less Deduct difference between physical and working life 20%	149,955,680	
Plus Interest on principal increased by revaluation		
1.5 years x 5% = 7.5%	11,246,676	
1 year x 2.5% = 2.5%	3,748,892	
		164,951,248
c) Moral damages		101,954,000

d) Medical costs, nursing care and special equipment		24,000,000
TOTAL DAMAGES		**494,813,248**

8c. Loss of eyesight – total blindness

Total blindness is normally regarded as a 100% disability, but in this case it has been supposed that the injured party would be able to undertake some sort of activity after he had recovered from the accident.

a) Biological damages		891,470
b) Damages for loss of earnings (90%) Lire 25,200,000 apply capitalisation factor 16.318	482,000,400	
Less Deduct difference between physical and working life 20%	385,600,320	
Plus Interest on principal increased by revaluation		
1.5 years x 5% = 7.5%	28,920,024	
1 year x 2.5% = 2.5%	9,640,008	
		424,160,352
c) Moral damages		445,735,000
d) Medical costs, nursing care and special equipment		240,000,000
TOTAL DAMAGES		**2,001,365,352**

9a. Deafness – total deafness

a) Biological damages		522,887,000
b) Damages for loss of earnings (60%) Lire 16,800,000 apply capitalisation factor 16.318	321,333,600	

	Less Deduct difference between physical and working life 20%	257,066,880	
	Plus Interest on principal increased by revaluation		
	1.5 years x 5% = 7.5%	19,280,016	
	1 year x 2.5% = 2.5%	6,426,672	
			282,773,568
c)	Moral damages		261,443,500
d)	Medical costs, nursing care and special equipment		12,000,000
	TOTAL DAMAGES		**1,079,104,068**

9b. Deafness – non-bilateral deafness

a)	Biological damages		35,567,000
b)	Damages for loss of earnings (12%) Lire 3,360,000 apply capitalisation factor 16.318	64,266,720	
	Less Deduct difference between physical and working life 20%	51,413,376	
	Plus Interest on principal increased by revaluation		
	1.5 years x 5% = 7.5%	3,856,003	
	1 year x 2.5% = 2.5%	1,285,334	
			56,554,713
c)	Moral damages		17,783,500
d)	Medical costs, nursing care and special equipment		12,000,000
	TOTAL DAMAGES		**121,905,213**

10. Repetitive strain injury

a) Moral damages		
1. Complete loss of function		70/80,000,000
2. Injury with significant permanent residual injury		50,000,000
3. Persistent pain and stiffness		35/40,000,000
4. If recovery is complete then the award will not be greater than:		18/20,000,000
a) Based on category 3 above Persistent pain and stiffness		40,000,000
b) General damages		
Assume that claimant is unable to resume her employment as secretary and takes on light duties after 6 months		40,000,000
c) Loss of income 0.5 years x 28,000,000		14,000,000
d) Miscellaneous expenses		2,000,000
e) Interest on damages for injury (2 years x 2.5%)		4,800,000
f) Future loss of earnings (20%) 5,600,000 x factor of 19.127	107,111,200	
Less Deduct difference between physical and working life 20%	85,688,960	
		85,688,960
TOTAL DAMAGES		**186,488,960**

LUXEMBOURG

Rene Diederich

Introduction

Under Luxembourg civil law the damages award will always have to take into account the real damages suffered by the injured person as it is a general rule under Luxembourg law that the indemnification has to be made "*in concreto*". This means that an injured person can in no way receive amounts that are lower or higher than the amount of the real damages suffered.

In order to determine the amounts payable to a victim, the Luxembourg courts will normally designate three experts to evaluate the damages accrued. However, it must be borne in mind that the Luxembourg courts have a considerable discretion to depart from the valuations produced by medical and other experts.

On the main principles according to which damages are recoverable for personal injuries, the Luxembourg courts tend to follow French and to a certain extent Belgian case law.

The main heads of damage recoverable under Luxembourg law for personal injuries are as follows:

a) The damages suffered by the injured person

(i) The pecuniary loss

The damage to the property of the injured person comprising the "*damnum emergens*" and the "*lucrum cessans*" with the interest accrued starting from the date of the event which caused the damage.

The damage to the person of the injured person such as the costs of the medical care, the damage to the integrity and the consequential detrimental effect on the actual and future income and on the pension benefits of the injured person.

(ii) The non pecuniary loss

Known in Luxembourg law as *préjudice moral* comprising the following kinds of damages:

- The moral part of the damage to the integrity of the injured person's body;
- The pain and the suffering of the injured person up to the date of the consolidation of his state of health (i.e. *pretium dolorosis*) in the case of the survival of the injured person;
- The sadness and humiliation caused by disfigurement (*préjudice esthétique*):
- The loss of amenities (*préjudice agrément*);
- The damage to the sexual life of the injured person comprising the impossibility to procreate and the deprivation of enjoyment of sex.

In the case of a young injured person, the damage suffered in relation to the diminution of the injured person's expectations of life.

b) The damages payable to the estate of the deceased injured person

Under Luxembourg law this is the so-called *actio ex haerede.*

These damages are composed of the personal damages suffered by the deceased person and will mainly compensate his moral damage for the pain he has suffered and possibly for the pangs of death. The amount of these damages will of course depend on the circumstances – whether the direct injured person died immediately after the accident or only some time later.

c) The damages payable to the indirect injured persons

The damages payable to the deceased person's wife and children will be of two different kinds; on the one hand, these indirect injured persons will be entitled to receive an indemnification for the moral injury they have suffered with respect to the death of their beloved close relative and, on the other hand, they will also be entitled to receive an indemnification for loss of support.

(i) The damages allocated to the family in order to compensate the moral injury suffered may vary. It will also be important to know whether the relatives and indirect injured persons lived together with the deceased in the same household. In the case of a middle aged married man having two dependent children, the Luxembourg courts for the time being allocated damages to 500,000 – 1,000,000 Luxembourg francs to the wife and 200,000 – 500,000 Luxembourg francs to the dependent children.

(ii) In order to calculate the loss of support suffered by the deceased person's relatives, for instance the wife and dependent children, the experts and the courts in Luxembourg will examine the average earnings of the deceased person, his normal life expectancy according to the statistical tables and they will also take into account the proportion of earnings the deceased used for personal expenses. The courts very often consider that an individual uses one third or one quarter of his earnings for personal expenses. They will of course take into account whether the deceased person had a more or less extravagant and expensive way of life.

Finally these indirect injured persons will also be entitled to receive an indemnification for all costs and expenses they had to bear in relation for their close relative's death.

It is worthwhile mentioning that the social security institutions are entitled under Luxembourg law to claim for the reimbursement of the costs and expenses they had to make in relation to the detrimental events.

With respect to the levels of personal injury awards given in the Grand Duchy of Luxembourg, I have examined the case studies and the schedules that have been prepared under French and Belgian law, respectively.

The main principles of indemnification are quite the same in France, Belgium and Luxembourg. This means that very often the personal injury awards given in Luxembourg are similar to those in Belgium or in France for the same kind of injury, very often the Luxembourg courts refer to the Belgian or French jurisprudence, save that certain amounts that would be awarded in order to compensate the moral damages suffered by the direct and indirect injured persons might be even higher in Luxembourg than in Belgium or France.

It is also important to mention that the Luxembourg courts evaluate the damages suffered by the direct and indirect injured persons as at the date of judgment.

In accordance with the rule that damages are evaluated as at the date of the judgment, the Luxembourg courts tend to adjust the awards to the variations in the cost of living.

Furthermore the Luxembourg courts will grant to the injured persons the interest accrued on the amounts that have been awarded from the date of the detrimental event or from the date of the consolidation of the victim's state of health up to the date of the judgment, at a rate which may vary from 5% to 10%, and from the judgment date at a rate that for the time being is 5% (this is the rate of the legal interest for the year 2000 and this rate will normally be determined at the beginning of each calendar year).

Table 1. Schedule A

Claimants :	Man
Age :	40
Status :	Married, 2 dependent children aged 5 and 7
Occupation	Doctor
Income :	LUF 100,000,000
Trial :	2.5 years after accident occurred in June 1997

1. Instant Death		LUF
A. For the widow		
a) Funeral expenses		80,000
b) Moral damage (for the loss of her husband)		1,000,000
c) Material or pecuniary damage – net value of income	2,100,000	
Less Deceased own expenditures (+/- 30%)	630,000	
Loss of income to date of trial	1,470,000	
2.5 years x 1,470,000		3,675,000
d) Future loss Age of the deceased at the date of trial 42.5 years – probable lucrative survival to 65 years = 22 years coefficient to capitalise at 5% annuities = 12.4575; 1,470,000 x 12.4575		18,312,530
e) Interest 2.5 years at 5% on 1,080,000 on items (a) and (b)	135,000	
1.25 years at 5% on 3,675,000 on item (c)	229,690	
	364,690	
		23,104,220

B. For the children

Moral damage for the loss of their father: 500,000 for each of them		1,000,000
Interest 5%		50,000
TOTAL AWARD: 23,687,500 + 1,050,000		**24,154,220**

2a. Burns (A, B, C)

Assume that the claimant is able to resume his employment two years after accident

a)	Loss of income 2 years x 2,100,000		4,200,000
	NB: If the victim receives a welfare benefit, this benefit will be subtracted from the above indemnity but the liable party (or his insurer) will have to reimburse the welfare service. For the liable party, there is therefore no difference.		
b)	Miscellaneous loss (medical expenses included), say		100,000
c)	Moral damage to date of trial		
	90 days' hospitalisation x 1,000	90,000	
	640 days without hospitalisation x 600	448,000	
	182.5 days hospitalisation x 600 x 20%	25,550	
		563,550	
	+10% =		619,905
d)	Interest 1.25 years 5% on 4,919,905 on items (a), (b) and (c)		307,495
e)	Future moral and material damage Assume there is no more loss of income 20 x 33,000		660,000
f)	*Préjudice esthétique* (for loss of looks)		220,000
	TOTAL AWARD		**6,107,400**

3. Quadriplegia

a) Loss of income to date of trial 2.5 years x 2,100,000		5,250,000
b) Cost of nursing care/medical expenses to date of trial 1,750,000 x 2.5 years		4,375,000
c) Cost of modifying home and special equipment, say		1,400,000
d) Moral damage until date of trial		
90 days' hospitalisation x 1,000	90,000	
822.5 days without hospitalisation x 600	575,750	
	667,750	
+10% =		732,325
e) Interest 1.25 years at 5% on 11,757,325 on items (a), (b), (c) and (d)		734,833
f) Future loss of income 42.5 years old at date of trial assume retirement at 65 years coefficient to capitalise at 5% annuities follow Levie's table = 12.4575 2,100,000 x 12,4575		26,160,750
g) Future costs of nursing probable survival at 42.5 years – 29 years coefficient to capitalise at 5% .annuities 3315.1411; 1,750,000 x 15.1411		26,496,925
h) Future moral damage 100 x 33,000		3,300,000
i) *Préjudice esthétique*		880,000
TOTAL AWARD		**69,329,833**

4. Paraplegia

a) Loss of income to date of trial 1.5 years' total disability: 2,100,000 x 1.5 =	3,150,000	

	1-70% disability 2,100,000 x 70%	1,470,000	
			4,620,000
b)	Cost of nursing and medical expenses to date of trial		1,400,000
c)	Cost of modifying home		700,000
d)	Moral damage 60.0 days' hospitalisation x 1,000	60,000	
	852.5 days without hospitalisation x 700	596,750	
		656,750	
	+10% =		722,425
e)	Interest 1.25 years at 5% on 7,442,425 on items (a), (b), (c) and (d)		465,152
f)	Future loss of income 2,100,000 x 70% x 12.4565		18,311,055
g)	Estimated future costs of nursing care/medical expenses 200,000 x 15.1411		3,028,220
h)	Future moral damage 70 x 30,000 + 10%		2,310,000
i)	*Préjudice esthétique*		660,000
	TOTAL AWARD		**32,216,852**

5a. Brain damage

a)	Loss of income to trial 2.5 years x 2,100,000	5,250,000
b)	Cost of nursing/medical care 2.5 years x 1,750,000	4,375,000
c)	Cost of modifying home and special equipment, say	500,000
d)	Moral damage until trial (same as for quadriplegia)	732,325

e)	Interest 1.25 years at 5% on 10,857,325 on items (a), (b), (c) and (d)	678,583
f)	Future loss of income 2,100,000 x 80% x 12.4575	20,928,600
g)	Estimated future cost of nursing care/medical expenses 200,000 x 15.1411	3,028,220
h)	Future moral damage 80 x 30,000 x 10%	2,640,000
i)	*Préjudice esthétique*	330,000
	TOTAL AWARD	**38,462,728**

5b. Brain damage with motor deficiency

a)	Loss of income to trial 2.5 years x 2,100,000	5,250,000
b)	Cost of nursing care/medical expenses	4,375,000
c)	Cost of modifying home equipment	1,400,000
d)	Moral damage until trial (same as for quadriplegia)	732,325
e)	Interest 1.25 years at 5% on 11,757,325 on items (a), (b), (c) and (d)	734,833
f)	Future loss of income (assuming he can still earn 10% of his former income) 2,100,000 x 90 x 12.4575 100	23,544,675
g)	Estimated future cost of nursing 1,750,000 x 15.1411	26,496,925
h)	Future moral damage 90 x 30,000 x 10%	2,970,000
i)	*Préjudice esthétique*	550,000
	TOTAL AWARD	**66,053,758**

6a. Amputation of leg above knee

Assumed claimant able to resume his employment 1.5 years after accident

a)	Loss of income 1.5 years at 2,100,000		3,150,000
b)	Miscellaneous losses		100,000
c)	Moral damage until date of trial		
	60 days' hospitalisation at 1,000	60,000	
	487.5 days' hospitalisation at 700	340,900	
	365 days without hospitalisation at 600 x 35% x 700 100	89,425	
		490,325	
	+10% =		539,358
d)	Interest 1.25 years at 5% on 3,789,358 on items (a), (b) and (c)		236,835
e)	Future moral damage and material damage (for the effort to work at 100% with a 35% disability) 35 x 45,000 + 10%		1,732,500
f)	*Préjudice esthétique*		660,000
	TOTAL AWARD		**6,418,693**

6b. Amputation of leg below knee

a)	Loss of income (same as preceding case)	3,150,000
b)	Miscellaneous losses	100,000
c)	Moral damage until trial	539,358
d)	Interest 1.25 years at 5% on 3,789,358 on items (a), (b) and (c)	236,835
e)	Future moral damage and material damage 30 x 45,000 + 10%	1,485,000

f) *Préjudice esthétique*		440,000
TOTAL AWARD		**5,951,193**

7a. Amputation of arm above the elbow

Claimant not able to resume his employment but takes up light duties 1.5 years after accident

a) Loss of income		
1.5 years at 2,100,000	3,150,000	
1 year x 1,200,000	1,200,000	
		4,550,000
b) Miscellaneous expenses		100,000
c) Moral damage until trial		538,368
d) Interest 1.25 years at 5% on 5,188,368 on items (a), (b) and (c)		324,273
e) Future loss of earnings (Belgian figure + 10%)		10,558,875
f) Future moral damage (Belgian figure + 10%)		1,155,000
g) *Préjudice esthétique*		660,000
TOTAL AWARD		**17,916,516**

7b. Amputation of arm below the elbow

a) Loss of income (7a)	3,150,000	
	1,200,000	
		4,550,000
b) Miscellaneous expenses		120,000
c) Moral damage until trial		525,305

d) Interest 1.25 years at 5% on 5,195,305 on items (a), (b) and (c)	324,707
e) Future loss of earnings (Belgian figure 10%) 850,000 x 12.4575	10,588,875
f) Future moral damage 30 x 30,000 + 10%	990,000
g) *Préjudice esthétique*	440,000
TOTAL AWARD	**17,538,887**

8a. Loss of eyesight – one eye without cosmetic disability

Assuming claimant able to resume his employment one year after the accident

a) Loss of income 1 year x 2,100,000	2,100,000
b) Miscellaneous losses	100,000
c) Moral damage until trial	417,538
d) Interest 1.25 years at 5% on 2,617,538 on items (a), (b) and (c)	163,596
e) Future moral and material damage 30 x 30,000 + 10%	990,000
f) *Préjudice esthétique* + 10% (Belgian figures)	220,000
TOTAL AWARD	**3,991,134**

8b. Loss of eyesight – one eye with cosmetic disability

Claimant able to resume his employment one year after the accident

a) Loss of income 1 year at 2,100,000	2,100,000
b) Miscellaneous losses	100,000

c) Moral damage until trial	417,538
d) Interest 1.25 years at 5% on 2,617,538 on items (a), (b) and (c)	163,596
e) Future moral and material damage 30 x 45,000 + 10%	1,485,000
f) *Préjudice esthétique*	330,000
TOTAL AWARD	**4,596,134**

8c. Total blindness

a) Loss of income until trial 2,100,000 x 2.5 years	5,250,000
b) Cost of care and medical expenses	700,000
c) Moral damage	633,600
d) Interest 1.25 years at 5% on 6,662,525 on items 2(a), (b) and (c)	416,408
e) Future loss of earnings 2,100,000 x 12.4575	26,160,750
f) Future moral damage (including *préjudice esthétique)* 45,000 x 100 + 10%	4,950,000
g) Future cost of replacement aids	660,000
TOTAL AWARD	**38,789,683**

9a. Deafness

Assume claimant able to resume his employment 1 year after accident at Lux. F. 1,250,000 p.a.

a) Loss of income until trial		
1.5 years at 2,100,000	3,150,000	
1 year x 2,100,000 – 1,250,000	850,000	
		4,000,000
b) Medical expenses and miscellaneous expenses to date of trial		100,000
c) Moral damage until date of trial		
30 days' hospitalisation x 1,000	30,000	
882.5 days' without hospitalisation x 700	617,750	
	647,750	
+10% =		679,725
d) Interest		
1.25 years at 5% on 4,779,525 on items (a), (b) and (c) for 1.25 years		298,720
e) Future loss of income		
13.2357 x 550,000		11,250,345
f) Future moral damage		
100 x 40,000 + 10%		4,400,000
g) Future costs of aid		300,000
h) *Préjudice esthétique*		100,000
i) *Pretium voluptatis*		600,000
TOTAL AWARD		**21,728,590**

Table 2. Schedule B

Claimant :	Woman
Age :	20
Status :	Single
Occupation :	Legal Secretary
Income :	LUF 700,000 p.a. increasing to LUF. 1,000,000 by age 30, and to LUF. 1,250,000 net by age 40
Trial :	2.5 years after accident

1. Instant Death

a) Funeral expenses		80,000
b) Moral damage of the father and mother 165,000 each		330,000
c) Interest 2.5 years x 5% on 410,000 on items (a) and (b) + moral damage for brother or sister where applicable (± 30,000 each more loss of part of income for the father and mother during ± 2 years)		51,250
TOTAL AWARD		**461,250**

2a. Burns (A, B, C)

Assume claimant able to resume her employment two years after the accident

a) Loss of income 700,000 x 2 years		1,400,000
b) Miscellaneous loss (medical expenses included)		100,000
c) Moral damage to date of trial		
90 days' hospitalisation x 1,000	90,000	
640 days without hospitalisation x 700	448,000	
182.5 days hospitalisation x 700 x 20%	25,550	
	563,550+10%	

		619,905
d) Interest 1.25 years 5% on 2,119,905 on items (a), (b) and (c)		132,494
e) Future moral and material damage (effort to work at 100% with 20% disability) 20 x 30,000 + 10%		660,000
f) *Préjudice esthétique* (for loss of looks) Belgian figure + 10%		275,000
TOTAL AWARD		**3,187,399**

3. Quadriplegia

a) Loss of income to date of trial 2.5 years x 700,000		1,750,000
b) Cost of nursing care/medical expenses to date of trial 2.5 year x 1,750,000		4,375,000
c) Cost of modifying home and special equipment		1,400,000
d) Moral damage until date of trial		
90 days' hospitalisation x 1,114	100,260	
822.5 days without hospitalisation x 700	575,750	
	676,010	
+10% =		743,611
e) Interest 1.25 years at 5% on 8,268,611 on items (a), (b), (c) and (d)		516,788
f) Future loss of income – age at the trial 22.5 years assuming retirement at 65 years coefficient to capitalise at 5% interest following		
Levie's table = 17.1465 7.5 years x 700,000	5,250,000	
9.6465 years x 1,125,000	10,852,312	
		16,102,312

g)	Future costs of nursing: likely survival at 22 years = 50 years coefficient to capitalise at 5% annuities of 1,750,000 during 50 years = 18,2559 1,950,000 x 18,2559	35,600,000
h)	Future moral damage 100% x 40,000 + 10%	4,400,000
i)	*Préjudice esthétique*	1,100,000
	TOTAL AWARD	**65,995,850**

4. Paraplegia

a)	Loss of income to date of trial 2.5 year x 700,000	1,750,000
b)	Cost of nursing care/medical expenses to date of trial	1,400,000
c)	Cost of modifying home	700,000
d)	Moral damage to date of trial (same as for quadriplegia)	665,750
e)	Interest 1.25 years at 5% on 4,515,750 on items (a), (b), (c) and (d)	282,234
f)	Future loss of income (assuming she still has a 30% work ability) 70% of 16,102,312 (see quadriplegia)	11,271,618
g)	Estimated cost of nursing care/medical expenses/aids 200,000 x 18.2559	3,651,180
h)	Future moral damage (Belgian figure + 10%)	3,080,000
i)	*Préjudice esthétique*	770,000
	TOTAL AWARD	**23,570,782**

5a. Brain damage

a) Loss of income to trial 2.5 years x 700,000	1,730,000
b) Cost of nursing care/medical expenses to date of trial 2.5 years x 1,750,000	4,375,000
c) Cost of modifying home and special equipment	1,400,000
d) Moral damage to date of trial (same as for quadriplegia: assuming 100% disability until trial)	665,750
e) Interest 1.25 years at 5% on 8,190,730 on items (a), (b), (c) and (d)	511,921
f) Future loss of income 80% of 16,102,312 (see quadriplegia)	12,881,845
g) Estimated costs of nursing care/medical expenses/aids 200,000 x 18.2559	3,651,180
h) Future moral damage 80 x 40,000 + 10%	3,520,000
i) *Préjudice esthétique*	440,000
TOTAL AWARD	**29,195,696**

5b. Brain damage

a) Loss of income 2.5 years x 700,000	1,750,000
b) Cost of nursing/medical expenses to date of trial 2.5 years x 1,750,000	4,375,000
c) Cost of modifying home equipment	1,400,000
d) Moral damage until trial	665,750

e) Interest 1.25 years at 5% on 8,190,730 on items (a), (b), (c) and (d)		511,921
f) Future loss of income 90% of 16,102,312		14,492,080
g) Estimated costs of nursing care/medical expenses/aids 1,750,000 x 18.2559		31,947,825
h) Future moral damage 90 x 40,000 + 10%		3,960,000
i) *Préjudice esthétique*		660,000
TOTAL AWARD		**58,187,576**

6a. Amputation of leg above knee

Assume claimant able to resume her employment 1.5 years after accident

a) Loss of income 1.5 years at 700,000		1,150,000
b) Miscellaneous losses		100,000
c) Moral damage		
60 days' hospitalisation x 1,000	60,000	
487.5 days' without hospitalisation x 700	340,900	
365 days without hospitalisation x 700 x 35% x 700	89,425	
	490,325	
+10% =		539,358
d) Interest 1.25 years at 5% on 1,622,065 on items (a), (b) and (c)		101,379
e) Future moral and material damage 35 x 50,000 + 10%		1,925,000
f) *Préjudice esthétique* + 10%		660,000
TOTAL AWARD		**4,375,737**

6b. Amputation of leg below knee

Assume claimant able to resume her employment 1.5 Years after accident

a) Loss of income		
1.5 years x 750,000		1,050,000
b) Miscellaneous losses		100,000
c) Moral damage		
60 days' hospitalisation x 1,000	60,000	
487.5 days without hospitalisation x 700	341,250	
365 days' hospitalisation x 700 x 30%	76,650	
	477,900	
+10% =		525,690
d) Interest		
1.25 years at 5% on 1,675,690 on items (a), (b) and (c)		104,731
e) Future moral damage and material damage		
30 x 50,000 + 10%		1,650,000
F) *Préjudice esthétique* (Belgian figure + 10%)		550,000
TOTAL AWARD		**3,980,421**

7a. Amputation of arm above the elbow

Claimant not able to resume her employment but takes up light duties 1.5 years after accident

a) Loss of income		
1.5 years at 700,000	1,150,000	
1 year x 190,000	190,000	
		1,240,000
b) Miscellaneous expenses		100,000

c) Moral damage		
60 days' hospitalisation x 1,000	60,000	
487.5 days without hospitalisation x 700	341,250	
365 days' hospitalisation x 700 x 35%	89,425	
	490,675	
+10%		539,743
d) Interest		
1.25 years at 5% on 1,879,743 on items (a), (b) and (c)		117,484
e) Future moral and material damage		
35 x 40,000 +10%		1,540,000
f) *Préjudice esthétique*		660,000
TOTAL AWARD		**4,197,227**

7b. Amputation of arm below the elbow

a) and b) Same as above		
1,240,000 + 100,000		1,340,000
c) Moral damage		
60 days' hospitalisation x 1,000	60,000	
487.5 days without hospitalisation x 700	341,250	
365 days' hospitalisation x 700 x 30%	76,650	
	477,900	
+10% =		525,690
d) Interest		
1.25 years at 5% on 1,865,690 on items (a), (b) and (c)		116,606
e) Future moral and material damage		
30 x 40,000 + 10%		1,320,000
f) *Préjudice esthétique*		550,000
TOTAL AWARD		**3,852,296**

8a. Loss of eyesight – one eye without cosmetic disability

Assume claimant is able to resume her employment one year after the accident

a) Loss of income 1 year x 700,000		700,000
b) Miscellaneous losses		100,000
c) Moral damage	416,240	
+10% =		458,062
d) Interest 1.25 years at 5% on 1,258,062 on items (a), (b) and (c)		78,629
e) Future moral and material damage 30 x 40,000 + 10%		1,320,000
f) *Préjudice esthétique*		275,000
TOTAL AWARD		**2,931,691**

8b. Loss of eyesight – one eye with cosmetic disability

(a), (b), (c), (d) & (e) same as above	2,656,691
f) *Préjudice esthétique*	660,000
TOTAL AWARD	**3,316,691**

8c. Total blindness

a) Loss of income until trial 2.5 years x 700,000		1,750,000
b) Cost of care/medical expenses/aids		700,000
c) Moral damage to date of trial	665,750	
+10% =		732,325

d)	Interest 1.25 years at 5% on 3,182,325 on items (a), (b) and (c)		199,083
e)	Future loss of income same as for quadriplegia		16,102,312
f)	Future moral damage (*préjudice esthétique* included) Belgian figure + 10%		6,600,000
g)	Future cost of aids		700,000
	TOTAL AWARD		**26,783,720**

9a. Deafness

Assume claimant able to resume her employment 1.5 years after accident at Lux. F. 1,250,000 p.a.

a)	Loss of income until trial 1.5 years at 700,000		1,050,000
b)	Medical expenses and miscellaneous losses to date of trial		400,000
c)	Moral damage		
	30 days' hospitalisation x 1,000	30,000	
	882.5 days' without hospitalisation x 700	617,750	
		647,750	
	+10% =		712,525
d)	Interest 1.25 years at 5% on 2,162,525 on items (a), (b) and (c) for 1.25 years		135,158
e)	Future loss of income: assume she will earn 500,000 p.a. for the rest of her life Age at the trial: 22.5 years Assuming retirement at 65 years, coefficient to capitalise at 4.75% interest over 42.5 years at 19.1368		
	8 years x 200,000	1,600,000	

	10 years x 500,000	5,000,000	
	24.5 years x 750,000	18,375,000	
		24,975,000	
			11,245,682
f)	Future moral damage 100 x 40,000 + 10%		4,400,000
g)	Future costs of aid		300,000
h)	*Préjudice esthétique*		100,000
i)	*Pretium voluptatis*		600,000
	TOTAL AWARD		**18,943,365**

THE NETHERLANDS

Marinus M. MacLean

Introduction

Under Netherlands law, damages for personal injury or death are assessed on the basis of concrete facts, i.e. taking into account all factual circumstances of the injured person or, in the case of death, those of the deceased and the surviving relatives, both at the time of the event and with a view to future developments reasonably expected to occur, such as pay rises, promotion opportunities, lost benefits, etc. The benefit of the doubt is given to the injured person in assessing the aforementioned future developments and the burden of proof is formulated as being relatively light by the Dutch Supreme Court. The injured party (the person injured or a dependant of the deceased) therefore receives no more – but also no less – than the amount of loss calculated on this basis. In case of injury losses can also be claimed by third parties in and as so far as the losses would have to be paid to the injured party as well (shifted losses).

Where an injured person is concerned the question whether he could bear his loss himself because he is wealthy is immaterial, but, in the case of surviving dependants of a deceased person that question does play a part to some extent. They are only entitled to damages to the extent that they have a "need" for them, which means that their financial position is taken into account when the amount of damages is assessed. There are cases where the liable party does not have to pay the deceased's surviving relations any damages, or only a very small amount.

Where claims or payments under life or personal accident insurance policies are concerned, such payments – whether received by injured persons or by dependants – may be fully or partly deducted for the purpose of assessing the damages.

The main items of loss that can be claimed in the case of personal injury are the following:

- Costs of medical treatment and convalescence, including hospital, doctors' and nursing fees. However, these expenses are almost always covered by insurance and are not usually claimed by the injured person himself; health insurance companies have their own right of recourse. The amount of medical expenses may vary strongly and for the purposes of this contribution is left aside:

- Other items of tangible loss such as the cost of domestic help during incapacity to work, travel expenses of visiting next-of-kin, etc. Recently attempts have been made to standardize certain costs, more notably travel expenses and an allowance for extra costs incurred during stay in hospital
- Loss of earning capacity; as a rule persons employed in private trade and industry receive their full wages during the first year of incapacity to work, after which in principle their disability benefit is reduced to 70% of their wages; civil servants are in a somewhat better position. As social security benefits have been reduced in the past ten years, claims for loss of income against the liable party have become higher; social security authorities have a right of recourse, except against employers. Parts of this recourse are collectivised by means of agreements between representative organisations of insurers on one hand and social security institutions on the other hand.
- Employers have a right of recourse for ongoing payments of wages.
- Further items of tangible loss, including reasonable legal or claims adjuster's fees.
- Compensation for pain and suffering. The main factors in deciding this amount are the nature of the injury, the medical treatment and operations the injured person has undergone, the nature and gravity of the permanent or temporary consequences of the injury, such as invalidity, mutilations, scars, etc. The largest amount in damages ever awarded in the Netherlands was NLG 300,000 (£81,967) to a patient infected with HIV through negligence of a hospital. Prior to this the largest amounts awarded were NLG 250,000 (£68,306) and NLG 200,000 (£54,645.) We may expect that in future awards for very serious injuries (such as paraplegia) will gradually become higher, but at present damages awarded in the Netherlands under this heading are still relatively modest compared with other Western European countries.

In the case of death, dependants have a (limited) right to damages. The term "dependants" includes:

- the deceased's husband or wife and children (both legitimate and illegitimate children);

- other surviving blood relations and relations by marriage, provided the deceased actually provided for them;
- other relatives for whose livelihood the deceased provided and would have continued to provide and who really need such financial help; since the new Civil Code came into force a claim may also be filed under this heading by a person's life companion outside marriage;
- a family member for part of whose livelihood the deceased provided by reason of the fact that he or she did the housekeeping.

The items which the above-mentioned surviving dependants may claim are the following:

- loss of provision for their livelihood; children can claim until the age at which they are supposed to finish their education – given the presumption that education would have been paid for by the deceased parent(s) – and (supposedly) will start earning their own income. Usually this age is set somewhere between 18 and 22 depending on the social environment of the deceased and surviving relatives.
- funeral expenses;
- reasonable legal or claims adjuster's fees.

Surviving relations or dependants are not entitled to damages for bereavement. This form of intangible loss is not recognised in the Netherlands and was rejected by the Supreme Court.

In settlements out of court this form of damage has been recognized in striking cases including for instance parents who witness the death of their own children and recently this view has also been adopted in a ruling by the Amsterdam Court of Justice.

Table 1. Schedule A

Claimant :	Man
Age :	40
Status :	Married – 2 dependent children, aged 5 and 7
Occupation :	Doctor
Income :	NLG 100,000 net p.a
Trial :	Not relevant

1. Instant death NLG

- Claim for funeral expenses 7,000 – 10,000
- Dependent wife and children would have separate claims for loss of maintenance. Deductible: benefits from National Widow and Orphans Pensions Act (ANW). The following computation is schematic
- Way of computing annual loss

Net Income		100,000	
Fixed costs (rent etc.)[1]		30,000	
Variable household costs		70,000	
Deceased's expenditure ¼		17,500	
		52,500	
Claim wife:			
13 years x ¼ variable costs	17,500		
2 x ¼ fixed costs	15,000		
		32,500	
Deductible: ANW (no recourse)		17,500	
			15,000

1 Till the age of majority or, as the case may be, the end of the children's education, a period of about 14 years, fixed costs are to be attributed proportionally to dependants (wife = 2 x children's portion: decision of Supreme Court, 1991)

13 years, interest 3%, factor 10.5		157,500
After 13 years until deceased's 65th year		
1/4 variable costs	17,500	
4/4 fixed costs	30,000	
	47,500	
Deductible ANW	17,500	
	30,000	
25-13 (12) years, interest rate 3%, fact 9.5	285,000	
Claim children per annum:		
1/4 variable costs	17,500	
1/4 fixed costs	7,500	
	25,000	
15 and 13 years respectively, say 14 years, factor 11.4 x 2		570,000

In Dutch law there is – in general see above – no compensation for bereavement of husband, father or any other relative of dependant

TOTAL AWARD	**1,012,500**

2. Burns (A, B, C)

– Pain and suffering 2 years' disablement; no permanent incapacity		
Severe scars		35,000
– Net loss of income 2 x 100,000	200,000	
– *less* National Disability Pension Act (WAZ) pays after 11 year of disablement (right of recourse)	20,000	
	180,000	
		180,000

–	Miscellaneous losses NB + medical expenses (subrogated insurer, see Introductory note)	4,000
	TOTAL AWARD	**219,000**

3.-5b. Quadriplegia-Paraplegia-Brain damage

a)	Pain and suffering	200,000/400,000
b)	Claimant not able to resume work; loss of income 25 years (minus benefits from AAW) 80,000; factor 18.5	1,480,000
c)	Various costs, not including medical expenses NB: medical expenses (see introductory note)	100,000/300,000
	TOTAL AWARD	**2,180,000**

6a. and 6b. Amputation of leg

a)	Pain and suffering	100,000/125,000
b)	Loss of earnings for 1.5 years	140,000
c)	Miscellaneous NB: medical expenses (see introductory note)	20,000
	TOTAL AWARD	**286,000**

7a. and 7b. Amputation of arm

a)	Pain and suffering	75,000/120,000
b)	Loss of income 50,000 pa minus WAZ 10,000 = 40,000 pa over 25 years; factor 18.5	740,000
c)	Miscellaneous NB: medical expenses (see introductory note)	100,000
	TOTAL AWARD	**960,000**

8a. and 8b. Loss of eyesight-one eye without permanent disablement

a) Pain and suffering		40,000/70,000
b) 0.5 years disabled		50,000
c) Miscellaneous NB: medical expenses (see introductory note)		10,000
TOTAL AWARD		**200,000**

8c. Loss os eyesight-total blindness

a) Pain and suffering		150,000/200,000
b) Loss of earnings (see 3 above)		
c) Miscellaneous NB: medical expenses (see introductory note)		20,000/60,000
TOTAL AWARD		**260,000**

9. Deafness (total)

a) Pain and suffering; 1.5 years disablement; partial permanent incapacity		75,000/100,000
b) Net loss of income 1.5 years 1.5 x 100,000	150,000	
c) *less* National Disability Pension Act (WAZ) after 1 year of disablement ceasing whem victim resumes work	5,000	
		145,000
d) Loss of earnings for 25 years 80,000 (100,000 minimum wage): factor 18.5		1,480,000
e) Various costs not including medical expenses nor hearing aid (AWBZ)		10,000
TOTAL AWARD		**1,735,000**

10. Repetitive strain injury

As it seems highly improbable for a doctor to suffer such an injury, let alone a thid party being liable for the consequences thereof, this has only been prepared for the secretary.

The highest amount awarded in Holland for pain and suffering is NLG 300,000. This was a decision by the Hague Court of Appeal: the Supreme court has rejected the appeal against this decision.

Statutory interest is charged at varying rates, set by the government, presently 6%; it runs on past losses; it can be claimed from the date of the accident for property losses and for other losses, such as expenses and income, from the date the loss is incurred. Future losses are generally awarded per date of settlement or court decision and discounted for future interest earnings, taxation on interest and inflation, however in a 1997 ruling the Dutch Supreme Court deemed it possible – in general – that future loss of earnings can be due from the date of the accident. Frequently a net discounting rate of interest of 2-3% is used so as to allow for inflation and for taxation of interest earnings.

Table 2. Schedule B

Claimant :	Woman
Age :	20
Status :	Single
Occupation :	Legal Secretary
Income:	NLG 23,500 – increasing to NLG 33,500 net by age 30 and remains at that level from there
Trial :	Not relevant

1. Instant death

a) Claim for funeral expenses	7,000 – 10,000
b) No dependants	10,000

In Dutch law there is no compensation for bereavement of any relative or dependant (see above). Only the injured party can claim its own material damages. See introductory note.

TOTAL AWARD	**20,000**

2. Burns (A, B, C)

a) Pain and suffering	35,000
b) Net loss of income; first year sickness benefit 70% (right of recourse), supplemented by the employer to 100% (recourse for net payment by employer)	
c) Employees' Disability Pension Act (WAO) pays to a single person after 1 year of disablement circa 75% of net income	
Loss of income 25% of 24,500	6, 125
Note: Other disability insurance benefits, Probably none (NB: private or state financed insurers may have a right of recourse)	
d) Miscellaneous losses NB: medical expenses (see introductory note)	4,000
TOTAL AWARD	**45,125**

3. – 5b. Quadriplegia-Paraplegia-Brain damage

a) Pain and suffering (maximum award) (Claimant not able to resume work)	200,000/400,000
b) Claimant not able to resume work; loss of income 44 years (minus benefits from AOW 6,000 rising to 20,000; right of recourse) roughly	485,000

c) Various costs NB: medical expenses (see introductory note)	100,000/300,000
TOTAL AWARD	**1,185,000**

6a. and 6b. Amputation of leg

a) Pain and suffering	100,000/125,000
b) Loss of earnings 1.5 years first year no loss; 2nd year 50% of 6,000	3,000
c) Miscellaneous NB: medical expenses (see introductory note)	20,000
TOTAL AWARD	**148,000**

7a. and 7b. Amputation of arm

a) Pain and suffering	75,000/125,000
b) Partial loss of earnings p.a. over 45 years; roughly	250,000
TOTAL AWARD	**475,000**

c) Miscellaneous NB: medical expenses (see introductory note) 100,000

8a. and 8b. Loss of eyesight – one eye without permanent disablement

a) Pain and suffering	40,000/70,000
b) 0.5 years disabled; no loss of income (sickness benefit 70%; right of recourse)	
c) Miscellaneous NB: medical expenses (see introductory note)	10,000
TOTAL AWARD	**80,000**

8c. Loss of eyesight – total blindness

a) Pain and suffering	150,000/200,000
b) Loss of earnings (see 3-5b, above)	485,000
c) Miscellaneous NB: medical expenses (see introductory note)	20,000
TOTAL AWARD	**705,000**

9. Deafness (total)

a) Pain and suffering; 1.5 years disablement; partial permanent incapacity	75,000/100,000
b) 1st year, no loss 2nd year 0.5 x (25% of 24,500)	3,062
c) Loss of earnings for 44 years (minus benefit light duties, minimum wage), roughly	400,000
d) Various costs, not including medical expenses nor hearing aid [AWBZ]	10,000
TOTAL AWARD	**513,062**

10. Repetitive strain injury

a) Pain and suffering, the figure is related to partial functional disablement of both arms; it is assumed that in daily life this disablement will not be very painful	20,000/30,000
b) Claimant not able to resume work (presumably not even light duties) loss of earnings (see 3-5b, above)	485,000
c) Various costs – miscellaneous losses NB: medical expenses (see introductory note)	10,000
TOTAL AWARD	**525,000**

PORTUGAL

Henrique dos Santos Pereira

Introduction

Portuguese Law does not provide fixed amounts to be attributed as personal injury awards in relation to instant death or other personal injuries. Beyond that, jurisprudence – case law – has not been uniform in all cases. The analysis of the more recent decisions of the Court of Appeal and Supreme Court (the decisions of first instance courts are not published), proves that the injury awards vary significantly even in very similar situations. The unique common characteristic of the judgments is the meagreness of the awards. The lack of uniformity extends to moral and pecuniary damages, not only to be attributed to the injured but also to his family.

In short, Portuguese law confers some freedom on the judge so that he can decide in accordance with the circumstances of each case. The following are the only exceptions to this rule:

1. Allowance to be paid as a consequence of an employment related accident

a) Incapacities

(i) Total incapacity for any work: life annuity of 80% of the salary, plus 10% for each son residing with the worker, up to the limit of 100% plus a subsidy for high permanent incapacity.

(ii) Total incapacity for the usual work: life annuity on the amount between 50% and 70% of the salary, depending on the capacity to perform other compatible work plus a subsidy for high permanent incapacity.

(iii) Permanent partial incapacity equal or higher than 70%: life annuity corresponding to 70% of the general earning ability plus a subsidy for high permanent incapacity.

(iv) Permanent partial incapacity inferior to 70%: life annuity corresponding to 70% of the general earning ability.

(v) Temporary absolute incapacity; daily indemnity corresponding to 70% of the daily salary.

(vi) Temporary partial incapacity; daily indemnity corresponding to 70% of the general earning ability.

b) Death

(i) Widow: 30% of the injured person's salary until his widow's 65th birthday and 40% there after.

(ii) Children: 20% of the injured person's salary if there is only one child, 40% if there are two and 50% if there are three, until their 24th birthday (maximum).

2. Indemnities to be paid as consequence of a traffic accident when the responsible party has no fault

a) In the case of physical injuries (including death) of one person, the maximum limit of indemnity is PTE 6,000,000 (£18,023.)

b) In the case of physical injuries (including death) of more than one person, as consequence of the same accident, the limit is PTE 6,000,000 for each injured person, up to PTE 18,000,000 (£54,069.)

c) If the award is fixed as an annual allowance, the maximum is PTE 750,000 (£2,253) per year for each injured person, up to PTE 2,250,000 (£6,759) for all, when there is more than one injured person.

d) If the accident is caused by public transportation, the limits referred to are raised to triple the amount.

e) If the accident is caused by a train, those limits are raised to ten times the amount.

(These rules are indicative of the meagre nature of injury awards).

There are some judgments that take into consideration some of these limits – mainly the allowances to be paid as consequence of an employment-related accident – but we cannot say that they represent the majority.

For all these reasons, it is impossible for us to indicate precisely the largest maximum personal awards – as our other European counterparts have done – and no one can do it in Portugal.

Consequently, bearing in mind these premises, we will only refer to the principal conclusions of the investigation that were made on the judicial decisions (beyond those mentioned above) and also some notes about the relevant rules.

Consideration about personal injury awards in Portugal

1. As mentioned above, personal injury awards in Portugal are usually very low.
2. Although the date of trial is not relevant, in the courts of Lisbon and Oporto these cases might take about two or three years (even less) but in provincial courts they might take longer.
3. In the case of death the moral damage of the deceased is transmissible to the heirs.
4. Funeral expenses are of about PTE 200,000 (£601.)
5. In general terms, the welfare benefits must be deducted from the indemnity and the liable party will not have to reimburse those benefits to the welfare service.
6. Taking into account the more recent decisions of the Portuguese courts, the maximum moral damages in case of death attributable to the widow or widower is of PTE 3,000,000 (£9,011) and the maximum moral damages attributable to the sons is of PTE 4,000,000 (£12,015.)
7. As to pecuniary damage, theoretically the indemnity must strive to re-establish the situation that would exist without the injuries event, so that it must represent an amount which will be extinguished at the end of the deceased's assumed working life (at about 65 years for men and at about 62 years for women) and will be able to provide, during that period, a periodical allowance correspondent to the loss of income.

So, some judicial decisions consider inflation, actual and foreseen (currently inflation in Portugal is about 2.3%) and also the banking interest rate. Unfortunately, this is not normal procedure.

Interest rates after judgment are 7%.

Legal costs

All civil and commercial lawsuits have a monetary value which is in principle the amount involved in the case (the indemnity claimed).

This value is the basis for calculation of legal fees:

Table 1.

Value of matter in controversy (PTE)	*Legal cost (PTE)*
100,000	10,000
200,000	14,000
300,000	18,000
400,000	22,000
500,000	26,000
600,000	30,000
700,000	34,000
800,000	38,000
900,000	42,000
1,000,000	46,000
1,400,000	50,000
1,800,000	54,000
2,300,000	60,000
2,900,000	68,000
3,500,000	76,000
4,100,000	84,000
4,700,000	92,000
5,500,000	100,000
6,500,000	108,000
7,500,000	116,000
8,500,000	124,000
9,500,000	132,000
10,000,000	136,000

NB: Over 10,000,000, for each 1,000,000 add 10,000.

Schedule A

DAC Notional Schedule based on Portuguese lawyers' information above.

1. Moral damages maximum applied to serious injury. Half maximum moral damages to lesser injuries. Portuguese assessed figures for two new injuries included since first edition.
2. Welfare benefits up to 30% of salaries have been deducted from award.
3. Medical expenses in Portugal deemed to be half English medical expenses.
4. Owing to the low level of limit on the most common physical injuries (traffic accident) PTE 6,000,000 (£ 18,023 per person) and PTE 18,000,000 (£ 54,069) for all persons injured in one accident, this schedule has an area of uncertainty for Portuguese lawyers, who say it is impossible to indicate precise injury awards. The schedule is for comparison purposes only, assuming no limits. Limits almost always apply. The notional figures for the more serious injuries in this schedule have never been seen.
5. Incomes – assessed by Portuguese lawyers.
6. We include this notional schedule in order to clarify the figures in the comparison schedules and to initiate discussion on the level of Portuguese awards. The percentages are based on employment- related accidents (not traffic etc.) as these are the only guide-lines ascertainable from the above.
7. To simplify, we have assumed no increase in salary, *but* have applied a full term of years rather than applying a capitalisation factor.

Table 2

Claimant :	Man
Age :	40
Status :	Married, 2 dependent children aged 5 and 7
Occupation :	Doctor
Income :	PTE 4,000,000 net (£12,015)
Trial :	2.5 years after accident

1. Instant death	PTE
a) Funeral expenses	200,000
b) Maximum moral damages paid to the estates	10,000,000
c) Moral damage of the deceased transmissible to the heirs	5,000,000
d) Loss of income	50,000,000
TOTAL AWARD	**65,200,000**

2. Burns (A, B, C)

Assume claimant is unable to resume employment for two years after the accident

a) Moral damages	1,000,000
b) Loss of income (2 years x P. Esc. 4,000,000)	8,000,000
less welfare benefits (30%)	2,400,000
TOTAL AWARD	**6,600,000**

3. and 5. Quadriplegia (and brain damage)

a) Moral damages	10,000,000
b) Cost of nursing care (half English of £236,485)	36,000,000
c) Loss of income	55,000,000
less welfare benefits (30%)	16,500,000
TOTAL AWARD	**84,500,000**

4. Paraplegia

a) Moral damages	10,000,000

b) Cost of nursing care (half English £46,312.50)	7,200,000
c) Loss of income	55,000,000
less welfare benefits (30%)	16,500,000
TOTAL AWARD	**55,700,000**

6a. and 6b. Amputation of leg

a) Moral damages	6,000,000
b) Loss of income 1.5 x P. Esc 4,000,000	6,000,000
c) Future loss of income	50,000,000
less welfare benefits (30%)	18,300,000
TOTAL AWARD	**43,700,000**

7a. and 7b. Amputation of arm

a) Moral damages	6,000,000
b) Loss of income 1.5 x P. Esc 4,000,000	6,000,000
c) Future loss of income	60,000,000
less welfare benefits (30%)	19,300,000
TOTAL AWARD	**52,200,000**

8a. and 8b. Loss of eyesight – one eye

a) Moral damages	4,000,000
b) 1 year at P. Esc 4,000,000	4,000,000
less welfare benefits (30%)	1,200,000
TOTAL AWARD	**6,800,000**

8c. Loss of eyesight – total blindness

a) Moral damages	9,000,000
b) Cost of nursing care (half English £ 10,937.50)	1,700,000
c) Future loss of income (see 3, above)	55,000,000
less welfare benefits (30%)	16,500,000
TOTAL AWARD	**49,200,000**

9. Deafness

a) Moral damages	7,000,000
b) Cost of nursing care	1,000,000
c) Future loss of income (see 3, above)	50,000,000
less welfare benefits (30%)	15,000,000
TOTAL AWARD	**43,000,000**

10. Repetitive strain injury

a) Moral damages	1,000,000
b) Cost of nursing care	350,000
c) Loss of income (0.5 years x P. Esc 4,000,000)	2,000,000
less welfare benefits (30%)	600,000
TOTAL AWARD	**2,750,000**

Table 3. Schedule B

Claimant :	Woman
Age :	20
Status :	Single
Occupation :	Legal Secretary
Income :	PTE 1,400,000 rising to PTE 1,750,000 by 30 and to PTE 2,300,000 by 40
Trial :	2.5 years after accident

1. Instant death

a) Funeral expenses	200,000
b) Maximum moral damages paid to the estates	10,000,000
c) Moral damage of the deceased transmissible to the heirs	5,000,000
TOTAL AWARD	**15,200,000**

2. Burns (A, B, C)

Assume claimant is unable to resume employment for two years after the accident

a) Moral damages	1,000,000
b) Loss of income (2 years x P. Esc. 1,400,000)	2,800,000
c) *less* welfare benefits (30%)	840,000
TOTAL AWARD	**2,960,000**

3. Quadriplegia

a) Moral damages	8,000,000
b) Cost of nursing care (half English of £236,485)	36,000,000

c) Loss of income	50,000,000
less welfare benefits (30%)	15,000,000
TOTAL AWARD	**79,000,000**

4. Paraplegia

a) Moral damages	8,000,000
b) Cost of nursing care (half English £46,312.50)	7,200,000
c) Loss of income	50,000,000
less welfare benefits (30%)	15,000,000
TOTAL AWARD	**50,200,000**

5a. and 5b. Brain damage

a) Moral damages	8,000,000
b) Cost of nursing care (half English £ 261,484)	40,000,000
c) Loss of income	50,000,000
less welfare benefits (30%)	15,000,000
TOTAL AWARD	**83,000,000**

6a. and 6b. Amputation of leg

a) Moral damages	6,000,000
b) Loss of income 1.5 x P. Esc 1,400,000	2,100,000
c) Future loss of income	30,000,000
less welfare benefits (30%)	9,630,000
TOTAL AWARD	**28,740,000**

7a. and 7b. Amputation of arm

a) Moral damages	5,000,000
b) Loss of income 1.5 x P. Esc 1,400,000	2,100,000
c) Future loss of income	35,000,000
less welfare benefits (30%)	11,130,000
TOTAL AWARD	**30,970,000**

8a. and 8b. Loss of eyesight – one eye

a) Moral damages	5,000,000
b) 1 year at P. Esc 1,400,000	1,400,000
less welfare benefits (30%)	420,000
TOTAL AWARD	**5,980,000**

8c. Loss of eyesight – total blindness

a) Moral damages	8,000,000
b) Cost of nursing care (half English £ 10,937.50)	17,000,000
c) Future loss of income (see 3, above)	50,000,000
less welfare benefits (30%)	15,000,000
TOTAL AWARD	**60,000,000**

9. Deafness

a) Moral damages	7,000,000
b) Cost of nursing care	1,000,000
c) Future loss of income (see 3, above)	30,000,000

less welfare benefits (30%)	9,000,000
TOTAL AWARD	**29,000,000**

10. Repetitive strain injury

a) Moral damages	1,000,000
b) Cost of nursing care	350,000
c) Loss of income (0.5 years x P. Esc 1,400,000)	700,000
less welfare benefits (30%)	210,000
TOTAL AWARD	**1,890,000**

SCOTLAND

Alastair H. Lockhart, Alan K. Brown and Fergus Thomson

Introduction

The Scottish legal system is separate and distinct from that of England and Wales. Awards for damages in personal injury cases are made largely on the basis of precedent and by comparing the individual circumstances of the instant case with previous decisions. There are no formal scales for assessing the appropriate award for *solatium* (pain and suffering) for a specific injury nor are awards calculated on the basis of an assessed percentage disability for a specific type of injury. The lawyer in Scotland requires as much of the following information and evidence as possible (the details being very similar to those required in England and Wales):

1. The claimant's dates of birth and National Insurance Number.
2. The claimant's marital status and family details.
3. Medical evidence as to the claimant's pre-accident (or disease) state of health, the injuries received in the accident (or details of the disease), the treatment given, degree and progress of recovery and future prognosis.
4. Details of the claimant's pre-accident gross and net earnings and any increases in earnings to which the claimant would have been entitled had he been working between the date of the accident and date of calculation.
5. The likely future earnings and earning capacity of the claimant.
6. The nature and security of the claimant's employment at the time of the accident and the future (whether the claimant is able to return to his pre-accident employment or not).
7. Details of 'personal services' rendered to the claimant in the period since the date of the accident to the date of calculation and details of such services liable to be provided in the future.

8. Details of services formerly provided by the claimant to others which as a result of the accident he was for a period and/or is and/or will be unable to provide currently or in the future.
9. The cost of past and likely cost of future medical treatment, nursing care and other assistance or special equipment made reasonably necessary by the injury.
10. Benefits and other monies paid to the claimant by the State or others (including company sick pay) as a consequence of the injury (or disease) and in particular details of Social Security benefits paid or likely to be paid from the date of the accident until the date payment is made (the treatment of DSS benefits is the same in Scotland as in England and in this respect we would refer to the Section on England).
11. Any element of conduct on the part of the claimant which contributed to causing the injury and on the basis of which the Defender has a prospect of obtaining a percentage reduction of the claim or of avoiding liability completely on the basis of contributory negligence by the claimant.

On the basis of the above information and evidence, the lawyer then calculates the likely value of the award which the court would make under the following heads of damage.

1. Solatium (Damages for Pain and Suffering)

Solatium or damages for pain and suffering (general damages) for personal injury is calculated by reference to the type and nature of the injury and comparison with previously decided cases. It is a system based on precedent. An allowance is made for inflation when considering previous causes; previous awards are 'updated' using a multiplier calculated on the basis of the rate of inflation since the decision in the previous analogous case. There are no formal scales for assessing *solatium* based on the type of injury nor is any attempt made to assess a percentage disability for any type of injury and to assess *solatium* with reference to that assessment. *Solatium* for the same injury may vary according to the age of the claimant and the speed and nature of recovery. In the specimen calculations we have based our figures on precedent where possible, given the very limited information provided as to the type of injury. For the more unusual injuries we have used our best estimate of what a court might award.

2. Loss of Earnings to Date

The claimant's loss of earnings to the date of calculation is based on his pre-accident average net earnings (i.e. gross earnings under deduction of tax, national insurance contributions and pension contributions). Average pre-accident net earnings are usually calculated by taking the net average weekly pay for the period of 13 weeks immediately prior to the accident. Any wage increases proved to have been awarded between the date of the accident and the date of calculation should be included in the calculation and the possibility of the claimant achieving promotion but for his absence due to injury may be taken into account. Appropriate and adequate documentation vouching loss of income should be produced by the claimant. It should prove possible to calculate fairly accurately past wage loss (i.e. loss of earnings to date of calculation).

In general if the claimant received sick pay from this employer this will have the effect of reducing his claim for past wage loss against the Defender. However some employers require by contract of employment that sick pay paid to an employee be refunded if the employee successfully recovers damages from a third party in respect of his injuries. If such an arrangement applies the amount of company sick pay should be ignored when calculating the actual loss of earnings.

In the event of the claim being made by a sole trader, equity partner or company director it is his personal claim for his personal loss of income, which is relevant, and not the loss of the company or partnership profits or the effect on goodwill of the undertaking. In the case of a company director account may be taken in assessing loss of earnings of benefits in kind such as health insurance, company car, payment of telephone expenses, loss of pension contributions etc.

3. Future Loss of Earnings

This is calculated by applying a multiplier to a figure for net annual loss (the multiplicand) calculated with reference to pre-accident net earnings and any increases in earnings from the date of the accident to the date of calculation. The calculation of future loss is based on what the claimant would actually have been earning as at the date of the calculation. In general no account is taken of prospective increases in earnings in real terms to which the claimant may have been entitled after the date of calculation but for his injuries. No allowance is made for inflation in the future. Multipliers, and choosing the appropriate multiplier in a particular case, are considered further below.

4. Loss of Employability/Compensation for Disadvantage on the Labour Market

In the harsh economic climate of recent years the courts have recognised that when jobs are scarce people with disabilities are at a disadvantage on the labour market. In England and Wales these are known as '*Smith & Manchester*' awards. Even when the claimant is in employment and will suffer no future loss of earnings as a result of his accident, an award for disadvantage on the labour market may be made. A loss of employability award may be made in addition to a claim for past and/or future wage loss. Awards have ranged from GBP 200 to 50,000, most often being a lump sum awarded, but occasionally being calculated on the basis of a multiplier and multiplicand. Most awards are in the GBP 3,000 – 6,000 range. In order to make the comparison award as realistic as possible we have, in line with our English colleagues, made no allowance for loss of employability awards in the specimen calculations. However such awards are not uncommon particularly where the claimant is able to return to pre-accident employment and would in fact be made in many of the examples considered.

5. Services

a) Where necessary services have been rendered to the claimant by a relative in consequence of the injuries (or disease) in question, then the claimant is entitled to be paid such sum as represents reasonable remuneration for those services and reimbursement of reasonable expenses incurred in connection with rendering these services. The claimant must then account to the relative for any sums recovered. In the event of a fatal accident the executor may pursue the claim and account to the provider of the services. For a claim to lie, services must have been provided by a relative and no other person. "Relative" is defined by statute. No claim shall lie if the relative has expressly agreed that no payment should be made in respect of the provision of the services in the knowledge that an action for damages has been commenced or is being contemplated by the injured person. Such circumstances must be rather rare, given human nature, and indeed we know of only one reported case where this has happened.

The actions which may constitute "necessary services" are many; they include providing nursing care, providing the services of a nursing auxiliary, washing, ironing, cooking, shopping, helping with bathing, shaving, dressing, driving the claimant about, undertaking paperwork resulting from the injury etc.

Valuing the claim may prove difficult and the courts have not taken a consistent approach as to what constitutes 'reasonable remuneration'. In general, the courts will take a broad approach. It is not generally appropriate to ask what it would cost to have a professional provide the services in question (e.g. if simple nursing services are provided it is not appropriate to ask what it would cost to have a nurse come to the claimant's house and provide these services). Such figures however may be of some assistance. It is not appropriate to ask what the provider of the services might otherwise have earned, unless the provider has had to give up their paid employment in order to provide the services, when their pre-accident wage may be relevant provided it was not disproportionately high (e.g. a Solicitor giving up work to perform household tasks!). In assessing claims in the specimen calculations we have made various assumptions as to what services might be provided for the injuries in question and looked simply to reported cases and our experience to assess a value.

An award for services to be provided in the future is competent. There is no consistent approach in selecting the appropriate multiplier, however, the current trend is for the courts to have regard to actuarial tables, at least to provide the base point for calculations.

b) Where as a result of the accident the claimant is no longer able to provide personal services a claim will lie. 'Personal' means no more than services rendered in person – it does not look to the nature or quality of the services rendered. Claims usually relate to DIY, gardening, car maintenance, household work etc. No guidance is given by statute as to what constitutes a 'reasonable sum' and in general the court takes a broad approach. There are some high awards made under this heading (e.g. where the mother of a 3 year old child was killed in a car accident and the father continued to work, an award was made under this heading for the cost of employing a housekeeper at a weekly cost of GBP 60 per week and a multiplier of 7 was applied.) In general, awards are lower. A multiplier is applied for future services. In determining the appropriate multiplier, the current trend is for the courts to have regard to actuarial tables but then to discount the multiplier in the tables on the basis that as the claimant becomes older the services which he would provide would diminish.

6. Cost of Care, Treatment and Equipment

A seriously injured claimant may require permanent nursing care or specialist equipment or medical treatment not available on the NHS. These costs may have been incurred by the time of the calculation or may be ongoing or future costs. For future costs, details of estimated costs based on current costs can be provided and an annual figure calculated to which an appropriate multiplier could then be applied. A discount on the annual figure may be required depending on the services to be provided in respect of living expenses which the claimant would have incurred notwithstanding his accident. A claimant who has been or will in the future be maintained in a NHS hospital, home or institution or otherwise wholly or partly at public expense, must set off any savings made as a result of such maintenance against any income lost by him as a result of his injuries. This will cover the cost of food and heating etc that the claimant will not be required to meet while in hospital. In practice this is rarely done and we have not provided for this in the specimen calculations. A disabled claimant may require alterations to his home. Where local or central government funding is unavailable, damages may be awarded for any necessary alterations. Damages may also be recovered for additional living expenses such as increased heating or laundry costs, travel expenses, medical supplies or special dietary requirements. Such costs to date of calculation are usually easily quantified. For the future an average annual figure should be calculated and an appropriate multiplier (based, increasingly on actuarial tables) applied.

7. Interest on Damages

By statute the court is required to include a sum in respect of interest on sums awarded under each Head of Claim in any action for personal injury. Interest is due from the date when the right of action arose (usually the date of the accident). Once Decree (Judgement) has been given for a specified sum, interest runs on the whole amount of the award (including the interest awarded to date of the Judgement) at the "judicial rate". With effect from 1st April 1993, the judicial rate has been 8% and this figure will be used in all cases where Decree (Judgement) is granted on or after that date. It is this figure which we have used in the specimen calculations. In calculating interest on various Heads of Claim from earlier dates the judicial rate is usually used as a point of reference.

1. Interest on Solatium

a) Where the claimant continues to suffer pain and suffering at the date of calculation a proportion of *solatium* is allocated to the past and a proportion to the future. For the sum allocated to the past interest runs at 4% per annum (half the judicial rate) from the date of the accident until the date of calculation.

b) Where the injury has resolved and there is no continuing pain or suffering at the date of calculation the whole *solatium* is allocated to the past, and, while the courts have not taken a consistent view on interest in these cases, the most likely approach is that interest will be applied on the whole amount of the award at the rate of 8% from the date on which the claimant was deemed to have become symptom free.

2. Interest on Wage Loss

Where the wage loss is continuing at Proof (Trial) interest is normally awarded on the whole amount of the past wage loss at half the judicial rate from the date of the accident to the date of Judgement. Where the injury has resolved and there is no continuing wage loss at the date of calculation the courts have not adopted a consistent approach. In our experience the most likely approach is for interest to be awarded on the whole sum at the judicial rate from the date on which the wage loss ceased.

3. Interest on Services Claims

In general the same principles apply to interest on services claims as for past wages loss. If services are still being rendered to the claimant or if he is still unable to provide services (i.e. the loss is continuing) interest runs on the whole sum at half the judicial rate from the date of accident to date of Proof (Trial). If services are no longer being rendered and the claimant is no longer disabled from providing services to others, interest runs at the judicial rate from the date on which the loss ceased.

4. Outlays

Where monies have been expended on medical expenses, travelling expenses, provision of equipment, modification of homes etc, interest will run at the full judicial rate from the date of outlay until the date of calculation. In the specimen calculations the date of outlay is not known. The assumptions, which we have made, are detailed in the specimen calculations.

5. Damage in Fatal Cases

In Scotland there is no equivalent to the English 'statutory bereavement damages'. Fatal claims in Scotland are regulated by the Damages (Scotland) Act 1976, as amended. The main Heads of Claim available to relatives of the deceased (as that term is defined in the 1976 Act) following a fatal accident are:

- Loss of Society etc

  The Act provides that if the relative is a member of the deceased's 'immediate family' (as defined) an award can be made by way of compensation for:

  a) the distress and anxiety endured by the relative in contemplation of the suffering of the deceased before his death;
  b) the grief and sorrow of the relative caused by the deceased's death; and
  c) the loss of such non-patrimonial benefit as the relative might have been expected to derive from the deceased's society and guidance if the deceased had not died.

  This Head of Claim is available to members of the deceased's immediate family as defined *i.e.* to the spouse, co-habitee, parent, parent-in-law, child of the deceased (including a child regarded by the deceased as part of his immediate family, i.e. his spouse's child by a previous marriage) and children-in-law. It should be noted each of the above parties has a separate and individual claim under this Head. An older spouse will not necessarily receive a lower award than a younger spouse but a younger child will usually receive a higher award than an older child. Past loss of society (i.e. to date of calculation) attracts interest at half the judicial rate from the date of death to the date of calculation. The courts tend to apportion 50% of the award to past loss.

- Where a person is injured or contracts a disease as a result of the fault or negligence of a third party and dies as a result (either shortly after the accident or contracting the disease or after a period of time) the deceased's executor has a claim in respect of *solatium* for pain and suffering experienced by the deceased in the period prior to death. The executor also has a claim for pecuniary losses (e.g. loss of wages, loss of pension payments, expenses and outlays) suffered or incurred by the deceased during the period prior to death. The value of the transmissible *solatium* claim will depend on the facts and circumstances of each case. Where death occurred shortly after the accident causing injury, any claim is likely to be small. Any award will be in respect of pain and suffering experienced by the deceased between the date of the accident (or contraction of disease) and death – no account is taken of future *solatium* and this must be taken into account when comparing transmissible *solatium* awards in fatal cases with awards made where the Pursuer remains alive, albeit disabled, as a result of the accident or disease.

- Funeral Expenses

  Funeral expenses are recoverable by the party paying these. Interest is due at the judicial rate from the date of payment.

- Loss of Support

  This claim is available to the deceased's spouse, divorced spouse, co-habitee, parent, parent-in-law, child, child-in-law, ascendants, descendants, brothers, sisters, uncles, aunts, nephews and nieces. Awards are made upon the basis of what support had actually been provided by the deceased during his life to the claimant. The degree of support has to be properly proved. The deceased's net income has to be established and evidence led as to what portion was used to support the claimant. Interest on claims for loss of support to date is at half the judicial rate on the full sum from the date of the accident to the date of calculation. Claims for future loss of support are based on a multiplier and multiplicand. In ascertaining the appropriate multiplier, reference is increasingly made to actuarial tables as the base point. In the case of children the age to which such support would have been rendered is relevant when calculating the appropriate multiplier.

- Services

  The executor may claim in respect of personal services rendered by a relative to the deceased prior to the deceased's death. The executor has an obligation to account to the provider of the services for sums recovered. A claim for services previously rendered by the deceased will accrue i.e. to those bereft of the services as a result of the death.

8. Multipliers

The calculation of future loss in both personal injury cases and fatal cases can only be by way of an estimate. The traditional method in Scotland of calculating future loss and expenditure was by estimating the average annual loss or expenditure and applying a multiplier to it. The appropriate multiplier was selected by reference to precedent with an assumption that the principle sum of damages if invested would earn interest at a rate of between 4 and 5% per annum. In 1984, in England and Wales, a working party chaired by Sir Michael Ogden QC recommended that actuarial tables should be used when selecting a multiplier and a set of such tables for use in personal injury and fatal accident cases was produced (the Ogden Tables) setting out a range of rates of net investment return and specifying a variety of multipliers dependent on which rate of return was deemed applicable. Initially, the use of the Ogden Tables in personal injury cases was met with some resistance by the courts but by the early 1990s Scotland's Senior Judge had indicated that in certain circumstances actuarial evidence and tables may provide a useful check upon a multiplier selected in the traditional way. In 1998 the House of Lords, in the case of *Wells v Wells* ruled that actuarial tables should provide the starting point when selecting a multiplier and that until the Secretary of State prescribed otherwise, the net investment returns should be assumed to be 3%. Although *Wells v Wells* was an English case, it has been followed in Scotland and until the Secretary of State prescribes otherwise, the assumed rate of return is 2.5%. The Secretary of State has power in terms of Section 1 of the Damages Act 1996 to prescribe the assumed rate of return. To date, he has not exercised this power.

9. Wage Loss

The multiplier selected may be influenced by many factors including primarily the age of the Pursuer, his usual retirement age, the nature of the injuries and the prognosis. Discounts are applied to reflect investments benefits in receiving a large capital sum. Discounts also apply due to the uncertainty that the Pursuer would live as long as expected, would remain unable to work, would have worked in any event and other various unpredictable turns of fate. The Ogden Tables multipliers take account of the various imponderables which might occur. The highest multiplier reported in Scotland is 17. In personal injury cases the multiplier is chosen with reference to and applied from the date of Proof and not the date of the accident. However, in fatal cases the multiplier is chosen with reference to the date of death and not from the date of Proof.

10. Services

It is less easy to determine an appropriate multiplier in the case of future services, as what is appropriate will depend very much on the circumstances of the case and the many and varied imponderables which may arise. In the specimen calculations we have simply take a "best guess". Recent developments indicate that the courts will use actuarial tables to provide initial guidance as to an appropriate multiplier and then discount to allow for the individual circumstances of the case and the various imponderables which may arise. Multipliers for future services are determined at the date of Proof except in fatal cases where they apply from the date of death. In fatal cases there is no consistent approach in assessing the multiplier but it may be similar to that applied for future wage loss.

11. Future Cost of Nursing Care

The cost of future nursing care is calculated on the basis of a multiplicand and multiplier with the appropriate multiplier being chosen with reference to actuarial tables. A distinction can be made between awards for future loss of earnings and awards for future costs to be incurred throughout the person's lifetime. Whereas with future loss of earnings there are many variables which may be taken into account, in considering the cost of future nursing care it is the life expectancy of the claimant only which is the measure of the period of loss. This is reflected in different actuarial tables being applicable for each head of claim. In a recent case (January 2000) a multiplier of 25.1 was held appropriate for the cost of future nursing care where the Pursuer was a 31 year old female.

12. Jury Trial

The option of a trial before a judge and jury in claims for damages for personal injury is a remedy open to parties only within the Court of Session, the Supreme, and Civil Court in Scotland. It is not available within the Sheriff Courts. In the Court of Session such claims must proceed by way of jury trial unless (a) parties otherwise agree of (b) special cause is shown justifying the withholding of the case from a jury. There is an exception to that rule where the claimant chooses a special "fast track" procedure also available only in the Court of Session (the Optional Procedure). By so doing he is held to waive his right a trial by jury. Despite the presumption in favour of jury trials, however, in the majority of cases (a ratio of 20-1) and usually by agreement, a proof (trial) before a single judge is fixed for the hearing of evidence.

All personal injury actions (other than under the Optional Procedure) follow the same procedure until the adjustment of the written pleadings has come to an end. At that stage a decision on further procedure requires to be made. In the absence of agreement, any party to the action may seek a jury trial and the other may object on the grounds of special cause. The question of suitability of the particular case for proof or jury trial is one to be assessed on the individual circumstances of each case. What constitutes special cause for withholding from a jury is within the discretion of the judge. If it is likely that the facts will throw up particularly complex legal or evidential issues either parties of the court may find a proof preferable to a jury trial. Typical examples of special cause would be where difficulties exist in relation to the relevance in law of the claims stated or where medical issues arising are particularly complex or novel.

The case is tried on the basis of formal "Issues" (written questions) on which the jury is asked to return their verdict. Appended to the pursuer's (claimant's) issue is a schedule enumerating the sum sued for and the various heads of damages claimed. The jury is the master of the facts in the case and the credibility of the witnesses and it is the jury which decides the factual questions at issue and awards damages under each of the heads of claim.

A jury is comprised of 12 persons selected in open court by ballot from a jury list drawn from the public living in Edinburgh (where the Court of Session is located) and its surrounding area. The court's business is not heard on circuit. Eligibility of persons for jury service is in accordance with the general statutory qualification and insofar as they are not exempt from service for any reason. Each party has an unlimited right of challenge of proposed jurors on cause shown and four rights of challenge without showing cause. It was once but is no longer possible to opt for a "single sex" jury of all men or all women.

Procedure at a jury trial differs to that at proof before a single judge in Scotland in that before the leading of evidence for each party, there are opening speeches by counsel for both parties. Evidence is then led in the normal way and at the conclusion of the evidence and after closing speeches of Counsel, the presiding judge charges the jury. This charge will consist of a summary of the facts which require to be established and a review of the evidence led. It also lays down the particular principles of law which apply to the case and which the jury must accept from the judge. Damages are solely within the province of the jury to assess. Counsel may not address the jury on the issue of damages with reference to precedent as is the practice in a hearing before a judge alone. However, Counsel, in their closing speeches, may be permitted to suggest that the claim is worth "several thousands of pounds" or "a three rather than four figure sum". It might be suggested to the jury that the sum sued for would represent a "reasonable award" or that they should be making a "substantial award". The position in relation to pecuniary loss is somewhat different in that it permissible to state e.g. what wage loss is and to suggest what multiplier might be applied to a yearly loss. The judge also outlines the principles which the jury must follow in awarding damages if they find these due.

A direction to a jury which has been generally approved and often used is such actions is:

> "that they ought not to attempt to fix damages at the full amount of compensation for the injury that a man has suffered but that they should take a reasonable view of the case and give what they consider in the circumstances to be fair compensation".

A jury may return a verdict by a simple majority of its number.

A jury's decision may be reclaimed (appealed) against both in relation to the issue of liability and the sum of damages awarded. The outcome of a successful Appeal is usually the ordering of a fresh trial either on liability or on damages or on both. The grounds for application for a new trial are as follows:-

a) Misdirection by the judge;

b) Undue admission or rejection of evidence;

c) That the verdict is contrary to the evidence;

d) The excess or inadequacy of damages;

e) *Res noviter veniens ad notitiam* (that new information has come to light); or

f) Such other ground as is essential to the justice of the case.

Where a new trial is sought only for the reason that damages are excessive or inadequate and the court so decides, it may grant a new trial restricted to the question of the amount of damages only. It may by consent of a party substitute a different award but it has now power of itself in the absence of consent to do so.

In determining a motion for a new trial on the grounds of excess of inadequacy of damages the appeal court will afford greater latitude for error to a jury than to a judge. The view taken is that judges in general should have knowledge of and access to the principles applicable when reaching their decision whereas a jury has no experience and only has guidance from the general principles mentioned in the judge's charge. Historically, the generally accepted test for excess of damages has been stated by the court thus:

> "It is evidently not enough in order to bring the damages within the description of excessive that they are more and even a great deal more than the amount at which the injury sustained might have been estimated in the opinion of the individual members of the court to whom this application is made. It is clear

> that in order to warrant the application of the term excessive, the damages must be held to exceed not what the court might think enough but even that latitude which in a question of amount so very vague, any set of reasonable men could be permitted to indulge. The excess must be such as to raise on the part of the court the moral conviction that the jury whether from wrong intention or incapacity or some mistake have committed gross injustice and have given higher damages than any jury of ordinary men, fairly and without gross mistake exercising their function could have awarded."

This approach has recently been confirmed by the House of Lords as the correct one and the modern statement of it is that to be "excessive" (or by extension inadequate) "the damages awarded have to exceed the latitude which any reasonable jury could be permitted to indulge and have to raise a conviction in the court that "a gross injustice" has been committed."

In deciding whether the jury has committed "a gross injustice" the matter must be considered in two stages. Firstly, the court should reach its own opinion as to the reasonable value of the claim taking into account judicial and jury awards. It must then consider the actual award of the jury. In relation to *solatium* (general damages), it is thought that there is a working rule of "100% permissible error" namely that a jury awarding more than twice as much or less than half as much as the court would have awarded is subject to its verdict being overturned and a new trial allowed. However, this working rule can only be properly applied to *solatium* and loss of society to family members upon the death of a relative. In the case of awards for pecuniary loss such as wage loss where a more precise calculation is possible, the jury's 'margin for error' is thought to be substantially reduced. It should be stressed that the working rule is not a formula simply a cross-check against which the court assesses the reasonableness of the award or otherwise on a case by case basis.

There is a general perception, well founded or not, that a jury is more likely to be generous in an award of damages to a 'sympathetic' Pursuer than a judge would be and for that reason Defenders advisors are thought to tend to resist the allowance of a jury. The risk to a Pursuer who does not impress the jury however is that they may award him less than a single judge applying established principles or indeed, that they may award him nothing at all!

Following recent approval by the upper courts, of what might once have been considered excessive jury awards, there is thought to be an increasing propensity for Pursuers to opt for their right to jury trial. This will lead to a greater number of jury awards and the respect which judges are now affording these is in turn likely to lead to increasing harmonisation of judge and jury awards (almost inevitably upwards). As was said in the leading case by a senior judge in the appeal court "12 jurors from different walks of life and with different incomes and needs might be thought to be better placed to understand the value of money than a judge such as myself."

It is clear that in this area of law the awards which juries will be 'permitted' to make without interference and the consequent effects upon the awards of judges are still in a state of development as at today's date.

13. Interim Damages

The court may make an award of interim damages on application by the claimant or the relatives of a deceased. Such an application may be made at any time after Defences have been lodged. If the Defendant has not admitted liability the court must be satisfied from the written pleadings and documents that if the action proceeded to Proof (Trial) the Pursuer would succeed in the action on the question of liability without any substantial finding of contributory negligence (i.e. the court must be of the opinion that the Pursuer would 'almost certainly' succeed). The amount to be awarded by way of interim damages may vary but it is not restricted to losses incurred to the date of the application.

14. Provisional Damages

Traditionally in Scotland damages for personal injuries were assessed once and for all at Proof. In certain personal injury cases the Pursuer may now choose to claim provisional damages if his condition is likely to deteriorate in the future. It must be proved or admitted that there is a risk that at some time in the future the claimant will, as a result of the accident, develop some serious disease or suffer some serious deterioration of is condition. The Defender against whom provisional damages are awarded must either be a public authority, public corporation or be insured or otherwise indemnified in respect of the claim. If an award of provisional damages is made the claimant will be given the court's permission to return to court for a further award to be made at any time during a specified period in the future. Examples of where provisional damages have been awarded include head injuries where there is a risk of epilepsy developing and cases of asbestosis where there is a future risk of cancer.

Table 1. Personal Injury Awards – Scotland

Claimant :	Man
Age :	40
Status :	Married, 2 dependent children aged 5 and 7
Occupation:	Doctor
Income:	GBP 36,000 net per annum
Date of Calculation:	2.5 years after the accident
Action for Damages:	Raised 1 year after accident. In Scotland, the date on which the action is raised is not relevant for the purposes of calculation interest. It is assumed the accident occurred after 1 January 1986 and compensation is paid on the date of Proof or calculating for the purpose of deduction of Welfare State Benefits.

1. Instant death		GBP
a) Loss of Society		
(i) Widows (50% to past 50%, to future)		
Interest on proportion allocated to past		15,000.00
4% x 5,500 x 2.5 years		750.00
(ii) Seven year old child		8,500.00
Interest on proportion allocated to past		
4% x 5, x 2.5 years		425.00
(iii) Five year old child		10,000.00
Interest on proportion allocated to past		
4% x 1,500 x 2.5 years		500.00
b) Funeral Expenses say:		
Interest due from date of outlay		300.00
c) Loss of Support		
(It is assumed that the deceased's wife did not work)		
Average net annual earnings per annum	36,000.00	

Less Deduct deceased's own expenditure Estimated @ 25%, subject to Proof	9,000.00	
Net annual loss of support per annum Assume 70% to widow and 30% to children (subject to Proof)	27,000.00	
Multiplier in fatal cases is assessed at date of death. Deceased's age at death 40. Multiplier to be applied is 17.09 17.09 x 27,000 =		461,430.00
Widow's loss of support (70%)	323,001.00	
Children's loss of support (30%)	138,429.00	
Total	**461,430.00**	
Interest on loss of support to date 2.5 x 27,000 x 4%		2,700.00

d) *Services provided by deceased per annum say 750 pa*

Multiplier to be applied 22.66	
Interest on loss of service to date of Proof	16,995.00
750 x 4% x 2.5 years	75.00
TOTAL AWARD	**518,175.00**

2. Burns (A)

a) *Services provided by deceased per annum say 750 pa*

Solatium (66% allocated to past, 33% to future)	25,000.00
Interest on proportion allocated to past 4% x 12,500 x 2.5 years	1,250.00

Assume claimant is able to resume his employment 2 years after the accident

b) *Loss of Income*

2 years at 36,000 pa	72,000.00	
Add Interest on past of income from date of return to work 72,500 x 8% x 0.5 years	2,880.00	
Less Deduct all Welfare State Benefits received as per CRU Certificate	18,000.00	
		56,880.00

c) *Miscellaneous Losses day:*

	1,800.00
Interest is due from date of loss; Assume losses incurred at date of accident 8% x 1,800 x 2.5 years	360.00

d) *Services rendered to Claimant by relative say:*

	5,000.00
Assume services rendered during absence from work and not continuing: Apply interest from date on which services ceased 5,000 x 8% x 0.5 years	200.00
No award for future	

e) *Services unable to be Provided by Claimant*

750 pa during period when claimant unable to work No future award	1,500.00
Interest from date claimant return to work 8% x 1,500 x 0.5 years	60.00
TOTAL AWARD	**92,000.00**

Burns (B)

a) Solatium *(66% allocated to past, 33% to future)*		
		12,000.00
Interest on proportion allocated to past 12,500 x 4% x 2.5 years		1,200.00
Assume that claimant is able to resume his employment 2 years after the accident		
b) Loss of income		
2 years @ 36,000 pa	72,000.00	
Add Interest on past loss of income from date of return to work 72,000 x 8% x 0.5 years	2,880.00	
Less Deduct all Welfare State Benefits received as per CRU Certificates	18,000.00	
		56,880.00
c) Miscellaneous Losses day:		
		1,800.00
Interest is due from date of loss; Assume losses incurred at date of accident 1,800.00 x 8% x 2.5 years		360.00
d) Services rendered to Claimant by relative say:		
		5,000.00
Assume services rendered during absence from work and not continuing; apply interest from date on which services ceased 5,000 x 8% x 2.5 years		200.00
No award for future		

e) Services unable to be provided by Claimant		
750 pa during period when claimant unable to work		1,500.00
No future awards		
Interest from date claimant return to work 8% x 1,500 x 0.5 years		60.00
TOTAL AWARD		**79,000.00**

Burns (C)

a) Solatium *(66% allocated to past, 33% to future)*		
		25,000.00
Interest on proportion allocated to past 4% x 16,000 x 2.5 years		1,650.00
Assume that claimant is able to resume his employment 2 years after the accident		
b) Loss of income		
2 years @ 36,000 pa	72,000.00	
Add Interest on past loss of income from date of return to work 72,000 x 8% x 0.5 years	2,880.00	
Less Deduct all Welfare State Benefits received as per CRU Certificates	18,000.00	
		56,880.00
c) Miscellaneous Losses day:		
Interest is due from date of loss;		
Assume losses incurred at date of accident		1,800.00
1,800.00 x 8% x 2.5 years		360.00

d) Services rendered to Claimant by relative:		
		5,000.00
Assume services rendered during absence from work and not continuing; apply interest from date on which services ceased 5,000 x 8% x 2.5 years		200.00
e) Services unable to be provided by Claimant,		
say 750 pa during period when claimant unable to work		1,500.00
Interest from date claimant return to work (i.e. no continuing loss) % x 1,500 x 0.5 years		60.00
TOTAL AWARD		**92,450.00**

3. Quadriplegia

Assume no reduction in life expectancy

a) Solatiuum *(40% allocated to past, 60% to future)*		
		130,000.00
Interest on proportion allocated to past 4% x 52,000 x 2.5 years		5,200.00
b) Loss of Income to Date of Proof		
2.5 years @ 36,000 pa	90,000.00	
Add Interest 4% x 90,000 x 2.5 years	9,000.00	
Less Deduct all Welfare State Benefits received as per CRU Certificate	30,000.00	
		69,000.00

c) Cost of Nursing Care/ Medical Expenses to date of Proof	
2.5 years @ 33,000 pa	83,750.00
Assume these costs are ongoing and incurred regularly since date of accident Interest @ 4% for 2.5 years	8,375.00
d) Services rendered to Claimant by relative	
Any award is likely to be small as full time hospital care is likely, say 750 pa to date of Proof	
2.5 years @ 750 pa	1,875.00
Interest thereon 1,500 x 4% x 2.5 years	187.50
Future Services, multiplier to be applied is 22.02	16,515.00
e) Services unable to be provided by Claimant say 750 pa	
to date of Proof	1,875.00
Interest thereon 4% x 1,875 x 2.5 years	187.50
Future Services Multiplier to be applied is 14	10,500.00
f) Cost of Modifying Home and Special Equipment, say:	
	25,000.00
Interest will be due from date on which expenses incurred @ 8%; assume incurred midway between date of accident and date of proof 25,000 x 8% x 1.25 years	2,500.00
g) Future Loss of Income	
(42.5 years old at date of Proof, assume retirement @ 65)	

	Multiplier to be applied is 16.12 @ 36,000 pa		580,320.00
h)	*Future Cost of Nursing Care*		
	Medical Expenses @ 33,600 pa		
	Multiplier to be applied is 22.02		739,872.00
i)	*Hospital Charges (maximum recoverable)*		
			10,000.00
j)	*Extra Holiday Costs @ 1,500 pa*		
	Multiplier to be applied is 22.02		33,030.00
k)	*Extra Transport Costs @ 1,500 pa*		
	Multiplier to be applied is 22.02		55,050.00
l)	*Aids and Equipment*		
			75,000.00
	TOTAL AWARD		**1,848,237.00**

4. Paraplegia

a)	Solatium *(40% allocated to past, 60% to future)*		
			115,000.00
	Interest on proportion allocated to past 4% x 46,000 x 2.5 years		4,600.00
b)	*Loss of Income to Date of Proof*		
	2.5 years @ 36,000 pa	90,000.00	
	Less Income earned in one year's sedentary work commencing 1.5 years after accident, say:	6,000.00	
		84,000.00	

Add Wage loss is continuing so allow interest @ 4% 4% x 84,000 x 2.5 years	8,400.00	
Less Deduct all Welfare State Benefits received as per CRU Certificate	30,000.00	
		62,400.00

c) *Cost of Nursing Care/ Medical Expenses/Aids Age to Date of Poof, say:*

	30,000.00
Interest is due from date of outlay or at 4% on whole sum if ongoing; assume interest @ 4% on 30,000 for 2.5 years	3,000.00

d) *Cost of Modifying Home, say:*

	14,000.00
Interest is due from date on which expenses incurred @ 8%; assume incurred midway between date of accident and date of Proof 8% x 14,000 x 1.25 years	1,400.000

e) *Services rendered to Claimant by relative to Date of Proof, say:*

	3,600.00
Interest thereon 3.600 x 4% x 2.5 years	360.00
Future Services, say, 400 pa Multiplier is 22.02	30,828.00

f) *Services unable to be provided by Claimant, say 750 pa*

to date of proof	1,875.00
Interest thereon 4% x 1,875 x 2.5 years (to nearest)	188.00
Future Services Multiplier to be applied is 14	10,500.00

g) Future Loss of Income

42.5 years old at date of Proof – assume retirement at 65		
Multiplier to be applied is 16.12 on 36,000 pa	580,320.00	
Less to be earned in sedentary work at 6,000 pa	96,720.00	
		583,600.00

h) Estimated Cost of Future Nursing Care/Medical Expenses/ Aids

@ 4,000 pa multiplier is 22.02	88,080.00

i) Hospital Charges (maximum recoverable)

	10,000.00

j) Extra Holiday Costs 500 pa

Multiplier to be applied is 22.02	11,010.00

k) Extra Transport Costs 1,000 pa

Multiplier to be applied is 22.02	22,020.00
TOTAL AWARD	**992,461.00**

5.a Brain Damage

a) Solatium *(33% allocated to past, 66% to future)*

	90,000.00
Interest on proportion allocated to past 4% x 30,000 x 2.5 years	3,000.00

b) Loss of Income to Date of Proof

2.5 years @ 36,000	90,000.00	

Add Interest thereon 4% x 90,000 x 2.5 years	9,000.00	
Less Deduct all Welfare State Benefits received as per CRU Certificate	30,000.00	
		69,000.00

c) *Cost of Nursing Care/Medical Expenses to Date of Proof 15,000 pa*

	37,500.00
Interest thereon 4% x 37,500 x 2.5 years	3,750.00

d) *Cost of Modifying Home and Special Equipment*

	14,000.00
Interest is due from date on which expense incurred @ 8%; assume incurred midway between date of accident and date of Proof 14,000 x 8% x 1.25 years	1,400.00

e) *Services rendered to Claimant by relative to date of Proof, say:*

	3,000.00
Interest thereon : 4% x 3,000 x 2.5 years	3000.00
Future services at 1,200 pa, multiplier is 22.02	26,424.00

f) *Services rendered to Claimant by relative to Date of Proof, say:*

750 per annum	1,875.00
Interest thereon 4% x 1,875 x 2.5 years (to the nearest)	188.00
Future services, multiplier is 14	10,500.00

g) *Future Loss of Income*

42.5 years old at the date of Proof, assume retirement at 65

Multiplier is 16.12 @ 36,000 pa	580,320.00	

Less To be earned in sheltered employment, likely to commence 6 months hence @ 2,500 pa	40,300.00	
		540,020.00
h) Future Cost of Nursing Care/Medical Expenses		
@ 5,000 pa		110,100.00
i) Hospital Charges (maximum recoverable)		
		10,000.00
TOTAL AWARD		**921,057.00**

5.b Brain Damage (Moderately Severe)

a) Solatium *33% allocated to past, 66% to future*		
		115,000.00
Interest on proportion to past 4% x 38,333 pa		3,833.00
b) Loss of Income to Date of Proof		
2.5 years @ 36,000 pa	90,000.00	
Add Interest thereon 90,000 x 2.5 x 4%	9,000.00	
Less Deduct all Welfare State Benefit received per CRU Certificate	30,000.00	
		69,000.00
c) Cost of Nursing Care/Medical Expenses to Date of Proof		
2.5 years @ 33,000 pa	83,750.00	

Interest is due from date of outlay or at 4% on whole sum if ongoing; assume interest @ 4% on 83,750 for 2.5 years	8,375.00
d) Cost of Modifying Home and Special Equipment, say:	
	25,000.00
Interest is due from date on which expenses incurred@ 8%; assume incurred midway between date of accident and date of Proof 8% x 25,000 x 1.25 years	2,500.00
e) Services rendered to Claimant by relative	
An award is likely to be small as full time hospital care is likely, say 750 pa to date of Proof 750 x 2.5 years	1,875.00
Interest thereon 1,875 x 2.5 years	187.50
Future Services: multiplier to be applied 22.02	16,515.00
f) Services unable to be provided by Claimant, say 750 pa to date of Proof	
	1,875.00
Interest thereon 4% x 1,875 x 2.5 years	187.50
Future Services, multiplier is 14	10,500.00
g) Estimated Future Cost of Nursing Care/Medical Expenses/Aids 33,500 pa	
Multiplier is 22.02	737,670.00
h) Future loss of income	
(42.5 years old to date of Proof assume retirement at 65)	

Multiplier is 16.12 @ 36,000 pa		580,320.00
i) Hospital Charges (maximum recoverable)		
		10,000.00
TOTAL AWARD		**1,666,588.00**

6.a Amputation of Leg above knee

a) Solatium *(50% allocated to past)*		
		55,000.00
Interest on proportion allocated to past 4% x 27,500 x 2.5 years		2,750.00
Assume claimant is able to resume his employment 1.5 years after accident		
b) Loss of Income		
1.5 years @ 36.000 pa	54,000.00	
Add Interest on past loss of income from date of return to work 54,000 x 8% x 1 year	4,320.00	
Less Deduct all Welfare State Benefits received as per CRU Certificate	18,000.00	
		40,320.00
c) Miscellaneous Losses		
		1,800.00
Interest is due from date of loss incurred; assume losses incurred at date of accident 1,800 x 8% x 2.5 years		360.00
d) Services rendered to Claimant by relative, say		
		1,800.00

Assume services rendered during absence from work and not continuing, apply interest from date on which services ceased 1,800 x 8% x 1 year		144.00
No award for future		
e) *Services unable to be provided by Claimant, say 750 pa*		
During period when claimant unable to work 750 x 1.5 years		1,125.00
Interest form date claimant returned to work 1,125 x 8% x 1 year		90.00
'Broad brush' award for future say:		10,000.00
Extra transport costs on 'Broadbrush' basis		10,000.00
g) *Hospital charges (maximum recoverable)*		
		10,000.00
TOTAL AWARD		**133,389.00**

6.b Amputation of leg below knee

a) Solatium *(50% allocated to past)*		
		50,000.00
Interest on past *solatium* 4% x 25,000 x 2.5 years		2,500.00
b) *Loss of Income*		
1.5 years @ 36,000 pa	54,000.00	
Add Interest on past loss of income from date of return to work 54,000 x 8% x 1 year	4,320.00	

Less Deduct all Welfare State Benefits received as per CRU Certificate	18,000.00	
		40,320.00
c) Miscellaneous Losses		
		1,800.00
Interest is due from date loss incurred; Assume losses incurred at date of accident 1,800 x 8% x 2.5 years		360.00
d) Services rendered to Claimant by relative, say		
		1,800.00
Assume services rendered during absence from work and not continuing, apply interest from date on which services ceased 1,800 x 8% x 1 year		144.00
No award for future		
e) Services unable to be provided by Claimant say 750 pa		
during period when claimant unable to work 750 x 1.5 years		1,125.00
Interest from date claimant returned to work 1,125 x 8% x 1 year		90.00
'Broad brush' award for future say:		10,000.00
f) Extra transport costs on 'Broad brush'		
		10,000.00
g) Hospital charges (maximum recoverable)		
		10,000.00
TOTAL AWARD		**128,139.00**

7.a Amputation of arm above elbow

(a) Solatium *(66% allocated to past)*			
			55,000.00
Interest on proportion allocated to past 4% x 36,000 x 2.5 year			3,630.00
Assume claimant not able to resume employment but takes up light duties 1.5 year after the accident			
b) Loss of Income			
1.5 years @ 36,000 pa		54,000.00	
Add 1 year's partial loss:			
Pre-Accident	36,000.00		
Light work	10,000.00		
		26,000.00	
		80,000.00	
Add Interest: Wage loss is continuing so allow interest @ 4% 4% x 80,000 x 2.5 years		8,000.00	
Less Deduct all Welfare State Benefits received as per CRU Certificate		12,000.00	
			76,000.00
c) Miscellaneous expenses			
			1,800.00
Interest is due from the date of outlay; Assume outlay at date of accident 1,800 x 8% x 2.5 years			360.00
d) Future loss of earnings			
Multiplier is 16.12 @ 26,000 pa			419,120.00

e) Services rendered to Claimant by relative, say		
		3,000.00
Assume services continue Interest at 4% x 3,000 x 2.5 years		300.00
'Broad brush' award for future, say		3,000.00
f) Services unable to be provided by Claimant, say 700 pa		
2.5 years x 750		1,875.00
Interest thereon 4% x 1,875 x 2.5 years (to nearest)		188.00
Future award at 750 pa, multiplier is 14		10,500.00
g) Future extra transport costs on 'Broad brush' approach		
		10,000.00
h) Hospital charges (14 days @ 435 per day)		
		6,090.00
TOTAL AWARD		**590,863.00**

7.b Amputation of arm below elbow

a) Solatium *(66% allocated to past)*		
		45,000.00
Interest on proportion allocated to past 4% x 30,000 x 2.5 years		3,000.00
b) Loss of income		
1.5 years @ 36,000 pa	54,000.00	

Add 1 year's partial loss:			
Pre-Accident	36,000.00		
Light work	10,000.00		
		26,000.00	
		80,000.00	
Add Interest: Wage loss is continuing so allow interest @ 4% 4% x 80,000 x 2.5 years		8,000.00	
Less Deduct all Welfare State Benefits received as per CRU Certificate		12,000.00	
			76,000.00

c) *Miscellaneous expenses*

	1,800.00
Interest is due form date of outlay; Assume outlay at date of accident 1,800 x 8% x 2.5 years	360.00

d) *Future loss of earnings*

Multiplier is 16.12 @ 26,000 pa	419,120.00

e) *Services rendered to Claimant by relative, say*

	3,000.00
Assume services continue Interest @ 4% x 3,000 x 2.5 years	300.00
'Broad brush' award for future, say	3,000.00

f) *Services unable to be provided by Claimant, say 700 pa*

2.5 years x 750	1,875.00
Interest thereon 4% x 1,875 x 2.5 years (to nearest)	188.00
Future award at 750 pa, multiplier is 14	10,500.00

g) Future extra transport costs on 'Broad brush' approach		
		10,000.00
h) Hospital charges (14 days @ 435 per day)		
		6,090.00
TOTAL AWARD		**580,233.00**

8.a Loss of Eyesight – One eye without cosmetic disability

a) Solatium *75% allocated to past*		
		20,000.00
Interest on proportion allocated to past 4% x 15,000 x 2.5 years		1,500.00
Assume that claimant is able to resume his employment one year after accident		
b) Loss of Income 1 year		
	36,000.00	
Add Interest from date of return to work 36,000 x 8% x 1.5 years	4,320.00	
Less Deduct all Welfare Benefits received per CRU Certificate	12,000.00	
		28,320.00
c) Miscellaneous losses, say		
		1,800.00
Interest is due from date of loss; Assume loss incurred at date of accident 1,800 x 8% x 2.5 years		360.00
TOTAL AWARD		**51,980.00**

8.b Loss of Eyesight – One eye with cosmetic disability

a) Solatium *50% allocated to past*		
		25,000.00
Interest on proportion allocated to past 4% x 12,000 x 2.5 years		1,250.00
b) Loss of Income		
1 year @ 36,000	36,000.00	
Add Interest from date of return to work 36,000 x 8% x 1.5 years	4,320.00	
Less Deduct all Welfare Benefits received per CRU Certificate	12,000.00	
		28,320.00
c) Miscellaneous losses, say		
		1,800.00
Interest is due from date of loss; Assume loss incurred at date of accident 1,800 x 8% x 2.5 years		360.00
TOTAL AWARD		**56,730.00**

8.c Loss of Eyesight – Total blindness

a) Solatium *33% allocated to past*	
	90,000.00
Interest on proportion allocated to past 4% x 30,000 x 2.5 years	3,000.00
Assume claimant unable to resume employment	

b) *Loss of Income*		
2.5 years @36,000 pa	90,000.00	
Add Interest thereon 90,000 x 4% x 2.5 years	9,000.00	
Less Deduct all Welfare Benefits received per CRU Certificate	30,000.00	
		69,000.00
c) *Cost of Care and Medical expenses to date of Proof*		
		13,400.00
Interest is due form date of outlay on whole sum if costs ongoing; assume interest at 4% 4% x 13400 x 2.5 years		2,680.00
d) *Services rendered to Claimant by relative*		
		3,000.00
Interest thereon 3,000 x 4% x 2.5 years		300.00
Future services @ 1,200 pa, multiplier is 22.02		26,424.00
e) *Services unable to be provided by Claimant, say 750 pa*		
2.5 years x 750		188.00
Future services, multiplier is 14 750 x 14		10,500.00
f) *Future loss of income*		
Multiplier is 16.12 @ 36,000 pa		580,320.00
g) *Future cost of replacement aids*		
		13,400.00
TOTAL AWARD		**812,747.00**

9. Deafness (Total)

Total deafness is a most unusual injury and it is therefore difficult to quantify with reference to precedent. Many cases of deafness relate to noise exposure at work. Such claims are usually settled in terms of Union/Employer Agreements and, in quantifying this claim, we have based our figures on experience of settlements achieved in such industrial deafness cases.

a) Solatium *25% allocated to past*			
			18,000.00
Interest on proportion allocated to past 4% x 4,500 x 2.5 years			450.00
Assume claimant unable to resume employment but takes up light work 1.5 years after accident			
b) Loss of Income			
1.5 years @ 36,000 pa		54,000.00	
Add 1 year's partial loss:			
Pre-Accident	36,000.00		
Light work	10,000.00		
		26,000.00	
		80,000.00	
Add Interest thereon 80,000 x 4% x 2.5 years		8,000.00	
Less Deduct all Welfare Benefits received per CRU Certificate		30,000.00	
			58,000.00
c) Miscellaneous expenses			
Interest is due from date of outlay; assume outlay incurred at date of accident 1,800 x 8% x 2.5 years			360.00

d) Future loss of income @ 26,000 pa			
Multiplier is 16.12			419,120.00
TOTAL AWARD			**497,730.00**

10. Repetitive Strain Injury

a) Range of Injury to wrist			
(i) Complete loss of function in wrist		15,500.00	
(ii) Injury with significant permanent residual disability		9,500.00	
(iii) Persistent pain and stiffness		7,500.00	
(iv) Complete recovery up to		3,600.00	
a) Persistent pain and stiffness			
Solatium 33% allocated to past			7,200.00
Interest on proportion allocated to past 4% x 2,400 x 2.5 years			240.00
Assume claimant unable to resume his employment as a surgeon and takes light duties 6 months after sustaining injury			
b) Loss of Income			
0.5 years @ 36,000 pa		18,000.00	
Add 2 years' partial loss: Pre-Accident @ 36,000 pa	72,000.00		
Less Light work @ 30,000 pa	60,000.00		
		12,000.00	
		30,000.00	
Add Interest thereon 4% x 30,000 x 2.5 years		3,000.00	

	Less Deduct all Welfare Benefits received per CRU Certificate	3,000.00	
			30,000.00
c)	*Miscellaneous expenses*		
			600.00
	Interest is due from date of outlay; assume expenses incurred at date of accident 8% x 600 x 2.5 years		120.00
d)	*Services unable to be provided by Claimant, say*		
			600.00
	For this type of injury a 'Broad brush' approach is likely and any award will be for all time inclusive of interest		
e)	*Future loss of income*		
	6,000 pa Multiplier is 16.12		96,720.00
	TOTAL AWARD		**135,480.00**

Schedule B

Claimant:	Woman
Age:	20
Status:	Single
Occupation:	Legal Secretary
Income:	GBP 10,000 net per annum (any potential future wage increase would not be taken into account by the Scottish Courts)
Date of Calculation:	2.5 years after the accident
Action for Damages:	Raised 1 year after accident. In Scotland, the date on which the action is raised is not relevant for the purposes of calculating interest. It is assumed the accident occurred after 1 January 1986 and compensation is paid on the date of Proof or calculation for the purpose of deduction of Welfare State Benefits.

1. Instant Death

	GBP
a) Funeral Expenses	
Say:	1,500
Interest due from date of outlay 8% x 1,500 x 2.5 years	300
TOTAL AWARD	**1,800**

Loss of Society awards may be made to parents, say 2,000 each, ½ allocated to past with interest accordingly @ 4% on 1,000.
Any loss of support would require Proof.

2. Burns (A)

a) Solatium *(66% allocated to past, 33% to future)*	
	30,000

Interest on proportion allocated to past 4% x 20,500 x 2.5 years		2,000
Assume claimant is able to resume his employment 2 years after the accident		
b) Loss of Income		
2 years at 10,000 pa	20,000	
Add		
Interest on past of income from date of return to work 20,500 x 8% x 0.5 years	800	
Less		
Deduct all Welfare State Benefits Received as per CRU Certificate	12,000	
		8,800
c) Miscellaneous Losses day:		
		1,800
Interest is due form date of loss;		
Assume losses incurred at date of accident 8% x 1,800 x 2.5 years		360
TOTAL AWARD		**42,960**

Burns (B)

a) Solatium *(66% allocated to past, 33% to future)*	
	15,000
Interest on past *solatium* 15,000 x 4% x 2.5 years	1,500
Assume that claimant is able to resume his employment 2 years after the accident	

b) Loss of Income		
2 years @ 10,000 pa	20,000	
Add		
Interest on past loss of income from date of return to work 20,000 x 8% x 0.5 years	800	
Less		
Deduct all Welfare State Benefits received as per CRU Certificates	12,000	
		8,800
c) Miscellaneous Losses day:		
		1,800
Interest is due form date of loss; Assume losses incurred at date of accident 1,800 x 8% x 2.5 years		360
TOTAL AWARD		**27,460**

Burns (C)

a) Solatium *(66% allocated to past, 33% to future)*		
		30,000
Interest on proportion allocated to past 4% x 20,000 x 2.5 years		2,000
Assume that claimant is able to resume his employment 2 years after the accident		
b) Loss of Income		
2 years @ 10,000 pa	20,000	

Add		
Interest on past loss of income from date of return to work 20,000 x 8% x 0.5 years	800	
Less		
Deduct all Welfare State Benefits received as per CRU Certificates	12,000	
		8,880
c) Miscellaneous Losses day:		
		1,800
Interest is due form date of loss; Assume losses incurred at date of accident 8% x 1,800 x 2.5 years		360
TOTAL AWARD		**42,960**

3. Quadriplegia

Assume no reduction in life expectancy

a) Solatium *(40% allocated to past, 60% to future)*		
		130,000
Interest on proportion allocated to past 4% x 52,000 x 2.5 years		5,200
b) Loss of Income to Date of Proof		
2.5 years @ 10,000 pa	25,000	
Add		
Interest 4% x 25,000 x 2.5 years	2,500	

Less		
Deduct all Welfare State Benefits received as per CRU Certificate	18,000	
		9,500

c) Cost of Nursing Care/Medical Expenses to date of Proof

2.5 years @ 33,000 pa	83,750
Assume these costs are ongoing and incurred regularly	

Since date of accident

Interest @ 4% for 2.5 years

8,375

d) Cost of modifying Home and Special Equipment, say:

	25,000
Interest will be due form date on which expenses incurred @ 8%; assume incurred midway between date of accident and date of Proof 25,000 x 8% x 1.25 years	2,500

e) Future loss of income:

(22.5 years at date of proof, assume retirement @ 65)	
Multiplier to be applied is : 23.97 @ 10,000 per annum	239,700

f) Future Cost of Nursing Care

Medical Expenses @ 33,600 pa	
Multiplier to be applied is 27.94	938,784

g) Hospital Charges (maximum recoverable)

	10,000

h) Extra Holiday Costs @ 1,500 pa

Multiplier to be applied is 27.94	41,910

i) Extra Transport Costs @ 1,500 pa		
Multiplier to be applied is 27.94		69,850
j) Aids and Equipment		
		75,000
TOTAL AWARD		**1,639,569**

4. Paraplegia

a) Solatium *(40% allocated to past, 60% to future)*		
		115,000
Interest on proportion allocated to past 4% x 46,000 x 2.5 years		4,600
b) Loss of Income to Date of Proof		
2.5 years @ 10,000 pa	25,000	
Less		
Income earned in one year's sedentary work commencing 1.5 years after accident, say:	6,000	
	19,000	
Add		
Wage loss is continuing so allow interest @ 4% 4% x 19,000 x 2.5 years	1,900	
Less		
Deduct all Welfare State Benefits received as per CRU Certificate	16,000	
		4,900
c) Cost of Nursing Care/Medical Expenses/Aids		
Age to Date of Poof, say:		30,000

Interest is due from date of outlay or at 4% on whole sum if ongoing; assume interest @ 4% on 30,000 for 2.5 years		3,000
d) Cost of Modifying Home, say:		
		14,000
Interest is due from date on which expenses incurred @ 8%; assume incurred midway between date of accident and date of Proof 8% x 14,000 x 1.25 years		1,400
e) Future Loss of Income		
22.5 years old at date of Proof – assume retirement at 65 Multiplier to be applied is 23.97 on 10,000 pa	239,700	
Less to be earned in sedentary work at 6,000 pa	143,820	
		95,880
f) Estimated Cost of Future Nursing Care/Medical		
Expenses/Aids @ 4,000 pa multiplier is 27.94		111,760
g) Hospital Charges (maximum recoverable)		
		10,000
h) Extra Holiday Costs 500 pa		
Multiplier to be applied is 27.94		13,970
i) Extra Transport Costs 1,000 pa		
Multiplier to be applied is 27.94		27,940
TOTAL AWARD		**432,450**

5.a Brain Damage

a) Solatium *(33% allocated to past, 66% to future)*		
		90,000
Interest on proportion allocated to past 4% x 30,000 x 2.5 years		3,000
b) Loss of Income to Date of Proof		
2.5 years @ 10,000	25,000	
Add		
Interest thereon 4% x 25,000 x 2.5 years	2,500	
Less		
Deduct all Welfare State Benefits received as per CRU Certificate	18,000	
		9,500
c) Cost of Nursing Care/Medical Expenses to Date of Proof		
15,000 pa		37,500
Interest thereon 4% x 37,500 x 2.5 years		3,750
d) Cost of Modifying Home and Special Equipment		
		14,000
Interest is due from date o which expense incurred @ 8%; assume incurred midway between date of accident and date of Proof 14,000 x % x 1.25 years		1,400
e) Future Loss of Income		
22.5 years old at the date of Proof, assume retirement at 65 Multiplier is 23.97 @ 10,000 pa	239,700	

Less		
To be earned in sheltered employment, likely to commence 6 months hence @ 2,500 pa	59,925	
		179,775
f) Future Cost of Nursing Care/Medical Expenses		
@ 5,000 pa, multiplier is 27.94		139,700
i) Hospital Charges (maximum recoverable)		
		10,000
TOTAL AWARD		**488,625**

5.b Brain Damage (Moderately Severe)

a) Solatium *33% allocated to past, 66% to future*		
		115,000
Interest on proportion to past 4% x 38,333 x 2.5 years		3,833
b) Loss of Income to Date of Proof		
2.5 years @ 10,000 pa	25,000	
Add		
Interest thereon 25,000 x 2.5 x 4%	2,500	
Less		
Deduct all Welfare State Benefit received per CRU Certificate	18,000	
		9,500
c) Cost of Nursing Care/Medical Expenses to Date of Proof		
2.5 years @ 33,000 pa		83,750

Interest is due from date of outlay or at 4% on whole sum if ongoing; assume interest @ 4% on 83,750 for 2.5 years	8,375
d) Cost of Modifying Home and Special Equipment, say:	
	25,000
Interest is due from date on which expenses incurred @ 8%; assume incurred midway between date of accident and date of Proof 8% x 25,000 x 1.25 years	2,500
e) Estimated Future Cost of Nursing Care/Medical	
Expenses/Aids 33,500 pa	
Multiplier is 27.94	935,990
f) Future loss of income	
(22.5 years old to date of Proof assume retirement at 65)	
Multiplier is 23.97 @ 10,000 pa	239,700
i) Hospital Charges (maximum recoverable)	
	10,000
TOTAL AWARD	**1,433,648**

6.a Amputation of Leg above knee

a) Solatium *(50% allocated to past)*	
	55,000
Interest on proportion allocated to past 4% x 27,500 x 2.5 years	2,750
Assume claimant is able to resume his employment 1.5 years after accident	

b) Loss of Income		
1.5 years @ 10,000 pa	15,000	
Add		
Interest on past loss of income from date of return to work 15,000 x 8% x 1 year	1,200	
Less		
Deduct all Welfare State Benefits received as per CRU Certificate	12,000	
		4,200
c) Miscellaneous Losses		
		1,800
Interest is due from date of loss incurred; assume losses incurred at date of accident 1,800 x 8% x 2.5 years		360
d) Extra Transport costs on 'Broad brush'		
		10,000
g) Hospital charges (maximum recoverable)		
		10,000
TOTAL AWARD		**84,110**

6.b Amputation of leg below knew

a) Solatium *(50% allocated to past)*	
	50,000
Interest on past *solatium* 4% x 25,000 x 2.5 years	2,500

b) Loss of Income		
1.5 years @ 10,000 pa	15,000	
Add		
Interest on past loss of income from date of return to work 15,000 x 8% x 1 year	1,200	
Less		
Deduct all Welfare State Benefits received as per CRU Certificate	12,000	
		4,200
c) Miscellaneous Losses		
		1,800
Interest is due from date loss incurred; assume losses incurred at date of accident 1,800 x 8% x 2.5 years		360
d) Extra transport costs on 'Broad brush'		
		10,000
g) Hospital charges (maximum recoverable)		
		10,000
TOTAL AWARD		**78,860**

7.a Amputation of arm above elbow

a) Solatium *(66% allocated to past)*	
	60,000
Interest on proportion allocated to past 4% x 40,000 x 2.5 year	4,000

Assume claimant not able to resume employment but takes up light duties 1.5 year after the accident

b) Loss of Income

1.5 years @ 10,000 pa		15,000	
Add			
1 year's partial loss			
Pre-Accident	10,000		
Light work	4,000		
		6,000	
		21,000	
Add			
Interest: Wage loss is continuing so allow interest @ 4% 4% x 21,000 x 2.5 years		2,100	
Less			
Deduct all Welfare State Benefits received as per CRU Certificate		12,000	
			11,100

c) Miscellaneous expenses

	1,800
Interest is due from the date of outlay; assume outlay at date of accident 1,800 x 8% x 2.5 years	360

d) Future loss of earnings

Multiplier is 23.97 @ 6,000 pa	143,820

e) Future extra transport costs on 'Broad brush' approach

	10,000

h) Hospital charges (14 days @ 435 per day)			
			6,090
TOTAL AWARD			**237,170**

7.b Amputation of arm below elbow

a) Solatium *(66% allocated to past)*			
			59,000
Interest on proportion allocated to past 4% x 38,940 x 2.5 years			3,894
b) Loss of income			
1.5 years @ 10,000 pa		15,000	
Add			
1 year's partial loss:			
Pre-Accident	10,000		
Light work	4,000		
		6,000	
		21,000	
Add			
Interest: Wage loss is continuing so allow interest @ 4% 4% x 21,000 x 2.5 years		2,100	
Less			
Deduct all Welfare State Benefits received as per CRU Certificate		12,000	
			11,100
c) Miscellaneous expenses			
			1,800

Interest is due form date of outlay; assume outlay at date of accident 1,800 x 8% x 2.5 years		360
d) Future loss of earnings		
Multiplier is 16.12 @ 26,000 pa		143,820
e) Hospital charges (14 days @ 435 per day)		
		6,090
TOTAL AWARD		**226,064**

8.a Loss of Eyesight – one eye without cosmetic disability

a) Solatium *75% allocated to past*		
		20,000
Interest on proportion allocated to past 4% x 15,000 x 2.5 years		1,500
Assume that claimant is able to resume his employment one year after accident		
b) Loss of Income		
1 year	10,000	
Add		
Interest from date of return to work 10,000 x 8% x 1.5 years	1,200	
Less		
Deduct all Welfare Benefits received per CRU Certificate	8,000	
		3,200
c) Miscellaneous losses, say		
		1,800

Interest is due form date of loss; assume loss incurred at date of accident 1,800 x 8% x 2.5 years		360
TOTAL AWARD		**26,860**

8.b Loss of Eyesight – one eye with cosmetic disability

a) Solatium *50% allocated to past*		
		30,000
Interest on proportion allocated to past 4% x 15,000 x 2.5 years		1,500
b) Loss of Income		
1 year @ 36,000	10,000	
Add		
Interest from date of return to work 36,000 x 8% x 1.5 years	1,200	
Less		
Deduct all Welfare Benefits received per CRU Certificate	8,000	
		3,200
c) Miscellaneous losses, say		
		1,800
Interest is due form date of loss; assume loss incurred at date of accident 1,800 x 8% x 2.5 years		360
TOTAL AWARD		**36,860**

8.c Loss of Eyesight – total blindness

a) Solatium *33% allocated to past*		
		100,000
Interest on proportion allocated to past 4% x 15,000 x 2.5 years		3,300
Assume claimant unable to resume employment		
b) Loss of Income		
1 year @ 10,000 pa	25,000	
Add		
Interest thereon 90,000 x 4% x 2.5 years	2,500	
Less		
All Welfare Benefits received per CRU Certificate	18,000	
		9,500
c) Cost of care and Medical expenses to date of Proof		
		13,500
Interest is due form date of outlay or at 4% on whole sum if costs ongoing; assume interest at 4% 4% x 13,500 x 2.5 years		1,350
d) Future loss of income		
Multiplier is 23.97 @ 10,000 pa		239,700
g) Future cost of replacement aids		
		13,400
TOTAL AWARD		**380,750**

9. Deafness (Total)

Total deafness is a most unusual injury and it is therefore difficult to quantify with reference to precedent. Many cases of deafness relate to noise exposure at work. Such claims are usually settled in terms of Union/Employer Agreements and, in quantifying this claim, we have based our figures on experience of settlements achieved in such industrial deafness cases.

a) Solatium *25% allocated to past*			
			24,000
Interest on proportion allocated to past 4% x 6,000 x 2.5 years			600
Assume claimant unable to resume employment but takes up light work 1.5 years after accident			
b) Loss of Income			
1.5 years @ 10,000 pa		15,000	
Add			
1 year's partial loss			
Pre-Accident	10,000		
Light work	6,000		
		4,000	
		19,000	
Add			
Interest thereon 19,000 x 4% x 2.5 years		1,900	
Less			
Deduct all Welfare Benefits received per CRU Certificate		12,000	
			8,900
c) Miscellaneous expenses			
			1,800

Interest is due from date of outlay; assume outlay incurred at date of accident 1,800 x 8% x 2.5 years		360
d) Future loss of income @ 26,000 pa		
Multiplier is 23.97		95,880
TOTAL AWARD		**131,540**

10. Repetitive Strain Injury

a) Range of Injury to wrist			
i) Complete loss of function in wrist		15,500	
ii) Injury with significant permanent residual disability		9,500	
iii) Persistent pain and stiffness		7,500	
iv) Complete recovery up to		3,600	
a) Persistent pain and stiffness			
Solatium 33% allocated to past			7,200
Interest on proportion allocated to past 4% x 2,400 x 2.5 years			240
Assume claimant unable to resume his employment as a surgeon and takes light duties 6 months after sustaining injury			
b) Loss of Income			
0.5 years @ 36,000 pa		5,000	
Add			
2 years' partial loss			
Pre-Accident @ 10,000 pa	20,000		
Light work @ 6,000 pa	12,000		
		8,000	
		13,000	

Add		
Interest thereon 4% x 13,000 x 2.5 years	1,300	
Less		
All Welfare Benefits received per CRU Certificate	3,000	
		11,300
c) Miscellaneous expenses		
		600
Interest is due from date of outlay; assume expenses incurred at date of accident 8% x 600 x 2.5 years		120
d) Future loss of income		
4,000 pa Multiplier is 23.97		95,880
TOTAL AWARD		**115,340**

SPAIN

Ms Mercedes Pallarés

Introduction

Under the Spanish legal system, the regulation of compensation for personal injury in tort is very similar to other Civil Code countries. The general and basic principle is, following Section 1902 of the Civil Code, that the damage caused must be totally indemnified. This compensation includes not only the damage arising from the injuries, but also consequential losses such as loss of earnings. This principle has an equivalent in Section 113 of the Criminal Code.

Prior to November 1995, the Courts evaluation of injuries arising from motor related accidents was based on the principle mentioned in the above paragraph. Therefore the Courts were solely tied by the *'free weight of evidence principle'*. Notwithstanding this, since 1991, some Courts have begun to apply, in order to calculate the amount of the compensation arising from motor accidents, a Rating System published by The Treasury and Economic Ministry (Order dated 5 March 1991). This included a document on compensation entitled '*System for the assessment of personal injuries derived from Traffic Accident*'. This Order had no purpose other than allowing insurance companies to make technical provisions for disaster coverage with a greater degree of certainty. This Ministerial Order (not compulsory) was well received by certain sections of our judiciary. Step by step, the spirit and general principles of this Order could be found after the decisions of some of our Courts.

Legislation enacted in 1995 produced the latest change of direction in this particular matter. This Act *30/1995 on the 'Regulation and supervision of Private Insurance'* was established as an annex to the '*Civil Liability and Motor Vehicles Traffic Insurance Act*' a '*Compulsory System for the Assessment of Personal Injuries derived from Traffic Accident*'. This was partially reformed by Act 50/1998 of 30 December.

Since the appearance of this System, there has been some controversy and a variety of reactions to it. In particular there is a strong debate as to whether the compulsory rating system which sets limits of indemnity is constitutional. Although there has been no particular decision of the Supreme Court related to the matter, some of it's members have already stressed that they are in disagreement with the binding and automatic nature of the System.

However, whilst the Constitutional Court has not decided the question, the '*System for the Assessment of Personal Injuries derived from Traffic Accident*' set out by the Act 50/1995, is enforceable, and applies to each and every case involving the valuation of injuries arising from motor accidents occurring in Spain. The only exception to this general principle is that the injuries are caused as a consequence of the commission of a deliberate crime.

Damage Recoverable under the Act 50/1995 Rating System

The general principles and guidelines of this system are as follows:

1. The Act considers as recoverable damage: death, permanent disability and temporary disability. As for the exact valuation of the damage the age of both the victim and the prejudiced person shall be taken into account.

DEATH: Quantum is established according to fixed amounts that are assigned according to the victim's age, as well as the familiar relationship with the prejudiced, the age of the latter and the number of prejudiced persons entitled to receive compensation.

PERMANENT DISABILITY: both the physical and functional sequels are compensated. The System includes a number of injuries/sequels, having assigned to each of them a maximum and minimum number of points. Where there are several sequels arising from the same event, the points' assignment is made through a formula. Once the final punctuation figure is made, according to the age of the damage and the number of points previously obtained. A given figure is therefore finally settled.

TEMPORARY DISABILITY: the Act defines temporary disability as the temporary loss of health. Under this concept, the System provides different valuation criteria according to the following situations:

- Number of days under hospital care: (assigned value of ESP 8,000/ £29 per day).
- Period of medical or sick leave, without hospital care. It is understood that the victim is unable to work, nor to carry out properly any of his daily duties (assigned value of ESP 6,500/ £23.50 per day).

- Period of healing. This is the period where the victim has not fully recovered from his injuries and sequels but he is able to work and carry out his normal daily duties (assigned value of ESP 3,500/ £12.67 per day).

2. The medical, surgical, nursing and pharmaceutical costs, along with costs arising from hospital care, are all recoverable. In addition, in the event of death, funeral and burial costs are recoverable too.
3. As a general rule, pain and suffering compensation is deemed to be equal for any victim. Without prejudice to it, the basic compensation figure obtained for death, permanent disability or temporary disability, can be increased in any of the following circumstances; limitation on the victim's working ability, loss of earnings, other needs eventually arising such as complementary pain and suffering, permanent personal assistance or care from a third person, accommodation needs, etc. All of these circumstances will be valued with the application of an adjusting index (within maximum and minimum limits).
4. The Valuation Table figures are updated on a yearly basis.
5. When the victim has contributed to the causation of the accident, the System provides the application of an adjusting index intended to reduce the compensation amount, including the recoverable costs.

Interest for delayed payment charged to Insurance Companies

This is sensible when related to compensation arising from personal injuries caused by motor accidents. It is quite normal that the Insurance Company has late notice of the extent and nature, and sometimes even the existence, of the injuries suffered by the victim. On the other hand, it is quite normal for the prejudiced person to fail to provide any information about his health situation at any moment prior to the trial. All these matters are regulated by Section 20 of the Act 50/1980 (Insurance Contract Law) and the Additional Provision of the 'Civil Liability and Motor Vehicles Traffic Insurance Act'.

The more significant provisions of the above are:

1. The Insurance Company eludes the interests for delayed payment when the compensation is paid to the beneficiary or deposited with the Court; within three months from the date of the accident.

2. When the sequels last for a period exceeding three months, or there is no possibility of properly determining their scope at the time the compensation is deposited with the Court, it is for the Courts to decide whether the amount deposited is or is not enough according to the known circumstances and the Rating System rules.

3. When no compensation is paid due to circumstances which are not attributable to the Insurance Company, there is no legal duty to pay default interest. This could be the case, for instance, of an accident that occurs in Spain and produces injuries to an Australian national within his holiday time. After undergoing medical assistance at a Spanish local hospital, the injured returns to Australia, without leaving a personal address and no further notice is given to the Insurance Company.

4. If none of the above-mentioned circumstances apply, then the Insurance Company has a legal duty to pay interests for delayed payment. The applicable rate is the current '*legal interest of money*' at the time the compensation should have been paid (4.25% for 1999) increased by 50%. Notwithstanding this, two years after the loss occurred without the Insurance Company having paid or having deposited the compensation before a Court, the interest rate applicable for delayed payment shall not be under 20% per year.

Therefore, most of thc Insurance Companies' practice is to deposit with the Court within three months from the accident the minimum amounts payable under the Rating System. This is to avoid the further possibility of facing huge interests for delayed payment.

Final Reminders

As to fully understand the extent of the amounts and concepts of the two practical schedules requested we provide details of the criteria according to which the calculations have been made.

1. For all purposes the reference date is 31 December 1999.

2. No calculations have been made for medical; pharmaceutical and hospital care costs and expenses, as the valuation arising from this concept strongly depends on the individual circumstances. However, such costs are clearly recoverable.

3. All injuries, sequels and recoverable subjects have been calculated taking into account the maximum figure or punctuation assigned by the current Valuation System. Therefore the amounts provided should be subject to later weighting, according to the particular case.
4. We have followed the same criteria for the calculation of interest for delayed payment by Insurance Companies. We have applied the figures arising from the rather extraordinary case of an Insurance Company not undertaking its legal duty to pay any compensation for a period of two and a half years from the date the accident occurred (i.e. a 20% interest rate).
5. Regarding loss of earnings, this is a matter of high controversy. There are serious doubts as to the application of the Rating System rules. The System does not provide the possibility of taking into account the loss of earnings via the application of an adjusting index on the basic compensation figure. This is the one we have used for this purposes. In addition, the majority of Courts are using these criteria, albeit some do not.

Table 1. Schedule A

Claimant:	Man
Age:	40
Status:	Married (children 5 and 7)
Occupation:	Doctor
Annual Income:	ESP 4,800,000 – net p.a.
Settlement:	2.5 years post accident

1. Instant Death	ESP
(a) For widow	
(i) All funeral expenses (with invoice)	–
(ii) Moral and pecuniary damages	12,808,524.–
Increases (%) for loss of earnings	2,469,483.–
(iii) Interest on item (ii) (2.5 years)	3,757,259.–

(b)	*For the children (two children)*	
(iv)	Moral and pecuniary damages	10,673,770.–
	Increase (%) for loss of earnings	2,057,902.–
(v)	Interest on item (i) and (ii), (2.5 years)	3,445,604.–
Total award (without expenses but with interest)		**35,212,542.–**

2a. Burns

Assume return to work after 2 years

(a)	*Burns to the face with permanent scarring*	
(i)	Fixed rate for compensation for the period of time elapsed until the date of medical discharge with sequels. As follows:	
	– Days spent at hospital (45 days)*	429,390.–
	– Days unable to work (685 days)*	5,310,805.–
(ii)	Medical, surgery and pharmaceutical expenses (with invoice)	–
(iii)	Moral and pecuniary damages	5,194,710.–
	Increase (%) for loss of earnings	1,001,540.–
(iv)	Interest on item (i) and (iii)	3,230,391.–
Total award (without expenses)		**15,166,836.–**

2b. Burns to the face without permanent scarring

(i)	Fixed rate for compensation for the period of time elapsed until the date of medical discharge with sequels. As follows:	
	– Days spent at hospital (45 days)*	429,390.–

* This amount includes the basic figure per day increased with an adjusting index for loss of earnings.

– Days unable to work (685 days)*	5,310,805.–
(ii) Medical, surgery and pharmaceutical expenses (with invoice)	–
(iii) Moral and pecuniary damages	1,845,600.–
Increase (%) for loss of earnings	355,832.–
(iv) Interest on item (i) and (iii)	2,149,261.–
Total award (without expenses)	**10,090,888.–**

2c. Burns to other parts of the body

(i) Fixed rate for compensation for the period of time elapsed until the date of medical discharge with sequels. As follows:

– Days spent at hospital (45 days)*	429,390.–
– Days unable to work (685 days)*	5,310,805.–
(ii) Medical, surgery and pharmaceutical expenses (with invoice)	–
(iii) Moral and pecuniary damages	2,802,780.–
Increase (%) for loss of earnings	540,376.–
(iv) Interest on item (i) and (iii)	2,458,251.–
Total award (without expenses)	**11,541,602.–**

3. Quadriplegia

(i) All medical, surgery, pharmaceutical and orthopaedic equipment expenses (unlimited but justified)	–
(ii) Housing adaptation (maximum)	10,673,770.–
(iii) General moral and pecuniary damages	35,812,900.–
Increase for loss of earnings	6,904,727.–

* This amount includes the basic figure per day increased with an adjusting index for loss of earnings.

(iv)	Complementary moral damages (maximum)	10,673,770.–
(v)	Total disability for any job and the necessity of third person (maximum)	64,042,617.–
(vi)	Moral injury to the family (maximum)	16,010,654.–
(vii)	Prospective medical and care expenses, nurse included, (in accordance with an estimation of an expert)	–
(viii)	Fixed rate of compensation for the period of time elapsed until the date of medical discharge with sequels (24 month). As follows:	
	All days spent at hospital or comparable situation*	6,965,660.–
(ix)	Interest on item (ii), (iii), (iv), (v), (vi) and (viii)	40,888,282.–
Total award (without expenses)		**191,972,380.–**

4. Paraplegia

(i)	All medical, surgery, pharmaceutical and orthopaedic equipment expenses (unlimited but justified)	–
(ii)	Housing adaptation (maximum)	10,673,770.–
(iii)	General moral and pecuniary damages	28,127,605.–
	Increase for loss of earnings	5,423,002.–
(iv)	Complementary moral damages (maximum)	10,673,770.–
(v)	Total disability for any job and the necessity of third person (maximum)	64,042,617.–
(vi)	Moral injury to the family (maximum)	16,010,654.–
(vii)	Vehicle adaptation costs (maximum)	3,202,131.–
(viii)	Prospective medical and care expenses, nurse included, (in accordance with an estimation of an expert	–

* This amount includes the basic figure per day increased with an adjusting index for loss of earnings.

(ix) Fixed rate of compensation for the period of time elapsed until the date of medical discharge with sequels (24th month). As follows:

All days spent at hospital or comparable situation*	6,965,660.–
(x) Interest on item (ii), (iii), (iv), (v), (vi) and (ix)	39,273,989.–
Total award (without expenses)	**184,393,198.–**

5a. Brain Damage

With loss of intellectual capacity (75 points allocated of a maximum of 100 points)

(i) All medical, surgery, pharmaceutical and orthopaedic equipment expenses (unlimited but justified)	–
(ii) General moral and pecuniary damages	22,694,625.–
Increase for loss of earnings	4,375,524.–
(iii) Total disability for his employment (maximum)	10,673,770.–
(iv) Moral injury to the family (maximum)	5,000,000.–
(v) Prospective medical and care expenses, nurse included, (estimated by an expert)	–
(vi) Fixed rate of compensation for the period of time which elapsed until the date of medical discharge with sequels (24th month). As follows:	
– Days spent at hospital (60 days)*	594,648.–
– Days unable to work (670 days)*	4,800,850.–
(vii) Interest on item (ii), (iii), (iv) and (vi)	13,027,997.–
Total award (without expenses)	**61,167,414.–**

* This amount includes the basic figure per day increased with an adjusting index for loss of earnings.

5b. Brain Damage with motor deficiency

(85 points allocated of a maximum of 100 points)

(i)	All medical, surgery, pharmaceutical and orthopaedic equipment expenses (unlimited but justified)	–
(ii)	General moral and pecuniary damages	28,127,605.–
	Increase for loss of earnings	5,423,002.–
(iii)	Total disability for his employment (maximum)	21,347,539.–
(iv)	Moral injury to the family (average)	8,000,000.–
(v)	Prospective medical and care expenses, nurse included, (in accordance with an estimation of an expert	–
(vi)	Fixed rate of compensation for the period of time elapsed until the date of medical discharge with sequels (18th month). As follows:	
	– Days spent at hospital (60 days)*	594,648.–
	– Days unable to work (670 days)*	4,800,485.–
(vii)	Interest on item (ii), (iii), (iv) and (vi)	18,482,388.–
Total award (without expenses)		**86,775,667.–**

6a. Amputation of leg above knee

Assume return to work after 1.5 years

(i)	Temporary disability: hospital days (40)*	396,432.–
(ii)	Temporary disability: days unable to work (508)*	4,090,684.–
(iii)	General moral and pecuniary damages (aesthetic damages included)	18,573,180.–
(iv)	Increase (%) for loss of earning item (iii)	3,580,909.–

* This amount includes the basic figure per day increased with an adjusting index for loss of earnings.

(v) All medical, surgery, pharmaceutical and orthopaedic equipment expenses (unlimited but justified)	–
(vi) Transport and prosthesis costs (unlimited but justified)	–
(vii) Interest on item (i), (ii), (iii) and (iv)	7,209,979.–
Total award (without expenses)	**33,851,184.–**

6b. Amputation of leg below knee

Assume return to work after 1.5 years

(i) Temporary disability hospital days (40)*	396,432.–
(ii) Temporary disability days unable to work (508)*	4,090,684.–
(iii) General moral and pecuniary damages (aesthetic damages included)	14,064,130.–
(iv) Increase (%) for loss of earning item (iii)	2,711,564.–
(v) All medical, surgery, pharmaceutical and orthopaedic equipment expenses (unlimited but justified)	–
(vi) Transport and prosthesis costs (unlimited but justified)	–
(vii) Interest on item (i), (ii), (iii) and (iv)	5,754,409.–
Total award (without expenses)	**27,017,219.–**

7a. Amputation of arm above elbow

Assume return to work after 1.5 years

(i) Temporary disability: hospital days (30)*	297,324.–
(ii) Temporary disability: days unable to work (518)*	4,171,209.–

* This amount includes the basic figure per day increased with an adjusting index for loss of earnings.

(iii) General moral and pecuniary damages (aesthetic damages included)	16,251,543.–
(iv) Increase (%) for loss of earning item (iii)	3,133,297.–
(v) Partial disability for his work (maximum)	2,134,754.–
(vi) All medical, surgery, pharmaceutical and orthopaedic equipment expenses (unlimited but justified)	–
(vii) Transport and prosthesis costs (unlimited but justified)	–
(viii) Interest on item (i), (ii), (iii) and (iv)	7,033,234.–
Total award (without expenses)	**33,021,361.–**

7b. Amputation of arm below elbow

Assume return to work after 1.5 years

(i) Temporary disability: hospital days (30)*	297,324.–
(ii) Temporary disability: days unable to work (518)*	4,171,209.–
(iii) General moral and pecuniary damages (aesthetic damages included)	12,015,047.–
(iv) Increase (%) for loss of earning item (iii)	2,316,501.–
(v) Partial disability for his work (maximum)	2,134,754.–
(vi) All medical, surgery, pharmaceutical and orthopaedic equipment expenses (unlimited but justified)	–
(vii) Transport and prosthesis costs (unlimited but justified)	–
(viii) Interest on item (i), (ii), (iii) and (iv)	5,665,649.–
Total award (without expenses)	**26,600,484.–**

* This amount includes the basic figure per day increased with an adjusting index for loss of earnings.

8a. Loss of eyesight – one eye without cosmetic disability

Return to work after 1 year

(i) Temporary disability: hospital days (30)*	297,324.–
(ii) Temporary disability: days unable to work (335)*	2,697,597.–
(iii) General moral and pecuniary damages	3,929,775.–
(iv) Increase for loss of earning item (iii)	757,661.–
(v) Partial disability for his work (maximum)	2,134,754.–
(vi) All medical, surgery, pharmaceutical and orthopaedic equipment expenses (unlimited but justified)	–
(vii) Transport and prosthesis costs (unlimited but justified)	–
(viii) Interest on item (i), (ii), (iii) and (iv)	2,656,830.–
Total award (without expenses)	**12,473,941.–**

8b. Loss of eyesight – one eye with cosmetic disability

Return to work after 1 year

(i) Temporary disability: hospital days (30)*	297,324.–
(ii) Temporary disability: days unable to work (335)*	2,697,597.–
(iii) General moral and pecuniary damages (aesthetic damages included)	5,714,181.–
(iv) Increase (%) for loss of earning item (iii)	1,101,694.–
(v) Partial disability for his work (maximum)	2,134,754.–
(vi) All medical, surgery, pharmaceutical and orthopaedic equipment expenses (unlimited but justified)	–
(vii) Transport and prosthesis costs (unlimited but justified)	–

* This amount includes the basic figure per day increased with an adjusting index for loss of earnings.

(viii) Interest on item (i), (ii), (iii) and (iv)	3,232,855.–
Total award (without expenses)	**15,178,405.–**

8c. Total blindness

Unable to return to work

(i) Temporary disability: hospital days (30)*	297,324.–
(ii) Temporary disability: days unable to work (335)* (compensation for the period of time passed until the date of medical discharge)	2,697,597.–
(iii) General moral and pecuniary damages	28,127,605.–
(iv) Increase for loss of earnings (iii)	5,423,002.–
(v) Total disability for any work (maximum)	21,347,539.–
(vi) Increase for the necessity of a third person to the ordinary matters of his life	15,000,000.–
All medical, surgery, pharmaceutical and orthopaedic equipment expenses (unlimited but justified)	–
(vii) Transport and prosthesis costs (unlimited but justificd)	–
(viii) Interest on item (i), (ii), (iii) and (iv)	19,727,240.–
Total award (without expenses)	**92,620,307.–**

9. Deafness – (Bilateral)

Return to light work after 5 months

(i) Temporary disability: hospital days (30)*	297,324.–
(ii) Temporary disability: days unable to work (120)*	966,303.–

* This amount includes the basic figure per day increased with an adjusting index for loss of earnings.

(iii) General moral and pecuniary damages	20,160,770.–
(iv) Increase for loss of earnings (iii)	3,886,996.–
(v) Partial disability for his work (maximum)	2,134,754.–
(vi) All medical, surgery, pharmaceutical and orthopaedic equipment expenses (unlimited but justified)	–
(vii) Transport costs (unlimited but justified)	–
(viii) Interest on item (i), (ii), (iii) and (iv)	7,427,822.–
Total award (without expenses)	**34,873,969.–**

Schedule B

Claimant:	Woman
Age:	20
Status:	Single
Occupation:	Legal Secretary
Annual Income:	ESP 1,920,000 – net p.a.
Settlement:	2.5 years post accident

1. Instant Death	ESP
Supposing that her parents live	
(a) All funeral expenses (with invoice)	–
(b) Moral and pecuniary damages	11,741,147.–
(c) Increases for loss of earnings item (b)	704,469.–
(d) Interest on item (a) and (b) 2.5 years	3,368,189.–
Total award (without expenses)	**15,813,805.–**

2a. Burns

Assume return to work after 2 years

(a) Burns to the face with permanent and severe scarring

(i)	Fixed rate for compensation for the period of time elapsed until the date of medical discharge with sequels. As follows:	
	– Days spent at hospital (45 days)*	381,600.–
	– Days unable to work (685 days)*	4,719,650.–
(ii)	Medical, surgery and pharmaceutical expenses (with invoice)	–
(iii)	Moral and pecuniary damages	10,497,105.–
	Increase (%) for loss of earnings	629,826.–
(iv)	Interest on item (i) and (iii)	4,391,875.–
Total award (without expenses)		**20,620,056.–**

2b. Burns to the face without permanent scarring

(i)	Fixed rate for compensation for the period of time elapsed until the date of medical discharge with sequels. As follows:	
	– Days spent at hospital (45 days)*	381,600.–
	– Days unable to work (685 days)*	4,719,650.–
(ii)	Medical, surgery and pharmaceutical expenses (with invoice)	–
(iii)	Moral and pecuniary damages	2,285,174.–
	Increase (%) for loss of earnings	137,110.–
(iv)	Interest on item (i) and (iii)	2,036,114.–
Total award (without expenses)		**9,559,648.–**

* This amount includes the basic figure per day increased with an adjusting index for loss of earnings.

2c. Burns to other parts of the body

(i) Fixed rate for compensation for the period of time elapsed until the date of medical discharge with sequels. As follows:	
– Days spent at hospital (45 days)*	381,600.–
– Days unable to work (685 days)*	4,719,650.–
(ii) Medical, surgery and pharmaceutical expenses (with invoice)	–
(iii) Moral and pecuniary damages	2,802,780.–
(iv) Interest on item (i) and (iii)	2,139,088.–
Total award (without expenses)	**10,043,118.–**

3. Quadriplegia

(i) All medical, surgery, pharmaceutical and orthopaedic equipment expenses (unlimited but justified)	–
(ii) Housing adaptation (maximum)	10,673,770.–
(iii) General moral and pecuniary damages	38,790,600.–
Increase for loss of earnings	2,327,436.–
(iv) Complementary moral damages (up to)	10,673,770.–
(v) Increase by total disability for any job and the necessity of third person (maximum)	64,042,617.–
(vi) Moral injury to the family (maximum)	16,010,654.–
(vii) Prospective medical and care expenses, nurse included, (estimated by an expert)	–
(viii) Fixed rate of compensation for the period of time elapsed until the date of medical discharge with sequels (24 months). As follows:	
All days spent in hospital or a comparable situation*	6,190,400.–

---

* This amount includes the basic figure per day increased with an adjusting index for loss of earnings.

(ix)	Interest on item (ii), (iii), (iv), (v), (vi) and (viii)	40,245,570.–
Total award (without expenses)		**188,954,817.–**

4. Paraplegia

(i)	All medical, surgery, pharmaceutical and orthopaedic equipment expenses (unlimited but justified)	–
(ii)	Housing adaptation (maximum)	10,673,770.–
(iii)	General moral and pecuniary damages	30,475,390.–
	Increase for loss of earnings	1,828,523.–
(iv)	Complementary moral damages (maximum)	10,673,770.–
(v)	Total disability for any job and the necessity of third person (maximum)	64,042,617.–
(vi)	Moral injury to the family (maximum)	16,010,654.–
(vii)	Vehicle adaptation costs (maximum)	3,202,131.–
(viii)	Prospective medical and care expenses, nurse included, (in accordance with an estimation of an expert)	–
(ix)	Fixed rate of compensation for the period of time elapsed until the date of medical discharge with sequels (24th month). As follows:	
	All days spent at hospital or in a comparable situation*	6,190,400.–
(xi)	Interest on item (ii), (iii), (iv), (v), (vi) and (xi)	38,726,782.–
Total award (without expenses)		**181,824,037.–**

* This amount includes the basic figure per day increased with an adjusting index for loss of earnings.

5a. Brain Damage

With loss of intellectual capacity (75 points allocated of a maximum of 100 points)

(i)	All medical, surgery, pharmaceutical and orthopaedic equipment expenses (unlimited but justified)	–
(ii)	General moral and pecuniary damages	24,598,275.–
	Increase for loss of earnings	1,475,896.–
(iii)	Total disability for her employment (maximum)	10,673,770.–
(iv)	Moral injury to the family (maximum)	5,000,000.–
(v)	Prospective medical and care expenses, nurse included, (estimated by an expert)	–
(vi)	Fixed rate of compensation for the period of time elapsed until the date of medical discharge with sequels (24th month). As follows:	
	– Days spent at hospital (60 days)*	508,800.–
	– Days unable to work (670 days)*	4,616,300.–
(vii)	Interest on item (ii), (iii), (iv) and (vi)	12,685,373.–
Total award (without expenses)		**59,558,414.–**

5b. Brain Damage with motor deficiency

(85 points allocated of a maximum of 100 points)

(i)	All medical, surgery, pharmaceutical and orthopaedic equipment expenses (unlimited but justified)	–
(ii)	General moral and pecuniary damages	30,475,390.–
	Increase (%) for loss of earnings	1,828,523.–
(iii)	Total disability for her employment (maximum)	21,347,539.–

* This amount includes the basic figure per day increased with an adjusting index for loss of earnings.

(iv)	Moral injury to the family (average)	8,000,000.–
(v)	Prospective medical and care expenses, nurse included, (estimated by an expert)	–
(vi)	Fixed rate of compensation for the period of time elapsed until the date of medical discharge with sequels (18th month). As follows:	
	– Days spent at hospital (60 days)*	508,800.–
	– Days unable to work (670 days)*	4,616,300.–
(vii)	Interest on item (ii), (iii), (iv) and (vi)	18,071,912.–
Total award (without expenses)		**84,848,464.–**

6a. Amputation of leg above knee

Assume return to work after 1.5 years

(i)	Temporary disability: hospital days (40)*	339,200.–
(ii)	Temporary disability: days unable to work (508)	3,500,120.–
(iii)	General moral and pecuniary damages (aesthetic damages included)	20,140,648.–
(iv)	Increase for loss of earning item (iii)	1,208,439.–
(v)	All medical, surgery, pharmaceutical and orthopaedic equipment expenses (unlimited but justified)	–
(vi)	Transport and prosthesis costs (unlimited but justified)	–
(vii)	Interest on item (i), (ii), (iii) and (iv)	6,816,772.–
Total award (without expenses)		**32,005,179.–**

* This amount includes the basic figure per day increased with an adjusting index for loss of earnings.

6b. Amputation of leg below knee

Assume return to work after 1.5 years

(i)	Temporary disability: hospital days (40)*	339,200.–
(ii)	Temporary disability: days unable to work (508)	3,500,120.–
(iii)	General moral and pecuniary damages (aesthetic damages included)	15,260,380.–
(iv)	Increase (%) for loss of earning item (iii)	915,623.–
(v)	All medical, surgery, pharmaceutical and orthopaedic equipment expenses (unlimited but justified)	–
(vi)	Transport and prosthesis costs (unlimited but justified)	–
(vii)	Interest on item (i), (ii), (iii) and (iv)	5,416,799.–
Total award (without expenses)		**25,432,122.–**

7a. Amputation of arm above elbow

Assume return to work after 1.5 years

(i)	Temporary disability: hospital days (30)*	254,400.–
(ii)	Temporary disability: days unable to work (518)	3,569,020.–
(iii)	General moral and pecuniary damages (aesthetic damages included)	17,628,093.–
(iv)	Increase (%) for loss of earning item (iii)	915,623.–
(v)	Total disability for her job as a secretary (maximum)	10,673,770.–
(vi)	All medical, surgery, pharmaceutical and orthopaedic equipment expenses (unlimited but justified)	–
(vii)	Transport and prosthesis costs (unlimited but justified)	–

* This amount includes the basic figure per day increased with an adjusting index for loss of earnings.

(viii) Interest on item (i), (ii), (iii) and (iv)	8,941,946.–
Total award (without expenses)	**41,982,852.–**

7b. Amputation of arm below elbow

Assume return to work after 1.5 years

(i) Temporary disability: hospital days (30)*	254,400.–
(ii) Temporary disability: days unable to work (518)	3,569,020.–
(iii) General moral and pecuniary damages (aesthetic damages included)	13,041,816.–
(iv) Increase (%) for loss of earning item (iii)	782,509.–
(v) Total disability for her job as a secretary (maximum)	10,673,770.–
(vi) All medical, surgery, pharmaceutical and orthopaedic equipment expenses (unlimited but justified)	–
(vii) Transport and prosthesis costs (unlimited but justified)	–
(viii) Interest on item (i), (ii), (iii) and (iv)	7,664,725.–
Total award (without expenses)	**35,986,240.–**

8a. Loss of eyesight – one eye without cosmetic disability

Return to work after 1 year

(i) Temporary disability: hospital days (30)*	254,400.–
(ii) Temporary disability: days unable to work (335)*	2,308,150.–
(iii) General moral and pecuniary damages	4,280,225.–
(iv) Increase for loss of earning item (iii)	256,814.–

* This amount includes the basic figure per day increased with an adjusting index for loss of earnings.

(v) All medical, surgery, pharmaceutical and orthopaedic equipment expenses (unlimited but justified)	–
(vi) Transport and prosthesis costs (unlimited but justified)	–
(vii) Interest on item (i), (ii), (iii) and (iv)	1,921,380.–
Total award (without expenses)	**9,020,969.–**

8b. Loss of eyesight – one eye with cosmetic disability

Return to work after 1 year

(i) Temporary disability: hospital days (30)*	254,400.–
(ii) Temporary disability: days unable to work (335)*	2,308,150.–
(iii) General moral and pecuniary damages (aesthetic damages included)	7,156,345.–
(iv) Increase for loss of earning item (iii)	429,381.–
(v) All medical, surgery, pharmaceutical and orthopaedic equipment expenses (unlimited but justified)	–
(vi) Transport and prosthesis costs (unlimited but justified)	–
(vii) Interest on item (i), (ii), (iii) and (iv)	2,746,454.–
Total award (without expenses)	**12,894,730.–**

8c. Total blindness

Unable to return to work

(i) Temporary disability_[16]: hospital days (30)*	254,400.–
(ii) Temporary disability: days unable to work (335)* (compensation for the period of time passed until the date of medical discharge)	2,308,150.–

* This amount includes the basic figure per day increased with an adjusting index for loss of earnings.

(iii) General moral and pecuniary damages	30,475,390.–
(iv) Increase (%)for loss of earnings (iii)	1,828,523.–
(v) Total disability for any work (maximum)	21,347,539.–
(vi) Increase for the necessity of a third person to the ordinary matters of his life	15,000,000.–
All medical, surgery, pharmaceutical and orthopaedic equipment expenses (unlimited but justified)	–
(vii) Transport and prosthesis costs (unlimited but justified)	–
(viii) Interest on item (i), (ii), (iii) and (iv)	19,272,831.–
Total award (without expenses)	**90,486,833.–**

9. Deafness – (Bilateral)

Return to light work after 5 months

(i) Temporary disability: hospital days (30)*	254,400.–
(ii) Temporary disability: days unable to work (120)	826,800.–
(iii) General moral and pecuniary damages	21,856,800.–
(iv) Increase (%) for loss of earnings (iii)	1,311,408.–
(v) Partial disability for her work (maximum)	2,134,754.–
(vi) All medical, surgery, pharmaceutical and orthopaedic equipment expenses (unlimited but justified)	–
(vii) Transport costs (unlimited but justified)	–
(viii) Housing adaptation (maximum)	400,000.–
(ix) Interest on item (i), (ii), (iii), (iv), (v) and (viii)	7,248,667.–
Total award (without expenses)	**34,032,829.–**

* This amount includes the basic figure per day increased with an adjusting index for loss of earnings.

SWEDEN

Göran Dahlström

Introduction

General insurance supplies both sickness care and basic protection in case of injury. The indemnity is paid by means of compensation from the sickness fund provided that the injured person is employed. In cases of permanent disability daily compensation is changed into a premature pension. Swedish sickness care is not completely free and the heavy costs are paid through the tax system. The personal charges for sickness care and medical expenses, including medicine and physiotherapy amounting to per annum of SEK 2,700 (£176) are paid by the injured person himself but are thereafter free. Care in hospital is SEK 80 (£5.23) a day. In cases of disability a special handicap indemnity may be granted with at the most SEK 25,000 (£1,634) p.a. For children under 16 years of age a treatment indemnity may be granted.

The most common reasons for personal injuries claims are traffic accidents. In Sweden, compensation for personal injury is paid according to the Swedish Damage Insurance Law, regardless of who is responsible for the accident. The Swedish Damage Insurance Law is also applicable in cases of third party liability accident damage. For injuries caused by traffic accidents, the indemnity limit is SEK 300,000,000 (£19,607,843.) In cases of third party liability damage, the limit depends on what kind of insurance has been underwritten.

According to the Damage Insurance Law compensation is paid for:

1. Medical expenses and other costs
2. Loss of income.
3. Pain and suffering, disability and detriment and inconvenience as a consequence of the injuries.

This means that the injured person receives payment for expenses incurred in respect of medical treatment, medicine and physiotherapy. Moreover "other expenses" can be indemnified as, for instance, household assistance, maintenance of building and other expenses incurred as a result of the injury.

Loss of income is covered according to the "difference" method, i.e. the gross sick indemnity or premature pension or other social compensation is deducted from the gross income (gross meaning income before deduction of taxes). Income loss is paid through an index-linked annuity to the age of 65. Thereafter an annuity may be paid if the injured person's pension is reduced through the consequences of the injury. The principle is that the injured person is as far as possible put into the same economic situation as if the accident had not occurred.

Compensation for pain and suffering is paid during a period during which the healing is still progressing, which means the acute sickness period. The indemnity follows a schedule and is independent of the insured person's age or type of injury.

Compensation for disability also is scheduled and is calculated by the Trafikskadenämnden (Traffic Injuries Commission). The degree of disablement is from 0-99%. The award is also based upon the age and type of injuries.

Compensation for inconvenience is calculated on an annual amount.

Consideration is taken of the fact that the injured person still goes to work in spite of a heavy strain [serious injury].

Payment for inconvenience is in most cases paid as a non-recurring amount. Compemsation for loss of income is taxable.

In fatal claims the funeral costs are paid. Should anyone have been dependent on the deceased, there is compensation for loss of maintenance.

Bereavement damages do not exist in Sweden. There are several no fault liability schemes in Sweden, of particular prominence are the pharmaceutical schemes. For motor claims there is a limit of SEK 300,000,000 per case.

Swedish traffic insurance may be described as a supplementary social insurance for motor traffic accident victims, with the high level of compensation characteristic of tort law. The link with the Tort Damages Act has been affected in a very simple manner. Section 9 of the Traffic Damages Act makes reference to the provisions of the Tort Damages Act that deal with determination of the amount of compensation and to legislation on modification of damages in the form of annuities.

The most important principles are the following:

- Compensation should be fully equivalent to the financial and non-financial loss suffered by the victims.

- Compensation is payable to the victim for expenses, loss of income, pain and suffering, disability and detriment, general inconvenience.

- In fatal claims, compensation is payable for funeral costs and other expenses resulting from death and any dependants are compensated for loss of maintenance.
- Compensation for future loss of income or loss of maintenance is paid in the form of an annuity or a lump sum, (an annuity is the most common form of compensation)
- Compensation payable in the form of a life annuity is index-linked.
- Certain benefits payable in connection with the loss are deducted from the compensation award principally, social insurance benefits, but other benefits are deducted including sick pay or pensions payable by employers under employment contracts.

Traffic insurance compensation-like damages, is the net amount remaining after the above-mentioned deductible benefits have been deducted. The principle is consistent with the principle that the social insurance scheme has no right to recovery of benefits it has paid out.

In severe cases of disability, death or in the cases where the disability has caused heavy loss of income the insurance companies are obliged to obtain an opinion regarding the issue of "Traffic Injuries Commission" before entering an agreement with the injured party. Some cases might also be the subject of legal proceedings in Court.

Table 1. Schedule A

Claimant:	Man
Age:	40
Status:	Married, 2 dependent children aged 5 and 7
Occupation:	Doctor
Annual Income:	SEK 500,000

1. Instant death	SEK
Funeral expenses (including gravestone, meals and clothes)	
Total award	max 50,000
The requirement for children is SEK 20,000 per year. As they get children's pension with, say, SEK 30,000 per year per child, they get nothing from insurance.	
The requirement of the wife is about 40-50% of total income. From this you have to reduce the widow's pension. If the widow's pension is about SEK 100,000, thc widow rcceives about SEK 150,000 from insurance until the children are about 12 years old and the widow can have a career of her own:	
150,000 x 7	1,050,000
TOTAL AWARD	**1,100,000**

2. Burns

Face and body 70% disability	
a) Pain and suffering during 2.5 years' acute illness	40,000
b) Disability and detriment about	400,000

c) Compensation for general inconvenience and expenses about 7,000 a year x factor of 16.5	115,000
d) Loss of income about 15% x 500,000 x 2.5 years	187,500
If not returning to work net income loss is paid out in the form of an annuity until 65 years, after that 66%.	
This man received compensation from his work and the social insurance in the form of an early retirement pension of about 70% of further income. Net loss from the insurance company SEK 150,000 per year until 65 years and 66% after that:	
150,000 x factor 31.7	4,755,000
TOTAL AWARD	**5,500,000**

Burns not so heavy and burns to other parts of the body

a) Pain and suffering (range SEK 10,000 – 30,000)	30,000
b) Disability and detriment (range SEK 5,000 – 40,000)	40,000
c) Loss of income: 15% x 500,000 x 1 year	75,000
No further loss of income if he returns to work	
TOTAL AWARD	**145,000**

3. Quadriplegia – 97% disability

a) Pain and suffering	25,000
b) Disability and detriment	595,000
c) Compensation for general inconvenience and expenses: 20,000 per year x factor of 16.5	330,000
(From general insurance you also get disablement benefit of SEK 24,000 per year)	

d) Loss of income 15% x 500,000 x 2.5 years	187,500
e) Future loss of income 150,000 per year x factor of 31.7	4,755,500
TOTAL AWARD	**5,892,200**

4. Paraplegia – 87% disability

a) Pain and suffering	25,000
b) Disability and detriment	480,000
c) The rest of the compensation is the same as c) to e) above, Quadriplegia	5,272,000
TOTAL AWARD	**5,777,500**

5.a. Brain damage – 60% disability

a) Pain and suffering 2.5 years' acute illness	40,000
b) Disability and detriment	265,000
c) Compensation for general inconvenience and expenses	165,000
d) Loss of income	187,500
e) Future loss of income	4,755,000
TOTAL AWARD	**6,402,500**

5.b. Brain damage with motor damage – 75% disability

a) Pain and suffering	40,000
b) Disability and detriment	368,000
c) General inconvenience and expenses: 10,000 per year x factor of 16.5	165,000

d) Loss of income: 15% x 500,000	187,500
e) Future loss of income: 150,000 per year x factor of 31.7	4,755,000
TOTAL AWARD	**5,515,500**

6.a. Amputation of leg above knee – 33% disability

a) Pain and suffering during 1 years's acute illness	25,000
b) Disability and detriment	177,000
c) Compensation for general inconvenience and expenses: 10,000 x factor of 16.5	165,000
d) Loss of income: 15% x 500,000 x 2.5 years	75,000
After that he is assumed to work again with the same income as before*	
TOTAL AWARD	**442,000**
*If not: 120,000 per year x factor of 31.735	3,808,200
TOTAL AWARD	**5,515,500**

6.b. Amputation of leg below knee – 12 to 19% disability

a) Pain and suffering during 1 year's acute illness	25,000
b) Disability and detriment	105,000
c) General inconvenience and expenses: 8,000 per year x factor of 16.5	132,000
d) Loss of income: 15% x 500,000 x 1 year	75,000
TOTAL AWARD	**337,000**

7.a. Amputation of arm above elbow – 46% disability

a) Pain and suffering during 1 year's acute illness	25,000
b) Disability and detriment	249,000
c) General inconvenience and expenses: 12,000 per year x factor of 16.5	198,000
d) Loss of income: 15% of income for 1 year	75,000
e) If not returning to work as a doctor, he receives net income loss: 150,000 x 31.7 until 65 years old, after that 66%	5,755,000
TOTAL AWARD	**5,302,000**

7.b. Amputation of arm below elbow – 42% disability

a) Pain and suffering during 1 year's acute illness	25,000
b) Disability and detriment	219,000
c) General inconvenience and expenses: 12,000 per year x factor of 16.5	165,000
d) Loss of income: 15% of income for 1 year	75,000
e) Loss of income: 15% x 500,000 x 1 year	4,755,000
TOTAL AWARD	**5,239,000**

8.a. Loss of eyesight, one eye – 17% disability

a) Pain and suffering during 1 year's acute illness	25,000
b) Disability and detriment	47,000
c) General inconvenience and expenses 4,000 per year x factor of 16.5	66,000

d) Loss of income 15% x 500,000 x 1 year	75,000
TOTAL AWARD	**213,500**

8.b. Total blindness – 68% disability

a) Pain and suffering during 1 year's acute illness	15,000
b) Disability and detriment	527,000
c) General inconvenience and expenses: 15,000 per year x factor of 16.5	247,000
d) Loss of income: 15% x 500,000 x 1 year	75,000
e) Future loss of income: 150,000 x factor 31.7	4,755,000
TOTAL AWARD	**5,619,500**

9. Deafness – 60% disability

a) Pain and suffering during 1 year's acute illness	25,000
b) Disability and detriment	255,000
c) General inconvenience and expenses: 8,000 per year x factor of 15.5	132,000
d) Loss of income: 15% x 500,000 x 1 year	75,000
e) If does not return to work: 150,000 x factor 31.7	4,755,000
TOTAL AWARD	**5,242,000**

10. Repetitive strain injury, can be 7% to 15% disability

a) Pain and suffering	15,000 –	20,000
b) Disability and detriment	17,000 –	117,000
c) General inconvenience: between 3,000 – 10,000 per year	49,000 –	165,000
d) Loss of income: 1 year		75,000
e) Future loss of income: 100,000 x factor 31.7 35		4,755,000
TOTAL AWARD	**156,500 –**	**5,132,000**

Table 2. Schedule B

Claimant:	Woman
Age:	20
Status:	Single
Occupation:	Legal Secretary
Annual Income:	SEK 180,000

1. Instant Death	SEK
Funeral expenses (the funeral, meals and clothes including gravestone)	max 50,000
TOTAL AWARD	**50,000**

2. Burns

Face and body 70% disability

(a) Pain and suffering during about 2.5 years' acute illness	40,000
(b) Disability and detriment about	500,000
(c) Compensation for general inconvenience and expenses about 7,000 a year x factor of 19.1	133,700
(d) Loss of income about: 15% x 2.5 years	67,500
If not returning to work net income loss is paid out in the form of an annuity compensation form social insurance in the form of an early disablement pension SEK 126,000 (70%)	
(e) Annuity 54,000 from traffic insurance until 65 years, after that 66% x 54,000 factor of 56.5	5,051,000
TOTAL AWARD	**3,793,000**

Burns, not so heavy and burns to other parts of the body

(a) Pain and suffering	10,000 –	30,000
(b) Disability and detriment (range SEK 5,000 – 40,000)	20,000 –	60,000
(c) General inconvenience and expenses	20,000 –	70,000
(d) Loss of income: 180,000 15% x 1 year		27,000
No further loss of income if she returns to work		
TOTAL AWARD	**77,000 –**	**187,000**

3. Quadriplegia – 97% disability

(a) Pain and suffering	25,000

(b) Disability and detriment	696,000
(c) Compensation for general inconvenience and expenses: 20,000 per year x factor of 19.1	382,000
(General insurance also provides disablement benefit of SEK 25,000 per year)	
(d) Loss of income 15% x 180,000 x 2.5 years	67,500
(e) Future loss of income: 54,000 per year x factor of 56.5	3,051,000
TOTAL AWARD	**4,222,000**

4. Paraplegia – 87% disability

(a) Pain and suffering	25,000
(b) Disability and detriment	565,000
(c) The rest of the compensation is the same as (c) to (e) above, Quadriplegia	3,500,500
TOTAL AWARD	**4,090,500**

5a. Brain damage – 60% disability

(a) Pain and suffering during 2.5 years' acute illness	40,000
(b) Disability and detriment	300,000
(c) Compensation for general inconvenience and expenses: 15,000 per year x factor of 19.1	286,500
(d) Loss of income: 15% x 180,000 x 2.5 years	67,500
(e) Future loss of income: 54,000 per year x factor of 56.5	3,051,000
TOTAL AWARD	**3,745,000**

5b. Brain damage with motor damage – 75% disability

(a) Pain and suffering	40,000
(b) Disability and detriment	433,000
(c) Compensation for general inconvenience and expenses: 15,000 per year x factor of 19.1	286,500
(d) Loss of income: 15% x 180,000 x 2.5 years	67,500
(e) Future loss of income: 54,000 per year x factor of 56.5	3,051,000
TOTAL AWARD	**3,870,000**

6a. Amputation of leg above knee – 33% disability

(a) Pain and suffering during 1 year's acute illness	25,000
(b) Disability and detriment	224,000
(c) General inconvenience and expenses: 10,000 per year x factor of 19.1	191,000
(d) Loss of income: 15% x 180,000 x 1 year	27,000
After that, she is assumed to work again with the same income as before*	
TOTAL AWARD	**467,000**

6b. Amputation of leg below knee – 19% disability

(a) Pain and suffering during 1 year's acute illness	25,000
(b) Disability and detriment	136,000
(c) General inconvenience and expenses: 10,000 per year x factor of 19.1	191,000

(d) Loss of income: 15% x 180,000 x 1 year	27,000
TOTAL AWARD	**379,000**

7a. Amputation of arm above elbow – 40% disability

(a) Pain and suffering during 1 year's acute illness	25,000
(b) Disability and detriment	262,100
(c) General inconvenience and expenses: 10,000 per year x factor of 19.1	191,000
(d) Loss of income: 15% x 180,000 x 1 year	27,000
(e) If not returning to work as a secretary she has to do lower paid work and the loss is 30,000 annually until 65 years old and after that 66% 30,000 x factor of 56.5	
	1,695,000
TOTAL AWARD	**2,200,000**

7b. Amputation of arm below elbow – 46% disability

(a) Pain and suffering during 1 year's acute illness	25,000
(b) Disability and detriment?	310,200
(c) General inconvenience and expenses: 12,000 per year x factor of 19.1	229,200
(d) Loss of income: 15% x 180,000 x 1 year	27,000
(e) Loss of income: 30,000 x factor of 56.5	1,695,000
TOTAL AWARD	**2,286,000**

8a. Loss of eyesight, one eye – 17% disability

(a) Pain and suffering during 1 year's acute illness	25,000
(b) Disability and detriment	55,000
(c) General inconvenience and expenses: 4,000 per year x factor of 19.1	76,400
(d) Loss of income: 15% x 180,000 x 1 year	27,000
(Returns to work)	
TOTAL AWARD	**183,000**

8b. Total blindness – 68% disability

(a) Pain and suffering during 1 year's acute illness	15,000
(b) Disability and detriment	622,000
(c) General inconvenience and expenses: 15,000 per year x factor of 19.1	286,500
(d) Loss of income: 15% x 180,000 x 2.5 years	67,500
(e) Future loss of income: 54,000 x factor 56.5 until 65 years old, after that 66%	3,051,000
TOTAL AWARD	**4,042,000**

9. Deafness – 60% disability

(a) Pain and suffering during 1 year's acute illness	25,000
(b) Disability and detriment	300,000
(c) General inconvenience and expenses: 8,000 per year x factor of 19.1	152,800
(d) Loss of income: 15% x 180,000 x 1 year	27,000

(e) If not returning to work total loss of income: 54,000 x factor 56.5		3,081,000
TOTAL AWARD		**3,555,800**

10. Repetitive strain injury can be 7% – 35% disability

(a) Pain and suffering	15,000 –	20,000
(b) Disability and detriment	20,000 –	138,000
(c) General inconvenience: between 3,000 – 10,000 per year	58,000 –	191,000
(d) Loss of income: 1 year		27,000
(e) If not returning to work: 54,000 x 56.5		3,051,000
TOTAL AWARD	**93,000 –**	**3,927,000**

Total damages for 21% disability about 1,440,000

EFTA COUNTRIES*

* Because of the number of jurisdictions involved in this comparative report, changes in law in the 20 jurisdictions after January 2001 have not been incorporated.

ICELAND

Ingólfur Hjartarson

Introduction

In the event of physical injury, the victim is usually entitled to compensation from various compensation systems. The social security systems covers all Icelanders, and does not demand that the victim took any particular advance measures in order to be entitled to compensation. If any accident causes permanent disability assessed as 75% or higher, a disability pension will be paid. Various benefits from the social security system are linked to income, and thus victims with low income may be entitled to disability compensation if they have suffered disability lower than 75%, or to a higher compensation than persons of higher income. Every person is entitled to an old age pension after having attained the age of 67 years. Disabled persons are entitled to child benefits. Benefits are also paid upon the death of a spouse.

A person who suffers injury at work will also be entitled to compensation through the occupational accident insurance plans (see below). That person, or a surviving spouse and children if the accident was fatal, may also be entitled to benefits from the victim's pension fund, and every person accepting wages is obliged to contribute to a pension fund which is also used to pay retirement pensions.

In addition to the compensation and insurance arrangements noted a victim is entitled to compensation from the person responsible for his physical injury. In 1993 the Icelandic legislature passed an Act on Damages, using laws passed in the Nordic countries as models. According to that Act the party responsible for physical injury shall compensate for loss of payment for work rendered by the victim in his or her occupation, for suffering, for medical expenses, and for other financial loss. If the harmful event has permanent consequences compensation shall also be made for non-financial loss and disability, i.e. a permanent loss or reduction in earning ability.

Compensation according to the Act is partially standardised but efforts are made to take the victim's age and occupation into account. Compensation for physical injury is reduced by the amounts received by the victim from the Social Security

Institution for that loss or for the loss of a supporter, and likewise by various other payments of a social nature received by the victim from the occupational accident insurance plan, and by payments from pension funds partially. The payments are calculated to conform to current price levels. On the other hand compensation through accident insurance or other compensation plans entered into by the victim at his own initiative and cost is not deducted. The interest accruing from the date of an accident or from the date a claim for permanent disability is calculated at 4.5% however a delay in settlement will not justify the application of overdue interest.

Temporary loss of income from occupation

Compensation for temporary loss of income from employment shall be calculated for the period from the date of an accident until the victim can resume work or his health condition has stabilised. This is determined on the basis of information on his loss of income while he remains unable to attend his work, and by reference to medical certificates on his inability. The compensation is reduced by wages paid by his employer and by the compensation to which he is entitled in the event of accident or sickness. Compensation for such temporary loss of income is taxable.

Compensation for suffering

Such compensation is standardised and paid for the period from the date of an accident until the victim's condition has stabilised. It amounts to ISK 1,500 for each day the victim must remain in bed, and ISK 850 for each day he remains ambulant without having recovered. This compensation is not taxable.

Medical expenses

A victim is entitled to a refund of any expenses incurred on account of his accident. Direct outlays for medical services and nursing are usually small, as such expenses are largely paid from public funds.

Non-financial loss

The amount of compensation for permanent non-financial loss is largely determined by medical assessment. According to the Act on damages such loss shall be determined in degrees, by reference to the medical nature and consequences of the injury, and to the difficulties caused to the victim's private life. The compensation is standardised, depending on the age of the victim and the amount payable to victims aged 49 years of age and younger, is ISK 4,615,500. In special cases the compensation may be increased by 50%. Such compensation is not taxable.

Permanent disability

Where physical injury permanently affects a victim's ability to earn income, he is entitled to permanent disability compensation. Such disability shall be assessed by reference to any options that may be available to the victim for earning income by work he may be reasonably expected to perform. The assessment is both financial and medical, and differs in nature from the assessment of permanent non-financial loss. Consequently the assessment of the degree of permanent disability frequently differs from the assessment of the degree of non-financial loss under the Act.

Permanent disability compensation under the Act on Damages shall be determined as a lump sum and not as annuities or other regular payments. The compensation is standardised to some extent. It is payable equally to victims who have earned income from work and to those who have received little or no income from such sources.

The amount of disability compensation depends on the disability stage as determined according to the above and by reference to the victim's age and income prior to his accident. For persons who have had little or no income from employment it is based on certain minimum annual reference income, ISK 1,384,500 for persons 66 years of age and younger, which is reduced gradually with increased age. The Act however limits the annual maximum reference income to ISK 5,192,500. Permanent disability compensation is tax-free.

Loss of a supporter

A surviving spouse, a surviving cohabiting partner and children under 18 years of age who were by law entitled to support by the deceased person are entitled to compensation. In addition to burial costs they are compensated by standardised amount. The compensation due to a spouse or cohabiting partner is 30% of the amount the deceased person would have received on account of 100% permanent disability. A person who intentionally or by gross negligence causes the death of another person may also be ordered by judgment to pay compensation for non-financial loss of that person's spouse, children or parents.

General rules of settlement

Compensation for physical injury is reduced by payments received by a victim from the social security system on account of the injury or the loss of a support, and by various other payments of a social nature to which the victim may be entitled on account of his injury. On the other hand no reduction is made on account of accident insurance or other compensation which the victim may have procured privately by the payment of a premium.

Non-financial loss and permanent disability is generally assessed by doctors. Their opinion can be referred for revision by a particular committee instituted for the purpose. The parties may also agree between themselves to refer the matter to the committee without having procured an expert opinion in advance. Two of the committee members are doctors, and one a lawyer. In the case of a dispute as regards the assessment of the committee or other experts, the matter may be referred to the courts.

According to the Act on Damages compensation claims bear interest from the date of the harmful event, except claims for permanent disability, which bear interest from the original date of the assessed disability. The interest rate is 4.5% per annum, until overdue interest can lawfully be claimed.

Method of calculation for the examples given

The examples given are calculated on the basis of the same degree of permanent disability as in the previous publication. Non-financial loss is assumed to be of the same degree as the permanent disability, except for burn injuries, where there is no permanent disability, but non-financial loss is assessed at 25%. A provision in the Icelandic Act on Damage allowing a 50% increase in the amount of compensation for non-financial loss in cases involving 100% permanent disability is furthermore used. Assessment of disability is assumed to take place one year after the accident. In the examples compensation for suffering is assessed by reference to the period during which the victim may be expected to be unable to attend work. That period is however limited by the date of assessment of permanent disability, i.e. one year.

No medical and nursing expenses are assumed; as such expenses are normally paid from public funds. Temporary loss of income from work is estimated by reference to the nature of the injury for one year at a maximum. Reduction in temporary loss due to the fact that a victim may be entitled to wages from an employer after the accident, and also to compensation from the social security system, is not taken into account.

Moreover no account is taken of possible payments form the Social Security and occupational insurance plans provided for by law or of payments from pension funds.

Wages are updated by reference to general wage increases since the time of the previous publication. They are determined at ISK 5,900,000 in the case of the doctor and at ISK 1,700,000 in the case of the legal secretary.

All amounts are stated in ISK. The interest rate is as provided for in the Act on Damages, 4.5% annually. Interest on disability compensation accrues on the date of its assessment one year after the accident, and interest on other compensation accrues from the date of the accident. The date of settlement is assumed to be two and a half years after the accident.

Table 1. Schedule A

Claimant:	Man
Age:	40
Status:	Married, 2 dependent children aged 5 and 7
Occupation:	Doctor
Annual Income:	ISK. 5.900.000 gross p.a (ISK. 3.700.000 net)
Settlement:	2.5 years after accident

* Note: Compensation for temporary loss of income is reduced by wages paid by his employer and by the compensation to which he is entitled in the event of accident or sickness. Compensation for such temporary loss of income is taxable.

Compensation for physical injury is reduced by the amounts received by the victim from the Social Security Institution for that loss or for the loss of a supporter, and likewise by various other payments of social nature received by the victim for the occupational accident insurance plan and by payments from pension funds partially. The payments are calculated to conform to current price levels.

1. Instant Death

	ISK
a) Funeral expenses	300.000
b) Wife: Compensation	16.500.000
c) Child 5 years: Compensation	2.000.000
d) Child 7 years: Compensation	1.700.000
TOTAL AWARD	**20.500.000**

* Deduct welfare state benefits. See Note. Plus interest.

2. Burns Assume no permanent disability

a) Temporary loss of income, one year (net)	3.700.000
b) Pain and suffering	300.000
c) Non-financial loss	1.200.000
TOTAL AWARD	**5,200,000**

* Deduct welfare state benefits. See Note. Plus interest.

3. Quadriplegia 100% disability

a) Temporary loss of income, one year (net)	3.700.000
b) Pain and suffering	300.000
c) Non-financial loss	6.900.000
d) Permanent disability	53.800.000
TOTAL AWARD	**64.700.000**

* Deduct welfare state benefits. See Note. Plus interest.

4. Paraplegia

a) 100% disability

Temporary loss of income, one year (net)	3.700.000
Pain and suffering	300.000
Non-financial loss	6.900.000
Permanent disability	53.800.000
TOTAL AWARD	**64.700.000**

* Deduct welfare state benefits. See Note. Plus interest.

b) 75% disability

Temporary loss of income, one year (net)	3.700.000
Pain and suffering	300.000
Non-financial loss	3.500.000
Permanent disability	40.300.000
TOTAL AWARD	**47.800.000**

* Deduct welfare state benefits. See Note. Plus interest.

5. Brain damage

a) 100% disability

Temporary loss of income, one year (net)	3.700.000
Pain and suffering	300.000
Non-financial loss	6.900.000
Permanent disability	53.800.000
TOTAL AWARD	**64.700.000**

* Deduct welfare state benefits. See Note. Plus interest.

b) and c) 55% disability

Temporary loss of income, one year (net)	3.700.000
Pain and suffering	200.000
Non-financial loss	2.500.000
Permanent disability	29.600.000
TOTAL AWARD	**36.000.000**

* Deduct welfare state benefits. See Note. Plus interest.

d) 25% disability

Temporary loss of income, one year (net)	3.700.000
Pain and suffering	200.000
Non-financial loss	1.200.000
Permanent disability	13.500.000
TOTAL AWARD	**18.600.000**

* Deduct welfare state benefits. See Note. Plus interest.

6. Amputation of leg above knee

a) 65% disability

Temporary loss of income, one year (net)	3.700.000
Pain and suffering	200.000
Non-financial loss	3.000.000
Permanent disability	35.000.000
TOTAL AWARD	**41.900.000**

* Deduct welfare state benefits. See Note. Plus interest.

Amputation of leg below knee

b) 45% disability

Temporary loss of income, one year (net)	3.700.000
Pain and suffering	200.000
Non-financial loss	2.000.000
Permanent disability	35.000.000
TOTAL AWARD	**30.100.000**

* Deduct welfare state benefits. See Note. Plus interest.

7. Amputation of arm above elbow

a) 75% disability

Temporary loss of income, one year (net)	3.700.000
Pain and suffering	300.000
Non-financial loss	3.500.000
Permanent disability	40.300.000
TOTAL AWARD	**47.800.000**

* Deduct welfare state benefits. See Note. Plus interest.

Amputation of arm below elbow

b) 65% disability

Temporary loss of income, one year (net)	3.700.000
Pain and suffering	200.000
Non-financial loss	3.000.000
Permanent disability	35.000.000
TOTAL AWARD	**41.900.000**

* Deduct welfare state benefits. See Note. Plus interest.

8. Loss of eyesight. One eye without cosmetic disability

a) 20% disability

Temporary loss of income, one year (net)	3.700.000
Pain and suffering	200.000
Non-financial loss	900.000
Permanent disability	10.800.000
TOTAL AWARD	**15.600.000**

* Deduct welfare state benefits. See Note. Plus interest.

Loss of eyesight. One eye with cosmetic disability

b) 25% disability

Temporary loss of income, one year (net)	3.700.000
Pain and suffering	200.000
Non-financial loss	1.200.000
Permanent disability	13.500.000
TOTAL AWARD	**18.600.000**

* Deduct welfare state benefits. See Note. Plus interest.

Loss of Eyesight. Total blindness

c) 100% disability

Temporary loss of income, one year (net)	3.700.000
Pain and suffering	300.000
Non-financial loss	6.900.000
Permanent disability	53.800.000
TOTAL AWARD	**64.700.000**

* Deduct welfare state benefits. See Note. Plus interest.

9. Deafness with loss of speech

a) 60% disability

Temporary loss of income, one year (net)	3.700.000
Pain and suffering	200.000
Non-financial loss	2.800.000
Permanent disability	32.300.000
TOTAL AWARD	**39.000.000**

* Deduct welfare state benefits. See Note. Plus interest.

Total loss of hearing in one year

b) 10% disability

Pain and suffering	100.000
Non-financial loss	500.000
Permanent disability	5.400.000
TOTAL AWARD	**6.000.000**

* Deduct welfare state benefits. See Note. Plus interest.

10. Repetitive strain injury. Complete loss of function in wrist

a) 25% disability

Temporary loss of income, one year (net)	3.700.000
Pain and suffering	200.000
Non-financial loss	1.200.000
Permanent disability	13.500.000
TOTAL AWARD	**18.600.000**

* Deduct welfare state benefits. See Note. Plus interest.

Repetitive strain injury with significant permanent and (c) persistent pain and stiffness

b) 15% disability

Temporary loss of income, one year (net)	1.800.000
Pain and suffering	100.000
Non-financial loss	700.000
Permanent disability	8.200.000
TOTAL AWARD	**10.800.000**

* Deduct welfare state benefits. See Note. Plus interest.

Table 2. Schedule B

Claimant:	Woman
Age:	20
Status:	Single
Occupation:	Legal Secretary
Annual Income:	ISK. 1,700.000 gross p.a (1.300.000 net)
Settlement:	2,5 years after accident

*Note: Compensation for temporary loss of income is reduced by wages paid by his employer and by the compensation to which he is entitled in the event of accident or sickness. Compensation for such temporary loss of income is taxable.

Compensation for physical injury is reduced by the amounts received by the victim from the Social Security Institution for that loss or for the loss of a supporter, and likewise by various other payments of social nature received by the victim for the occupational accident insurance plan and by payments from pension funds partially. The payments are calculated to conform to current price levels.

* Deduct welfare state benefits. See Note. Plus interest.

1. Instant Death

a) Funeral expenses	300.000

2. Burns Assume no permanent disability

a) Temporary loss of income, one year (net)	1.300.000
b) Pain and suffering	300.000
c) Non-financial loss	1.200.000
TOTAL AWARD	**2.800.000**

* Deduct welfare state benefits. See Note. Plus interest.

3. Quadriplegia 100% disability

a) Temporary loss of income, one year (net)	1.300.000
b) Pain and suffering	300.000
c) Non-financial loss	6.900.000
d) Permanent disability	30.800.000
TOTAL AWARD	**39.300.000**

* Deduct welfare state benefits. See Note. Plus interest.

4. Paraplegia

a) 100% disability	
Temporary loss of income, one year (net)	1.300.000
Pain and suffering	300.000
Non-financial loss	6.900.000
Permanent disability	30.800.000
TOTAL AWARD	**39.300.000**

* Deduct welfare state benefits. See Note. Plus interest.

b) 75% disability

Temporary loss of income, one year (net)	1.300.000
Pain and suffering	300.000
Non-financial loss	3.500.000
Permanent disability	23.100.000
TOTAL AWARD	**28.200.000**

* Deduct welfare state benefits. See Note. Plus interest.

5. Brain damage

a) 100% disability

Temporary loss of income, one year (net)	1.300.000
Pain and suffering	300.000
Non-financial loss	6.900.000
Permanent disability	30.800.000
TOTAL AWARD	**39.300.000**

* Deduct welfare state benefits. See Note. Plus interest.

b) and c) 55% disability

Temporary loss of income, one year (net)	1.300.000
Pain and suffering	200.000
Non-financial loss	2.500.000
Permanent disability	17.000.000
TOTAL AWARD	**21.000.000**

* Deduct welfare state benefits. See Note. Plus interest.

d) 25% disability

Temporary loss of income, one year (net)	1.300.000
Pain and suffering	200.000
Non-financial loss	1.200.000
Permanent disability	7.700.000
TOTAL AWARD	**10.400.000**

* Deduct welfare state benefits. See Note. Plus interest.

6. Amputation of leg above knee

a) 65% disability

Temporary loss of income, one year (net)	1.300.000
Pain and suffering	200.000
Non-financial loss	3.000.000
Permanent disability	20.000.000
TOTAL AWARD	**24.500.000**

* Deduct welfare state benefits. See Note. Plus interest.

Amputation of leg below knee

b) 45% disability

Temporary loss of income, one year (net)	1.300.000
Pain and suffering	200.000
Non-financial loss	2.000.000
Permanent disability	13.900.000
TOTAL AWARD	**17.400.000**

* Deduct welfare state benefits. See Note. Plus interest.

7. Amputation of arm above elbow

a) 75% disability

Temporary loss of income, one year (net)	1.300.000
Pain and suffering	300.000
Non-financial loss	3.500.000
Permanent disability	23.100.000
TOTAL AWARD	**28.200.000**

* Deduct welfare state benefits. See Note. Plus interest.

Amputation of arm below elbow

b) 65% disability

Temporary loss of income, one year (net)	1.300.000
Pain and suffering	200.000
Non-financial loss	3.000.000
Permanent disability	20.000.000
TOTAL AWARD	**24.500.000**

* Deduct welfare state benefits. See Note. Plus interest.

8. Loss of eyesight. One eye without cosmetic disability

a) 20% disability

Temporary loss of income, one year (net)	1.300.000
Pain and suffering	200.000
Non-financial loss	900.000
Permanent disability	6.200.000
TOTAL AWARD	**8.600.000**

* Deduct welfare state benefits. See Note. Plus interest.

Loss of eyesight. One eye with cosmetic disability

b) 25% disability

Temporary loss of income, one year (net)	1.300.000
Pain and suffering	200.000
Non-financial loss	1.200.000
Permanent disability	7.700.000
TOTAL AWARD	**10.400.000**

* Deduct welfare state benefits. See Note. Plus interest.

Loss of eyesight. Total blindness

c) 100% disability

Temporary loss of income, one year (net)	1.300.000
Pain and suffering	300.000
Non-financial loss	6.900.000
Permanent disability	30.800.000
TOTAL AWARD	**39.300.000**

* Deduct welfare state benefits. See Note. Plus interest.

9. Deafness with loss of speech

a) 60% disability

Temporary loss of income, one year (net)	1.300.000
Pain and suffering	200.000
Non-financial loss	2.800.000
Permanent disability	18.500.000
TOTAL AWARD	**22.800.000**

* Deduct welfare state benefits. See Note. Plus interest.

Total loss of hearing in one year

b) 10% disability

Pain and suffering	100.000
Non-financial loss	500.000
Permanent disability	3.200.000
TOTAL AWARD	**3.800.000**

* Deduct welfare state benefits. See Note. Plus interest.

10. Repetitive strain injury. Complete loss of function in wrist

a) 25% disability

Temporary loss of income, one year (net)	1.300.000
Pain and suffering	200.000
Non-financial loss	1.200.000
Permanent disability	7.700.000
TOTAL AWARD	**10.400.000**

* Deduct welfare state benefits. See Note. Plus interest.

Repetitive strain injury with significant permanent and (c) persistent pain and stiffness

b) 15% disability

Temporary loss of income, one year (net)	700.000
Pain and suffering	100.000
Non-financial loss	700.000
Permanent disability	4.700.000
TOTAL AWARD	**6.200.000**

* Deduct welfare state benefits. See Note. Plus interest.

LIECHTENSTEIN

Dr Andreas Girsberger

Introduction

Detailed awards in personal injury matters are scarce in the Principality of Liechtenstein with a population of hardly 30,000 and therefore little litigation of that kind is on record compared to larger jurisdiction such as Germany or even Switzerland.

The basic legal provisions for the determination of damages in cases of fatal and non-fatal personal injuries are sections 1325 and 1327 of the Austrian General Civil Code (ABGB) which codification has been integrated into Liechtenstein law to a considerable extent. Article 1325 provides compensation in cases of non-fatal injuries as follows:

> Whoever causes personal injury is bound to compensate the injured person for medical expenses. He also has to compensate any loss of gain which the injured person has suffered or is about to suffer in future as a result of having become incapacitated for work. Moreover, upon special demand, adequate compensation is to be paid for pain and suffering.

Article 1327 is specifically directed to case of fatal injuries by providing:

> If the injury has resulted in death, full compensation is due not only for all costs involved but also for any loss sustained by those who through the death of the injured person have been deprived of their support.

As far as the so-called pecuniary damages for pain and suffering are concerned the basic principle expressed in the last sentence of Article 1325 is supplemented by a number of further provisions, partly derived from Swiss law, which gives the judge a large measure of discretion in awarding such a particular indemnity in addition to damages in the strict meaning of the word.

From the few reported cases the following awards can be noted:

A decision of the Liechtenstein Supreme Court headed by a prominent Austrian professor of law was rendered on 6 May 1991. Although the injury was a relatively minor one the decision is interesting for the general principles expressed in it as to the mechanics of personal injury assessments. The injury consisted in a perforation of the eardrum. Instant surgery had resulted in complete recovery but the injured party had felt severe pain during a certain period of time and there had even been some reason to fear that the ear would remain slightly affected permanently. Medical expenses and temporary loss of gain were not in dispute. The controversy which occupied first the trial court, then the Court of Appeals and finally the Supreme Court of the Liechtenstein Principality was restricted to the question of adequate indemnification for pain and suffering.

In its initial statement the Supreme Court pointed out that Liechtenstein practice in personal injury matters mainly followed Austrian doctrine and jurisprudence. Measuring the case by Austrian precedents the court came to the conclusion that the particular injury with its effects on the person who had suffered it would have deserved compensation of ATS 10,000 for pain and suffering. In order to compensate for the differences existing between Austrian and Liechtenstein economically and with regard to currency fluctuations the court applied a multiplier first of 1.3 for the currency factor and subsequently of 1.7 for the cost of living factor, thereby reaching a sum of CHF 2,700, which was reduced to CHF 2,500 after taking into account contributory negligence.

That Liechtenstein also takes into account personal injury awards rendered in Switzerland is evidenced by a decision of the country's Appellate court of 28 June 1984 (published in *Liechtenstein court Reports 1987*, pp. 29-31). The plaintiff was the victim of a motor-car accident. He suffered various fractures which required repeated surgery. He was unable to work for the greater part of 1981 and 1982. Although his working capacity was finally restored there remained residual effects such as an increased sensibility to changes of weather and a swollen knee after hours of walking. In determining the amount payable for pain and suffering the appellate judge looked for comparable cases from Austria as well as from Switzerland. After quoting an example from Austria with an indemnity of ATS 100,000 in 1980 the court referred to a number of awards taken from the Swiss jurisdiction and accordingly fixed its award for pain and suffering at CHF. 35,000.

Increased reliance on Swiss practice is often explained in Liechtenstein legal circles by the fact that motor-car liability insurance is mostly written by Swiss companies which tend to apply their own standards of indemnification. This aspect of insurance gave rise to a decision of the Liechtenstein Court of Appeals of 9 September 1982 (*Liechtenstein Court Report 1983*, pp 132-134). There, a man had been injured in a motor-car accident. After long and complicated medical treatment he was again able to do his job without any future loss of salary which amounted to CHF. 30,000 annually. Medically, however, his general faculties appeared to be diminished which induced the liability insurer to agree on a payment for a so-called abstract or theoretical impairment of the man's physical integrity. Compensation was calculated by capitalising 20% of the salary based on the actuarial tables with a resulting amount of CHF 122,700. Since there was no proof of an actual loss of salary, however, this sum was reduced to 50% of it and the remaining CHF 61,350 were once more reduced to a final CHF 50,000 in a purely pragmatic fashion. A settlement was accepted on that basis.

When the liability insurer then sought to recover at least part of this expense from its insured who was apparently grossly negligent, the court denied the claim on the grounds that a lenient insurance practice was not binding in law. The payment was not designated as an indemnity for pain and suffering but as an item of pecuniary damages for which there was not sufficient evidence, given the fact that the man was still earning the same salary as before including all future benefits.

To summary the situation in Liechtenstein, it can be safely stated that irrespective of whether Austrian law or also to a certain extent, Swiss law is applied the practice tends to follow the example of the leading Swiss liability insurers in assessing the settling damages as a result of fatal as well as non-fatal injuries.

Future Developments

Presently, in Switzerland as well as in Liechtenstein, legislative steps are being taken to improve the situation of plaintiffs in personal injury cases. Higher standards of care are applied and the requirements for proving negligence are lowered. The particular items of damages and their computation, however, remain more or less the same. A project for a reform of the law of torts containing 55 Articles came out in 1996 but will not be enacted in the foreseeable future. It can be safely stated, therefore, that for at least the first decade of the new millennium personal injury claims will be dealt with in Switzerland as well as in Liechtenstein in the same may as in the previous decade .

NORWAY

Pål Mitsem

Introduction

Norway has a system of comprehensive National Health coverage. In accidents or in the case of occupational injuries, the coverage would comprise:

- All hospital costs
- All doctors' bills
- All costs of medicines
- Scheduled travel costs to hospitals and doctors
- Costs of special equipment necessitated by disability, such as wheelchair, modification to car, special lift, etc.
- Schedule contributions during temporary disablement and for retraining.
- Schedule contribution for extra help at home
- Schedule costs of funerals
- Special contribution for a spouse bereaved of a supporter, with a view to facilitate the spouse's own professional career.
- Special child contribution for children under 18 bereaved of a supporter.

In the case of other injuries, for instance for which no specific cause can be pointed out, most of the items will be covered. However, there will be deductibles from the coverage of doctors' bills and the cost of medicines.

In most cases, actual costs may exceed scheduled costs. Tort law damages for the economic loss should cover the discrepancy. No effort will be made to assess what the discrepancy might be in the cases below; this should be covered by the tortfeasor or the insurance company in addition to the figures given.

The contributions for bereaved persons and children will never compensate the actual loss, but will reduce the said loss. This mitigating factor is taken into account below.

All employers are obliged by law to have occupational injuries insurance.[1] These injuries are covered according to special schedules, which for most people are about the same as tort law damages. Schedule A below is assumed to be an occupational injury. In other examples, normal tort law calculations have been applied. The occupational injury coverage does not require a specific calamitous event. Injuries caused by exposure to harmful substances, noise, light etc. will be covered. However, repetitive strain injuries, of the kind set out in the examples, will not be covered under the occupational injury insurance.

A distinction is made between economic and non-economic damages. The economic damages should cover the loss of earnings as well as costs not covered by the comprehensive National Health coverage. An example could be the cost of modifying a house which are not picked up by the National Health coverage.

Compensation for past loss of income up to the date of the award is taxable as is the interest on the loss for each year. Thus, full compensation must include the tax element in respect of the interest which will be assessed,[2] and should leave the injured party with the same net amount as if the income had been earned and taxed in the normal manner.[3]

Compensation for *permanent* loss of future income is not taxable, thus, it is the net annual loss after deduction of taxes which should be computed, and discounted to the date of the award.[4] The method of actuarial discounting assumes that both the capital amount and future interest on the remaining capital amount will be available to provide the annual amount of compensation. This assumption is not valid, however, in as much as the annual amount of interest is subject to income tax and as the remaining capital is subject to net wealth tax. Thus, an additional amount of compensation must be paid to cover future income tax on interest and net wealth tax. Since this additional amount, referred to as *tax disadvantage compensation,* is also subject to tax on interest and net wealth the tax on the tax must

---

1 In the case that an employer fails to arrange an insurance policy the compensation to the employee is paid from a pooling arrangement between the insurance companies.

2 Including a tax element in respect of the interest.

3 The process of calculating the amounts inclusive of tax is referred to as grossing up.

4 In the case of occupational injuries, covered by insurance, the amount of compensation follows from a schedule, which is based on the percentage of occupational disability. In establishing the schedule, account has been taken of the likely loss of income with a calculation as described here.

also be taken into account. Only the advent of personal computers and spreadsheet programs have made it possible for lawyers to prepare actuarial calculations covering these points.

All calculations of economic damages are made on a differential basis. On the one hand there is the question of what the injured party would have earned had he not been injured. On the other, the question is what income and social security benefits the injured party will enjoy, despite his injuries. The calculation of the gross amount of damages, with deduction of the amount of social security payments, is not made. It is the difference in income on a year to year basis which is subject of the calculation of damages.

Insurance payments, other than National Health coverage are deducted in full if the insurance has been provided by the paying party. If the insurance was obtained by the injured party for his own benefit it is up to the discretion of the court to make deductions; a reasonable amount will be deducted if the insurance payments are considerable.

The Non-economic damages consist of two elements. The most important element is medical disability compensation, which is a scheduled compensation amount from a table which is based on the degree of lasting medical disability. A table has been established, and most injuries will be assigned a percentage – on a scale from 0% to 110%.[5]

The actual medical disability is calculated from the percentage, the age of the injured person at the time of the accident and the so-called basic amount of the National Health coverage at the time of the award. The income of the injured party is not relevant. There is a possibility of "upgrading" an injury that causes a greater harm to the enjoyment of life than the actual injury, and related percentage, indicates.

In the calculations below, I have used the disability percentages stipulated by the publishers. This is the only way we can compare the cases between the various countries. The differences that existed previously between Norwegian disability percentages, and those of the continent, have been considerably reduced with the new disability percentages introduced in 1997.

There is also the possibility of claiming common law non-economic damages for pain and suffering or other limitations to the fulfilment of life that a court finds

---

5 Actually, the regulations specify injuries up to 100% and establish a new class for injuries which are considerably more burdensome than those to which a percentage of 100 have been assigned.

to be compensatable (confinement to a bed for a year, etc.) However this requires gross negligence by the responsible party, which in most instances must be a physical person. Common law non-economic damages awards have traditionally been very conservative. I will disregard this element in the actual examples, but for your information, such compensation would typically be of the order of a NOK 50,000 (£3,791) lump sum payment.

I am assuming for the purpose of the calculations below that legal liability has been established, and that it is only a matter of calculating the compensation. I am further assuming that the discretionary powers of the court to reduce the award in view of the circumstances of the responsible party will not be exercised. The calculations are actuarial spreadsheet calculations that will not lend themselves to easy explanation. Thus the results only will be given.

The assumptions made in the English calculations have been followed, with any modifications specifically stated.

Table 1. Schedule A

Claimant :	Man
Age :	40 (at the time of accident)
Status :	Married – 2 dependent children aged 5 and 7 (at the time of the accident)
Occupation :	Doctor
Income :	NOK 500,000 (low average for the position)
Trial :	2½ years from accident to award

1. Instant death NOK

It is assumed that compensation will be paid by the occupational injury Insurer. If this was not the case the actual income of the wife would have to be taken into account

a) Funeral expenses (supplemental to scheduled National Heath coverage), incl. Interest		30,500
b) Wife		
c) Compensation	704,300	
d) Interest	208,200	
		912,500
e) Child, 5 years		
f) Compensation	234,800	
g) Interest	69,400	
		304,200
h) Child, 7 years		
i) Compensation	187,800	
j) Interest	55,600	
		243,400
TOTAL AWARD		**1,490,600**

2. Burns (A, B, C)

It is assumed that sickness benefits will cover the loss of earnings for the first year. It is further assumed that temporary disablement/retraining contributions will be available for a further year, in an amount of NOK 205,000.

a) Medical disability compensation	74,000

b) Economic damages		
a) Loss of (past) income	412,600	
b) Interest	20,000	
		432,600
TOTAL AWARD		**506,600**

3. Quadriplegia

Assumptions in relation to sickness benefits as above. After this period, a National Health pension in an amount of NOK 185,000, with the addition of child supplement, is assumed.

a) Medical disability compensation		665,200
b) Economic damages		
Loss of past income	412,600	
Interest	20,000	
		432,600
Future loss	1,895,500	
Tax compensation	513,200	
		2,408,700
TOTAL AWARD		**3,506,500**

4. Paraplegia

a) Medical disability compensation		443,500
b) Economic damages		
Loss of past income	412,600	
Interest	20,000	
		432,600

Future loss	1,895,500	
Tax compensation	513,200	
		2,408,700
TOTAL AWARD		**3,284,800**

5a. Brain damage, 80% disability

a) Medical disability compensation		549,100
b) Economic damages		
Loss of past income	412,600	
Interest	20,000	
		432,600
Future loss	1,895,500	
Tax compensation	513,200	
		2,408,700
TOTAL AWARD		**3,390,400**

5b. Brain damage, 90% disability

a) Medical disability compensation		665,200
b) Economic damages		
Loss of past income	412,600	
Interest	20,000	
		432,600
Future loss	1,895,500	
Tax compensation	513,200	
		2,408,700
TOTAL AWARD		**3,506,500**

6a. Amputation of leg above knee

It is assumed that work is resumed after a 2½ year period of recovery

a) Medical disability compensation		191,000
b) Economic damages		
Loss of past income	412,600	
Interest	20,000	
		432,600
TOTAL AWARD		**622,700**

6b. Amputation of leg below knee

It is assumed that work is resumed after a 2½ period of recovery

a) Medical disability compensation		126,700
b) Economic damages		
Loss of past income	412,600	
Interest	20,000	
		432,600
TOTAL AWARD		**559,300**

7a. Amputation of arm above elbow

It is assumed that work is resumed after a 2½ year period of recovery

a) Medical disability compensation		190,100
b) Economic damages		
Loss of past income	412,600	
Interest	20,000	
		432,600
TOTAL AWARD		**622,700**

7b. Amputation of arm below elbow

It is assumed that work is resumed after a 2½ year period of recover

a) Medical disability compensation		126,700
b) Economic damages		
Loss of past income	412,600	
Interest	20,000	
		432,600
TOTAL AWARD		**559,300**

8a. Loss of eyesight in one eye, without cosmetic disability

It is assumed that sickness benefits will cover the period until work can be resumed

a) Medical disability compensation	126,700
TOTAL AWARD	**126,700**

8b. Loss of eyesight in one eye, with cosmetic disability

It is assumed that work is resumed after a 2½ year period of recovery period

a) Medical disability compensation	126,700
TOTAL AWARD	**126,700**

8c. Total blindness

a) Medical disability compensation		665,200
b) Economic damages		
Loss of past income	412,600	
Interest	20,000	
		432,600

Future loss	1,895,500	
Tax compensation	513,200	
		2,408,700
TOTAL AWARD		**3,506,500**

9. Deafness

It is assumed that work is resumed after a 2½ year period of recovery but with reduced income

a) Medical disability compensation		264,000
b) Economic damages		
Loss of past income	412,600	
Interest	20,000	
		432,600
Future loss	617,200	
Tax compensation	107,800	
		725,000
TOTAL AWARD		**1,421,600**

10. Repetitive Strain Injury

It is assumed that the doctor in question will suffer from persistent pain and stiffness. It is further assumed that he will be able to resume lighter duties, with a total income of NOK 400,000 per year, six months after the injury.

a) Medical disability compensation		74,000
b) Economic damages		
Loss of past income	199,800	
Interest	11,400	
		211,200

Future loss	617,200	
Tax compensation	107,800	
		725,000
TOTAL AWARD		**1,101,200**

Table 2. Schedule B

Claimant :	Woman
Age :	20 (at the time of the accident)
Status :	Single
Occupation :	Legal Secretary
Income :	NOK 184,000 pa (low) NOK 197,700 pa (average) NOK 220,100 pa (high)
Trial :	2½ years from accident to award. Calculations made for salary of NOK 197,700

1. Instant death

It is assumed that compensation will be paid by the occupational injury insurer.

a) Funeral expenses (supplemental to scheduled National Health coverage) inclusive of interest 30,500

2. Burns (A, B, C)

It is assumed that sickness benefits will cover the loss of earnings for the first year. It is further assumed that temporary disablement/retraining contributions will be available for a further year in an amount of NOK 135,000.

a) Medical disability compensation 85,200

b) Economic damages		
Loss of (past) income	78,800	
Interest	4,900	
		83,700
TOTAL AWARD		**168,900**

3. Quadriplegia

Assumptions in relation to sickness benefits as above. After this period, a National Health pension in an amount of NOK 120,000, is assumed, after a year with NOK 135,000.

a) Medical disability compensation		766,200
b) Economic damages		
Loss of past income	78,800	
Tax compensation	4,900	
		83,700
Future loss	728,700	
Tax compensation	230,000	
		958,700
TOTAL AWARD		**1,808,600**

4. Paraplegia

a) Medical disability compensation		510,800
b) Economic damages		
Loss of past income	78,800	
Interest	4,900	
		83,700

Future loss	728,700	
Tax compensation	230,000	
		958,700
TOTAL AWARD		**1,543,200**

5a. Brain damage, 80% disability

a) Medical disability compensation		632,400
b) Economic damages		
Loss of past income	78,800	
Interest	4,900	
		83,700
Future loss	728,700	
Tax compensation	230,000	
		958,700
TOTAL AWARD		**1,674,800**

5b. Brain damage, 90% disability

a) Medical disability compensation		766,200
b) Economic damages		
Loss of past income	78,800	
Interest	4,900	
		83,700
Future loss	728,700	
Tax compensation	230,000	
		958,700
TOTAL AWARD		**1,808,600**

6a. Amputation of leg above knee

It is assumed that work is resumed after a 2½ year period of recovery.

a) Medical disability compensation		218,900
b) Economic damages		
Loss of past income	78,800	
Interest	4,900	
		83,700
TOTAL AWARD		**302,600**

6b. Amputation of leg below knee

It is assumed that work is resumed after a 2½ year period of recovery.

a) Medical disability compensation		146,000
b) Economic damages		
Loss of past income	78,800	
Interest	4,900	
		83,700
TOTAL AWARD		**229,700**

7a. Amputation of arm above elbow

It is assumed that work is resumed after a 2½ year period of recovery.

a) Medical disability compensation		218,900
b) Economic damages		
Loss of past income	78,800	
Interest	4,900	
		83,700
TOTAL AWARD		**302,600**

7b. Amputation of arm below elbow

It is assumed that work is resumed after a 2½ year period of recovery.

a) Medical disability compensation		146,000
b) Economic damages		
Loss of past income	78,800	
Interest	4,900	
		83,700
TOTAL AWARD		**229,700**

8a. Loss of eyesight in one eye without cosmetic disability

It is assumed that sickness benefits will cover the period until work can be resumed.

a) Medical disability compensation	146,000
TOTAL AWARD	**146,000**

8b. Loss of eyesight in one eye, with cosmetic disability

It is assumed that work is resumed after a 2½ year period of recovery.

a) Medical disability compensation	146,000
TOTAL AWARD	**146,000**

8c. Total blindness

a) Medical disability compensation		766,200
b) Economic damages		
Loss of past income	78,800	
Interest	4,900	
		83,700

Future loss	728,700	
Tax compensation	230,000	
		958,700
TOTAL AWARD		**1,808,600**

9. Deafness

It is assumed that work is resumed after a 2½ year period of recovery.

a) Medical disability compensation		304,100
b) Economic damages		
Loss of past income	78,800	
Interest	4,900	
		83,700
Future loss	504,200	
Tax compensation	129,500	
		633,700
TOTAL AWARD		**1,021,500**

10. Repetitive strain injury

It is assumed that the legal secretary in question will suffer from persistent pain and stiffness. It is further assumed that she will be able to resume lighter duties, with a total income of NOK 150,000 per year, six months after the injury.

a) Medical disability compensation		85,200
b) Economic damages		
Loss of past income	95,300	
Interest	7,100	
		102,400

Future loss	504,200	
Tax compensation	129,500	
		633,700
TOTAL AWARD		**821,300**

SWITZERLAND

Dr Andreas Girsberger

Introduction

All personal injury awards, once liability has been established, are based on either Article 45 of the Swiss Federal Code of Obligation (in case of fatal injuries) or Article 46 of the Code (in case of non-fatal injuries). These two provisions are worded as follows:

> Article 45
>
> Where a person has been killed, the damages include expenses, particularly the funeral expenses.
>
> Where death did not immediately follow, the compensation will include the cost of medical treatment and the damages resulting from the inability for work.
>
> Where death causes any dependents to lose their support, the damages resulting therefrom must also be paid.

> Article 46
>
> The person who has been injured is entitled to compensation for the expenses as well as the losses resulting from total or partial disability for work, due regard being had to the detriment inflicted on the economic future of the injured party.
>
> Where the consequences of the injury cannot be ascertained with sufficient certainty at the time when judgment was rendered, the court may reserve the right to have it amended within two years after the date thereof.

In cases of fatal injuries, those who were close to the deceased such as the surviving spouse, children, the fiancé(e), persons living together in a quasi-marital relationship and sometimes even brothers and sisters are entitled to special compensation for grief and bereavement based on Article 47 of the Swiss Code of Obligations. In cases of non-fatal injuries similar compensation in addition to pecuniary damages may be claimed by the injured party equally based on Article 47 of the Code, particularly when the injury has resulted in permanent mental or bodily harm.

The prevailing parameters for personal fatal and non-fatal injury awards were fixed by the Federal Supreme Court of Switzerland in the following decisions:

Fatal injuries

By a judgment of 2 June 1987 the Swiss Supreme Court (*Supreme Court Reports,* Civil Law Part, Volume 113, pp. 323-344) settled a dispute where the victim of a motorcar accident was a 36-year-old married man who left a 33-year-old widow and three children. The accident happened in 1980. The income earned by the man as an employee in the year prior to the accident amounted to Swiss Francs (Sw Fr.) 41,753. The children's loss of support was mainly covered by the Federal Accident Insurance Board which automatically acquired their claims against the party liable for the accident. The Supreme Court held that in the case of an average wage earner the amount of his income required to support his wife and children varies between 65-70%.

In this case the youngest of the three children became self-supporting by 1988, i.e. eight years after their father's accidental death. As long as the widow and children continued to live together the widow was compensated for 40% of what her husband would have continued to earn and each child for 10%. National Accident Insurance took care of that part and obtained recovery from the liable party in a separate negotiation.

What remained to be determined were pecuniary damages for the widow based on Article 45 of the Code for the period after 1988 as well as non-pecuniary damages (so-called *tort moral* in the French wording of the Code) based on Article 47 of the Code both for the widow and for each of the three children. All the respective items of damages were taken up by the Supreme Court in a way which can serve as a model for determining personal injury awards in fatal accident cases generally. The first and principal item of pecuniary damages was the loss of future support which would have been provided by the husband. As pointed out before, his annual income prior to death was Sw Fr. 41,753. The Supreme Court followed the trial court in that it adjusted the income for the calculation of future damages to an amount of Sw Fr. 50,000 by taking into account various economic factors such as the general depreciation of monetary value of a successively higher salary of the husband. The widow's hypothetical quota of her husband's income was assumed to be 57.5%, i.e. Sw Fr 28,750 annually once the children had become self-supporting. By then the widow would be 41 years old.

The rule in Switzerland for compensating annual support is to award capital instead of an annuity. The standard method consists applying the actuarial tables of Stauffer/Schaetzle which are based on statistical material in evaluating life expectancy and average periods of professional activity. In that particular case the Supreme Court took the middle between life expectancy and professional activity by multiplying Sw Fr. 28,750 by a factor of 12.13, effective from 1988, for the remaining period of the combined lives of husband and wife. This produced a capital sum of Sw Fr. 353,912 which was reduced by 21% on account of the so-called remarrying expectancy statistically established for a 41-year-old widow with grown-up children. From this amount there had to be deducted the capitalised served by the National Accident Insurance Board on the one hand (amounting to Sw Fr. 12,510 annually) and by the National Pension Scheme on the other hand (amounting to Sw Fr. 9,750 annually) which left a net amount of Sw Fr. 70,931 to be awarded against the motor-car insurer of the party liable for the accident. Again, however, one has to bear in mind that the National Accident Insurance Board as well as the carrier of the National Pension Scheme probably succeeded in recovering their accumulated annuity payments against the liable party in a separate negotiation.

Funeral expenses, recoverable under Article 45 of the Code were fixed at Sw Fr. 5,189.20. A further amount of Sw Fr. 700 was awarded for black dresses in connection with the funeral but a claim for expenses required for the maintenance and upkeep of the grave was denied. A last item concerned additional non-pecuniary damages for grief and bereavement. Finding that there had been contributory negligence on the husband's part the Court awarded the widow Sw Fr. 20,000 and each child Sw Fr. 10,000.

Independently of the distribution of Court and lawyers' fees for the proceedings, the Court awarded an additional amount of Sw Fr. 3,130 for so-called pre-trial legal expenses which were considered to be part of the damages comparable to medical expenses or similar costs accruing to the party affected by the event out of which liability arises.

The above case and the way it was decided by the Supreme Court are illustrative for awards in fatal injury matters generally. Without the husband's contributory negligence the special payment for grief and bereavement would probably have reached Sw Fr. 30,000 for the widow and Sw Fr. 15,000 for each child. Otherwise, the parameters fixed by the Court for the widow and Sw Fr 15,000 for each child be applied in almost every fatal injury case .

Non-fatal injuries

The most recent non-fatal injury case was dealt with by the Supreme Court in a judgment of 8 May (*Supreme Court Reports*, Civil Law Part, Volume 116, pp. 295-300). It involved a man whose left leg had remained partly paralysed due to negligence of a surgeon. The surgery had taken place prior to 1978. After having been completely unable to work during a long recovery period the man – a trained electrician – resumed after December 1978 but only on a half-time basis due to the malfunctioning of his left leg. His work pre injury income amounted to approximately Sw Fr. 40,000 per year.

At the time of the damaging event the man was in his mid-thirties. The liability insurer offered and paid out an amount of Sw Fr. 436,500 which the injured man felt was insufficient. He sued for an additional Sw Fr. 650,000. It took until 1989 for the trial Court to give a judgment and the Plaintiff was awarded Sw Fr. 300,000. On appeal the Supreme Court raised the award to Sw Fr. 365,000. The essential factors in determining compensation for loss of gain and for pain and suffering were as follows:

The trial Court adjusted Plaintiff's income for the 10 years up to 1989 to an average of Sw Fr. 55,000 by taking into account the higher cost of living as well as probable increases in the Plaintiff's income. Damages for loss of salary during the recovery period and for the time after December 1978 to the date of judgment in 1989 reached approximately Sw Fr. 380,000 on account of which (and on account of future damages) the liability insurer had already paid out Sw Fr. 436,500.

Future loss of income had to be capitalised, again by applying the actuarial tables of Stauffer/Schaetzle which are standard in Switzerland.

Plaintiff had reached the age of 47 in 1989.

The multiplier for a 47-year-old male based on his remaining period of professional activity is 12.21. The applicable income for that period was assumed to be an average of Sw Fr. 61,000, again taking into account increases in living costs and salary. The multiplication of 50% of Sw Fr. 61,000 by 12.21 produced a capital of Sw Fr. 372, 405.

The Plaintiff sustained a further loss since his employer had only to make pension contributions on half of the salary instead of the entire one as before. Capitalisation of those contributions produced a further amount of Sw Fr. 26,630, thus raising the total sum to Sw Fr. 399,035.

The pain and suffering the Plaintiff had asked an additional Sw Fr. 40,000 but received only Sw Fr. 20,000.

Since approximately Sw Fr. 55,000 of the above amounts was already included in the insurer's initial payment of Sw Fr. 436,000 the balance to be awarded amounted to Sw Fr. 365,000. Altogether the victim of the accident thus received from the liable party a total sum of Sw Fr. 800,000 in round figures (insurer's initial payment of Sw Fr. 436,500 plus additional Sw Fr. 365,000 awarded by the Supreme Court).

Swiss legal interest of 5% was payable as from the date of the trial Court's judgment.

It goes without saying that medical expenses too are deemed to be compensable, but apparently had not been covered by the National Health Scheme so that they were not an issue in the litigation.

The above case offers a good example of what a professionally active person can expect to be awarded by way of damages for loss of income resulting from a reduced capacity for work. In this case the Claimant was an average wage-earner injured in his mid-thirties with a pre-accident salary of around Sw Fr. 40,000 which the courts thought would have gone up to a maximum of approximately Sw Fr. 60,000 in the course of his professional career.

The corresponding personal injury payment without medical expenses totalled Sw Fr. 800,000. Higher salaries and losses thereof resulting from a reduced capacity for work are therefore apt to produce compensation in excess of one million and up to two million Swiss Francs or, in exceptional cases, even more depending on the circumstances.

A final example may be mentioned for high non-pecuniary damages in a case awarded involving severe injuries. This case concerned an Italian woman employed as a laundress in a Swiss firm who, having been terribly injured in a blast accident caused by the Swiss Army, came to the Supreme Court on the question of how much she would be entitled to for pain and suffering on the basis of Article 47 of the Swiss Code. Pecuniary damages for loss of income were not in dispute. The woman was 38 years old at the time of the accident in 1978. She became totally disabled for the rest of her life. The Federal Military Administration recognised a liability for damages to the extent of Sw Fr. 922,000 (*Supreme Court Reports*, Administrative Law Part, Volume 111, pp. 192-200) which capital may have been based on an average annual salary of a laundress within the range of Sw Fr. 40,000-50,000.

The only controversy related to the amount payable for non-pecuniary damages, i.e. for pain and suffering. The Military Administration was prepared to pay Sw Fr. 60,000 whereas the victim asked for Sw Fr. 140,000. The Supreme Court considered that the Plaintiff had been perfectly healthy and good looking before the accident. The various injuries caused by the blasting had completely disfigured her. She lost one eye and had been traumatised mentally to a degree which left her a total invalid. All these circumstances combined called for special compensation of Sw Fr. 110,000 in addition to the sum of almost one million Swiss Francs for the purely pecuniary damages not including the considerable medical expenses covered under a special arrangement (*Supreme Court Reports*, Civil Law Part, Volume 112, pp. 131-138).

Future Developments

Presently, in Switzerland as well as in Liechtenstein, legislative steps are being taken to improve the situation of Claimants in personal injury cases. Higher standards of care are applied and the requirements for proving negligence are lowered. The particular items of damages and of their computation, however, remain more or less the same. A proposal to reform tort law containing 55 Articles was made in 1996 but will not be enacted in the foreseeable future. It can be safely stated, therefore, that for at least the first decade of the new millennium personal injury claims will be dealt with in Switzerland as well as in Liechtenstein as in the previous decade.

Table 1. Schedule A

Claimant :	Man
Age :	40
Status :	Married, wife aged 35, 2 dependent aged 5 and 7
Occupation :	Doctor
Annual Income :	CHF 100,000 net pa
Settlement :	2.5 years after accident

1. Instant Death		CHF
a) Claim for funeral expenses		8,000
Interest on funeral expenses at 5% for half of the period until settlement		500
b) Dependent wife and children would have separate claims for loss of maintenance. Social security payments to widow and orphans are deductible but will be claimed back by the social security institutions from the liable party		
Net income	100,000	
1. Wife's share in case of more than average income 40%	40,000	
Maintenance until settlement		100,000
Interest on maintenance until settlement at 5% for half of the period		6,250
Future loss of maintenance based on adjusted income of Sw Fr. 120,000 taking into account expected increases until retirement multiplied by a factor of 16.5 on basis of Swiss actuarial tables: i.e. 48,000 x 16.5		792,000
Non-pecuniary damages for grief and bereavement		20,000 – 30,000

2. Children (10% each)	10,000	
Maintenance until settlement for both children		50,000
Interest on maintenance until settlement at 5% for half of the period		3,125
Future loss of maintenance based on adjusted income of Sw Fr. 120,000 until age 25 of each child according to Swiss actuarial tables for 5-year-old child capitalised as from date of settlement		144,000
For 7-year-old child equally capitalised as form date of settlement		132,000
Non-pecuniary damages for grief and bereavement for each child	10,000	20,000
	1,275,875	1,285,875

2. Burns

Assume that claimant is able to resume his employment two years after accident

a) Pecuniary losses	
1. Medical expenses	–
2. Loss of income	200,000
Interest on maintenance until settlement at 5% for half of the period	12,500
b) Non-material losses, ie. pain amd suffering	10,000
TOTAL AWARD	**222,500**

3. Quadriplegia

a) Pecuniary losses	
1. Medical expenses	–
2. Loss of income	250,000
Interest on maintenance until settlement at 5% for half of the period	15,125

Future loss of income (age 42 at time of settlement; adjusted average income Sw Fr. 120,000 p.a. multiplied by a factor of 17 according to Swiss actuarial tables)	2,040,000
b) Pain and suffering	100,000
TOTAL AWARD	**2,405,125**

4. Paraplegia

a) Pecuniary losses (see 3 above)	
b) Pain and suffering	80,000 – 100,000

5. Brain damage (entailing complete incapacity for work)

a) Pecuniary losses (see 3 above)	
b) Pain and suffering	80,000 – 100,000

6. Amputation of leg

Assume that claimant is able to resume his employment 1.5 years after accident

a) Pecuniary losses	
1. Medical expenses	–
2. Loss of income	150,000
Interest on maintenance until settlement at 5% for half of the period	9,375
Miscellaneous losses, i.e. damage for diminished physical integrity and general economic disadvantage if compared on an unharmed person in the same profession, normally compensated by a percentage of 25% of the damages for full incapacity	500,000
TOTAL AWARD	**659,375**

7. Amputation of arm

Assume that claimant is able to resume his employment 1.5 years after accident at Sw Fr 60,000 net pa

a) Pecuniary losses	
1. Medical expenses	–
2. Loss of income	190,000
Interest on maintenance until settlement at 5% for half of the period	11,875
Future loss of income (Sw Fr. 40,000 multiplied by a factor 17,for a man 42 years of age at the time of settlement during his remaining period of professional activity according to Swiss actuarial tables.)	680,000
3. Miscellaneous losses There is a likelihood that the capital of Sw Fr. 680,000 for the remaining loss of future income would be increased by 25% or even more as an equitable compensation for general disadvantage to a partially disabled person in a competitive market	170,000
b) Pain and suffering	50,000
TOTAL AWARD	**1,101,875**

8a. and 8b. Loss of eyesight – one eye

Assume that claimant is able to resume his employment one year after accident

a) Pecuniary losses	
1. Medical expenses	–
2. Loss of income	100,000
Interest on maintenance until settlement at 5% for half of the period	6,250

3. Miscellaneous	–
b) Pain and suffering included an equitable amount for indiscriminate negative effects of disability on claimant's economic future, approximately	100,000
TOTAL AWARD	**206.250**

8c. Loss of eyesight – total blindness

Assume that claimant is able to resume his employment

a) Pecuniary losses (as with 3)	
1. Medical expenses	–
2. Loss of income	–
3. Miscellaneous losses	–
b) Pain and suffering	80,000 – 100,000
TOTAL AWARD	**2,385,125 – 2,405,125**

9. Deafness

Assume that claimant is able to resume his employment

a) Pecuniary losses	
1. Medical expenses	–
2. Loss of income until settlement	250,000
Interest 5% for half of the period until settlement	15,625
Future loss of income (age 42 at time of settlement, adjusted average income Sw Fr. 120,000 p.a. multiplied by a factor of 7 according to Swiss actuarial tables)	2,040,000

(However, even being completely deaf and unable to resume his former employment claimant would be expected to derive some income form a suitable activity, presumably an amount of approximately Sw Fr. 30,000 p.a. which would have to be deducted, leaving a loss of income of only Sw Fr 90,000 multiplied by a factor of 17 = 1,530,000)

b) Non-material losses ie. pain and suffering	50,000 – 80,000
TOTAL AWARD	**2,355,625 – 2,385,625**

10. Repetitive strain injury

a) Complete loss of function in wrist, but no loss of income, estimated	25,000
b) Injury with significant permanent residual disability The disability would probably be assimilated to a (theoretical) 10% reduction of claimant's earning capacity, even with no proof of an immediate loss of income, and capitalised accordingly, i.e. Sw Fr. 12,000 multiplied by a factor of 17, that amount also taking care of pain and suffering	204,000
TOTAL AWARD	**229,000**

Table 2. Schedule B

Claimant :	Woman
Age :	20
Status :	Single
Occupation :	Legal Secretary
Annual Income :	CHF 36,000 net p.a increasing to Sw Fr. 46,000 net
Settlement :	2.5 years after accident

1. Instant Death		CHF
a) Funeral expenses, average of		6,000
b) Interest on funeral expenses at 5% for half of the period		375
Loss of maintenance		–
(Except if it could be proved that she would, in all probability, have supported her parents or other dependants.)	100,000	
c) Compensation for grief and bereavement, assume two parents alive	30,000	

(Might be due to persons closely related to her such as parents, brothers and/or sisters living with her in the same household, a possible fiancé etc.: amounts varying between Sw Fr. 10,000 and 20,000)

TOTAL AWARD	**36,375**

2. Burns

Assume that claimant is able to resume her employment two years after accident

a) Pecuniary losses	
1. Medical expenses	–
2. Loss of income	72,000

Interest on maintenance unil setttlement at 5% for half of period	4,500
3. Miscellaneous losses	–
b) Non-material losses, i.e. pain and suffering if no residual effects of the injury are left such as scars etc	5,000
(Otherwise Sw Fr. 10,000 to 20,000 depending on extent of residual effects)	
TOTAL AWARD	**81,500**

3. Quadriplegia

a) Pecuniary losses	
1. Medical expenses	–
2. Loss of income	90,000
Interest on maintenance until settlement	5,625
Future loss of income (calculated on an average income of presumably Sw Fr. 40,000 multiplied by a factor of 23.7 for a female person between 22 and 23 years at time of settlement according to Swiss actuarial tables)	948,000
b) Pain and suffering – at least	100,000
TOTAL AWARD	**1,143,625**

4. Paraplegia

Assume income earned Sw Fr. 15,000 p.a. in sedentary job 1.5 years after accident

a) Pecuniary losses	
1. Medical expenses	–
2. Loss of income	75,000

Interest on loss of income until settlement at 5% for half of the period	4,687.50
Future loss of income (calculated on an average income of presumably Sw Fr. 25,000 multiplied by a factor of 23.7)	592,500
Miscellaneous losses	–
b) Pain and suffering, up to	100,000
TOTAL AWARD	**772,187.50**

5. Brain damage

a) Pecuniary losses (see 3 above)	
b) Pain and suffering	100,000 or even more

6. Amputation of leg

Assume that claimant is able to resume her employment 1.5 years after accident

Pecuniary losses	–
Medical expenses	
Loss of income	54,000
Interest on maintenance until settlement at 5% for half of the period	3,375

For the reasons already explained in Schedule A, 6(iii), above, claimant would be entitled to a further equitable amount to be calculated as follows: from a purely medical point of view the loss of one leg is assimilated to a 50% reduction of the total physical integrity of a person. If claimant were to suffer a 50% loss of income she would be entitled to a compensation of approximately half a million Sw Fr. Since it is not at all

certain whether or not she will be capable of maintaining her level of income for all the years to come in spite of her physical disability she would probably be awarded an equitable amount of at last half that sum i.e.	250,000
Pain and suffering, at least	50,000
TOTAL AWARD	**357,375**

7. Amputation of arm

Assume that claimant is not able to resume her employment but takes up light duties 1.5 years after accident at Sw Fr. 25,000 net p.a. until age 30 and Sw Fr. 25,000 net p.a. by age 40

a) Pecuniary losses	
1. Medical expenses	–
2. Loss of income until settlement	75,000
Interest on maintenance until settlement at 5% for half of the period	4,687.50
Future loss of income (calculated on average amount of presumably Sw Fr. 20,000 multiplied by a factor of 23.7)	474,000
3. Miscellaneous losses	–
b) Pain and suffering	30,000 – 50,000
TOTAL AWARD	**585,687 – 603,687**

8a. and 8b. Loss of eyesight – one eye

Assume that claimant is able to resume her employment one year after accident

a) Pecuniary losses	
1. Medical expenses	–
2. Loss of income until settlement	36,000

Interest on maintenance until settlement at 5% for half of the period	2,250
b) Pain and suffering, including an equitable amount for indiscriminate negative effects of disability on claimant's economic future, approximately	100,000
TOTAL AWARD	**138,250**

8c. Loss of eyesight – total blindness

Assume that claimant is unable to resume his employment

a) Pecuniary losses (as with 3)	1,043,625
1. Medical expenses	–
2. Loss of income	–
b) Pain and suffering, at least	100,000
TOTAL AWARD	**1,143,625**

9. Deafness (total)

Assume that claimant is able to resume his employment but takes up light duties 1.5 years after accident with a corresponding income of Sw Fr. 18,000 net p.a.

a) Pecuniary losses	
1. Medical expenses	–
2. Loss of income until settlement	72,000
Interest 5% for half of the period until settlement	4,500
Future loss of income based on adjusted average income of Sw Fr. 40,000 less residual income of Sw Fr. 18,000 for light duties. The difference of Sw Fr. 22,000 would be multiplied by a factor of 23.7 for a female	

person between 22 and 23 years at time of settlement according to Swiss actuarial tables	521,400
b) Non-material losses, i.e. pain and suffering	50,000 – 80,000
TOTAL AWARD	**647,900 – 677,900**

10. Repetitive strain injury

a) Complete loss of function in wrist, but without any (present and future) loss of income	10,000 – 20,000
b) Injury with significant permanent residual disability	
The disability would probably be assimilated to a (theoretical) 10% reduction of claimant's earning capacity, even with no proof of an immediate loss of income, and capitalised accordingly, i.e. Sw Fr. 4,000 multiplied by a factor of 17, that amount also taking care of pain and suffering	94,800
TOTAL AWARD	**104,800 – 114,800**

INDEX